language acquisition

Palgrave Advances in Linguistics

Consulting Editor:
Christopher N. Candlin,
Macquarie University, Australia

Titles include:

Noel Burton-Roberts (*editor*)
PRAGMATICS

Susan Foster-Cohen (*editor*)
LANGUAGE ACQUISITION

Monica Heller (*editor*)
BILINGUALISM: A SOCIAL APPROACH

Martha E. Pennington (*editor*)
PHONOLOGY IN CONTEXT

Ann Weatherall, Bernadette M. Watson and Cindy Gallois (*editors*)
LANGUAGE, DISCOURSE AND SOCIAL PSYCHOLOGY

Forthcoming:

Charles Antaki (*editor*)
APPLIED CONVERSATIONAL ANALYSIS:
CHANGING INSTITUTIONAL PRACTICES

Barry O'Sullivan (*editor*)
LANGUAGE TESTING: THEORIES AND PRACTICES

Palgrave Advances
Series Standing Order ISBN 978–1–4039–3512–0 (Hardback) 978–1–4039–3513–7 (Paperback)
(outside North America only)

You can receive future titles in this series as they are published by placing a standing order.
Please contact your bookseller or, in the case of difficulty, write to us at the address below
with your name and address, the title of the series and one of the ISBNS quoted above.

Customer Services Department, Macmillan Distribution Ltd, Houndmills, Basingstoke,
Hampshire RG21 6XS, England

language acquisition

edited by
susan foster-cohen

palgrave
macmillan

First published 2009 by
PALGRAVE MACMILLAN

Palgrave Macmillan in the UK is an imprint of Macmillan Publishers Limited,
registered in England, company number 785998, of Houndmills, Basingstoke,
Hampshire RG21 6XS.

Palgrave Macmillan in the US is a division of St Martin's Press LLC,
175 Fifth Avenue, New York, NY 10010.

Palgrave Macmillan is the global academic imprint of the above companies
and has companies and representatives throughout the world.

Palgrave® and Macmillan® are registered trademarks in the United States,
the United Kingdom, Europe and other countries.

ISBN-13: 978–0–230–50029–7 hardback
ISBN-10: 0–230–50029–3   hardback
ISBN-13: 978–0–230–50030–3 paperback
ISBN-10: 0–230–50030–7   paperback

This book is printed on paper suitable for recycling and made from fully
managed and sustained forest sources. Logging, pulping and manufacturing
processes are expected to conform to the environmental regulations of the
country of origin.

A catalogue record for this book is available
from the British Library.

A catalog record for this book is available
from the Library of Congress.

10   9   8   7   6   5   4   3   2   1
18   17   16   15   14   13   12   11   10   09

Printed and bound in Great Britain by
CPI Antony Rowe, Chippenham and Eastbourne

contents

series preface

christopher n. candlin

This new *Advances in Linguistics Series* is part of an overall publishing programme by Palgrave Macmillan aimed at producing collections of original, commissioned articles under the invited editorship of distinguished scholars.

The books in the Series are not intended as an overall guide to the topic or to provide an exhaustive coverage of its various sub-fields. Rather, they are carefully planned to offer the informed readership a conspectus of perspectives on key themes, authored by major scholars whose work is at the boundaries of current research. What we plan the Series will do, then, is to focus on salience and influence, move fields forward, and help to chart future research development.

The Series is designed for postgraduate and research students, including advanced level undergraduates seeking to pursue research work in linguistics, or careers engaged with language and communication study more generally, as well as for more experienced researchers and tutors seeking an awareness of what is current and in prospect in adjacent research fields to their own. We hope that the some of the intellectual excitement posed by the challenges of linguistics as a pluralistic discipline will shine through the books!

Editors of books in the Series have been particularly asked to put their own distinctive stamp on their collection, to give it a personal dimension, and to map the territory, as it were, seen through the eyes of their own research experience.

There are few sites of scholarly engagement in linguistics as rich in potential for interdisciplinary study as that of language acquisition. It is hardly possible, one would imagine, for such a site not to encompass the range of disciplinary fields evidenced in this remarkable collection commissioned and brought together so expertly by Susan Foster-Cohen. Yet, as the history of the broad field also evidences, this harmonization and integration has been perhaps rather the exception than the rule. Partly this is a consequence of the existence of professional boundaries, as between, say, scholars in first and second language acquisition, communication disorders, bilingualism and neuroscience, and partly because of corresponding distinctions and divisions in the academy. Yet, were one to approach the field from the perspective of investigative and research-based practice, it would be precisely that interdisciplinarity that one would be seeking to draw upon, whether in response to challenges that arise in the mundane or the professional world, or, indeed, to address the theoretical and descriptive issues to which such challenges give rise.

Accordingly, this imaginative volume in the *Advances in Linguistics Series* has an innovative thematic purpose; more than that, however, it has an equally important and parallel methodological purpose, namely to bring together a number of research paradigms and to display how these, taken together, can reveal more of the processes and outcomes of language acquisition than could any single mode of research. This is more than advocating a mixing of the qualitative and the quantitative, popular though that now is; what this collection shows is that warranting claims with evidence, properly gathered and systematically analysed, will always lead us to eschewing a single framework, however trenchantly espoused, in favour of a more comprehensive explanatory paradigm. This is true of all scientific endeavour but none more apposite than in the study of the acquisition of human language in all its complexity. As Popper reminds us: 'at any moment we are prisoners caught in the framework of our theories: our expectations: or past experiences; our language. But we are prisoners in a Pickwickian sense; if we try, we can break out of our framework at any time. Admittedly, we shall find ourselves again in a framework, but it will be a better and a roomier one, and we can at any moment break out of it again' (1970, p. 56). The authors in this collection of papers show us exactly how one can construct just such a roomier framework, and Susan Foster-Cohen deserves all our thanks for designing the architecture to make this possible.

Christopher N. Candlin
Macquarie University, Sydney

preface

This book provides a snapshot of the field of language acquisition at
the beginning of the twenty-first century, together with some attempts
to speculate about the future. It is, first and foremost, a book of *ideas*;
ideas which you are invited to challenge. The advancement of the field
requires no less of you. Your challenge should be on the basis of other
ideas that you can argue are better and/or are supported by empirical
data. Your challenge should not be based on disliking the framework in
which ideas are couched, disliking the person who is proposing them,
or finding the ideas hard to understand.

Knowing where a field has come from, as preparation for understanding where it is going, is a vital component of good scholarship;
and in the field of language acquisition there are many histories that
intertwine. The field has engaged, and continues to engage, those in
linguistics, philosophy, psychology, anthropology, neuroscience, sociology, education, and more. This volume respects that multidisciplin-
arity of research and understanding, and attempts to reflect the rich
range of approaches with which more advanced students and beginning researchers ought to be familiar. The chapters provide readers with
a review of current topics and debates, as well as addressing some of
the connections between sub-fields and the possible future directions
for research, including in first language, second language, bilingualism and language disorder in languages that are spoken, manual and
written.

To have been asked to put a volume of this kind together is an honour; and it has been a delight to have so many respected colleagues in

the field accept my offer to contribute. I have solicited contributions from those whose ideas excite me; some who are established and long-standing members of the child language community, and some who have joined more recently. I'm just sorry I could not invite everyone I would have liked to include. However, taken together, I hope the papers in this volume will give the student of language acquisition a feel for the many ideas that have been, and are still waiting to be, explored.

Susan Foster-Cohen
Christchurch, New Zealand

acknowledgements

My first thanks must go to Chris Candlin, who as series editor had the confidence in my abilities to ask me to put this volume together. My next thanks, and the biggest, goes to the authors who have contributed. They reflect the places I've been, the people I've met, and the things I've read over the years, as I've explored, in my typically eclectic fashion, early mother–infant interaction, generative syntax, developmental bilingualism, cognitive approaches to pragmatics, second language acquisition, and, most recently, early intervention. Reading all the wonderful material the contributors have sent me has reminded me of why I'm still excited by this field and how much there is still to find out.

For the past several years I have been Director of the Champion Centre, which provides individualized multi-disciplinary early intervention programmes to children with developmental disabilities and their families in Christchurch, New Zealand. This has been, and continues to be, the most interesting experience of my professional life. I have learnt and continue to learn so much about human development in general, language development in particular, and about the incredible neuroplasticity to be seen on a daily basis when children who have been dealt some of the worst hands on the planet are raised by knowledgeable and emotionally connected families. I am so privileged to work with such a wonderful group of smart, wise and funny women, and I thank them all for their support in allowing me the time to put this volume together. My heartfelt thanks go particularly to Patricia Champion, who saw that I could contribute to the programme she developed over 30 years.

Finally, I thank the Department of Linguistics and the Department of Communication Disorders at the University of Canterbury, who, by giving me opportunities to teach language acquisition courses, have ensured that I can continue to exercise my first love of educating students.

list of tables and figures

tables

figures

contributors

Meaola Amituanai-Toloa is Associate Director of the Woolf Fisher Research Centre, and Lecturer and Associate Dean Pasifika at the University of Auckland, New Zealand. Her general research interests are literacy and language development, particularly as it relates to Pasifika student achievement. Recent work has explored effective teaching of reading comprehension of Samoan students in bilingual and mainstream contexts.

Ruth A. Berman is Professor Emeritus in Linguistics at Tel Aviv University, Israel. Among her fields of interest are Modern Hebrew grammar and lexicon; cross-linguistic language acquisition, narrative development, and school-age text construction abilities. Major publications include *Acquisition of Hebrew*, 1985; *Relating Events in Narrative*, 1994 with Dan I. Slobin; and *Language Development across Childhood and Adolescence* (ed.), 2004.

Georgie Columbus is a phraseologist working in corpus linguistics and psycholinguistics with additional interests in the variation in discourse markers between English varieties. Georgie is currently completing her PhD at the University of Alberta, Canada, on the processing of multi-word units in native and non-native speakers.

Susan Gass is University Distinguished Professor at Michigan State University, USA. She has published widely in the field of second language acquisition including numerous books and articles. She served as President of the International Association of Applied Linguistics and is the recipient of the Distinguished Service and Scholar Award of the American Association for Applied Linguistics.

Maria Teresa Guasti is Professor of Linguistics at the University of Milano–Bicocca, Italy. She has carried out research at MIT and the Psycholinguistic Laboratory in Paris, and has held positions at the San Raffaele Hospital in Milan, and the University of Siena. She is the author of books and articles in theoretical linguistics and language acquisition, with a special focus on Romance languages.

Maya Hickmann is Research Director at the CNRS and joint Director of the Laboratory Structures Formelles du Langage at the University of Paris 8, France. Her publications concern the development of discourse organization in a functional and cross-linguistic perspective, as well as typological constraints on first and second language acquisition.

Koenraad Kuiper is Professor of Linguistics at the University of Canterbury, New Zealand. He has written widely on the phrasal lexicon. A new book, *Formulaic Genres*, is to appear with Palgrave Macmillan in 2009.

Stuart McNaughton is Professor of Education and Director of the Woolf Fisher Research Centre at the University of Auckland, New Zealand. His research interests are literacy and language development, the design of effective educational programmes for culturally and linguistically diverse populations and cultural processes in development.

Natascha Müller is Professor of Romance Linguistics (French, Italian, Spanish) at Bergische Universität Wuppertal, Germany. Her research focuses on the syntax of Romance languages and the acquisition of Romance syntax by bilingual children. In 1999 she received the Venia Legendi for Romance Linguistics from the University of Hamburg.

Ann M. Peters is Professor Emerita of Linguistics, University of Hawai at Manoa, USA. She focuses on early stages of language acquisition with emphasis on the interaction of linguistic, cognitive, social and biological development; the roles of prosody, speech formulas and verbal routines; the influence of phonology on the acquisition of morphology; and individual differences.

Nausicaa Pouscoulous received her PhD from the Institut Jean Nicod and the Institut des Sciences Cognitives. Then, as a Marie Curie Fellow at the Max Planck Institute for Evolutionary Anthropology, she studied the development of pragmatic processes in children. Currently, she is a Lecturer in the Linguistics Department at University College London, UK where she continues to combine experimental and theoretical approaches in her research on pragmatic inferences.

Ira A. Noveck is Director of the Laboratoire sur le Langage, le Cerveau et Cognition (L2C2) and its Reasoning, Development and Pragmatics team at the Institut des Sciences Cognitives (CNRS) near Lyon, France. His interests lie in experimental approaches to developmental semantics/pragmatics and reasoning and he is the author of articles and chapters on these topics and co-editor (with Dan Sperber) of a book entitled *Experimental Pragmatics*.

Judy S. Reilly is a developmental psycholinguist with a long-standing interest and 20 years of experience in studying the developing relations between language and emotion in both typically and atypically developing children. She is currently a Professor of Developmental Psychology at San Diego State University, USA and the University of Poitiers in France.

Matthew Saxton trained in psychology, linguistics and applied linguistics at the Universities of Edinburgh and Oxford. He is currently Senior Lecturer in Psychology at the Institute of Education, University of London, UK. His research on negative evidence in first language acquisition was recognized by the Paul Pimsleur Award in 1999.

Norbert Schmitt is Professor of Applied Linguistics at the University of Nottingham, UK. He is interested in all aspects of second language vocabulary studies and has just completed a research manual on that topic.

Marilyn Vihman is Professor of Language and Linguistic Science at the University of York, UK. Her research focuses on early word learning in infants acquiring various languages (US and UK English, Estonian, Finnish, French, Italian, Japanese, Welsh), and includes both observational and experimental studies of infant word form recognition and segmentation.

Jill G. de Villiers is Professor of Psychology and Philosophy at Smith College, USA. She has published on a wide array of topics in language acquisition, particularly on syntax development and the interface of language and cognition. She helped to develop a new language assessment test, the DELV, designed to neutralize dialect differences.

Peter A. de Villiers is Professor of Psychology at Smith College, USA. He is deeply interested in language acquisition and language disorders and has worked in research on the cognitive effects of language delay in deaf children for many years. Most recently he is working on assessing pragmatics in children with autism.

Ema Wolfgramm-Foliaki is Lecturer at the Centre for Academic Development at The University of Auckland, New Zealand. She has carried out research in the area of literacy development within Pacific Island families. 'Ema's current research work is in the area of student learning.

introduction

There have been, and probably always will be, two rather different approaches to language acquisition, which I have referred to as the 'observational' and the 'logical' (Foster-Cohen, 1999), and which, while not being entirely separable in practice, help us understand some of the key debates in language acquisition studies. In the first approach, the aim is to observe children acquiring languages in a range of circumstances and to capture those observations in whatever form current technologies make possible (pencil and paper, video, audio, etc.). Many of these observations are based on data now housed in corpora such as the CHILDES database at Carnegie Mellon University, developed and maintained by Brian MacWhinney. The second approach starts from the premise that to understand how language is acquired, we must first understand exactly what is being acquired and then try to, as it were, *fill in the gaps* between the capacities of the novice (infant, child or adult) and the competent language user: given their destination, what must the learner both bring to the task and experience along the road to get there?

To some extent, the differences between the 'observational' and the 'logical' are methodological, since no one ever goes looking at learners without some understanding of the task learners are expected to achieve. And in both approaches there is the need to know what the learner brings to the task of language acquisition, and what they can glean from the input. However, in practice, those (notably linguists) who have placed the initial focus on the endpoint of acquisition have come to rather different conclusions from those who have focused on the path, particularly those who have started at the very earliest stages of acquisition in infancy (notably anthropologists and psychologists). Not only do these researchers not share a common view as to the endpoint of acquisition, they also do not share a view of what is understood to be the input to language acquisition.

In general, those who view the nature of language as a body of overt constructions which form a toolbox for communication (e.g. Tomasello, 2003) view it as revealed by the language that learners hear, see and read (i.e. what speakers can and do say/write). They then tend to see the task of language acquisition as one of coming to mirror the language of the input by observation, imitation, pattern extraction and adjustment towards the adult model. Those who see language as a much more complex system, containing fine distinctions and subtle interpretations that are *not* revealed directly by the language to which learners are exposed, tend to see the task as involving much more complex interactions between the nature of the human animal and the input language. These researchers argue that equally as important as explaining what children come to understand they *can* say (or interpret linguistic strings as meaning) is explaining how they come to understand what they *cannot* say (or interpret).

Both the perspectives outlined above are represented in this volume because it is important to follow both the logic and the empirical findings of both approaches. I personally think that the story Tomasello (2003) tells about the emergence of symbolic communication in infants from the interpretation of other intentions in an excellent one. I remain unconvinced that the same story can be told about advanced syntax (Foster-Cohen, 2006). This then raises other questions about the nature of language development: is it a single path that needs the same sort of explanation throughout its trajectory? Or could different sorts of explanations come into play at different times? (This is the 'continuity of explanations' problem.) At the present state of our knowledge, I would argue that we must remain open to both possibilities: on the one hand that language is a system, or more likely a collection of systems, that can be constructed or reconstructed by each child through relatively straightforward pattern recognition strategies; and on the other that language, because of its inherent complexity of constraints and disallowed possibilities, must be, to a greater or lesser extent, built into the nature of the human brain. If we don't *welcome* this tussle, we will have no hope of correctly interpreting either current or future data.

Part of the reason why a variety of different perspectives holds sway in the study of language acquisition is because so many different disciplines contribute to it. Linguistics, psychology, anthropology, education and, more recently, cognitive science and neuroscience, are all disciplines that have contributed significantly to our understanding of language acquisition, both first and second, monolingual and bilingual, typical and atypical (disordered), in languages around the world.

While such multidisciplinary activity has contributed significantly to the richness of our understanding of language acquisition, it has also been a source of tension. Each discipline comes with its theoretical assumptions and preferred methodologies for research, and as each discipline has independently matured and developed its own theoretical basis, it has become more and more difficult to reach across discipline boundaries and truly understand alternative perspectives. I am hopeful that in the future this chasm will begin to close, as our understanding of both the psychological and the social become more grounded in our understanding of the workings of the brain.

We are still a long way off being able to observe, through brain scans and other devices, the moment-by-moment acquisition of a language or languages by a child or adult, and even further away from understanding exactly what the brain activity we will be able to observe might actually reflect. However, though the neuroscience of language acquisition is very much in its infancy, it is the natural progression for a field that began by examining the *external* behaviour of language users (at a time when cognitive processes were not even accepted objects of research), and might now be able to examine the *internal* behaviour of language learners' brains. In between, we have enriched the study of language acquisition through examination of the cognitive and interactional aspects of acquisition, with a focus on a range of different levels of language from the phonetic to the pragmatic, viewed as the development of the individual and as the development of the individual in social and psychological connection with another. Along the way, language acquisition researchers have had long and heated debates about nature versus nurture, though now most recognize that these debates were based on a false dichotomy, since nothing in human development springs fully made from genetic instructions. As Matt Ridley puts it, it is always nature through nurture (Ridley, 2003). And if language is part of the human endowment, as Chomsky has always insisted it is, then it too will emerge through interaction, both internal and external to the human learner.

The question remains, however, whether there is anything that can be sensibly described as a domain-specific language acquisition mechanism as opposed to domain-general capacities that are called into service for language acquisition. Elizabeth Bates, who endeavoured more than anyone to make sense of our emerging understanding of the 'cascading consequences' nature of human development for language development, was convinced that language was 'a new system made up of old parts' and that a specifically evolved mechanism purely for language development was extremely unlikely, given the nature of evolution (Bates et al., 2005). Even while there is a strong tendency for certain neuronal assemblies to fire in response to certain language tasks, she and others would argue that this does not mean there is a genetic programme for such similarity across individuals. Some, like Paula Tallal (2003), would argue that the left hemisphere is particularly attuned to fine auditory discrimination and that that is why language ends up being in the left hemisphere; unless of course that part of the brain is damaged, when other areas may step up to take on the task. Along the same lines, (Karmiloff-Smith, 1996) argues that there is a progressive modularization for language; and brain science now tells us that modules need not be anatomically localized, but are rather assemblies of interconnected neurons with fast connections.

These are interesting and valuable ideas; and there is no doubt that the staunchest supporter of Universal Grammar needs to take account of the nature of brain development in the young infant/child and the extent and limits of neuroplasticity in the older learner who is trying to add another language (or reclaim one that has been lost to trauma or disease). We must not, however, forget the point made earlier, that there are still questions to answer around the complexity of linguistic knowledge, and around the species specificity of complex language. To use an analogy Chomsky has used many times: humans will grow arms and not wings no matter what environment we put them into. And why is it that even though intact children are exposed to only a fraction of the possible data from a language or languages, they form quite clear intuitions about the limits on how language can/cannot be constructed and what it can/cannot mean? And why are these limits and possibilities of language so common across languages that differ widely one from another in so many other ways? And why are children's 'mistakes' almost always possible in some other human language, even while they are not possible in the one they are learning (Yang, 2006)?

There are those (several of whom appear in this volume) who think the similarities are because of similarities of cultural transmission and exposure to language input. However, we still need to account for the fact that languages only appear to be able to change within certain limits (Lightfoot, 2006), and that children acquiring language in the absence of a culturally transmitted model create and change their systems in only certain ways (Bickerton, 1992). (Several of the chapters in this volume make reference to the Nicaraguan Sign Language data, which can be used to address this issue.)

Will we ever agree on how learners, generation after generation, succeed in mastering the most wonderful and intricate systems of communication that we call language? Probably not. But we certainly will not
agree on the 'how' unless we can agree on the 'what'. Exactly what is it
that children and older learners are acquiring? Exactly what help can
and does the surrounding world give them? And exactly what is the
path of acquisition at whatever age and with whatever linguistic background (in the case of bilinguals) they already have? As you will see in
this volume, interesting ideas on all these topics have been proposed for
first language acquisition in infancy and early childhood and for bilingual and second language acquisition in childhood and later.

One area that will, I believe, continue to be of acute interest to those
studying language acquisition is the variation between individuals
acquiring language: neurological variation, variation in input, variation
in path and variation in endpoints (Foster-Cohen, 1999). It is vitally
important that we do not simplify this variability by lumping learners
into groups, but rather strive to understand the full complexity of the
different ways learners acquire languages. A certain degree of idealiza-
tion of the data is needed, of course, but I would like to think that, as we
get better at understanding just how individuals are both similar and
different, we can dispense with a number of demarcations that we have
been making. Do we really know what makes for typical versus atypical
development, for example? Are children with the same genetic markers
(e.g. trisomy 21) really more similar to each other than they are different in language development? Is there really a single condition we can
call specific language impairment (SLI), given the interrelationships in
the development of the human phenotype (Laws and Bishop, 2004)?
Why do certain features in first language acquisition get a designation
as disordered when the same features in second language acquisition
pass without comment as simply immature or errorful forms? The fact
is that we are far from knowing the true extent of the ways individuals
vary one from another in language development. We use notions of
'normal', 'disordered', 'typical', etc. as if we actually knew on what basis
we were doing so. Those bases are almost entirely behavioural, whereas
in fact two children with very similar paths may actually be acquiring
language very differently. Two other children with very different paths
as revealed by their comprehension and production may actually be
acquiring language very similarly, but using their systems in ways that
make them appear more different than in fact they are.

Rather than pre-empt discussions which I suspect will get more and
more interesting as the limits and capacities for neuroplasticity are

investigated, I would like this volume to be clear in stating that all learners contribute to our understanding of the rich tapestry of human development. This means that they must all be referred to in terms that are respectful and open about the success they may achieve in developing our most human of capacities (Roeper, 2007). It is for that reason that, in this volume, learners will be referred to (where this needs to be done) as 'typical' and 'atypical' learners, rather than as 'normal', 'disordered' or 'impaired'. I have also made a conscious choice when talking about children with various disabilities to refer to them as 'children with Down syndrome', 'children with autism', etc. rather than 'Down syndrome, or autistic, children'. They are children first and foremost, and the particular aspect of them that makes them interesting from a language acquisition perspective is secondary from a human rights and humanitarian point of view.

I hope readers will agree that this volume contains some of the 'hottest' topics in language acquisition. Readers will certainly find some of the same issues being raised by writers coming from very different perspectives and covering a wide range of different aspects of acquisition. In order to facilitate finding the threads through the various chapters, I have noted many of them in the following summaries of each section of the book (with bolded key terms for convenience), and others can be accessed via the index.

part 1. explaining language acquisition

The first four chapters in this collection provide an overview of current thinking about language acquisition from very different perspectives. At the same time, they each raise several of the same issues as each other.

The first chapter, by Marilyn Vihman, provides an account of the movement from babbling to first words and on to the development of a phonological system. She appeals to the notion of **attention** as key, both in its presence (in explicit learning) and in its absence (in implicit learning), arguing that attention is involved in the acquisition of first words, but not in the approximation of babbling to the ambient language or in the emergence of the phonological system. Attention is also a key component in Susan Gass's account of the Input/Interaction/Output model of second language acquisition. Here, though, the focus is on its role in the development of morphosyntax and pragmatics rather than phonology or lexis.

Gass's chapter makes another important connection with those that are concerned with first language acquisition, since her interest in attention is principally around its role in a learner's being able to take on board the kind of feedback that comes from **recasts** or reformulations of learner utterances. The importance to acquisition of these kinds of responses of the interaction partner is at the heart of Matthew Saxton's contribution in which he argues that children can and do make use of so-called corrective input in moving towards adult language. Gass and Saxton are both interested ultimately in the use that learners make of the **input** language to which they are exposed, an issue that has always been at the heart of language acquisition research.

In her chapter, Ann Peters focuses largely on the stage of child language development at which early words are separated out from the incoming speech stream and begin to be combined. She examines ways in which children can use the nature of the speech stream itself to help in carving it up; in cracking the linguistic code. Maria Teresa Guasti, on the other hand, has a very different take on the role of the input. Focused as she is on the complexities of advanced grammar, she makes the case that the input is inadequate in multiple ways to allow children to come to the conclusions about interpretations and possible constructions that they do. The tension between different conceptions of the nature of the **endpoint** of acquisition could not be any clearer when Guasti's chapter is compared to the others in this section. (I should note that, later in the volume, both de Villiers and de Villiers, and Pouscoulous and Noveck provide further detailed evidence for the complexity of the endpoint.)

Vihman, Peters, Saxton and Gass are all, in their different ways, focused on understanding just what learners can make of the input without any special help from preconceptions about the endpoint. Gass, however, because of her focus on a second language opens up the discussion to include situations where, unlike in first language acquisition, there must perforce always be linguistic preconceptions in the learner's mind. She is also, in contradistinction to Saxton, less hopeful that recasts and reformulations can actually do the work that is claimed for them, at least when it comes to adult learners. Guasti, for her part, opens up not only the issue of the complexity of what is to be explained, but also the depth of the issues surrounding the role and possible roles of the input in her discussion of the argument from the poverty of the stimulus. It is not just that the input can be unhelpful, a point which Saxton goes some considerable way towards countering, but that it simply does not show the complexity of the system that is acquired. This, however, means that we need to think carefully about Saxton's claim that grammar is both the input and the output to acquisition. Guasti would heartily disagree, since, from her point of view, children do not have access to grammar in the input. Utterances do not bear their analysis on their sleeves.

Finally, and relatedly, these first four chapters raise the issue not just of input, but of **interaction**. While Saxton remarks in his contribution that the social interactional approach to language acquisition that was the focus of much work in the 1970s has been ignored in recent years, I believe these papers show that it still underlies much thinking in language development; as well it should. The problem with the earlier work was that while it showed quite clearly that social and emotional exchanges between individuals are necessary for language development, it was not able to show the mechanism by which interaction worked its wonders. It will, I believe, be one of the most exciting hallmarks of the next generation of research that the impact of interaction will be tackled in a whole new way through neuroscience techniques that were not available 40 years ago. We will, I believe, finally get some traction on the kinds of **internal and external drivers** of acquisition identified by Peters, including individual learning preferences, cultural differences in interaction and the context of learning, emerging desires for control over the environment through skill development, and memory development.

The four papers in this section, each in their own way, make an extremely important point: that the language acquisition process is **dynamic**. As Ann Peters puts it in her chapter, paraphrasing Heraclitus, learners never put their toes into the same linguistic river twice. As learners learn, the background against which they make each new step is different from the background against which they made the previous step. This is also the point of the cascading consequences model of human brain development (e.g. Stiles, 2008): each development impacts those that follow. Moreover, this is true no matter what approach to language acquisition is taken. We would do well to keep this in mind as we progress through the rest of the contributions.

part 2. windows on language acquisition

Language acquisition researchers have always understood that the only way to get a fix on language acquisition is to explore it through a variety of lenses. Researchers such as the late Elizabeth Bates, who gave so much to the field, helped open our eyes to the huge amount of **variation** in path and approach to development that could be understood by looking both at variation within the so-called typical language learning population and through the lens of those acquiring language in unusual circumstances, or acquiring languages typologically distant from those most studied (cf. Bates, Tomasello and Slobin, 2005).

The four papers in this second section drill down into the question of the relationships between language and other forms of communication, and between language and thought. In so doing, they bring to the fore the issue of the complexity of what needs to be explained in language acquisition. Reilly, de Villiers and de Villiers, and Pouscoulous and Noveck all explore the **interface** between language and non-linguistic **emotion** and **thought**. These three papers use, in various ways and to various extents, the windows on language use and interpretation that are provided by atypical populations. Deaf children show us how separate linguistic and non-linguistic forms of communication are (Reilly), and how intertwined are the development of complex syntax and of reasoning about false beliefs (de Villiers and de Villiers). Children who have suffered perinatal stroke show us how language is differently organized from emotional aspects of communication in infancy (Reilly). Children with Williams syndrome (Reilly) and autism (Pouscoulous and Noveck) show how structural characteristics of language (morphosyntax) can fall out of step with pragmatic aspects of language use: in Reilly's case, in the context of evaluations in narratives; in the case of Pouscoulous and Noveck's work, in the disambiguation of possible interpretations of complex sentences.

De Villiers and de Villiers, Pouscoulous and Noveck, and Kuiper, Columbus and Schmitt provide a hugely important focus on the **hidden complexities** of language. Like Guasti, they urge us not to underestimate learners' grasp of how linguistic strings are constructed or how they can be interpreted. This puts an enormous importance on getting to grips with not only language production, but also language **comprehension**. Like Guasti in Part 1, de Villers and de Villiers and Pouscoulous and Noveck put the focus directly on comprehension; vital if we are to understand the complexities of acquisition. They also put the focus on the degree of complexity of the representations and interpretations children have/make. And here, of course, we meet the limitations of corpora. A corpus of utterances can shed huge light on what children produce, but is severely limited in revealing what they understand; a challenge that Kuiper et al. take up in relation to second language acquisition. Despite the ubiquity of phrasal vocabulary in corpora of English, and thus the enormous exposure to these forms that learners in a range of environment have, their performance in cloze test evaluations of this exposure is, frankly, abysmal. As with the discussion around input in Part 1 of this collection, input does not equal uptake, and we need to understand why.

One idea that recurs across many of the contributions to this volume is the notion of where the **seams in language** actually are. Kuiper et al., Reilly, and Peters emphasize the notion of chunks, either as a transitory phase or as a permanent state. In so doing, they lead us to pose questions about analysis and about control, along the lines suggested for second language acquisition by Bialystok (2001). **Chunking** (a neuroscientifically respectable notion, by the way) may be a necessary waystation on the road to analysis (as argued by Peters and by Reilly), but it is also a necessary endpoint for fluency and speed of language production (as argued by Kuiper et al.).

part 3. language acquisition, culture and linguistic diversity

The importance of casting the net as wide as it is cast deep in language acquisition studies cannot be over-emphasized. The previous section drilled down; this one will expand outwards to embrace the full richness of language acquisition as a human capability for communication and thought.

In a sense, every child in every generation goes it alone in language acquisition. They don't know about how languages other than the one(s) they are learning work, any more than they know the history of the language(s) to which they are exposed. Nonetheless, language comes in the context of a culture that is passed from generation to generation, and the history of each language is built into the way it is now. It is important, therefore, that we are always looking at how things work elsewhere: other languages, multiple languages at once, different cultural contexts.

Natascha Müller's paper, which opens this final section, challenges us to think carefully about the level at which we consider our analyses. Comparing the ways in which different children acquire various combinations of languages bilingually, she suggests that we cannot think in terms of languages compared as wholes. Rather, we need to think in terms of **subsystems** of languages in relation to each other and the interactions between these subsystems in the language-acquiring child. Like Susan Gass, in her discussion of second language acquisition, the question Müller poses is how children make sense of data from more than one language, in this case presented simultaneously. It is thus the question of **dynamism** and the impact of existing knowledge on knowledge currently being acquired. How does knowing some part of language or having some aspect of language acquired or partially acquired impact that Heraclitan river of language acquisition? Like Peters' paper in Part 1, Müller's paper addresses the question of the interfaces between areas of language development, and of the processing requirements posed by systems and subsystems of language.

And finally, we move back (or up) from the microstructures of individual sentences and subsystems to the kinds of **macrostructures** that are represented by oral and written narratives, and to the impact of sociolinguistic variables on language development. Maya Hickmann focuses on children's ability to regulate the flow of information as it unfolds across utterances in discourse (discourse cohesion), with specific reference to referential domains of narrative discourse (entities, time and space) across child languages. Ruth Berman also focuses on narrative, drawing out underlying properties and principles by reviewing different approaches to the study of narrative development, surveying form–function relations in different domains of developing narrative production, and tracing the developmental path from interactive, conversation-embedded narration in childhood to autonomous text construction in adolescence and adulthood. Hickmann and Berman also address how the nature of the language being learned impacts on this development, just as it did on the kinds of issues addressed by Müller.

The final paper, by McNaughton, Amituanai-Toloa and Wolfgramm-Foliaki, addresses the impact of cultural expectations on literacy practices in Tongan and Samoan communities, and connects back to notions addressed in the first section around cultural expectations for first words (Peters), how one talks to children (Saxton) and what one expects of bilingual children (Müller).

references

Bates, E., Tomasello, M. and Slobin, D. I. (2005). *Beyond Nature–Nurture: Essays in honor of Elizabeth Bates.* Mahwah, NJ; London: Lawrence Erlbaum Associates, Publishers.

Bialystok, E. (2001). *Bilingualism in Development: Language, Literacy, and Cognition.* Cambridge, UK; New York: Cambridge University Press.

Bickerton, D. (1992). *Language and Species.* Chicago, IL: University of Chicago Press.

Foster-Cohen, S. (1999). *An Introduction to Child Language Development.* London: Longman.

Foster-Cohen, S. (2006). 'Review of Tomasello, M. and Slobin, D. I. (2005) *Beyond Nature–Nurture: Essays in Honor of Elizabeth Bates'. Studies in Second Language Acquisition,* 28: 4, 659–60.

Karmiloff-Smith, A. (1996). *Beyond Modularity: A Developmental Perspective on Cognitive Science* (1st MIT Press paperback ed.). Cambridge, MA: MIT Press.

Laws, G. and Bishop, D. V. M. (2004). 'Pragmatic language impairment and social deficits in Williams syndrome: a comparison with Down's syndrome and specific language impairment. *International Journal of Language & Communication Disorders*, 39: 1, 45–64.

Lightfoot, D. (2006). *How New Languages Emerge*. Cambridge, UK: Cambridge University Press.

Ridley, M. (2003). *Nature via Nurture : Genes, Experience, and What Makes Us Human* (1st ed.). New York: HarperCollins.

Roeper, T. (2007). *The Prism of Grammar: How Child Language Illuminates Humanism*. Cambridge, MA: MIT Press.

Stiles, J. (2008) *The Fundamentals of Brain Development: Integrating Nature and Nurture*. Cambridge, MA: Harvard University Press.

Tallal, P. (2003). 'Language learning disabilities: Integrating research approaches.' *Current Directions in Psychological Science*, 12: 6, 206–11.

Tomasello, M. (2003). *Constructing a Language: A Usage-Based Theory of Language Acquisition*. Cambridge, MA: Harvard University Press.

Yang, C. D. (2006). *The Infinite Gift: How Children Learn and Unlearn the Languages of the World*. New York: Scribner.

part 1
explaining language acquisition

1
word learning and the origins of phonological systems

marilyn vihman

introduction

Although attention is clearly required for certain aspects of language development (Tomasello, 2003; Ruddy and Bornstein, 1982), recent experimental work with adults, infants and children has provided strong evidence of the power and importance of *implicit* learning that takes place outside of attentional focus (Gomez and Gerken, 1999). In this chapter, the role of implicit learning in the development of words will be examined from the earliest stages through to the development of the adult phonological system.

distributional or statistical (probabilistic, 'implicit' or 'procedural') learning

The conceptual distinction between explicit and implicit learning is not new (Reber, 1967), but only recently have experimental findings revealed that both children and adults automatically tally distributional regularities to which they are incidentally exposed while attending to other tasks (Saffran et al., 1997). Implicit learning has been shown to occur even in infants when they are exposed to uninterrupted sequences of syllables lacking any natural speech prosody (Saffran et al., 1996). These studies reveal probabilistic (statistical, distributional) rather than categorical learning or 'symbol manipulation'. Together with other experimental studies of prelinguistic responses to speech (Jusczyk, 1997), the research suggests that infants gradually gain a sense of the patterns in the ambient input language at the level of segments, syllables, accentual patterns, words, phrases and clauses, without any intention to learn. Moreover, this learning capacity seems to be a general one, applying to any regularly recurring sequences (aural, visual, tactile, etc.) in the infants' environment (Kirkham et al., 2002).

Studies of infant responses to speech have revealed emergent sensitivity to what is known as 'prosodic coherence' in ever smaller prosodic units over the course of the first year. That is, infants listen longer to infant-directed speech sequences that reflect natural prosodic units: clauses as early as 4-and-a-half months, then phrases at 9 months and finally words at 11 months (Jusczyk, 1997). It is highly likely that these effects are achieved through implicit learning, because although this kind of learning is not strictly speaking 'statistical' or 'distributional', it is not arbitrary, symbolic or based on attention either. It can safely be termed implicit learning, or learning in the absence of voluntary or focused attention to the stimuli, intention to learn or conscious awareness of learning.

The effect of implicit perceptual learning can also be seen as infants shift the production of their vowels in babbling towards those in the language(s) to which they are exposed (Boysson-Bardies et al., 1989). Similar production effects are reported for prosody (rising pitch is more common in the babbling of French than in that of American infants in the age range 6–12 months (Whalen et al., 1991)) and for consonants (a larger proportion of labials are found in the vocalizations of 10-month-olds exposed to English and French than in those of infants exposed to Japanese or Swedish (Boysson-Bardies and Vihman, 1991)). In each case the differences mirror those in the relevant adult languages.

An instructive test of the idea of implicit (or frequency-based) vs. explicit (or lexically based) learning can be seen in a comparison between infants exposed to Finnish and infants exposed to Welsh. Finnish has a systematic distinction between long (geminate) and short consonants. Welsh, on the other hand, lengthens consonants between vowels under accent. Thus, children exposed to Welsh tend to hear more long consonants than those exposed to Finnish, since in Welsh they occur regularly in running speech whereas in Finnish they occur in only about a third of the content words mothers use with their children. The median length in Welsh mothers' child-directed disyllables is 118 milliseconds, vs. 75 milliseconds for Finnish, a highly significant difference. As predicted by implicit learning Welsh infants produce longer consonants, on average, in babble and first words than do Finnish infants (170 milliseconds vs. 116 milliseconds). However, by the time the children reach the end of the single-word period the situation has reversed, as Finnish children have learned enough words to have picked up on the occurrence of long consonants. Direct measurement reveals that Finnish medial consonants attain a mean of 223 milliseconds at this point, while Welsh children show little change from the earlier stage (Vihman, 2001; Vihman and Kunnari, 2006).

Implicit pattern learning has a less direct effect on production, because production is only a secondary reflection of the child's perception of adult speech. To account for an effect on production we must assume that infants are biased to *reproduce* more often the vocalizations they perceive as better matches to what they are *hearing* with greatest frequency in input speech. If this interpretation is correct, the effect should be seen only in patterns that have a solid grounding in the infants' production repertoire, i.e. that are also *produced* with sufficient frequency to be subject to such a 'pruning' effect of the perception/production match. This seems to be the case. Phonetic categories such as coda consonants (consonants that end syllables), which are rare in infant babbling, show the impact of distributional learning at a later stage than phonetic categories that come under infant control earlier, such as the long consonants between vowels mentioned above (Vihman and Boysson-Bardies, 1994).

In fact, ease of production and input frequency interact. Children exposed to English and French, on the one hand, and Finnish, on the other, show similar ranges of medial consonant duration at the earliest stages of word production, with some children in each group producing far longer consonants than are typical of adult English or French (Vihman and Velleman, 2000). The Welsh children followed in the study summarized above showed the effect of adult long consonant production already at this early stage, reflecting *both* the relative ease of production and the relatively high input frequency of this phonetic feature in Welsh. As word learning progresses in each group, infants exposed to English and French restrict the length of their medial consonants in accordance with adult norms while Finnish children increase theirs. The Welsh children show no further lengthening, since in their case lexical learning does not increase the salience of the (purely phonetic) long medial consonants in the input.

In contrast, by the end of the single-word period Finnish children are producing even more long consonants, proportionately, than are found in input speech: a mean of 47 per cent of their words are transcribed as including a long consonant, even though only 38 per cent of their words have long consonants as produced by adults. It seems that once one or two of the common words with geminates (such as *anna* 'give', *kukka* 'flower', *loppu* 'finished, all done', *pallo* 'ball', *tyttö* 'girl') have been produced, practice leads children to focus on words with long medial consonants in Finnish despite their relatively low overall frequency in the input. This reflects an effect of 'top-down' (cognitive, lexical) processing in contrast to the 'bottom-up' or purely 'signal-based' salience of long medial consonants in a language like Welsh, where they occur more frequently due to their status as phonetic markers of accent. I return to this issue below.

lexical or symbolic (categorical) learning ('explicit' or 'declarative')

Lexical learning must depend at least in part on infant attention. Specifically, the first 'true' referential or symbolic word is demonstrated when a child either comprehends or produces an adult-based word pattern in a new situation (Bates et al., 1979; Vihman and McCune, 1994). Before that can happen, however, the child must have attended to adult use of the word in a situation in which both form and use were clear and salient. Indeed, before word use becomes well established children spontaneously deploy markers of attention, e.g. pointing, 'showing' and grunting, all good indicators of intentional communication (Vihman, 1996). (See Gass , this volume, on attention in second language acquisition: SFC)

By the first half of the second year infants typically demonstrate an interest in language and an intention to learn as well as a capacity for explicit attention to, and memory for, word use. Furthermore, in mothers' speech to their one-year-old infants, words used repeatedly in isolation – that is, words which can most easily capture the child's attention – have been shown to correlate significantly with first word production (Ninio, 1992; Brent and Siskind, 2001). Thus, despite the well-established abilities of prelinguistic infants to make implicit use of phonetic cues in the input as to how to segment the speech stream (Jusczyk, 1997), words or phrases that are readily available to the child's attention *without* the need for segmentation of the speech stream (because they have been heard in isolation) seem to be the most readily incorporated into the emerging *production* lexicon. It is plausible, then, to make a distinction between learning with and without attention, corresponding roughly to the distinction between explicit and implicit learning in adults. The distinction is supported by current thinking in neuroscience about dual memory systems (Squire, 1992; Baddeley et al., 2001; Ellis, 2005).

integrating distributional with lexical learning: the spiral model

It seems plausible to distinguish three types of learning for first language acquisition. Two of these are the product of 'implicit' processing by the 'non-declarative' or 'procedural' system (Squire and Kandel, 1999), and the third requires processing by the declarative system.[1] The three types of learning are:

- type 1: procedural tallying of *regularities perceived in sensory data* of any kind (e.g. of frequencies of occurrence, sequencing or rhythmic patterning);
- type 2: declarative (categorical, symbolic) registering of arbitrary form-meaning co-occurrences or associations, leading to a *mental lexicon of linguistic items*;
- type 3: 'secondary' procedural induction (a kind of 'tallying') of the *regularities inherent in the linguistic items* registered in the mental lexicon, ultimately resulting in *abstract knowledge of the linguistic system* – the basis for the purely language-internal components of phonology and morpho-syntax.

Type 1 learning is sufficient to account for language development in the first year of life. It requires no pre-established 'knowledge base' (Murphy et al., 2003) and can begin to 'inform the child about the world' as soon as the infant's sensory organs are complete. As the child gains increasing knowledge, first of prosody (especially rhythmic patterning: (Nazzi et al., 2000)), then of segmental sequences, this type of learning will yield a more detailed analysis of the ambient language.

The second type of processing and learning typically comes 'on-line' during the first half of the second year. It makes possible the declarative learning of linguistic units, and once children have achieved the 'nominal insight' (i.e. that individual word tokens or exemplars refer to word categories or 'types'), each new encounter with a given word form in an identifiably related situation is taken to belong to the same word type or 'lexical category' as on the previous occasion. For example, the live dog barking next door can be referred to using the same word form as the stylized doggy found in the picture book or on the side of a cup.

This understanding, and thus this kind of access to the mental representation of experiences, cannot be expected to emerge until a stable base of frequently heard words or phrases has developed, along with a capacity for rapidly retaining both phonetic and semantic representations. This is necessary to free up the attentional resources required for declarative ('explicit' or conjunctive) learning: Attention is needed to enable the child to relate new forms to new referents (Werker et al., 2002). Once such voluntary access to lexical representations becomes possible, a lexical knowledge base will begin to be established, somewhat different for each child at first (because experiences differ), but converging over a period of years on a lexicon very similar to that of other members of the same speech community.

Finally, once a child has begun to establish a lexicon of words or phrases with both phonological form and semantic content, 'secondary' procedural or distributional learning will automatically occur, as the neocortex again goes to work on recurrent regularities (type 3 learning). The input to that implicit or procedural processing is now no longer at the level of direct perceptual input but is rather a representational derivative of the cognitive processing that created the lexical entries – what Karmiloff-Smith (1992) has termed 'representational redescription'. Beyond a difference in 'raw material' or input to the processor, however, the learning process itself must be the same as in type 1. This secondary procedural learning can now be understood as gradually building up the abstract knowledge of system or structure to which we generally apply the term 'grammar' (Pierrehumbert, 2003). Importantly, this kind of pattern induction is a good candidate for a pattern recognition system able to account for language learning without the need for innate 'foreknowledge' of linguistic structure in the form of Universal Grammar.

We are assuming that 'primary' (type 1) and 'secondary' (type 3) procedural learning are separate contributions, with declarative learning (type 2) serving as the mediator between the two. Figure 1.1 (adapted from Vihman and Kunnari, 2006) illustrates this conceptualization in the form of a 'spiral model', by which procedural or implicit learning 'sets the stage' while declarative or explicit learning adds concrete lexical items to the mix. Once the process has functioned repeatedly to this point, yielding a small lexicon, procedural or implicit memory is triggered again, resulting in new levels of phonological knowledge. The process may be supposed to function continuously over the life-span, although new lexical learning becomes less frequent in the native language once an adultlike level has been achieved, typically late in the teenage years.

the articulatory filter

It is likely that first word use reflects the implicit matching of vocal production to perceived word forms (Vihman, 1993; see also Locke,

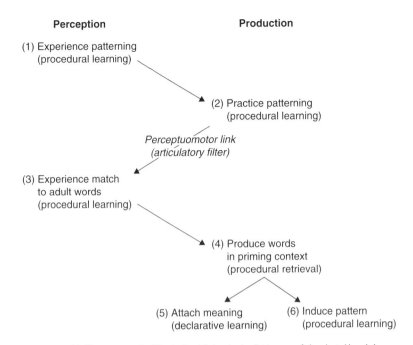

Figure 1.1 Model of learning: procedural (implicit) and declarative (explicit) sources of phonological knowledge

1986; Kuhl and Meltzoff, 1988). The concept of an 'articulatory filter' conveys the idea that the child's familiarity with his or her own vocal production patterns makes sequences in input speech that are like those patterns particularly salient. This idea is in line with a range of other evidence that there is continuity between babbling and speech, both in the general patterning of babble in relation to early word production (Oller et al., 1976) and in the particular babbling of individual children in relation to their own first word forms (Vihman et al.,1985), including prelinguistic gesture in relation to first signed words (Cheek et al., 2001).

At this developmental point the range of different word forms in terms of length in syllables, syllable shapes and consonant and vowel types is limited and is broadly the same regardless of ambient language. However, within those limits, individual children learning the same language differ in vocal patterns and draw their particular word forms from their own personal repertoire. That is, each child's early word patterns can be traced to that particular child's vocal practice or babbling.

The apparently nonlinear advance in the accuracy of first words has been a topic of interest for several decades. Over thirty years ago Ferguson and Farwell (1975) suggested that the very first identifiable words children produce are relatively accurate. After the rather slow initial build-up of new words, however, there seems to be an overall reduction in accuracy accompanied by an increase in systematicity or inner coherence among the child's own forms (the so-called U-shaped developmental curve), as well as a more or less abrupt shift to more rapid lexical learning. As well as being (relatively) accurate, first words have been found to be based on a highly restricted set of adult forms (Ferguson et al., 1973; Schwartz and Leonard, 1982).

Table 1.1 provides examples of early words from four children each acquiring one of three languages: British English, Estonian and Italian. The English and Italian children have been selected from a larger group of longitudinally recorded children (12 and 11, respectively), to illustrate relatively rapid and relatively slow first word production. (See Vihman, 1996 and Vihman and Kunnari, 2006 for details on these studies.) We will return to an analysis of the 'accuracy' of these first words below. In Table 1.1, target words that the child's form closely matches are in bold; words that the child changes by virtue of more radical changes than omission or simple consonant substitution – i.e. words that show reduplication or harmony – are in italics. There are no cases of metathesis in these first words.

Returning to the issue of implicit learning, we can propose that once children are able to combine rhythmic jaw movement with voice to produce 'canonical' babbling, or CVCV vocalizations with adult-like timing (Oller, 2000; Davis and MacNeilage, 2000), they have access to the first truly adult-like production patterns. From this point on they can begin to gain 'inside knowledge' of what it feels like to produce particular sound patterns in familiar situations. That is, children implicitly 'learn' both the 'feel' and the 'sound' of the vocal patterns they produce the most consistently. This idea, that the child may be 'experiencing the flow of adult speech through an 'articulatory filter' which selectively enhances motoric recall of phonetically accessible words' (Vihman, 1996, p. 142), is based on the following logic:

1. An (implicit) match of child vocal pattern to adult speech can provide infants with 'inside knowledge' through distributional learning of their own repeated articulatory production.
2. The 'selection' evidenced in accurate first word forms must result from *including known patterns in the selection*, not from excluding what is not known. That is, what is familiar becomes salient in the

input and is registered or remembered more robustly than what is unfamiliar (Fennell and Werker, 2003).

We turn now to experimental evidence in support of the articulatory filter.

experimental evidence

My colleagues and I recently undertook a series of studies designed to test the articulatory filter hypothesis, using the notion of 'vocal motor scheme' (VMS) (McCune and Vihman, 2001). A VMS is 'a generalized action plan that generates consistent phonetic forms... a formalized pattern of motor activity that does not require heavy cognitive resources to enact' (McCune and Vihman, 2001, p. 152). In practice, a VMS was a consonant used ten or more times in at least three out of four longitudinal sessions (based on monthly recording and transcription). Vihman and Nakai (2003) recorded infants bimonthly, from 10-and-a-half to 12 months of age, and tested them for a perception effect two weeks later, at 12-and-a-half months, using the Head Turn Preference Procedure (Kemler Nelson et al., 1995). Based on data from 27 children acquiring English and 26 children acquiring Welsh in North Wales a small overall effect of production on perception was found. Specifically, non-words, including a glottal or glide (taken to be pre-canonical and thus neutral in relation to the issue of production practice) and either

Table 1.1 Early Words

a. British English (North Wales)

Jude (10–11 mos.)		Ian (10–11 mos.)		Ali (13–15 mos.)		Helena (19–23 mos.)	
mum	mʌm	**yeah**	jæ	[peek-a-boo, I] **see ya**	diːː jaːː, diːːjæʔ, diˈda	**mum**	mɑm
hiya	aɪja	**who's [th]at?**	həʒa, huʒa, husə	**good-girl**	kʌᵏkaː	**car** [kaː]	ikɑː
cat	ka	**bang (bang)**	ʌba, babə, papa	**see-saw**	didaʔ, diːdaː, diˈdaː	**bird**	bɜːɪd
[grand]ma	ma	**catch**	kæ, kɛ, kə	**gone**	gʌ, ga	**I see**	aisiː
barnaby	babi	**hiya**	hʌɪ, heja, heaː	**oh dear**	ʌdɛː	**baby**	beibi
caterpillar	biɔ	**ball**	bo, boː, bul, bulː, buːl	**hi(ya)**	aja, ai		
yes, yeah	jə	**up**	ʔʌp				

Source: Keren-Portnoy et al., 2005: first ten words produced, based on bimonthly 30-minute recording sessions.

b. Estonian

Virve (10–12 mos.)		Raivo (13–14 mos.)		Eriku (from 17 mos.)		Madli (11–16 mos.)	
hi	[hai]	<u>shoe</u>	[ʃ, ç]	tiss 'nipple'	[tss]	**auto** 'car'	[auto]
pai 'nice'	[pai]	viska 'throw'	[is, iɫ, ɫ]	*päkapikk* 'elf'	[pæpa]	**kaka** 'poo'	[kaka]
aitäh	[aita,	põmm 'boom'	[bm bim,	tita 'girl'	[tit]	**kuu**	[kuːː]
/aitæh/	aida]		bëm:]			'moon'	
'thanks'							
allo 'hello	[ao]	aitäh	[ta, taʔ]	*paber* 'paper'	[paba]	kass 'cat'	[asˡ:]
(telephone)'		/aitæh/ 'thanks'					
see 'this'	[se]	**ei** 'no'	[ei:]	onu 'uncle'	[en:]	**auh** 'woof'	[auh]
tere 'hello'	[te,	vesi 'water'	[s̩]	suur 'big'	[u:]	naba 'belly	[aba]
	teðe,					button'	
	tete]						
kikerikii 'cock-	[titi:]	pall 'ball'	[bæ, pæ	väike	[æ:]	**nämm**	[næm:]
a-doodle-do'			bæbæ]	'small'		'yum'	
habe 'beard'	[abə]	<u>hiya</u>	[aja]	vanaema	[ana]	**aiai** 'ow'	[aiai]
				'grand-mom'			
cookie, cracker	[kɔ̥kɔ̥]	banaan	[ba,	ammuu 'moo'	[am:]	kott, kotid	[kotˡi]
		'banana'	babæ]			'bag, bags'	

Sources: Vihman, 1976 (Virve); Vihman, 1981 (Raivo); Kõrgvee, 2001 (Madli); Salo, 1993 (Eriku): first words produced, based on diary records. Underlined words are English.

c. Italian

Anna (10–13 mos)		Luca (10–13 mos)		Nicola (10–16 mos)		Nina (13–18 mos)	
<u>**mamma**</u>	mamːa	mamma	momːœ	**mamma**	mama	**mio**	mio
'mummy'		'mummy'		'mummy'		'mine (m.)'	
bebè 'baby'	bebɛ	**bella** 'pretty/	beja	**nonna** 'granny'	nenːa,	baubau	baːˈbaː
		nice (f.)'			nonːa	'bowwow'	
nonna	nonːa	**bimba**	bimba	**nanna** 'to sleep	nanːa	mamma	mem
'granny'		'child (f.)'	ɔˈchildˈ fˑ	(BT)'		'mummy'	
nanna 'to	nanːa	cocò 'hen (BT)'	kaˈka	**papà** 'daddy'	papːa	zia 'aunt'	ia
sleep (BT)'							
caffè	kakɛ	**pappa**	papːa	bimba 'child (f)'	bœbːɛ	**bimbo** 'child	bibːo
'coffee'		'food (BT)'				(f.)'	
papà	paːpa	**mimi** 'candy,	miˈmi	**tata** 'auntie'	tata	caffè 'coffee'	aɛ
'daddy'		sweet'					
		occhio 'eye'	aˈgo	vale 'goodbye'	ae		
		acqua	akwa				
		'water'					
		tata	titːa				
		'child (BT)'					
		bebè 'baby'	beˈbɛ				

Source: (adapted from Keren-Portnoy et al., 2009): first ten words produced, based on bimonthly 30–45 minute recording sessions. Key: m. = masculine; f. = feminine; ipv = imperative.

/t/ or /s/ for English and either /b/ or /g/ for Welsh (the two members of each pair being roughly equal in input frequency) elicited a novelty response, such that infants who were producing /t/d/ tended to look longer in response to /s/ while infants who were producing either /p/b/ or /k/g/ tended to look longer in response to the stop that they were not yet producing. A subsequent reanalysis showed that the effect, at least in English, was driven largely by the response of 11 children, each of whom produced over 200 tokens of the VMS consonant across the four recording sessions (/t/d/ in all cases for English, /s/ being relatively rarely produced at this age). Thus, we found that the extent of a child's use of a particular consonant in production did, as hypothesized, affect the level of the child's perceptual attention to that consonant: a consistently produced consonant elicited less attention than a rarely produced consonant.

DePaolis (2006) undertook a finer grained longitudinal study, recording the infants every one or two weeks from the age of 9 or 10 months and testing them as soon as they appeared to master at least one consonant to VMS level. In order to be able to administer the perception test as soon as the child showed a reliable production preference, VMS was defined operationally either in the same way as in Vihman and Nakai (2003) or, alternatively, as 50 or more occurrences in the course of one to three sessions. Testing involved randomly ordered presentations of each of three brief contrasting passages of five sentences each, with nine uses of non-words featuring (a) the child's VMS (e.g. for /p/b/, *bapeb*), (b) another child's VMS (e.g. for a child producing /t/d/ to less than VMS criterion, *deeted*), or (c) the fricatives /f/v/, which are seldom if ever used to VMS criterion in this period (e.g. *vufev*). The passages consisted of simple sentences with one or two content-word slots filled with the relevant non-word type (e.g. for /p/b/: *Wow, my pabep is a buppeb one. Did the bapeb go pubbep below? We pubbep call buppeb a lot. Are your bapeb too pabep over there? I see the bapeb here!*). Differing passages were used for each of the stop consonants. The fricative passage, used as a control for all of the infants, was recorded in three forms to ensure that each child heard three distinct passages, one each for the VMS- and non-VMS stop non-words and a third for the fricative.

Testing the children within a week of the recording session in which they first produced one or more consonants to VMS level proved critical, as it revealed a bipolar response to the non-word passages: Of the 18 children tested successfully, half had only a single VMS; of those nine children, six showed greater attention to the passages featuring their own VMS stop, while of the nine with multiple

VMS, all but one showed the reverse pattern, greater attention to the non-VMS stop passage – reproducing the novelty effect found in Vihman and Nakai (2003).

The differences between the two sets of results appear to be a consequence of the differences in design of the two studies. First, the perception test in DePaolis (2006) was more challenging than that used in Vihman and Nakai (2003). In the DePaolis study, the child could only identify the presence of a particular consonant after some degree of segmentation of the passage into words, whereas the earlier study provided the easier and evidently less appealing task of attending to words listed in isolation (looking times were shorter in that study). Second, and most importantly, DePaolis found that infants moved rapidly from practice with a first consonant to practice with one or more others. His 'multiple VMS' sample showed a novelty effect, as had the earlier study, which tested somewhat older children. The novelty effect in the earlier study was also weaker, presumably because it combined the responses of both infants with multiple VMS (who could be expected, in hindsight, to have been more attentive to the novel consonant) and infants with only a single VMS (who would likely have attended longer to the familiar consonant). Given the relatively long delay between the final production session and the perception test in the earlier study it was not possible to determine the exact production status of these infants, but by 12-and-a-half months we can assume that the majority were producing more than one consonant to VMS criterion.

The implication of both these studies is that production practice affects the way children listen to speech. In fact, the DePaolis study suggests that the shift from attention to the child's *own* VMS at the stage of single-VMS production to attention to *other* VMS at the subsequent stage implies 'a powerful mechanism for segmentation…An infant should be predisposed to segment words that contain sounds that they are producing' (DePaolis, 2006, p. 152), an effect that is consistent with the relative phonological accuracy of the first words.

item learning and 'selected' word forms

Let us consider again the word forms presented in Table 1.1. Some are, as expected, quite close to the target word forms (those in bold face), while others are less accurate. All of the English children produce over half of their early words relatively accurately; Helena, who makes the latest start, produces all of her first words as good matches. In the case of the other British children the less accurate forms generally involve final consonant omission (as in Jude's *cat,* Ian's *bang, catch* and Ali's *gone*). Jude unusually targets two longer words, omitting the medial syllable in *Barnaby* and the initial trochee in *caterpillar*. In Estonian the two girls (Virve and Madli) similarly produce more than half of their early words in a way that quite closely matches the target. The two boys make more changes, although the changes largely involve omissions – of whole syllable (Eriku's *väike, ammuu*; Raivo's *viska, aitäh, banaan*), vowel (Eriku's *tiss, tita, onu*; Raivo's *shoe, põmm, vesi*) or consonant (including onset consonant, which is rarely omitted in English: Eriku's *suur, väike, vana(ema)*; Raivo's *viska, hiya*). Finally, the first words of the Italian children are also largely either excellent matches to the target (as in Anna's case) or involve unsystematic consonant or vowel changes (Luca, Nicola) or omissions (Nicola, Nina). In just one case we see consonant harmony, suggesting that Anna is making a systematic change to align the word *caffè* with her other words, which have consonant harmony in the target forms as well as in her production.

In general, the early word sets (the first several recorded words of each child) do not appear to reflect a pre-existing template or production pattern (with the possible exception of Anna's). Most of the early word forms of each of the children are fairly distinct from one another, although in Estonian, for example, three out of Virve's first nine words have the diphthong [ai] and both Raivo and Eriku produce disyllables only in the case of target words with an onset labial stop (*pall, banaan*; *päkapikk, paber*). In Italian almost all of the early word forms are disyllabic and both Anna and Nicola favour disyllables with harmonizing adult initial and medial consonants. This appears to be a characteristic of early words in a language with a great many simple reduplicated words in infant-directed speech. In contrast, no one pattern dominates the output for any of the British children. Note that in a comparison of first word forms in English, French and Welsh in relation to the early acquisition of rhythm, Vihman et al. (2006) found that the disyllabic words most often used by five children acquiring French were all characterized, like the Italian data here, by simple CVCV structures (with harmonizing consonants in *maman* 'mama', *papa*, *poupée* 'doll', but not *chapeau* 'hat') while each of the (American) English children's often-used disyllabic words that included a diphthong, coda, syllabic consonant, C_1VC_2V sequence, or more than one of these sources of difficulty (*apple, baby, Big Bird, button*).

Returning to Table 1.1 once again, we can also see that the range of phonetic patterns produced is largely limited in all three languages to one- or two-syllable word forms with stops, nasals, glides and glottals – but with language-specific differences in the patterns. For example, only in Estonian does [s] occur in all four samples. By contrast, word-onset consonants occur in half or more of the early word forms for most of the children in all three languages, but vowel-onsets or syllabic consonants are prominent for two of the Estonian children only. Use of two different 'true' consonants in a word form is rare overall (i.e. excluding glottals and glides, which are already present in pre-canonical vocalizations). Such a limited range of consonant types and phonotactic structures, cross-linguistically, supports the idea that children are depending on their babbling practice, which is highly similar across differing ambient languages, to lead them into word production. They are also consistent with the hypothesis that 'selection' reflects the child's experience of a match between his or her babbling patterns and often heard, situationally salient, input words or short phrases (*who's that, see ya, good girl, oh dear, I see*).

lexical advance and the emergence of phonological systematicity

So far development is the product of the implicit matching process, with the articulatory filter resulting in the first (context-limited) word production. The period of first words by 'item learning' reflected in Table 1.1 provides, by hypothesis, the database on which the implicit distributional learning mechanism can again begin to operate, leading to a new level of lexical growth. Once a few words have begun to be produced, children's repertoires and their attention to the arbitrary relationship between form and meaning can both be expected to expand, with wide individual differences in the speed of this advance and in the extent to which it is driven by vocal skill and learning or by independent cognitive or semantic development.

Bates et al. (1979) and Vihman and McCune (1994) have emphasized the shift in word learning as the early context-bound words are supplemented by more 'context-flexible' word use, with generalized meanings. The proposed sequence – first context-limited, then flexible word acquisition – is not uncontroversial (Barrett, 1995; Harris et al., 1995; Ninio, 1993). And while the disparity in results from different studies may, in part, reflect differences in the definition of the two word types, it is probably sensible to view the distinction itself as gradient rather than categorical. In particular, first flexible or 'referential' words are more likely to be among children's first words if they are children whose comprehension is well in advance of their production. That is, children who begin to talk early typically produce some context-bound words in the earliest period, while children who begin somewhat later may produce words of both kinds from the start (McCune and Vihman, 2001).

The first flexible or 'referential' words express children's emerging understanding of the relationship between lexical categories (types) and their uses on particular occasions (tokens) (Vihman, 1996), and typically fall into two categories: nominals, which refer to familiar objects or animals in the child's world (not typically to persons, who tend to be referred to by 'context-bound' proper-name terms unique to specific individuals: *mama, papa, baby*) and 'relational words' (McCune-Nicolich, 1981) or predicates (Deuchar and Vihman, 2005). The latter may take the form (in English) of verb particles (*up/down, in/out, on/off*), expressing path or location, or of forms belonging to a variety of word classes which are used to comment on one or another of the dynamic aspects of events (*bye-bye, all gone, thank you, mine, more, no, uh-oh, back*), variously expressing ideas such as occlusion, deictic path, iteration, negation or reversal with the same referential generality that characterizes the symbolic use of nominals. These single-word predicates are harbingers of syntactic advance because they signal readiness to form the longer, more complex structures of the first word combinations (Vihman, 1999; Ninio, 2001; McCune, 2006).

the emergence of phonological systematicity

How does the move to more flexible word use, with referential meanings, relate to emergent phonological knowledge? Logically, there need be no direct relationship between these parallel cognitive and phonological advances, nor is there evidence to suggest a causal relationship (Vihman, 1976). Instead, the child's increasing awareness that 'things have names' leads to more proactive word learning – the 'explicit' learning referred to earlier, with focused attention and a greater degree of both intentionality and effort. This in turn generally leads to more rapid lexical advance (although this need not take the form of a 'vocabulary spurt' (Ganger and Brent, 2004)).

According to one current account, the growing density of (largely receptive) lexical neighbourhoods provides the pressure that drives holistic word learning to yield to segmental analysis and storage (Walley, 1993; Metsala, 1999). However, doubt has recently been cast on both the extent to which 'holistic word learning' can be supported (Swingley, 2003), and on the validity of the connection between vocabulary growth and segmental knowledge (e.g. Ballem and Plunkett, 2005). The hypothesis that whole word representation precedes more detailed, segmental representation (Waterson, 1971) has a long tradition (e.g. Ferguson and Farwell, 1975; Macken, 1979; Menn, 1983) and was first tested in relation to word recognition with 11-month-old French infants (Hallé and Boysson-Bardies, 1996). Hallé and Boysson-Bardies found that although *omitting* the word-initial consonant effectively masked the familiar (iambic) words, word-initial consonant *change* did not. Change to the medial consonant produced mixed results. However, Vihman et al. (2004) showed that the accentual pattern of the language of exposure was critical: In English, in which the most common words to children bear initial-syllable stress, change to the onset consonant masked the familiar words whereas change to the medial syllable did not. Thus the nature of the language involved is crucial, but is not always recognized in the literature, where infants' failure to recognize English words with changed first consonants is often interpreted to mean that they have 'detailed phonological representations' even at 7-and-a-half months (e.g. Jusczyk and Aslin, 1995). Also important is matching of the ages and stages of children to be compared, since Swingley (2003) tested 19-month-olds, at the opposite end of a steeply rising word comprehension curve (Oviatt, 1980) from the 11-month-old subjects of the French study.

Our discussion of learning mechanisms above provides an alternative account of the relationship of lexical growth to phonological learning. Once the child's productive lexicon begins to increase, giving the child repeated opportunities to hear and practise a range of phonetic patterns, distributional learning results in the growth of production routines, as illustrated below. Further experience with lexical units will lead to the reanalysis of the wholes into often-used component parts, yielding familiar phonotactic sequences which themselves support new representational learning of unfamiliar word forms (Storkel, 2001; Peters, this volume). Production practice – first with babbling, then with word forms – is one source of advances in phonological memory (Fennell and Werker, 2003). The product of more efficient word learning is more word production, more production practice, and consequently more implicit pattern-learning.

later words: both 'selected' and 'adapted'

Table 1.2 provides examples of the phonological pattern-learning exhibited in later word forms, based on data from two of the four children learning each of the languages represented in Table 1.1. For the children followed longitudinally (i.e. the English and Italian children) the data are taken from the first session in which the child produced at least 25 different word types spontaneously; this typically corresponds to a

Table 1.2 Later Words

a. British English (North Wales)

Jude (15 mos) T = 43 words				Ali (25 mos) T = 28 words			
<CV>				**<(CV)CVC>**			
select		adapt		select		adapt	
blue	[bʌ]	ball	[bɔ]	back	[pæʲkʰ, baʲk]	(another) one	[məm, məməm]
car	[kʰaː]	book (im.)	[bʊ]	bed	[pat, bad, bət, baʲç, bəbaʲtʰ]	biscuit	[əpɪʃ]
no	[nɔ, dɔː]	cake	[kʰi]	crash	[oːən kəɫː]	Tamar	[nĭmaːt]
sky	[kʰa]	cheese (im.)	[kʰi̥]	feet	[əhᵒmːiːtʰ]	yeah	[jˑam]
square	[wɛ]	flower	[la]	mam	[maˑmː]		
star	[daː]	mouth	[ma]	mess	[mːæːs, mæːːɫ]		
ta	[tʰaː]	teeth	[tiːː]	pump	[bɔːp]		
there	[dɛː]						

Source: See Keren-Portnoy et al., 2005. The words listed for each child are taken from the first biweekly session with close to 25 words.

b. Estonian

Virve (17–18 mos)				Raivo (15–16 mos)			
<Ca/ɔ s/n i/u s/n i/u> [see text]				**<C₁VC₁ >**			
select		adapt		select		adapt	
banaani 'banana'	[paːnini]	tagasi 'back (verb prt.)'	[tasisi]	kiik (i) 'swing'	[kikː]	lind (i) 'bird'	[nɪŋ]
		lennukit ' airplane, obj.'	[nanunu]			rind 'breast'	[nən]
		maasikas 'strawberry'	[maːsini]			king 'shoe'	[nɪŋ, nɪn, nɛŋ, næŋ]
		porgandit 'carrot, obj.'	[pɔnini]			banaan 'banana'	[pamː, bamː, pap]
		raamatut 'book, obj.'	[maːnunu]			karp 'small box'	[pap]
		rosinad 'raisins'	[oːsini]			kits 'goat'	[tits, titˡ]
						trepp 'step, stair'	[papː]

Sources: Vihman, 1996 (Virve), 1981 (Raivo). Diary data are chosen to reflect imposition of a template on adult words (i.e. of 'adapting' targets to child system) within first 50-word period. English words are underlined. F = fricative; N = nasal.

c. Italian

Anna (20 mos) T = 27 words			Nicola (22 mos) T = 25 words		
< C₁VC₂V >			<VCV>		
select		adapt	select		adapt
bimba 'child (f.)'	[bimba]	*ancora* 'again'	[kora]	*alta* 'high'	[atːa]	*cade* 'fall down, s3 pres.'	[ade]
cadi 'fall down, s2 pres.'	[kadi]	*animali* 'animals'	[mali]	*aria* 'air'	[aja]	*cavallo* 'horse'	[alːo]
cane 'dog'	[kane]	*coperta* 'blanket'	[pɛtːa]	*erba* 'grass'	[ɛbːa]	*chiudo* 'close, s1 pres.'	[udu]
coda 'tail'	[koda]	*maialone* 'big pig'	[mone]			*indietro* 'back'	[etro]
dritte 'straight'	[ditːe]	*seduta* 'sit, s3 pres.'	[duta]			*pronto* 'hello (telephone)'	[onto]
gallo 'rooster'	[galːo]					*trattore* 'tractor'	[are]
mucca 'cow'	[mukːa]					*vieni* 'come, s2 pres.'	[ɛni]
metto 'put, s1 pres.'	[metːo]					*zitto* 'silent'	[itːo]

Source: (Adapted from Keren-Portnoy et al., 2009): The words listed for each child are taken from the first bimonthly 30–45 minute recording session with 20 or more words. (s1/2/3 'first/second/third person singular'; pres. 'present tense'; f. 'feminine'.)

cumulative lexicon, based on a diary record, of 50–75 words. To match this, the Estonian children's words are taken from the time when they had approximately 50 recorded words. In Table 1.2, child words that closely match the target are termed 'select(ed)'; words that the child changes systematically, so that there is more internal similarity among child word forms than between child and adult target, are termed 'adapt(ed)'. Imitated words are marked (im).

For each child Table 1.2 shows a single pattern chosen to illustrate the processes of 'selection' and 'adaptation'. In the case of 'selection' the adult model is reproduced relatively accurately (allowing for some typical immaturity in production), while in the case of 'adaptation' the adult target is more radically changed and the child forms are more similar to one another than to the target. Note that the standard for 'accuracy' has now changed, as the children's phonetic skills have advanced. Coda omission, for example, is not typical of all children and tends to be sufficiently systematic at this point to be considered an 'adaptation' where it occurs. In all cases the child's pattern or 'template' is informally expressed (in angle brackets) to account for the two sets of forms, where the source of the child's 'adapted' forms is at least partially to be found in the 'selected' models which serve as representatives of the adult language to which the child is exposed.

This next step in phonological learning, which we take to reflect the beginnings of phonological organization or systematicity, is illustrated by both the commonalities and the differences between the different children's patterns, both within and across language groups. For English, one of the children with rapid lexical learning, Jude, is contrasted with one of the children who made slower progress, Ali. In Jude's case we see a simple template, the open <CV> syllable, expressed in eight 'selected' forms and seven 'adapted' forms. The selected forms constitute good matches (are 'accurate') except for cluster reduction and, in one case, vowel change (*blue*). The adapted forms reflect the processes of coda omission or, in one case (*flower*), truncation of the disyllable to a mono-syllable. In addition, we see monophthongization (in *mouth*) and, in the case of *cake* and *cheese*, an unusual substitution of [i] for [e] and of [k] for [tʃ], possibly reflecting a single output solution for two problematic forms.

In Ali's case we find more 'selected' than 'adapted' forms for her pri-mary pattern, expressed as the template <(CV)CVC>. The 'selected' words are all closed monosyllables (CVC), although a 'filler syllable' appears to be prefixed in some cases (cf. *bed*, *crash*, *feet*). The adapted forms include longer target words, however, and reflect a range of dif-ferent phonological processes, all of which produce a one- or two-syl-lable word ending in a closed syllable (labial harmony in *(another) one*, perhaps inspired by the /w/ of *one* /wʌn/, truncation in the case of *bis-cuit*, metathesis in the case of *Tamar* [tamaːr]).

For Estonian, we see phonological patterning of quite different kinds in the case of the two siblings, Virve and Raivo. For Virve we see one relatively 'accurate' or selected form, *banaani*. The adapted forms are all trisyllabic and reflect a bias toward the vowel melody <a…i> (as in *banaani*, a bias apparent already in Virve's first words: see Table 1.1) or <a…u>. The choice of high vowel for the unstressed syllable appears to follow the implicit rule, 'use [u] if the target includes [u]; otherwise use [i]'. The last two (unstressed) syllables also show full or partial con-sonant harmony, with a nasal or /s/ as target consonants (again, as in *banaani*), or the melody <s…n>, specifically in the two cases – *maasikas* and *rosinad* – in which the target word form includes both a nasal and /s/ (regardless of their sequencing in the target word). The word-initial /m/ in *maasikas* is retained and the medial /m/ of *raamatut* moved to word-initial position; again as in *banaani,* only the two unstressed sylla-bles are constrained by the place harmony of the template, which is also observed in the child's more numerous disyllabic word forms (through 22 months: Vihman, 1996, p. 224).

As in the English cases, the overall templatic patterning applies to all of the forms. The extent of 'selection' of potential targets even in the case of the adapted forms is striking: Only words with a high vowel in one of the last two syllables are targeted for trisyllabic production, and only words with either /s/ or a nasal in one of the three syllables. In *lennukit* we also see the imposition of [a] for adult [e] in the first syllable; all of the child's forms have a low or lower-mid back vowel in the stressed syllable. (For a template of similar complexity applied to English, see Priestly, 1977.)

Whereas Virve's template applies only to long words, Raivo (like Jude) shows a template that constrains production to monosyllables, with the further requirement that the monosyllable take the shape CVC with harmonizing onset and coda consonants. The one selected form (an imitation) is accurate except for the displacement of vowel length to the coda consonant. The seven adapted forms actually involve only three fully distinct output forms: <nVn>, <pap> and <tit> (where the angle brackets indicate abstraction away from the variant phonetic detail of the child's forms). This tendency to settle on a small number of homophonous forms to express a large number of target words (Vihman, 1981; Waterson, 1971) was a successful strategy leading to rapid increase in vocabulary; it also demonstrates the same distributional learning or systematizing that we see in the other children at this stage.

Finally, for Italian, we again have one relatively early word learner and one with slower progress. Anna's selected forms reflect her ability not only to change consonants within a disyllabic form but also to produce medial nasal-stop clusters (although not the onset cluster in *dritte*). The adapted forms all involve truncation, reducing three- and four-syllable words to disyllabic forms. As in Virve's case, the particular form that the disyllables take depends on the target – especially the rhythmic pattern, with penultimate accent in all of the words targeted – but also on Anna's practised consonant repertoire. Anna produces [mone] for *maialone,* for example, profiting from her production experience with [m] at word onset but otherwise omitting all but the last two syllables to match her disyllabic template.

Nicola's template is one also found in languages like Finnish or Hindi which, like Italian, have medial geminates (Vihman and Croft, 2007): VCV, with omission even of (early learned) onset stops (*cade, pronto*) in the adapted forms. Again we see the targeting of long words (difficult to avoid in Italian); and again the truncated forms reflect the accentual pattern but also show sensitivity to the rest of the word, with [are] for *trattore,* for example (see Wijnen et al., 1994). Note, too, that Nicola preserves clusters, whether heterogeneous or geminates, when they occur within the final (accented) disyllable of the model.

Overall, the individual children's patterns and preferences differ considerably in the complexity of the constraints exhibited even in this small sample. There are also language-specific characteristics. But the data sets share the feature that the output patterns do not obviously derive directly from the adult languages. They are neither directly input-frequency based nor closely modelled on the target word forms in all cases. Nor are they the product of a single dominant phonological process or of universal markedness conditions or stages of development (Keren-Portnoy et al., 2009). Instead, the patterns reflect the *individual* child's perceptual experience of the input *in relation to* his or her motoric experience or practice – resulting in differences that are as great within as across language groups.

conclusion

This chapter has focused on the early stages of word production, bringing experimental evidence of the effects of production practice on perception to bear on the shaping of first word forms. It has attempted to illustrate 'secondary procedural induction' through the regression in accuracy reflected in the later 'adapted' word forms. Above all, it has sought to indicate that both implicit (procedural) and explicit (declarative) learning play a role in phonological and lexical development and has provided a model in outline of how these two kinds of learning become integrated over the period of single-word production.

note

1. Following Squire and Kandel I use the terms 'procedural' and 'declarative' here, in lieu of the more widely used terms 'implicit' and 'explicit', to avoid the difficulties of applying the notion of 'explicit' or 'conscious awareness' to infants for whom no such awareness can be clearly established.

references

Baddeley, A. D., Vargha-Khadem, F. and Mishkin, M. (2001). Preserved recognition in a case of developmental amnesia. *Journal of Cognitive Neuroscience, 13,* 3, 357–69.

Ballem, K. D. and Plunkett, K. (2005). Phonological specificity in children at 1; 2. *Journal of Child Language, 32,* 159–73.

Barrett, M. (1995). Early lexical development. In P. Fletcher and B. MacWhinney (eds), *Handbook of Child Language* (pp. 362–92). Cambridge, MA: Blackwell.

Bates, E., Benigni, L., Bretherton, I., Camaioni, L. and Volterra, V. (1979). *The Emergence of Symbols*. New York: Wiley.

Boysson-Bardies, B. de, Hallé, P., Sagart, L. and Durand, C. (1989). A crosslinguistic investigation of vowel formants in babbling. *Journal of Child Language,* 16, 1–17.

Boysson-Bardies, B. de and Vihman, M. M. (1991). Adaptation to language: Evidence from babbling and first words in four languages. *Language*, 67, 297–319.

Brent, M. R. and Siskind, J. M. (2001). The role of exposure to isolated words in early vocabulary development. *Cognition*, 81, B33–B44.

Cheek, A., Cormier, K., Repp, A. and Meier, R. P. (2001). Prelinguistic gesture predicts mastery and error in the production of early signs. *Language,* 77, 292–323.

Davis, B. L. and MacNeilage, P. (2000). An embodiment perspective on the acquisition of speech perception. *Phonetica*, 57, 229–41.

DePaolis, R. A. (2006). The influence of production on the perception of speech. In Bamman, D., Magnitskaia, T. and Zaller, C. (eds), *Proceedings of the 30th Boston University Conference on Language Development*. Somerville, MA: Cascadilla Press.

Deuchar, M. and Vihman, M. M. (2005). A radical approach to early mixed utterances. *International Journal of Bilingualism*, 9, 137–57.

Ellis, N. C. (2005). At the interface: dynamic interactions of explicit and implicit language knowledge. *Studies in Second Language Acquisition,* 27, 305–52.

Fennell, C. T. and Werker, J. F. (2003). Early word learners' ability to access phonetic detail in well-known words. *Language and Speech,* 46, 245–64.

Ferguson, C. A. and Farwell, C. B. (1975). Words and sounds in early language acquisition. *Language,* 51, 419–39.

Ferguson, C. A., Peizer, D. B. and Weeks, T. A. (1973). Model-and-replica phonological grammar of a child's first words. *Lingua*, 31, 35–65.

Ganger, J. and Brent, M. R. (2004). Reexamining the vocabulary spurt. *Developmental Psychology,* 40, 621–32.

Gómez, R. L. and Gerken, L. A. (1999). Artificial grammar learning by one-year-olds leads to specific and abstract knowledge. *Cognition*, 70, 109–35.

Hallé, P. and Boysson-Bardies, B. de. (1996). The format of representation of recognized words in infants' early receptive lexicon. *Infant Behavior and Development*, 19, 435–51.

Harris, M., Yeeles, C., Chasin, J. and Oakley, Y. (1995). Symmetries and assymmetries in early lexical comprehension and production. *Journal of Child Language*, 22, 1–18.

Jusczyk, P. W. (1997). *The Discovery of Spoken Language*. Cambridge, MA: MIT Press.

Jusczyk, P. W. and Aslin, R. N. (1995). Infants' detection of the sound patterns of words in fluent speech. *Cognitive Psychology*, 29, 1–23.

Karmiloff-Smith, A. (1992). *Beyond Modularity*. Cambridge, MA: MIT Press.

Kemler Nelson, D. G., Jusczyk, P. W., Mandel, D. R., Myers, J., Turk, A. and Gerken, L. (1995). The Head Turn Preference Procedure for testing auditory perception. *Infant Behavior and Development*, 18, 111–16.

Keren-Portnoy, T., DePaolis, R. A. and Vihman, M. M. (2005). The articulatory filter and the creation of sound-meaning links. Presented at the conference on Emergence of Linguistic Abilities, Lyon.

Keren-Portnoy, T., Majorano, M. and Vihman, M. M. (2009). From phonetic to phonology: The emergence of first words in Italian. *Journal of Child Language,* 36, 235–67.

Kirkham, N. Z., Slemmer, J. A. and Johnson, S. P. (2002). Visual statistical learning in infancy: evidence for a domain-general learning mechanism. *Cognition,* 83, B35–B42.

Kõrgvee, K. (2001). Lapse sõnavara areng vanuses 1;8–2;1 ('A child's lexical development, 1;8–2;1'). Bachelor's dissertation, Tartu University.

Kuhl, P. K. and Meltzoff, A. N. (1988). Speech as an intermodal object of perception. In A. Yonas (ed.), *Perceptual Development in Infancy. The Minnesota Symposia on Child Psychology, 20.* Hillsdale, NJ: Lawrence Erlbaum.

Locke, J. (1986). Speech perception and the emergent lexicon. In P. Fletcher and M. Garman (eds), *Language Acquisition* (2nd edition). Cambridge: Cambridge University Press.

Macken, M. A. (1979). Developmental reorganization of phonology. *Lingua,* 49, 11–49.

McCune, L. (2006). Dynamic event words. *First Language,* 26, 233–55.

McCune-Nicolich, L. (1981). The cognitive basis of early relational words. *Journal of Child Language,* 8, 15–36.

McCune, L. and Vihman, M. M. (2001). Early phonetic and lexical development. *Journal of Speech, Language and Hearing Research,* 44, 670–84.

Menn, L. (1983). Development of articulatory, phonetic, and phonological capabilities. In B. Butterworth (ed.), *Language Production* (Vol. 2). London: Academic Press.

Metsala, J. L. (1999). Young children's phonological awareness and nonword repetition as a function of vocabulary development. *Journal of Educational Psychology,* 91, 3–19.

Murphy, K., McKone, E. and Slee, J. (2003). Dissociations between implicit and explicit memory in children: The role of strategic processing and the knowledge base. *Journal of Experimental Child Psychology,* 84, 124–65.

Nazzi, T., Jusczyk, P. W. and Johnson, E. K. (2000). Language discrimination by English-learning 5-month-olds: Effects of rhythm and familiarity. *Journal of Memory and Language,* 43, 1–19.

Ninio, A. (1992). The relation of children's single word utterances to single word utterances in the input. *Journal of Child Language,* 19, 87–110.

Ninio, A. (1993). Is early speech situational? In D. J. Messer and G. T. Turner (eds), *Critical Influences on Child Language Acquisition and Development.* New York: St. Martin's Press.

Ninio, A. (2001). Pragmatic keywords and the first combining verbs in children's speech. *First Language,* 21, 433–60.

Oller, D. K. (2000). *The Emergence of the Speech Capacity.* Mahwah, NJ: Lawrence Erlbaum.

Oller, D. K., Wieman, L. A., Doyle, W. J. and Ross, C. (1976). Infant babbling and speech. *Journal of Child Language,* 3, 1–11.

Oviatt, S. (1980). The emerging ability to comprehend language. *Child Development,* 50, 97–106.

Pierrehumbert, J. (2003). Phonetic diversity, statistical learning, and acquisition of phonology. *Language and Speech,* 46, 115–54.

Priestly, T. M. S. (1977). One idiosyncratic strategy in the aquisition of phonology. *Journal of Child Language,* 4, 45–66.

Reber, A. S. (1967). Implicit learning of artificial grammars. *Journal of Verbal Learning and Verbal Behavior,* 6, 855–63.

Ruddy, M. G. and Bornstein, M. H. (1982). Cognitive correlates of infant attention and maternal stimulation over the first year of life. *Child Development,* 53, 183–8.

Saffran, J. R., Aslin, R. N. and Newport, E. L. (1996). Statistical learning by 8-month-old infants. *Science,* 274, 1926–8.

Saffran, J. R., Newport, E. L., Aslin, R. N., Tunick, R. A. and Barrueco, S. (1997). Incidental language learning: Listening (and learning) out of the corner of your ear. *Psychological Science,* 8, 101–5.

Salo, A. (1993). Muutelõppude ilmumine ühe eesti lapse keelde vanuses 1; 5–2; 5. [The emergence of inflectional endings in the language of one Estonian child aged 1; 5–2; 5.] Undergraduate thesis, Finno-Ugric Languages Department, Tartu University.

Schwartz, R. and Leonard, L. (1982). Do children pick and choose? *Journal of Child Language,* 9, 319–36.

Squire, L. R. (1992). Memory and the hippocampus: A synthesis from findings with rats, monkeys, and humans. *Psychological Review,* 99, 195–231.

Squire, L. R. and Kandel, E. R. (1999). *Memory: From Mind to Molecules.* New York: Henry Holt.

Storkel, H. L. (2001). Learning new words: Phonotactic probability in language development. *Journal of Speech, Language, and Hearing Research,* 44, 1321–37.

Swingley, D. (2003). Phonetic detail in the developing lexicon. *Language and Speech,* 46, 265–94.

Tomasello, M. (2003). *Constructing a Language.* Boston, MA: Harvard University Press.

Vihman, M. M. (1976). From prespeech to speech: on early phonology. *Stanford Papers and Reports on Child Language Development,* 12, 230–44.

Vihman, M. M. (1981). Phonology and the development of the lexicon. *Journal of Child Language,* 8, 239–64.

Vihman, M. M. (1993). Variable paths to early word production. *Journal of Phonetics,* 21, 61–82.

Vihman, M. M. (1996). *Phonological Development.* Oxford: Blackwell.

Vihman, M. M. (1999). The transition to grammar in a bilingual child: Positional patterns, model learning, and relational words. *International Journal of Bilingualism,* 3, 267–301.

Vihman, M. M. (2001). A cross-linguistic study of the acquisition of geminate consonants. End of award report, Economic and Social Research Council Award R000223134.

Vihman, M. M. and Boysson-Bardies, B. de. (1994). The nature and origins of ambient language influence on infant vocal production and early words. *Phonetica,* 51, 159–69.

Vihman, M. M. and Croft, W. (2007). Phonological development: Toward a 'radical' templatic phonology. *Linguistics,* 45, 683–725.

Vihman, M. M. and Kunnari, S. (2006). The sources of phonological knowledge. *Recherches Linguistiques de Vincennes,* 35, 133–64.

Vihman, M. M., Macken, M. A., Miller, R., Simmons, H. and Miller, J. (1985). From babbling to speech. *Language,* 61, 397–445.

Vihman, M. M. and McCune, L. (1994). When is a word a word? *Journal of Child Language,* 21, 517–42.

Vihman, M. M. and Nakai, S. (2003). Experimental evidence for an effect of vocal experience on infant speech perception. In M. J. Solé, D. Recasens and J. Romero (eds), *Proceedings of the 15th International Congress of Phonetic Sciences, Barcelona* (pp. 1017–20).

Vihman, M. M., Nakai, S. and DePaolis, R. A. (2006). Getting the rhythm right: A cross-linguistic study of segmental duration in babbling and first words. In L. Goldstein, D. Whalen and C. Best (eds), *Laboratory Phonology 8* (pp. 341–66). Mouton de Gruyter: New York.

Vihman, M. M., Nakai, S., DePaolis, R. A. and Hallé, P. (2004). The role of accentual pattern in early lexical representation. *Journal of Memory and Language,* 50, 336–53.

Vihman, M. M. and Velleman, S. L. (2000). The construction of a first phonology. *Phonetica,* 57, 255–66.

Walley, A. C. (1993). The role of vocabulary development in children's spoken word recognition and segmentation ability. *Developmental Review,* 13, 286–350.

Waterson, N. (1971). Child phonology: A prosodic view. *Journal of Linguistics,* 7, 179–211.

Werker, J., Fennell, C., Corcoran, K. and Stager, C. (2002). Infants' ability to learn phonetically similar words: Effects of age and vocabulary size, *Infancy,* 3, 1–30.

Whalen, D. H., Levitt, A. G. and Wang, Q. (1991). Intonational differences between the reduplicative babbling of French- and English-learning infants. *Journal of Child Language,* 18, 501–16.

Wijnen, F., Krikhaar, E. and Den Os, E. (1994). The (non)realization of unstressed elements in children's utterances. *Journal of Child Language,* 21, 59–83.

2
cracking the language code: processing strategies in first language acquisition

ann m. peters

introduction

By the end of their first year, children are on the threshold of being able to extract and internally represent meaningful chunks of language (Fernald, 1991), i.e. to crack the language code. During the first year they have been discovering which sounds and sound contrasts are important in the ambient language, and are becoming familiar with the dominant stress and melodic patterns of utterances; information that will be used to target speech chunks to extract. They have also been developing articulation and memory skills that will enable them to make passable attempts at repeating (imitating) words they hear. Articulatory skills are further refined by these attempts to imitate salient chunks of the ambient language.

The creation of adult-like representations of 'words' in memory is a fairly slow process (at least to begin with), 'fed' both by hearing multiple repetitions of a word and by multiple attempts to articulate it (Vihman, this volume). The ability to recognize and recall stretches of several syllables makes such chunks accessible for retrieval, affording ever more 'hooks' to which a learner can connect new chunks and compare them with remembered chunks, both in real time and in memory. This leads to the discovery of similarities and differences, providing ever more material for comparison and analysis into components and patterns. Imitation and practice prepare infants to recognize and remember the sounds of recurring chunks of language. It does not really matter whether these chunks correspond to adult words or phrases or even to whole sentences. What matters is the developing ability to recognize, remember and eventually to reproduce them.

Children expend a great deal of effort acquiring language, driven by powerful desires to interact socially with caregivers, to anticipate what will happen next, and to exert increasing control over the environment. This theme of the power of internal drives is one that will recur throughout this chapter. In line with Halliday's account of the different functions early language serves pre-school children (Halliday, 1973), the desire to interact affectively with caregivers leads to the realization that one can use speech to achieve a whole range of social goals: social interaction (Halliday's *interpersonal* function), control of others' behaviour (*instrumental* and *regulatory* functions), prediction of what will happen next (*heuristic* function), and learning about the world (*mathetic* function). Trying to achieve these goals motivates remembering and producing early chunks of language. As noted, unanalysed forms extracted in this way become available for linguistic analysis, forming the material out of which a learner can begin to construct her own linguistic system (Peters, 1983).

In addition to becoming proficient at engaging in social communication through turn-taking, infants in their first year have been learning about objects and people in the world: their physical characteristics and that they have names. At first these names are just sounds that caregivers regularly (though not always) use in the presence of specific objects. Once the 'nominal insight' has occurred (i.e. that sound sequences can be used to *refer* to objects, in their presence and then in their absence) children have a new kind of power over the environment that forms a powerful motivation for learning ever more words and their meanings. At the same time, infants are beginning to learn about *categories* of things, and that words can be used to refer to categories of objects. These new tools lead to a growing comprehension vocabulary between 10 and 12 months, even though no or very few words may yet be produced. This forms a foundation which babies can use to attach meanings to newly extracted chunks of language.

Learners eventually have to integrate and interconnect all these kinds of development. This can be conceptualized as the construction of overlapping networks of connections between attributes of remembered pieces of language. One network connects chunks that sound similar; another might connect chunks that feel similar in the mouth; another, chunks that occur in specific (routine) contexts (e.g. mealtime, diaper changing, going for a walk); yet another, those that contain some of the same components (e.g. 'whats-that' with 'whats-this'). The expansion of all these networks assists both memory and analysis, and eventually forms the basis for the discovery of combinatorial patterns (see below).

Access to such overlapping networks also accounts for adults' ability to retrieve words on the basis of a range of small clues, e.g. to solve crossword puzzles.

attributes of the linguistic environment

The kind of language that children can begin to extract from the ambient speech stream will depend on what that stream is like. One infant might only ever hear single-word utterances spoken in an exaggerated 'baby talk' sort of intonation, while a second infant (say one who is riding in a sling on his mother's back) might only ever (over-) hear adults talking to each other in full sentences. (See Saxton, this volume.) Assuming that the caregivers are speaking the same language (e.g. English) we would expect these two infants to extract very different kinds of language, e.g. single words vs. whole phrases. Heath (1983) describes language learning in Trackton, a community of the second sort. She observed babies in their second year sitting on the floor near adults who were talking, literally, over their heads. These children, not directly interacting with anyone, nevertheless began to extract and imitate small pieces from this language flow, often the tag ends of overheard phrases. A few months later they began manipulating overheard chunks, adding to them, deleting parts, or varying the intonation or structure. Heath calls this activity 'repetition with variation'; it makes manifest what most babies probably do more covertly in the process of analysis of extracted units into their components (Peters, 1983).

Other critical attributes of the early linguistic environment are cultural expectations about when a child's 'first words' will appear, what they are likely to sound like, and when a child is expected (allowed) to take the floor on his own. In the USA (and other countries) a child's first word is popularly anticipated to be 'mama' or 'dada'. However, as recent debate on the child language exchange system revealed (CHILDES TalkBank, September 2006), first words actually range from 'hi!' or 'hiya!' to 'juice', 'bye-bye', 'uh-oh' and 'trash-truck'.

Caregivers' expectations are important because infant vocalizations receive feedback based on them. If a child is producing a phonetically consistent form in a predictable context, this would be a good candidate for an early 'word'. However, if it does not fit the caregiver's expectations, it may not be recognized or acknowledged and runs the risk of dying out for lack of support. Along the same lines, if, as in Trackton, babies' early vocalizations are interpreted as 'just noises' rather than as attempts to communicate, children will have to rely on their own efforts to break into the language system. In contrast, an empathetic caregiver who is willing to recognize a child's consistent forms as 'words' can facilitate the child's move into communication with adults.

Finally, if the speech which babies hear routinely contains long morphologically complex words this will pose different segmentation problems to learners than if the speech routinely contains monosyllabic words. In the former case, babies' early productions are much more likely to consist of morphologically complex chunks (Peters, 1997). Learners of some agglutinative and polysynthetic languages (e.g. Japanese or West Greenlandic Eskimo) have been observed to produce combinations of two bound morphemes earlier than combinations of two 'free' words (Clancy, 1985; Fortescue and Lennert Olsen, 1992). We will revisit these issues below when we reconsider environmental influences on the strategies learners employ.

In what follows, we will consider how learners progress from prelanguage into 'real' language, discussing the kinds of strategies they use and what is known about individual differences in the strategies selected. Finally, we will look at how the learning process itself changes with development and at some of the forces that move the process along.

steps and strategies

In order to learn language, mere extraction and representation of sound sequences is not enough. The learner also has to be able to attach meanings to extracted chunks, by connecting them to what is happening in the contexts in which they are heard. Strong motivations to accomplish this are being able to anticipate what will come next (e.g. 'when Mommy says *bath time*, I know what kind of activity to expect') and to effect changes in one's own environment (equivalents of *up* and *down* are generally produced very early). Accumulating such knowledge empowers a child to participate increasingly in social interactions, as well as to exert more and more control over those interactions.

The next two tasks are segmentation and pattern extraction and these must proceed in parallel. Segmentation is the discovery of smaller units latent in extracted chunks and pattern extraction concerns how those units can be combined to construct new meanings. It is important to bear in mind that if learners were only able to remember and extract single adult words, they would have no way to gather information about how words are combined. It is in the process of comparing larger with smaller chunks of language that learners discover the inherent combinatorial patterns. This implies that a necessary prerequisite for acquiring syntax is the ability to remember (extract) chunks longer than a single word, and analyse (segment) them both into their components and into their combinatorial patterns, with both tasks proceeding in tandem, each feeding the other. Let us consider these tasks further.

In the simplified variety of English addressed to children, the 'smallest units' tend to be single words. Nonetheless, children have been observed trying to decompose monomorphemic disyllables into smaller components (Peters, 1983). For instance, the word *behave* is prone to misanalysis into *be* + /heyv/, probably on analogy with *be good*, *be quiet*, etc. Children have also been observed to use a perceptual strategy in which 'filler syllables' such as schwa (/ə/) represent unclear syllables in an otherwise faithfully reproduced utterance (Peters and Menn, 1993; Peters, 2001b). Fillers provide scaffolds for trying to say things that have not yet been fully analysed, providing handy places to park material to be analysed later, once perception of their phonological content has improved (Peters, 2001a). In order to analyse large chunks of speech, if the initially extracted chunks do not map cleanly onto the words of the adult language, children will use any perceivable boundary, such as a pause or a syllable break to create their own units. For instance, a frequent question, *whassat?*, may be extracted as a single chunk. When it is realized that this chunk is related to, say, *what's-this?* It will assist the segmentation of the original *whassat* into two pieces: *whats* + *that*? And when it is discovered that *whats* actually contains two pieces (*what* + *is*) the original chunk will be fully analysed into its adult components.

extraction strategies: identifying useful chunks of language

Taking children's early language productions to be evidence of the kinds of extraction strategies they are using, we can infer the following list of strategies: (see Peters, 1983, for a fuller discussion)

1) Extract <u>whole utterances</u> if they are short enough to remember and are bounded by silence. It helps if they are repeated, either exactly or with slight alterations. (e.g. *Ball. That's a ball.*)
2) Extract the perceptually salient <u>ends of utterances</u>, even if it isn't clear what they mean (e.g. *ge da ka* extracted from *But you wanna get down on the <u>couch</u>.*)
3) Extract <u>suprasegmentally delineated intonational packages</u>, including tags such as *isn't-it?* or *I believe*. Good candidates are clear speech tunes that are easily identifiable with a particular context (*Hi!*, *Uh-oh!*, *Gimme <u>five</u>!*, *Lookit-that!*) and phrases repeatedly uttered by an older

sibling (*Open-the-door!* or *Don't-touch-that-it's-mine*) or a parent (e.g. /aydlæsam/ which turned out to be *No thanks, I still have some*).

4) Extract sound sequences that can be <u>identified as producing useful results</u>. (e.g. *chih*, used to get picked up, and extracted from *Do you want to come up on Daddy's chest?* Eventually *chih* was replaced with *piyaup* (extracted from *Do you want me to <u>pick you up</u>*).

5) Extract <u>rhythmic stretches</u>, replacing less clearly perceived syllables with fillers (e.g. *Cross-uh-street, down-uh-stairs, sitcha-potty, cuppa-milk*).

segmentation strategies: finding smaller components within extractions

In order to move beyond recognition and production of initially extracted units, children must realize that every extracted string is potentially composed of smaller units that can be segmented out and stored as independent units. With this realization, the general strategy is to try to segment all extractions into smaller pieces. The phonological salience of a specific part of an extraction, such as a stressed syllable, can enhance focus on it. This leads to several identifiable sub-strategies:

1) Segment off the <u>final</u> syllable or foot from an utterance (e.g. pick out *five* from *gimme <u>five</u>*; *high* from *we jump so <u>high</u>*; *by-you* from *Daddy's gonna sit down <u>by you</u>*).

2) Segment out a <u>stressed</u> syllable or foot (e.g. pick out *toothbrush* from *Oh you jus' do like your <u>toothbrush</u>, dontcha*).

3) Segment off the <u>first</u> syllable from the rest (e.g. Ruth Weir's observation that her son produced [wIs] for *whistle* (when used as a verb) and [mezh] for *measure* (Weir, 1962, p. 74).

4) Segment sub-units that are somehow <u>salient</u> (e.g. pick out *back-a-house* from *Do you wanna go <u>back ta the house</u>, an' swing*).

5) Segment off sub-units that are <u>repeated</u> within the same unit. This last strategy is supported by the observation that repetition of elements appears to increase their salience, as in languages such as Hebrew where gender or number agreement is multiply marked, or Xhosa where gender-class agreement is marked on both noun and modifying adjective by prefixing.

analysis strategies: discovering how units can be combined

As already noted, if learners were only able to remember and extract single units, they would have no way to discover how units can be combined. It is in the process of comparing larger with smaller units that learners discover how systematic combinations of units can create new meanings. A prerequisite for acquiring syntax is therefore the ability to extract, segment, and compare chunks to discern combinatorial patterns. But how do children do this? Let's return to the analysis of the frequent question, *whassat?*, described briefly above, which involved three steps:

1) Note when two extracted units share a phonologically similar portion (*whassat, whassis*).
2) Remember the similar portion (*whas*) as a new unit in the lexicon.
3) Pay attention to the dissimilar portions (*sat, sis*), too, and remember them.

Segmentation of a long unit into shorter ones thus yields structural as well as lexical information. From the simple juxtaposition of units, the realization that two such juxtapositions have a unit in common leads to the abstraction from <u>unit + unit</u> to <u>unit + (closed) list</u>:

4) Posit a simple pattern consisting of a fixed item plus a list: (*whats +___{sat, sis}*). Then as further segmented sequences sharing a common element (*whats + your-name, whats + up, whats + cookin', whats + sa-matter*) are recognized, the list both grows and generalizes (*whats + ___*).

The next step is to note that the slot can be treated more abstractly, supporting a move from <u>unit + (closed) list</u> to <u>unit + (open)</u> class. This requires two realizations: recognition of some feature that characterizes all the members of the list, and that any other unit that shares this feature can also be combined with this particular (constant) unit.

5) Generalize the contents of a slot as more and more likely candidates are encountered.

Sometimes this process can backfire, as in the case of 'behave' mentioned above where *be* + [human quality] seems to have been extracted from *be quiet, be good, don't be so noisy*, etc. leading to '*I'm going to be very very /heyv/*' or '*She's not being /heyv/*' based on an exhortation such as *Now I want you to behave!* (See Peters, 1983, Chapter 3, for more examples of oversegmentation, and one example of a child correcting this misanalysis 'on line', moving from *I am /heyv/* to *I /heyv/* to *I am behaving*.)

6) At this stage a new tool can emerge: once learners realize that frames recur, they can use the frame itself as a segmentation aid. For example, the frame *all* + adj, (*all gone, all done, all clean*) can, on the basis of hearing *all over*, allow the inference that *over* is a new word, and that it belongs to the list of words that can occur with *all*.

For this gradual sort of expansion to result in an adult-like grammar, primitive frames must be abstracted to more general patterns such as Sentence = Subject + Predicate as advocated by construction theorists (e.g. Goldberg, 1995; Tomasello, 1998). This is made possible by the fact that a great deal of language use is quite formulaic (See Kuiper et al., this volume). For efficiency of communication, speakers rely on formulaic frames that are only as general as they need to be, with fairly simple slots to be rapidly filled in as the situation warrants (Fillmore, 1978; Nagy, 1978; Peters, 1983). Only rarely do speakers struggle to say some-thing entirely new, for which already assembled formulaic construc-tions are inadequate.

Evidence for the abstraction of construction frames comes from 'dense data' such as that collected nearly daily over a six-week period by Lieven et al. (2003). Similarly dense data is provided by my record of Seth, such as the following, which shows he begins marking tran-sitivity on a verb-by-verb basis. The very first hint of a verbal object appears at 1;7,17 when he produces 7 tokens of 3 verbs with some sort of object: *find'it* (3), *hold'it* (3), and *get ball* (1). The next week, 1;7.26, he produces 7 tokens of *get* + NP: (*get (da) ball* (6), *get block* (1)), as well as 1 token of *get down*. Two weeks later (1;8.00) he produces four verbs with objects: *hold'it* (1), *kiss'it* (2), *get'it* (3), *get ball* (1), *see da thunder* (1). (*See* also occurs intransitively, as in *wan' see*.) The number of different verbs he uses with *it* slowly increases; at 1;10.05 he produces *it* with 6 different verbs: *close'it* (17), *put'it* (14), *get'it* (7) , *fix'it* (5), *push'it*, (2), and *take'it* (2). Simultaneously, but a little more slowly, he adds to the set of verbs that he uses with noun objects. At 1;10.05 there are 4 of these: *take* (10) (*a cup* (2), *a'bath* (8)), *see* (4) (*cup, trees, stones* (2)), *close a tape recorder* (1), and *get a cup* (1). These frames still seem to be quite item-specific: the overlaps are *close* and *get* (both of which he mostly uses with *it*), and *take* (mostly in the phrase *take-a-bath*). The verb that he first generalizes to use with a list of nouns is *see*. In one hour at 1;10.16 *see* + *N* occurs 81 times(!), with 10 different nouns (*stone(s)* 50, *water* 10, *hedge* 5, *window* 5, *trunk* (of tree) 4, *bark* (of tree) 3, *flowers* 1, *roots* 1, *wall* 1, *Sandra* 1).

As development proceeds the lists of verbs that he uses in different constructions slowly increases, and tracking in detail becomes all but impossible. Nonetheless, these sorts of multi-dimensional analyses show slow accrual of patterns and verbs into patterns, rather than sudden leaps to the kinds of abstract 'rules' claimed by other approaches to language acquisition.

production strategies: combining units

In considering early attempts to combine units, it is important to remember that multiple kinds of development are taking place simultaneously. In order to produce a two-unit utterance, the child needs to:

1) Have developed lexical representations of the required units;
2) Be able to retrieve their pronunciations (using fillers for hard or unclear parts);
3) Decide which order to produce them in;
4) Articulate them sufficiently clearly.

On-line help may come from piggy-backing on an immediately preceding self- or other-produced utterance; what Clark (1974) called build-ups.

As a means of classifying Seth's early attempts at combination, I differentiated between build-ups (BU), spontaneous frame-inserts (FI) and imitated frame-inserts (FIM). The following are examples:

Imitated Frame-Inserts (FIMs): Because they make use of material just produced by another, FIMs require the least competence by the child.

a) Seth is 1;8.02: *had chocolate; had cake.*
   Dad: *when we went ta supper last night didju have <u>pudding</u>?*   3 sec
         an' <u>milk</u>? <u>choc</u>'late milk?   3 sec
   Seth: <u>cha</u> kut.
         <u>cha</u> kut.
         <u>cha</u> ka.
         mmuk!
   Dad: *choc'late <u>milk</u>. that's <u>right</u>.*
         an' we had last- an' <u>last</u> <u>night</u> late we had choc'late <u>cake</u>.   5.4 sec
   Seth: <u>ha chak</u>ut.   3.4 sec
         ha cake   'cake' is soft but clear
   Dad: *yeah. <u>choc</u>'late cake.*

b) Seth is 1;8.09: *I throw, canya throw, can ball, can throw*
   Dad has been trying to elicit actions by asking a lot of *can you VP* questions: *c'n you give that Teddy a <u>kiss</u>? c'n you <u>throw</u>'it? c'n you play with'it? can'you pick'it'up an' <u>walk</u> with'it? can you <u>walk</u> with'it?* Now they are playing with a ball:

Dad:	*here comes the <u>ball</u>.*	3.2 sec
	you don't <u>catch</u> very well.	
Seth:	*um fro.*	
	I fra.	overlapped by D
Dad:	*you <u>threw</u>'it.*	
Seth:	*canya <u>fra</u>?*	1.5 sec
Dad:	<u>*here*</u> *lemme throw'you the <u>Teddy</u>.*	13 sec
Seth:	*canyu <u>ball</u>?*	
	can <u>fra</u>?	
	kin <u>frah</u>?	

c) Seth is 1;9.16: *Mommy shoe, Mommy shirt*

Dad:	*c'n you say <u>Mommy's shoe</u>.*	
Seth:	<u>*ma-iy*</u> *shuws.*	= 'Mommy shoe(s)'
	maniy shut.	= 'Mommy shirt' substitution in a frame
Dad:	*Mommy's shoe.*	still trying to elicit <u>shoe</u>
Seth:	<u>*mommy*</u> <u>*shut*</u>.	= 'Mommy shirt'
Dad:	*Mommy shirt?*	recognizing what S said

<u>Build-ups (BUs)</u>: Early build-ups can make use of material just produced by another, or, as competence increases, be accomplished by oneself.

d) Seth is 1;9.09: *tree trunk*

Dad:	*wha'did we see outside when we went for a walk.*	
Seth:	<u>*chu*</u>*-unk.*	= 'trunk'
	chiys.	= 'tree(s)'
Dad:	*trees. trunk.*	
Seth:	*bak!*	= 'bark'
Dad:	*bark.*	
Seth:	*chunk!*	= 'trunk'
Dad:	*trunk.*	
Seth:	<u>*chiy*</u> *chunk.*	= 'tree trunk' articulatory effort
Dad:	*tree trunk.*	
Seth:	*liys.*	= 'leaves'
Dad:	*leaves.*	
Seth:	<u>*chih*</u> *chruk.*	= 'tree trunk' articulatory effort
Dad:	<u>*tree*</u> <u>*trunk*</u>.	
Seth:	<u>*chiy*</u> *chrunk.*	= 'tree trunk' articulatory effort
Dad:	<u>*tree*</u> <u>*trunk*</u>. *that's <u>right</u>.*	

e) Seth is 1;9.22: *down a slide*
Dad is feeding Seth and they are talking about Seth's school.

Seth:	*swayt.*	
	slite.	effort at pronunciation

Dad: *wha'da'ya <u>do</u> on the <u>slide</u>.*
Seth: *<u>dan</u> da <u>slide</u>.*
Dad: *down the slide. tha's right.*

f) Seth is 1;10.00: *drain drip*
Dad is feeding Seth and they are talking about what they see out walking.

Dad: *an' whatta they <u>have</u> right down there by the <u>water</u>.*
        by the <u>water</u> hydrant.
Seth: *drip<u>drip</u>?*   high pitch; lo-hi
Dad: *dripdrip?*
        here.   softly, giving S a bite
Seth: *drip<u>drip</u>?*   very high pitch on 2nd syll; lo-hi
Dad: *dripdrip?*
Seth: *drain <u>drip</u>!*

g) Seth is 1;10.06: *put (it) away*
Seth has been playing with the telephone; now he wants Dad to take it away. He expends a lot of effort trying to get his message across.

Seth: *um put'it?*
        a-w-way?
        puh <u>away</u>?
        em puh <u>away</u>?
        'm put'i t?
        'm <u>put</u>'it?
        please.
        puh 'way?
Dad: *y'wan'put away?*
Seth: *please.*

Frame-Inserts (FIs):

h) Seth is 1;9.09: *take ya toy(s)/it/ball*
Seth: *uh <u>take</u> ya <u>to(y)</u>.*
        <u>take</u> a <u>toys</u>?
        <u>take</u> i' + ...
        take ya <u>toys</u>?   effortful
        uh take'it.
        uh take y'r <u>toys</u>?
        take-ay ya ball?

i) Seth is 1;11.06: *dry + bodypart*
Dad is helping Seth dry off after a bath, eliciting names for body parts:

Dad: *well what're you <u>drying</u>.*   6 sec

Seth: *da <u>eyes</u>?*
        day <u>botto(m)</u>?
Dad: *dry y'r <u>eyes</u>?*
        dry <u>bottom</u>?
Seth: *dayt <u>ne-eck</u>?*
Dad: *<u>dry</u> y'r <u>neck</u>?*   overlap at "y'r"
Seth: *de.*
        da <u>nose</u>?
Dad: *dry your <u>nose</u>?*

These are all examples of early combinations. As children acquire more vocabulary and more automatized control over articulation, the length and complexity of what they can produce increases. In the process, more and more combinatorial possibilities can be discovered as well. A common stereotype of early combinations in English has been that they consist of the juxtaposition of two adult units, as in the preceding examples. However, they can use (relatively) unanalysed chunks, as in the following examples from two-year-old Kelly (Horgan, 1980) in which she combines whole adult utterances with a suggestion-making unit, *how'bout*:

How'bout + daddy go get a hamburger.
How'bout + open more presents.   said the day after Christmas
How'bout + what do you want to eat.   meaning 'Ask me what I want to eat'

internal and external influences on strategies

Now that researchers have collected language-acquisition data from a wide range of children learning both English and other languages (see the many corpora available through CHILDES TalkBank) it has become evident that, even within a single language, it is possible to observe quite a wide range of strategies. We can divide the influences on strategy choice and implementation into two major kinds: internal and external. We consider first, internal influences.

Katherine Nelson (1973), studying the early vocabulary development of 18 children, found that some children (the ones she called Expressive), tended to pick up language that was useful in social interaction. Interestingly, their early vocabularies often contained what to adults are multi-word phrases such as *thank-you, all-gone, come-see-me*. Other children (the ones she called Referential) tended to focus on single adult words which tended to be labels for objects or people. This difference illustrates how social and cognitive pressures can lead to differential awareness of 'long units' vs. short ones. (See Peters, 1983, chapter 2 for a fuller discussion; also Bates et al., 1980; Lieven et al., 1992; Lieven and Pine, 1995.)

Another internal influence on the kinds of early units that children focus on seems to be phonological-prosodic. There is now considerable evidence that children vary in the amount of attention they allocate to different aspects of the sound signal, i.e. syllables and segments vs. prosodic 'tunes' (Echols and Newport, 1992; Echols, 1993; Macken, 1979; Peters, 1997; Plunkett, 1993). A striking example is found in Klein's (1978) study of the ways in which young children who are barely beginning to combine words (re)produce two- to five-syllable words. The data from her four subjects suggests that two of them were able to produce the most salient syllable or pair of syllables with a fair degree of fidelity. A third mostly reproduced the stressed syllable plus those following it, also with a fair degree of fidelity. Interestingly the fourth child usually produced the right number of syllables, but none very accurately. For instance, *astronaut* came out as /æwæwæ/, *motorcycle* as /mumulalak/, and *hippopotamus* as /bibibababa/. It seems clear that this last sort of 'tune' focus, coupled with a social orientation would push learners first to extract whole phrases and only later to analyse them, rather than extracting single syllables or words later to be juxtaposed into longer utterances.

This phonetic bias seems to carry over into the acquisition of the morphosyntactic system. Peters and Menn (1993) traced the early morphological development of two children: Seth, whose development has already been illustrated, was a 'tune-child', while Daniel was a 'syllable/segment-child'. Daniel focused on the word-final Z-morphemes (/s/z/iz/) of single English words. While his initial hypothesis seems to have been that they were governed by a phonological rule, we showed how, as he learned to mark possession and then plurals, he slowly converted the basis of their appearance to a morphological one. Seth, on the other hand at about 19 months began to approximate grammatical morphemes with rhythmically appropriate schwa-like fillers (e.g. *ng go*, *um frow*, *a down*). Two months later he started producing three-syllable utterances with internal fillers (e.g. *cross a street*, *down a stairs*). Over the next six to eight months, these syllables gradually approached their adult targets, both phonologically and grammatically. (Peters (2001b) presents a detailed tracing of the development of Seth's pre-verbal fillers into auxiliaries, modals and catenatives, such as *wanna* and *gonna*.)

Turning now to external influences we can ask whether variations in characteristics of the input would influence whether a child takes a bottom-up (syllable/segment) approach or a more top-down (tune before the words) approach. There are at least two important variables here: the assumptions adults make about appropriate ways to speak to children, and the morphophonological characteristics of the language being learned. With respect to the first question, I firmly believe that the forms of children's utterances will make sense if we pay as careful attention to what children are hearing and the context in which it occurs as we do to the forms of their utterances. An example from Seth's language development illustrates how understanding the input can help explain a child's seemingly anomalous productions:

At 31 months Seth started producing questions which began with an element which I transcribed as *whatta*: *whatta you're gonna smell?* [31 mo.], *whatta we're gonna buy at the store? whatta we saw at the zoo?* [32 mo.], *whatta we call that?* [33 mo.], *whatta we do at Kailua beach? whatta I'm doing?* [34 mo.], *whatta I was doing on my plastic bag?* Listening to these utterances in isolation gave the impression that Seth was perhaps doubling his auxiliaries, as in *what're you're gonna smell?* But more attention to the input revealed the near homonymy of his father's pronunciation of *what are*, *what do*, *what did* and *what a*. In light of this, my preferred explanation for Seth's questions is that he extracted his own multi-purpose *wh*-word, *whatta*, which he used as needed until he had sorted out the auxiliaries *are*, *do* and *did*.

The lesson gained from this, and from some other idiosyncrasies of Seth's speech, is always to check what the input might <u>sound like to the child</u>; a task made easier by today's easily searchable digitized sound files.

Another important external influence on children's segmentation and analysis (discovery of adult sub-units and combinatorial patterns) comes from cultural assumptions. Many middle-class English speakers talk to babies using reductions, expansions, substitutions and variations intended to enhance comprehension. However, as noted earlier, in the community Heath calls Trackton, speech to children lacks these kinds of 'enhancements'. [But see Saxton, this volume: SFC.] And yet, as Trackton children's linguistic skills develop, they can be heard not only imitating phrases, but also playing with them and manipulating the parts in various ways, suggesting that this is how they go about doing their analysis (Heath, 1983, Chapter 3). Heath's description of a language-acquisition process where children start with long chunks that they then learn to vary on their own, without specially tailored input language from their caretakers, seems particularly important for understanding segmentation (and language acquisition in general). It suggests that children do not need to have the input predigested, nor do they have to start at the level of single words to acquire language satisfactorily; segmentation can take place on a wide range of input. For this reason, when studying how language acquisition proceeds it is crucial to do enough background research on how caregivers talk to their babies so that the input can be adequately understood and characterized. Children can only acquire what they hear, and the way they go about it will depend to some extent on the structure of the input. [See Saxton, this volume: SFC]

Finally, the nature of the language being learned is a key external influence. For example, we can infer that while the perception and segmentation of words will be an early accomplishment for learners of more isolating languages like English or Mandarin, the segmentation of bound morphemes may be important much earlier for learners of highly inflecting languages like Turkish or Georgian or West Greenlandic. (See the volumes edited by Dan Slobin, 1985–97 for accounts of acquisition of these languages and many more.) The variation between languages leads to a 'clingability index' for each language that is the result of the rhythmic, phonetic and morphological characteristics of the language leading to words and morphemes tending either to cling together into complex units or to fall apart at the seams. This parameter will clearly influence the sorts of units that are easy to extract. Features that are likely to be important include the presence or lack of prosodic highlights (such as strong contrast between stressed and unstressed syllables vs. little stress contrast); the degree to which morphophonemic changes or resyllabifications occur at morpheme boundaries (which may serve to obscure these boundaries); the degree to which syllable boundaries and morpheme boundaries coincide; and the degree to which grammatical morphemes draw from a restricted pool of phonemes (e.g. the English *th*-morphemes). We will return again to these themes below.

The three major variables that influence children's strategies for early language acquisition: individual differences, cultural differences, and linguistic structural differences interact with each other, and we now have descriptions of children taking different paths into quite a range of different languages. Both 'word' and 'tune' children have been observed acquiring Danish (Plunkett, 1993), German (Stern and Stern, 1928), and Norwegian (Simonsen, 1990). Tune children have also been reported in data from French (Veneziano and Sinclair, 2000), Italian (Pizzuto and Caselli, 1992) and Portuguese (Scarpa, 1993). (See Peters,

2001a.) Thus, although the research is only just beginning, we should expect the three variables to interact in all possible ways to produce a range of language development profiles within any given language, and to understand the developmental strategies used by a particular child, we need to know as much as possible about the input as well as what the child is doing.

changes in strategies as development proceeds

As language mastery increases, we need to know how changes in the kinds of linguistic tasks that can be accomplished affect how and what the learner can extract and how that in turn affects the kinds of linguistic input the learner receives. The following observations may seem self-evident, but a consideration of their consequences for language learning is important. First, developing abilities affect not only the kinds of input received (longer utterances, more complex constructions, larger vocabulary) but also how the 'same' input is perceived at different stages of development. Second, the more vocabulary and syntax a child knows, the easier it is to figure out as yet unacquired aspects of language, leading to an acceleration of the process. Third, changes in the learner's own expectations and increasing desires to exert control over his environment also influence the process. We will defer until the next section consideration of consequences of children's drives for mastery (efforts and off-line practice) and for social interaction and control. The major point to keep in mind is that language learning changes as it proceeds; it is a dynamic process.

language development as a dynamic process

As a learner grows physically, mentally and socially, the abilities available for learning language are constantly expanding. For example, increasing familiarity with the sounds and sequences of the ambient language enable perception and retention of ever longer stretches of speech. Independently, memory span also increases, which contributes to the ability to retain chunks of language. Moreover, with constant practice, articulatory ability is also becoming more automatic. This supports the production of ever longer utterances. Finally, an increasing familiarity with the world facilitates the expansion and generalization of word meanings. One consequence of all these influences is that, to paraphrase Heraclitus, a child doesn't step in the same linguistic river twice. In other words, an identical utterance will be perceived and analysed differently by a learner at different stages of development.

Hirsh-Pasek and Golinkoff (1996) present a 'coalition model' of language comprehension that suggests how the major weights given to different kinds of information shift with development from birth to about 36 months. They recognize six kinds of cues that are always present in the environment; four are primarily linguistic (prosodic, semantic, syntactic and lexical/morphological), while two (physical and social) pertain more to the general context. But Hirsh-Pasek and Golinkoff note that young language learners cannot pay equal attention to all these kinds of cues all through the language learning process. They suggest that, for the first nine months or so, infants give the greatest weight to prosodic cues, which help them extract chunks of language. Once they have extracted a critical mass of potential lexical items (whether or not they yet match the adult lexicon) learners begin to shift their focus to cues that help them analyse what they have already extracted, as well as to extract and analyse ever more. Hirsh-Pasek and Golinkoff suggest that semantic cues bear the greatest burden up to about 24 months, although all six kinds of cues are actually being apprehended and used to some extent. They argue that by two years, the greatest burden of linguistic attention has shifted to syntactic cues.

Another way to conceptualize the ever-shifting nature of the acquisition process is to think of language as a mass of interwoven details which can only be grasped a little at a time, by focusing attention on a single kind of information; but at the same time attention to specific details builds understanding of the overall task. It is as if each learner were equipped with two kinds of lights to shine on the language. One light is a spotlight that can be aimed at a small area. The other is a general background light which grows ever brighter as more details are worked out. The choice of portion to be spotlighted is determined partly by the learner's proclivities, partly by the nature of the input, and partly by how much the learner already knows. As one part of the system is made some sense of, the learner shifts the spotlight to illuminate some other area. But also, as more and more of the whole system is sorted out, more and more of the mass is covered by the background illumination.

This sort of focus-shifting also accounts for the phenomenon of the 'U-shaped performance curve', characterized by seemingly good performance on some task, which then temporarily falls off before returning to the previous level and then continuing to improve (e.g. Bever, 1970). In the kind of dynamic account being described here, U-shaped performance is plausibly explained by assuming that the learner is dealing with a multi-dimensional problem; one dimension is under reasonable control but the process of shifting focus to a second dimension leads to allocation of fewer processing resources to the first, resulting in apparent loss of mastery. An example from very early in language production is a decrease in accuracy of pronunciation when longer utterances are attempted. For instance a child may be producing clear CVC utterances when producing single syllables (e.g. /bɪg/ and /bʊk/) but these "regress" to CV syllables when they are combined (/bɪ bʊ/). Or a child may temporarily manifest a 'stutter' when he is struggling with a new syntactic construction.

interactions between input and learning

Verbal input provides the raw materials from which a learner must eventually extract a working knowledge of the whole language system. To the extent that it is tailored to the child's developmental level, it can provide a 'scaffold' that supports the kinds of changes the child is ready to embark on, as described by Vygotsky in his description of the Zone of Proximal Development (Vygotsky, 1978, p. 86). In middle-class American households, where it is common to speak directly to babies, toddlers and pre-schoolers, one can document changes in the nature of this input as a result (partly) of the caregiver's perception of the child's ability to comprehend and respond. An anecdotal description of Minh's mother's utterances to her son illustrate these changes: at first, when he was 7-and-a-half months old she had no expectation of his comprehension of her speech and used long utterances designed simply to provide reassurance. When he was 14 months old, and just beginning to produce one-word utterances, her mean length of utterance (MLU) dropped dramatically, seemingly in an attempt to promote both comprehension and production. At 17 months, just when Minh was starting to combine words, his mother's MLU was higher; but it wasn't until he was 26 months old that her MLU was again as long as it had been when he was 7-and-a-half months.

These sorts of changes in input, driven by parental assessment of the child's ability to interact linguistically, are reasonably common, although not universal. Where they occur, there are changes in both overall length of utterances and in complexity, with more multi-clause constructions appearing as a child nears 2;0. Other changes include an increase in the overall vocabulary employed and changing expectations about how the child can and should respond. Of course, this sort of tailoring is generally geared to promoting a child's understanding of any communication directed at him rather than specifically to scaffolding his language acquisition. After all, a caregiver's immediate goal is to assure the child's appropriate participation in whatever social event is going on at the moment. Language lessons just happen in the process. The good news for language learners is that the more they know about the language, the more they can understand, and the more information they can glean for working out the as yet unknown parts.

changes in social and cognitive goals

Finally, we can consider why children bother improving their language. Once they are managing to communicate at all, what motivates them to move from isolated chunks to combinations to grammar? Four inextricably intertwined forces are: children's increasing desire for control of the environment and the realization that language can help; children's desire for increasingly complex social interactions; cognitive changes which lead children to want to express ever more complex ideas; and children's internal desire for mastery of a complex skill. Let us briefly consider each of these.

Typically developing children have a powerful urge to learn to participate in and exert control over the adult world as fast as they are able. Much of this participation must be deferred, of course, until certain conditions are fulfilled, including physical, social and cognitive developments. But this does not stop children from observing how the world works and from trying to insert themselves into its workings whenever and however possible. In Seth's interactions with his father, there were a number of situations where Seth behaved like a 'language sponge', imitating and repeating whatever his father said, and then trying to put it to use. For example, as he learned to build and knock down small towers with large blocks, he first just asked *help me*, but soon diversified to *put da o(ther) one, help me put'it top, knock'it down* and eventually *help buil' tower*. One can hypothesize that his desire for control over this specific new situation led to the diversification of his language.

If a child has caregivers who support this kind of participation (through attention and scaffolding) the learning process is relatively smooth and trouble-free. But if a child's ambitions outreach his skill, he may become very frustrated. This sort of mismatch between ability and desire may be part of what underlies the 'terrible twos' phenomenon. Acredolo and Goodwyn (1998) have found that teaching toddlers to communicate with manual signs can help to relieve some of this pressure. Frustration at not being able to communicate can also develop if caregivers do not pay attention to a child's efforts.

The drive to express more complex ideas is another force in language development. As children come to think about the world in ever more complex ways, it seems plausible that they would find ways to talk about it in more complex language. Children also discover that language can be a tool for finding out about the world and how it works, progressing from asking the names of things to wondering how and why things work the way they do. Children are continually searching for how to accomplish things with language, and then trying them out. They want to be able to greet others, make requests, resist demands, acquire information, make or deny claims, narrate past experiences, anticipate future events, etc. and are ever alert to how language can serve each of these goals.

Along with such cognitive developments come increasing social expectations and desires to make oneself heard in diverse contexts. Halliday (1973), discussed briefly above, proposes three early social functions of language: Regulatory ('do what I want'), Interpersonal ('my relationship to you') and Interactional ('let's do this together'). Children have to learn how to interact, not only with their closest caregiver(s), who are likely to anticipate what the child wants at the moment, but also with less cooperative others, such as children and less familiar adults.

Finally, it seems that children have some sort of innate drive for mastery of language, 'just because it is there'. A great deal has been said about young children's ability to master language with a minimum of effort. However, close observation reveals they are, in fact, working hard at it. In the tapes of Seth, there were many examples of 'effort sequences' between 19 and 22 months, including both spontaneous (non-elicited) imitations of his father's speech and 'practice' on difficult targets. The criteria used to identify effort sequences were that they should be spontaneous (i.e. self-motivated); that there should be a sequence of attempts; and that there should be some sort of improvement across the sequence. In the earlier sequences he seems to be focusing on improving his pronunciation, which suggests both that he has a mental representation of the word that somehow differs from his first try and that he has a feeling that he can 'do better'. (See Seth's attempts to say *tree trunk* and *put it away* discussed above.) Thus these diverse and sometimes conflicting forces collectively propel a child along the path of language learning.

references

Acredolo, L. P. and Goodwyn, S. W. (1998). *Baby Signs: How to Talk with Your Baby before Your Baby Can Talk*. Chicago: NTB/Contemporary Publishers.

Bates, E., Bretherton, I. and Snyder, L. (1980). *From First Words to Grammar: Individual Differences and Dissociable Mechanisms*. Cambridge: Cambridge University Press.

Bever, T. G. (1970). The cognitive basis for linguistic structures. In J. R. Hayes (ed.), *Cognition and the Development of Language*. New York: John Wiley and Sons.

Clancy, P. M. (1985). The acquisition of Japanese. In D. I. Slobin (ed.), *The Crosslinguistic Study of Language Acquisition*, Vol. 1 (pp. 373–524). Hillsdale, NJ: Lawrence Erlbaum Associates.

Clark, R. (1974). Performing without competence. *Journal of Child Language*, 1, 1–10.

Echols, C. H. (1993). A perceptually-based model of children's earliest productions. *Cognition*, 46, 245–96.

Echols, C. H. and Newport, E. L. (1992). The role of stress and position in determining first words. *Language Acquisition*, 2, 189–220.

Fernald, A. (1991). Prosody in speech to children: Prelinguistic and linguistic functions. In R. Vasta (ed.), *Annals of Child Development*, Vol. 8 (pp. 43–80). London: Jessica Kingsley Publishers.

Fillmore, C. J. (1978). On the organization of the semantic information in the lexicon. *Papers from the Parasession on the Lexicon*, Chicago Linguistic Society, 148–73.

Fortescue, M. and Lennert Olsen, L. (1992). The Acquisition of West Greenlandic. In D. I. Slobin (ed.), *The Crosslinguistic Study of Language Acquisition*, Vol. 3 (pp. 111–219). Hillsdale, NJ: Lawrence Erlbaum Associates.

Goldberg, A. (1995). *Constructions: A Construction Grammar Approach to Argument Structure*. Chicago: University of Chicago Press.

Halliday, M. A. K. (1973). *Explorations in the Functions of Language*. London: Edward Arnold.

Heath, S. B. (1983). *Ways with Words: Language, Life and Work in Communities and Classrooms*. Cambridge: Cambridge University Press.

Hirsh-Pasek, K. and Golinkoff, R. (1996). *The Origins of Grammar: Evidence from Early Language Comprehension*. Cambridge, MA: The MIT Press.

Horgan, D. (1980). Nouns: love 'em or leave 'em. In V. Teller and S. I. White (eds), *Studies in Child Language and Multilingualism*, New York: Annals of the New York Academy of Sciences.

Klein, H. B. (1978). *The Relationship between Perceptual Strategies and Production Strategies in Learning the Phonology of Early Lexical Items*. Bloomington: Indiana University Linguistics Club.

Lieven, E. V. M., Behrens, H., Speares, J. and Tomasello, M. (2003). Early syntactic creativity: a usage-based approach. *Journal of Child Language*, 30, 333–70.

Lieven, E. V. M. and Pine, J. M. (1995). Comparing different views of early grammatical development. *Proceedings of the 27th annual Child Language Research Forum*.

Lieven, E. V. M., Pine, J. M. and Barnes, H. D. (1992). Individual differences in early vocabulary development – redefining the referential-expressive distinction. *Journal of Child Language*, 19, 287–310.

Macken, M. (1979). A developmental reorganization of phonology: a hierarchy of basic units of acquisition. *Lingua*, 49, 11–49.

Nagy, W. (1978). Some non-idiom larger-than-word units in the lexicon. *Papers from the Parasession on the Lexicon*, Chicago Linguistic Society, 289–300.

Nelson, K. (1973). Structure and strategy in learning to talk. *Monographs of the Society for Research in Child Development,* 39 (1–2, Serial No. 149).

Peters, A. M. (1983). The Units of Language Acquisition Cambridge. *Monographs and Texts in Applied Psycholinguistics.* Cambridge: Cambridge University Press.

Peters, A. M. (1997). Language typology, prosody and the acquisition of grammatical morphemes. In D. I. Slobin (ed.), *The Crosslinguistic Study of Language Acquisition,* Vol. 5 (pp. 136–97). Hillsdale, NJ: Lawrence Erlbaum Associates.

Peters, A. M. (2001a). Filler syllables: what is their status in emerging grammars? *Journal of Child Language, 28.1,* 229–42; 283–9.

Peters, A. M. (2001b). From prosody to grammar in English: the differentiation of catenatives, modals, and auxiliaries from a single protomorpheme. In J. Weissenborn and B. Höhle (eds), *Signal to Syntax II: Approaches to Bootstrapping in Early Language Development* (pp. 121–56), Amsterdam: Benjamins.

Peters, A. M. and Menn, L. (1993). False starts and filler syllables: ways to learn grammatical morphemes. Language, 69, 742–77.

Pizzuto, E. and Caselli, M. C. (1992). The acquisition of Italian morphology: implications for models of language development. *Journal of Child Language,* 19, 491–557.

Plunkett, K. (1993). Lexical segmentation and vocabulary growth in early language acquisition. *Journal of Child Language,* 20, 43–60.

Scarpa, E. (1993). Models in the description of phonological acquisition. Paper at Sixth International Conference for the Study of Child Language. Trieste.

Simonsen, H. G. (1990). *Barns fonologi: System og variasjon hos tre norske og et samoisk barn* (Child phonology: system and variation in three Norwegian children and one Samoan child). Doctoral dissertation, Department of Linguistics and Philosophy, University of Oslo.

Slobin, D. I. (ed.) (1985–97). *The Crosslinguistic Study of Language Acquisition,* Vols 1–5. Hillsdale, NJ: Lawrence Erlbaum Associates.

Stern, C. and Stern, W. (1928). *Die Kindersprache.* Leipzig: Barth. Reprinted in 1965, Darmstadt: Wissenschaftliche Buchgesellschaft.

Tomasello, M. (1998). The return of constructions. *Journal of Child Language,* 25, 431–47.

Veneziano, E. and Sinclair, H. (2000). The changing status of 'filler syllables' on the way to grammatical morphemes. *Journal of Child Language,* 27, 461–500.

Vygotsky, L. S. (1978). *Mind in Society: The Development of Higher Psychological Processes.* Cambridge, MA: Harvard University Press.

Weir, R. H. (1962). *Language in the Crib.* The Hague: Mouton.

3
the inevitability of child directed speech
matthew saxton

introduction

This chapter will consider the nature and function of Child Directed Speech (CDS), the special register adopted by parents and others when talking to young children. Interest in CDS was at its zenith in the 1970s, partly in response to Chomsky's (1965) characterization of the input to language acquisition as a stuttering mass of false starts, hesitations and flawed models of grammar. However, a landmark study by Snow (1972) provided an empirical refutation. This study, and numerous subsequent studies, proved Chomsky wrong. The speech directed at children was found to provide a remarkably clear, simplified and well-formed entry point into the complexities of language learning. Nonetheless, the significance of CDS continues to be disregarded in certain quarters (e.g. Pinker, 1994; Hornstein, 2005), typically on the grounds that CDS is only experienced by a handful of well-educated, Western, middle-class children. The argument runs: If CDS is not universally available, then it can be disregarded as a necessary or even important feature of language acquisition. I will argue below that this assumption is unwarranted, because the available evidence about universality from cross-cultural research has been persistently misrepresented. I will further argue that there is, in fact, something inevitable about CDS. If one wants to engage a young child in a language-based interaction, then many of the features of Child Directed Speech that are, by now, so well documented, simply fall out naturally as an artefact of successful communication.

a note on terminology

Over the years, there has been a proliferation of terms for the register used to infants and children, including: *baby talk*, *motherese*, *caregiver talk, caretaker talk, input language, linguistic input, verbal stimuli, exposure language* and *infant-directed speech,* among others. However, *Child Directed Speech,* or CDS (Warren-Leubecker and Bohannon, 1984), a term which contrasts with *Adult Directed Speech,* or ADS, now holds sway within the child language community (Saxton, 2008). The term CDS avoids most of the inappropriate connotations of other terms, though it does retain the limitation that it excludes ambient language that children are exposed to but which is not aimed directly at them. Radio, television and the conversations of others all provide input that may conceivably contribute to language learning (but see below).

characteristics of child directed speech

Chomsky (1965, p. 31) described the input available to the language learning child as 'fairly degenerate in quality', characterized by 'fragments and deviant expressions of a variety of sorts' (ibid., p. 201). However, as soon as researchers began to examine the input supplied to children, it became apparent that adults adapt their speech in numerous ways at every level of linguistic analysis (Snow, 1972; Phillips, 1973). It is not the intention here to provide an exhaustive description of CDS (for fuller accounts, see Clark, 2003; Owens, 2005), but a brief summary is in order.

Phonological features of CDS include exaggerated intonation and stress; higher pitch overall and a greater pitch range; slower speech, with syllable-lengthening, longer pauses and fewer dysfluencies. These adaptations figure most prominently during the first year of life, becoming far less extreme by the time the child is beginning to talk. Features of vocabulary in CDS include a greatly restricted range of vocabulary items (around 100 words in the early stages, compared to the many thousands of words used in ADS (Ferguson, 1977), and a marked emphasis on words for concrete, rather than abstract, concepts. Five topics in particular seem to recur frequently: kin, animals, parts of the body, food and clothing. Evidently these reflect topics dictated by the child's interests, and contribute to maintaining the child's interaction with others. Overall, then, there is a strong sense in which the lexical input to young children is both simplified and adapted to the needs of a cognitively naive interlocutor.

From a syntactic point of view, CDS utterances tend to be shorter and grammatically simpler than in ADS. Studies of the prevalence of particular structures suggest a paucity of subordinate clauses, relative clauses, sentential complements and negations, and as many as

50 per cent of adult utterances comprise single word utterances or short declaratives (Owens, 2005). Moreover, contrary to Chomsky's claim, the sentences addressed to young children are remarkably well formed grammatically, and although children may hear a considerable number of incomplete sentences, they are nevertheless complete syntactic phrases. One survey, by Newport et al. (1977), found just one instance of adult ungrammaticality in a corpus of 1,500 utterances. Overall, it is now clear that young children are not exposed to the deviant model of language anticipated in the 1960s. Moreover, the structural characteristics of CDS are sufficient to mark it out as a distinct form of address.

Much of adult communication with infants is geared towards gaining and maintaining their attention. From birth, infants demonstrate an interest in attending to the mother's face and voice, and from the fifth or sixth week, they show an increase in smiling and cooing. This inherent sociability of infants is reciprocated by mothers through increases in their own vocalizations and displays of interest and affection. The interaction between mother and child then undergoes a transformation as the child becomes more interested in the physical world of objects. By about 3 months of age, the infant is less willing to gaze solely at the mother and is more prone to explore the world around them. In response, mothers typically become less gentle in the timbre of their vocalizing and adopt a more vigorous, playful approach, typified by a more excited, arousing mode of speech (Brand et al., 2007; Papousek, 2007). Of course, infants do not lose interest in their mothers. On the contrary, an increasingly sophisticated set of routines, games and rituals develops.

Adults' ability to capture and hold children's attention, and to direct that attention elsewhere, seems to be critical for language development (Scaife and Bruner, 1975; Dominey and Dodane, 2004). The level of shared attention witnessed in adult–child discourse is positively correlated with both later vocabulary development (Tomasello et al., 1986; Akhtar et al., 1991) and syntax (Rosenthal Rollins and Snow, 1998). It appears that the isolation of objects and actions, together with appropriate verbal labels and key gestures such as maternal pointing at key referents, facilitates vocabulary learning. Similarly, 2-year-olds whose mothers indulge in high levels of these attention-holding devices score highly on general measures of later verbal learning one year later (Schmidt and Lawson, 2002).

As children begin to talk, typically in the second year, the linguistic interaction between child and adult is marked by significant levels of repetition. Adults repeat themselves a lot, and they also repeat what the child says, in one form or another. When repeating *themselves*, adults often rely on a restricted repertoire of verbal routines, in order to intro-duce new information (Broen, 1972; Ferguson et al., 1973). *Look at NP, Here's NP* and *Let's play with NP* are typical of the sentence frames used by adults, with the noun in the noun phrase often being produced with exaggerated intonation and heavy stress. The new information is placed in sentence-final position in these frames (Slobin, 1973). Fernald and Mazzie (1991) report that new information features utterance-finally in 75 per cent of CDS utterances, while the comparable figure is just 53 per cent for ADS. Consequently, new information is more exposed, and is thus more easily processed, allowing children to respond more accur-ately to new information (Shady and Gerken, 1999). Thus, children are exposed to new linguistic information in a format that best suits their cognitive abilities.

Adult repetitions, both of their own and of the child's speech, are often characterized by minor variations to the original utterance (although verbatim repetitions are not infrequent, either). This is not a new observation. Jespersen (1922, p. 142) noted how 'understanding of language is made easier by the habit that mothers and nurses have of repeating the same phrases with slight alterations'. This kind of repe-tition, often called an expansion or a recast, was studied extensively by Roger Brown and his students (Brown and Bellugi, 1964; Cazden, 1965). The following examples are from Brown (1973), archived in the CHILDES corpus (MacWhinney and Snow, 1990).

(1) Eve: *More cookie.*
    Mother: *You have another cookie right on the table.*
    Eve: *That finger.*
    Mother: *Where is your finger?*
    Eve: *Play Eve broom.*
    Mother: *Yes, you play with Eve's broom. That's a girl.*

The potential value of expansions for language development is read-ily apparent. Children supply the raw material for the adult reply, so one can be fairly confident that at least part of the adult utterance will be comprehensible and of interest to the child. Parental recasts thus provide a good example of so-called scaffolding (Vygotsky, 1978). New linguistic material is supplied within a context that the child can read-ily apprehend. Many studies have demonstrated an association between expansions/recasts and linguistic development in both typically and atypically developing children (e.g. Seitz and Stewart, 1975; Nelson et al., 1984; Hoff-Ginsberg, 1985; Forrest and Elbert, 2001; Eadie et al., 2002; and Swensen et al., 2007).

the direct contrast hypothesis

Recasts, or rather, a specific subset of recasts, have been the focus of research on corrective input, or *negative evidence* (Saxton, 2005; Gass, this volume). The widespread belief that grammatical errors are not corrected originates in a paper by Brown and Hanlon (1970), but the empirical evidence they report was confined to an unlikely, behaviourist-inspired version of correction, namely, overt markers of disapproval, like *'Don't say that'*. Ironically, Brown and Hanlon (1970, p. 197) were well aware that recasts could often provide a more plausible source of corrective information, remarking that 'repeats of ill-formed utterances usually contained corrections and so could be instructive'. Thus, exchanges of the following kind (Saxton, 1995) have been well documented (errors and corrections appear in italics, while stress is marked by underlining):

(2) Child: I don't even know *what is* a patient.
    Adult: You don't know *what* a patient *is?*

    Adult: Hey, don't walk on my scarf.
    Child: You *should've* dropped it.
    Adult: <u>You</u> *shouldn't've* walked on it.

    Child: Yeah, so they won't come *to apart.*
    Adult: Well, they won't come *apart* if we put this on.

    Child: I *thinked* it with my brain.
    Adult: *I thought* about it and told you.

    Child: You *walked him* the plank.
    Adult: No, I didn't *make him walk* the plank.

In each case, the child's grammatical error is followed immediately by the correct adult alternative. Exchanges of this kind have been reported in more than twenty empirical studies (e.g. Hirsh-Pasek et al., 1984; Bohannon and Stanowicz, 1988; Farrar, 1992; Strapp and Federico, 2000; Chouinard and Clark, 2003), and for every child on whom individual data have been gathered, and for every grammatical structure investigated, corrective input of this kind has been documented. In each case, a unique discourse context is created in which the erroneous child form is directly juxtaposed with the correct adult alternative. The Direct Contrast hypothesis (Saxton, 1997) predicts that this conjunction of linguistic forms can provide the child with two pieces of information: (1) their own selection is disfavoured; and (2) the adult form is preferred instead. Arguably, the contrast between child and adult forms is especially salient, given the joint attention and shared topic of conversation. The form preferred by the adult is thus thrown into sharp relief when set against the child's selection.

To test the Direct Contrast hypothesis, children were taught novel verbs prior to eliciting past tense forms (Saxton, 1997). Unbeknownst to the children, the verbs were designated as irregular, so that the default production of regular past tense forms could be corrected by the experimenter, via contrastive discourse. For the novel verb *streep* (modelled on *creep/crept*), negative evidence could be supplied as follows:

(3) Experimenter: *What happened?*
    Child: *He streeped his nose.*
    Experimenter: *Oh, yes, he strept his nose.*

To demonstrate the importance of discourse context, children were also exposed to irregular past tense forms in a non-contrastive (positive input) condition. In this case, a video narrative, used to create a past tense context, would be paused, allowing the experimenter to say (for *streep*), *Oh look! He strept his nose.* Thus, the linguistic information, in both positive and negative input conditions, was identical. The child is exposed for the first time to the (correct) irregular past tense form. The sole difference between the two was contingency versus non-contingency of the adult model on a child error. The results suggested that children were far more likely to produce the adult model in the negative evidence condition (see also Saxton et al., 1998). Evidence is also now forthcoming to show both the immediate and longer-term effects of negative evidence on the grammaticality of child speech (Saxton, 2000; Saxton, Backley and Gallaway, 2005).

In addition to the kind of negative evidence described by the Direct Contrast Hypothesis, a corrective function can also be exerted by *negative feedback*. Here, the adult provides a prompt to previously learned forms. Error-contingent clarification requests provide the paradigm example:

(4) Child: *Knights have horse, they do.*
    Adult: *They what?*

    Child: *He slided down the door.*
    Adult: *He what?*

    Child: *Ouch! It hurted.*
    Adult: *Eh?*

While clarification requests can have many functions (Saxton, 2000), I have suggested that one of these can be to focus the child's attention on the grammatical form of their utterance, prompting them to recall an alternative formulation. In this way, negative feedback is a weaker form of correction than negative evidence, since it does not model the correct alternative for the child. Its corrective potential rests on the assumption that the child has already been apprised of the adult form, but has produced an error that one might characterize as performance-based, rather than competence-based (Chomsky, 1965). Evidence in support of the Prompt Hypothesis is forthcoming from both observational and experimental work (Saxton, 2000; Saxton, Houston-Price and Dawson 2005).

An opposing view of the input, generally advocated by nativist researchers, entirely precludes any possible role for the discourse context as a source of information about grammaticality (e.g. Lightfoot, 1991). On this view, all input is positive input. But this position is difficult to square with the fact, noted above, that children respond differently according to whether or not the adult form is contingent on a child error. Moreover, child intuitions about grammaticality more closely resemble adult norms when the child has been exposed to error-contingent, rather than non-error-contingent, models (Saxton et al., 1998). More broadly, these findings are consistent with a large body of research showing that particular aspects of adult–child interaction are intimately associated with language growth in the child.

How children overcome their language errors must be addressed in all approaches to language acquisition. Negative input provides a straightforward solution to this problem. Yet few, if any, authors would argue that corrective input is *necessary* for language development. Perhaps the best we can do is to demonstrate the extent to which a given input feature *facilitates* language development. In this regard, negative input appears to be a viable candidate.

the dynamics of talking to children: finetuning

The way adults interact with children changes as they grow and develop (Snow, 1972). The child's increasing linguistic prowess is matched by changes in the content and style of CDS; changes that have been characterized by Snow (1995) as 'finetuning' to reflect the continual sensitivity of caregivers to the child's communicative needs. For example, the high pitch and exaggerated intonation contours in speech to newborns, noted above, have all but disappeared by the time the child is 5 years old (Englund and Behne, 2006). Similarly, in the syntactic complexity of adult speech, Sokolov (1993) reports very high positive correlations between child omissions of key morphemes (modals, nouns and pronouns) and the rate at which mothers supply these morphemes. As the child's speech becomes grammatically more accurate, the rate at which errors of omission are corrected declines. In a similar vein, Pan et al. (1993) showed that the complexity of adult speech increased in the speech to children between the ages of 14 months and 32 months. Over this period, parental utterances became longer and more lexically diverse. Moreover, these changes are predicted by growth in child language, as measured by the same indices.

The process of finetuning sheds light on adult sensitivity to the child's changing needs. [See Peters, this volume: SFC] For example, adult MLU starts fairly high and decreases across the first six months of their child's life (Murray et al., 1990). Evidently, gaining the newborn's attention is far more important than the lexical or syntactic content of adult utterances. At around 6 months of age, though, when the child is on the verge of producing their own first words, lexical content and grammatical complexity become critical factors in CDS, and adult–child exchanges take on a genuinely linguistic character. The MLU of adult speech then begins to increase again throughout the second year of life (Bellinger, 1980), a pattern that is predictable from the child's improving powers of comprehension and production during this period. Thus while taxonomies of CDS may give the impression that CDS is constituted by a static set of features, applicable to children at all stages of development, it is actually dynamic, changing in tandem with the child's communicative development (Warren-Leubecker and Bohannon, 1983; Snow, 1995). Bohannon and Warren-Leubecker (1985, p. 194), observe that, 'since the complexity of speech addressed to children is largely determined by cues from the children themselves ... one might think of language acquisition on this view as a self-paced lesson'.

non-interactive input

Television offers the child exposure to linguistic information in the absence of a communicative partner, that is, in the absence of interaction. This observation holds true even though fellow viewers will sometimes engage the child in conversation about a TV programme (Naigles and Mayeux, 2000). The interaction here is between the two viewers, not between the child and the television. Other sources of non-interactive input include overheard conversations, radio, song lyrics and, eventually, printed material. The impact of non-child-directed input on language development is meagre (though see Akhtar, 2005). The central issue, of course, is the importance of interaction per se. If language development could proceed in the complete absence of interaction, then support would be accrued for the nativist view of the input, whereby the child simply needs to hear key linguistic forms to trigger development (Lightfoot, 1989). In the event, though, there is no support for this view, at least not in the first two years of life. During infancy, children seem remarkably immune to the effects of television (Kuhl et al., 2003; Mumme and Fernald, 2003; Anderson and Pempek, 2005).

By the age of two years, typically developing children experience a rapid acceleration in both vocabulary and grammar learning (Bates et al., 1995). From this age onwards, some studies have shown weak effects of TV on vocabulary acquisition. Thus, Rice and Woodsmall (1988) report that 3-year-olds showed immediate recall for, on average, 1.56 novel words out of 20 target words. The superiority of interaction was demonstrated by Patterson (2002). In this study, shared book reading had a greater impact on child learning than television, for 21- to 27-month-olds. For older children, Rice et al. (1990) report vocabulary learning from the television programme *Sesame Street*. They found that regular viewing of *Sesame Street* functioned as a predictor of later vocabulary growth for 3-year-olds, though not for 5-year-olds. They also found that other kinds of TV viewing, including non-informative programmes for children, had no discernible effect on vocabulary development. These two findings point to the crucial nature of the programming in studies of this kind. *Sesame Street* is not only more relevant for 3-year-olds than for 5-year-olds, but the kind of input provided bears a much closer affinity with Child Directed Speech (albeit minus interactional features) than many other kinds of programming. In a similar vein, Uchikoshi (2005) demonstrated that kindergartners' narrative skills improved through exposure to television, but only to programmes in which emphasis was placed explicitly on narrative structure.

It is perhaps not surprising that older children can learn some vocabulary from television, since they are increasingly well equipped, both cognitively and linguistically, to infer word meanings for themselves in the absence of interactive support. At the same time, even these relatively weak effects are not always observed (Snow et al., 1976). Evidently, there are very strong limitations on the language-teaching potential of television. When input is presented without interaction, the results are generally disappointing.

The non-effects of television are especially clear in the case of a hearing child born to deaf parents studied by Sachs et al. (1981). This child was exposed to English almost exclusively via extensive TV-watching, and by the age of 3;9, had acquired some vocabulary. However, his language was not merely delayed; it appeared to be disordered (breaking numerous precepts of Universal, or any other, Grammar). Typical productions included *I want that make*, *This is how plane* and *House chimney my house my chimney*. Apparently, children beyond the age of 2 can learn some vocabulary from television, but overall, it is apparent that the role of television as a language teacher is strictly limited. Currently at least, there is no substitute for live interaction with an engaged, linguistically mature conversational partner.

frequency of linguistic forms

The frequency with which children hear key linguistic forms is often taken to be the crux of the child's linguistic experience (e.g. Nicoladis and Palmer, 2007). Undoubtedly, input frequency does have a direct influence on the timing and rate of learning in many cases. For example, Gordon and Chafetz (1990) estimate that full passives occur only rarely in the input to English-speaking children, on the order of one in every 20,000 utterances. In other languages, including K'iche' Mayan, Zulu and Inuktitut, full passives are more frequent and acquisition is earlier than for children acquiring English. Brooks and Tomasello (1999) found that acquisition of the passive could be accelerated by artificially increasing levels of exposure to passives for 3-year-old children. Artificial acceleration of this kind has also been observed by Nelson (1977) for yes/no questions and complex verb phrases. In a similar vein, there are numerous examples of how enriched forms of input, as provided in therapeutic interventions, can enhance language acquisition for children with Specific Language Impairment (e.g. Fey et al., 2003). Conversely, limited exposure to parental speech is associated with delays in language acquisition (Culp et al., 1991; D'Odorico and Jacob, 2006).

While frequency of exposure is clearly an important factor, our understanding of threshold frequencies for successful learning is generally very hazy. Word learning provides an exception, since children have been observed to acquire at least some information about new vocabulary items from a single exposure, a phenomenon known as *fast mapping* (Carey, 1978). In most cases, though, we simply do not know how much input is required. One consideration in this respect is what Bates and MacWhinney (1989) describe as *functional readiness*, that is, the child's ability to take on board the information on offer. Thus, the linguistic, cognitive and perceptual faculties of a 6-month-old will cope less well with passive constructions than those of a typical 3-year-old. Hence, no amount of input will help the neonate acquire passives. We must also take into account that, for many linguistic forms, children are probably exposed to far more input than is actually needed to guarantee acquisition. In this regard, Snow (1995) makes a simple, but powerful, observation that underscores the fact that many children receive more input than is strictly necessary for successful acquisition. She notes that many children (many millions, in fact) are raised as bilingual or even trilingual with no decrement in performance across different languages, despite the fact that the amount of input supplied per language must be severely fractionated when compared with monolingual learners.

Frequency has not always been so strongly emphasized. CDS was a central component in social-pragmatic approaches to language acquisition developed in the 1970s (Bruner, 1974; Bateson, 1975; Snow, 1979). Language in this approach was seen as a social skill that children are motivated to acquire, as a means to attaining their social goals, and the structure of interaction was key to providing children with language models that they could successfully internalize. However, social learning theories foundered rather quickly, succumbing to justified criticisms of vagueness and untestability (Gleitman et al., 1984). Ascendant in their place have been the nativist approach (e.g. Ayoun, 2003) and the usage-based constructivism of Tomasello and colleagues (Tomasello, 2003; Rowland et al., 2003). In both these frameworks the role of interaction is downplayed and simple frequency of occurrence is emphasized instead.

In nativist approaches, the input is portrayed as a set of triggers, exposure to which somehow permits innate categories of syntax to manifest themselves in the child's grammar. On this view, the child needs to be exposed to a small subset of available input, since only a narrow range of key input experiences is required to act as triggers for setting the parameters of Universal Grammar (Gibson and Wexler, 1994; Snyder, 2007). In principle, a single exposure to a key triggering stimulus might be sufficient for parameter setting to proceed. Any notion that interaction might play a role in providing key language learning experiences is simply not entertained. The nativist view of the input reduces, then, to limited exposure to a limited range of key linguistic structures.

In the constructivist approach the role of the input is also, largely, reduced to a mechanistic matter of quantity. Frequency of exposure to given forms is regarded as the critical aspect of the child's linguistic environment (Tomasello, 2003, p. 173). As with the nativist approach, the emphasis on frequency neglects the role of interaction as a critical constraint in much current theorizing about language development. However, as the foregoing discussion has emphasized, frequency of exposure alone will not suffice in explaining the role of input in acquisition. The case of negative evidence shows that the interactive context in which linguistic items are introduced to the child can affect the quality of information supplied. There is, then, a pervasive neglect in current theorizing about the full richness of the child's linguistic environment. If nothing else, it should be borne in mind that linguistic forms are very rarely presented to children in isolation. In fact, the notion of input without interaction is very difficult to entertain. Instead, the default is for language to be used with the child in communicative exchanges, and it is the structure of communication that provides the basis for language acquisition.

universality and necessity of CDS

Child language researchers agree that linguistic input is necessary for language acquisition. Moreover, one does not need cases of abused or feral children to support this claim (e.g. Lane, 1976; Curtiss, 1977). It simply stands to reason that unless the child is exposed to language, they will not acquire it. A possible caveat here includes cases where children seem to have created a grammatical system spontaneously, as in the celebrated case of Nicaraguan deaf children documented by Goldin-Meadow and others (e.g. Goldin-Meadow and Mylander, 1998; Senghas et al., 2004). The language used by these children, and transmitted to subsequent generations, was structured both at the level of the word and the sentence. Moreover, spatial modulations, a linguistic feature unique to signed languages, emerged to denote shared reference, a feature enabling the expression of long-distance grammatical relationships among words. Arguably, therefore, certain aspects of what the children came to know about grammar was not sourced directly from the input (although see Russo and Volterra, 2005, for an opposing view). However, this does not mean that everything the children knew about grammar, or language more widely, emerged spontaneously. Nor does it mean that even spontaneous expressions of grammatical relations could have been possible without some form of linguistic input. Indeed, we know that these children were supplied with linguistic input, in the form of spoken Spanish and lip-reading from parents and teachers, in addition to gestures and signing from other children. The Nicaraguan deaf children, therefore, do not provide clear evidence against the necessity of linguistic input as a component in language acquisition.

While linguistic input is clearly necessary for language learning, it is less obvious whether Child Directed Speech is necessary. That is, do parents need to make the many fine adjustments and simplifications typical of CDS, in order to guarantee successful language acquisition in their children? The answer to this latter question is much more difficult to answer, even though, in principle, it looks quite straightforward. All one need do is find even a single child who has been deprived of this special input, but who has nevertheless acquired language normally. In this regard, Pinker (1994, p. 40) asserts that 'in many communities of the world, parents do not indulge their children in Motherese'. Pinker is especially scathing on this subject: 'the belief that Motherese is essential to language development is part of the same mentality that sends yuppies to "learning centers" to buy little mittens with bull's-eyes to help their babies find their hands sooner' (ibid., p. 40). In fact, Pinker has set up a straw man, since it is surpassingly difficult to find anyone who has actually made a case for the necessity of motherese/CDS (the case for mittens with bull's-eyes is even less clear). Instead, the argument has been made in the reverse direction, with Pinker to the fore in the claim that CDS is *not* necessary for language acquisition.

In essence, the implication is that as soon as one steps outside the comfort zone of educated, white, Western parenting, one finds cases where children are not prized as conversational partners and are not deemed to merit either specialized input or even any input at all. In fact, though, the evidence is drawn from a very limited range of cross-cultural sources. Three cases are continually cited in this regard: (1) the African American community of Trackton in South Carolina (Heath, 1983); (2) parents in Western Samoa (Ochs, 1982); and (3) the K'iche' Mayan community of Guatemala (Pye, 1986). These three studies have been cited numerous times by authors who seem not to have read the original sources, leading to considerable misrepresentation of the findings that were originally reported. Collectively, they have inspired the myth that certain cultures exist where CDS is absent. It is worthwhile, therefore, examining the empirical evidence actually supplied by these (and other) sources in some detail.

In the first example, the linguistic anthropologist, Shirley Brice Heath, provides a comparative study of child rearing practices in Roadville and Trackton, two communities in South Carolina. What caught the attention of nativists was Heath's (1983) assertion that, in the African American community of Trackton, the adults were dumbfounded by the idea that parents should modify their speech when talking to infants. This aspect of Heath's work has been retailed in the psycholinguistic literature so often that errors have crept in, Chinese Whispers-style. For example, 'Trackton' is sometimes rendered as 'Tracton' (Hamilton, 1999, p. 430), while the name of the best-known informant has been distorted from 'Annie Mae' to 'Aunt Mae' (Pinker, 1994, p. 40). This latter infelicity is significant because Annie Mae is actually the grandmother (not aunt or mother) of the child (Teegie) of whom she says:

> Now just how crazy is dat? White folks uh hear dey kids say sump'n, dey say it back to 'em, dey aks 'em 'gain 'n' 'gain 'bout things, like they 'posed to be born knowin'. You think I kin tell Teegie all he gotta know? Ain't no use me tellin' him: learn dis, learn dat. What's dis? What's dat? He just gotta learn, gotta know. (Heath, 1983, p. 84)

What we have, then, is an informant who is not the main caregiver of the child and who is reporting on her *beliefs* about child rearing. What her actual practices are remain unclear. Heath's data are anthropological in nature and were not designed to address psycholinguistic research questions with any rigour, as she readily allows (ibid., p. 7).

The contrast between what people *say* they do in talking to children and what they *actually* do is demonstrated vividly in a recent study by Haggan (2002). Interviews with 82 Kuwaiti adults were held on the general topic of child rearing, including questions on whether the participants felt they addressed small children in a special way when compared to they way they spoke with adults. Eighteen of these Kuwaiti adults were adamant that they made no concessions when talking to children. A commonly held view among this group was that language acquisition might even be delayed by the use of 'special ways' to communicate (Haggan, 2002, p. 22). Each member of this group of 'CDS-sceptics' was then recorded interacting with a child aged 2–3 years. Haggan thus provides a controlled comparison of ADS with CDS. Strikingly, every single one of these gainsayers was discovered to modify their speech in ways that are entirely typical of Child Directed Speech. Among several other standard modifications, Haggan (2002) reports the use of short, semantically simple sentences, concrete referents based on the child's own interests and extensive repetitions. Had Haggan stopped her study at the interview stage, she would have been left with a fundamentally mistaken view of how Kuwaiti adults interact linguistically with their young children. At the very least, we are provided with a salutary reminder that anthropological studies like Heath's (1983) need to be approached by psycholinguists with extreme caution.

Even treading with the care engendered by Haggan (2002), it is worth pointing out that Heath (1983) provides some clues that Trackton parents may, in fact, provide elements of CDS. For example, 'when adults do not understand what point the young child is trying to make, they often repeat the last portion – or what is usually the predicate verb phrase – of the child's statement' (Heath, 1983, p. 93). This kind of interaction sounds remarkably like the recasting so prevalent in standard CDS. There is also a hint that older children may be supplying specially modified input for their younger siblings and peers (ibid., p. 93). More concrete empirical evidence is required from Trackton, but it seems that, as it stands, there is no basis for dismissing CDS from the repertoire of Trackton parents.

There does remain a question mark over the very youngest children in Heath's sample. Heath asserts that 'during the first six months or so, and sometimes throughout the entire first year, babies are not addressed directly by adults' (ibid., p. 77). One reason for this attitude towards infants is that 'for an adult to choose a preverbal infant over an adult as a conversational partner would be considered an affront and a strange behavior as well' (ibid., p. 86; cf. Pye, 1986). But many Western parents might behave in a similar fashion, when friends and family are gathered around. It might be considered odd in *any* cultural setting to talk to an infant to the exclusion of any adults present. Again then, what we need here is evidence of how mothers and others interact with their babies when they are *alone* together, a form of evidence that is, by definition, impossible when using the anthropological method of participant-observation (Young, 1979). It is, of course, conceivable that very young children in certain cultures are denied any substantial form of linguistic input for a period of time. But even if such cases could be established, any such period must surely be limited in scope since parents and others must start talking to the infant at some point.

The second resort of nativists, in asserting the non-universality of CDS, is provided by Ochs (1982). In her study of Western Samoan society, Ochs reports that parents spend little time interacting directly with very young children and provide few of the features of child directed speech familiar in Western settings. Again, the evidence of how parents actually converse with their children in private is lacking. Moreover, the task of interacting with very young children is commonly assigned to older siblings in Western Samoa. Given that children as young as 4;0 produce the modifications associated with Child Directed Speech (Shatz and Gelman, 1973; Weppelman et al., 2003), the possibility is open that older siblings may provide the CDS. Beyond that, Ochs (1982, p. 101) observes that parents do in fact *paraphrase* their children's speech. No category definition is supplied, but like the Trackton parents' repetitions of child speech, there is every possibility that a rich form of interaction is being supplied by parents in this setting.

Finally, in his study of K'iche' Maya, a native language of Guatemala, Pye (1986, 1992) reports that a number of classic features of CDS are absent, specifically the phonological adaptations of cluster reduction, liquid substitution, reduplication and the use of special sounds, reported by Ferguson (1977). However, a number of other features of CDS *are* present, even in Pye's very small sample of three children. For example, the MLU for Pye's three adults is reported at 4.63, 5.31 and 8.43, respectively, not greatly dissimilar to the range of 4.1–5.4 reported by Cross (1977) for conventional CDS in Australia. Moreover, as in Trackton and Western Samoa, adults are reported to provide repetition of child utterances. Again, the precise nature of the repetitions supplied would bear closer examination, but one has a tantalizing clue that adults interact with their young children in remarkably similar ways, in diverse cultural settings.

The example of K'iche' Maya demonstrates that not all of the many recorded features of CDS may be present simultaneously. Instead, one finds cases where some features are present, while others are absent. One of the most robust features is the practice of repeating what children say back to them in one form or another. Repetitions, elicited repetitions and expansions have been recorded in a wide range of languages. Mead (1930, p. 35) remarks of the Manus people of New Guinea that the adult's 'random affection for repetitiousness makes an excellent atmosphere in which the child acquires facility in speech'. Other examples include Danish (Jespersen, 1922), French (Chouinard and Clark, 2003), Warlpiri (Bavin, 1992), Hebrew (Berman, 1985), Mandarin (Erbaugh, 1992), Japanese (Clancy, 1985) and Korean (Clancy, 1989). Ironically, they also seem to include Trackton, Guatemala and Western Samoa. Clearly, the evidence that, in some cultures, parents do not specially modify the speech addressed to young children, is extremely weak. Unfortunately, this does not prevent some authors from claiming that 'motherese is not a universal part of L1 acquisition' (Ayoun, 2003, p. 51).

I suggest that the myth that CDS is a middle-class Western peculiarity has grown up for two reasons. First, nativists have selectively focused on statements made by anthropologists that do not bear up to close, scientific scrutiny. Second, indications that aspects of CDS *are* present in non-Western cultures have been ignored. Without a much stronger evidence base, we must conclude that, in every culture examined so far, some aspects of Child Directed Speech have been recorded, including, critically, some version of interaction based on parental expansions of child utterances.

the inevitability of CDS

The only way to test whether CDS is necessary for language acquisition would be to systematically deny such input to a typically developing child. One might imagine trying the exclusive use of Adult Directed Speech to young children. However, ethical considerations aside, this would be difficult to sustain in practice for any length of time because it would fail to gain, let alone maintain, a 2-year-old's attention. Most adults and even older children (Weppelman et al., 2003) unconsciously realize that the cognitive immaturity of a small child requires certain adaptations when attempting conversation. Without such modifications, one will not be acknowledged or understood. Even those individuals who lack this insight will quickly be rebuffed by signs of incomprehension and will, perforce, have to make concessions to the communicative needs of the child if they are to have any success at all (Warren-Leubecker and Bohannon, 1983). In fact, one might argue that the *only* way to engage an infant in conversation is to take the lead from the child and follow their interests. It is little wonder, therefore that parents spend so much time recasting child speech, effectively reflecting back the child's own speech with a range of modifications. On this view, Child Directed Speech is inevitable. One cannot avoid adopting a special register if one wants to have any kind of successful conversation with a very young child.

Even if CDS is inevitable, however, it does not mean that adults and older children are explicitly using CDS to *teach* language to the young child (except perhaps some vocabulary; Harris, 1992). Rather, the overriding aim is to maintain communication. It just so happens that simplified input of a kind that is tailored to the needs of language learners falls out naturally from the process of communication. CDS can be seen, therefore, as a serendipitous artefact of conversation between a linguistically sophisticated speaker and a less advanced interlocutor. This process can be observed at work beyond CDS in other simplified registers, including Foreigner Talk, the register used with second language learners (Ferguson, 1975; Freed, 1980; Ravid et al., 2003) and even in the speech style adopted with pets (Hirsh-Pasek and Treiman, 1982; Mitchell, 2001).

input and endpoint: formal similarities

An unusual characteristic of language development is that the input to development is itself a product of the fully developed system. The child hears sentences of the target language and must use this raw material to produce a system capable of producing sentences of their own. If one compares this situation to the growth of a plant, the contrast is dramatic. The input to a seed includes water, nutrients in the soil and particular conditions of light and heat. Thus, none of the input bears any structural resemblance either to the initial state (the seed) or to the endpoint of development (the mature plant). A celery seed does not develop into water or nitrogen or an ambient temperature of 50°F. A further difference between plant and language learner is in the range of different forms the input can take. In the case of the plant, the range of inputs required to permit successful growth is extremely rigid. But for the language learner, the input can vary in form quite dramatically. The range of different human languages that the child might be exposed to runs into the thousands with significant variations in phonology, lexis and grammar. And each of these unique inputs produces a unique output: the child exposed to Greek input acquires Greek, not Urdu. In consequence, the intimate relationship between the input and what actually develops in the child makes it difficult to disentangle, empirically, the separate contributions made by genes versus environmental factors.

One might argue that the case of grammar is somewhat different. The child is exposed to the outputs from grammatical rules, rather than the rules themselves. But even here, one must allow that the input to the child nevertheless bears a striking resemblance to the final outcome of development. The child acquires grammar when exposed to grammar. Moreover, a child exposed to Catalan will acquire the grammar of Catalan, not that of Warlpiri. The formal similarity between input and endpoint extends to other cognitive domains, for example, musical and mathematical cognition. In consequence, language development could not proceed unless the previous generation replicated not only their genes but supplied the necessary environment also. In this regard also, the situation is very different from that faced by the plant seed. At the very least, the task of identifying the genetic influences on language learning is rendered especially difficult (cf. Scholz and Pullum, 2006). It is one thing to argue that the form of language is closely governed by genetic factors (Chomsky, 1986). It is quite another to demonstrate the truth of that hypothesis empirically when the input is so closely aligned in its formal characteristics to what is actually acquired.

concluding remarks

For more than thirty years, researchers have been compiling a lengthy catalogue of special features that together characterize Child Directed Speech (CDS). We now also have a substantial body of research which shows that the special features of CDS can have a direct impact on specific language learning outcomes. Moreover, I have argued that claims that CDS is absent in certain cultures are not supported empirically. On the contrary, it is difficult to imagine how communication could be at all successful without resorting to at least some of the characteristic features of Child Directed Speech. It has also been suggested that current theories of language acquisition could benefit from closer attention to the issue of adult–child interaction in a move beyond considerations of simple input frequency. The facilitative effects of Child Directed Speech are by now well established. The extent to which CDS is *necessary* for language acquisition remains to be determined.

references

Akhtar, N. (2005). The robustness of learning through overhearing. *Developmental Science*, 8: 2, 199–209.

Akhtar, N., Dunham, F. and Dunham, P. J. (1991). Directive interactions and early vocabulary development: The role of joint attentional focus. *Journal of Child Language*, 18, 41–9.

Anderson, D. R. and Pempek, T. A. (2005). Television and very young children. *American Behavioral Scientist*, 48: 5, 505–22.

Ayoun, D. (2003). *Parameter Setting in Language Acquisition*. London: Continuum.

Bates, E., Dale, P. S. and Thal, D. (1995). Individual differences and their implications for theories of language development. In P. Fletcher and B. MacWhinney (eds), *The Emergence of Language* (pp. 29–79). Mahwah, NJ: Lawrence Erlbaum.

Bates, E and MacWhinney, B. (1989). Functionalism and the competition model. In B. MacWhinney and E. Bates (eds), *The Cross-linguistic Study of Sentence Processing*. Cambridge: Cambridge University Press.

Bateson, M. C. (1975). Mother–infant exchanges: The epigenesis pf conversational interaction. In D. Aaronson and R. W. Rieber (eds), *Developmental Psycholinguistics and Communication Disorders* (pp. 101–13). New York: New York Academy of Sciences.

Bavin, E. L. (1992). The acquisition of Warlpiri. In D. I. Slobin (ed.), *The Crosslinguistic Study of Language Acquisition* Vol. 3. Hillsdale, NJ: Erlbaum.

Bellinger, D. (1980). Consistency in the pattern of change in mothers' speech: Some discriminant analyses. *Journal of Child Language*, 7, 469–87.

Berman, R. (1985). The acquisition of Hebrew. In D. I. Slobin (ed.), *The Crosslinguistic Study of Language Acquisition* Vol. 1. Hillsdale, NJ: Erlbaum.

Bohannon, J. N. and Stanowicz, L. (1988). The issue of negative evidence: adult responses to children's language errors. *Developmental Psychology,* 24, 684–9.

Bohannon, J. N. and Warren-Leubecker, A. (1985). Theoretical approaches to language acquisition. In J. Berko Gleason (ed.), *The Development of Language* (pp. 173–226). Columbus: C.E. Merrill.

Brand, R. J., Shallcross, W. L., Sabatos, M. G. and Massie, K. P. (2007). Fine-grained analysis of motionese: eye gaze, object exchanges, and action units in infant-versus adult-directed action. *Infancy,* 11: 2, 203–14.

Broen, P. A. (1972). The verbal environment of the language-learning child. *Monograph of the American Speech and Hearing Association* 17.

Brooks, P. J. and Tomasello, M. (1999). How children constrain their argument structure constructions. *Language,* 75: 4, 720–38.

Brown, R. (1973). *A First Language.* London: George Allen and Unwin.

Brown, R. and Bellugi, U. (1964). Three processes in the child's acquisition of syntax. *Harvard Educational Review* 34, 133–51.

Brown, R. and Hanlon, C. (1970). Derivational complexity and order of acquisition in child speech. In J. R. Hayes (ed.), *Cognition and the Development of Language.* New York: John Wiley.

Bruner, J. S. (1974). The organization of early skilled action. In M. R. M. Richards (ed.), *The Integration of a Child into a Social World* (pp. 167–84). Cambridge: Cambridge University Press.

Carey, S. (1978). The child as a word learner. In M. Halle, J. Bresnan and G. A. Miller (eds), *Linguistic Theory and Psychological Reality* (pp. 264–93). Cambridge, MA: MIT Press.

Cazden, C. B. (1965). Environmental assistance to the child's acquisition of grammar. Unpublished Ph.D. thesis, Harvard University.

Chomsky, N. (1965). *Aspects of the Theory of Syntax.* Cambridge, MA: MIT Press.

Chomsky, N. (1986). *Knowledge of Language: Its Nature, Origin and Use.* New York: Praeger.

Chouinard, M. M. and Clark, E. V. (2003). Adult reformulations of child errors as negative evidence. *Journal of Child Language,* 30, 637–69.

Clark, E. V. (2003). *First Language Acquisition.* Cambridge: Cambridge University Press.

Clancy, P. (1985). The acquisition of Japanese. In D. I. Slobin (ed.), *The Crosslinguistic Study of Language Acquisition,* Vol. 1. Hillsdale, NJ: Erlbaum.

Clancy, P. (1989). A case study in language socialisation: Korean wh-questions. *Discourse Processes,* 12, 169–91.

Cross. T. G. (1977). Mothers' speech adjustments: The contribution of selected child listener variables. In C. E. Snow and C. A. Ferguson (eds), *Talking to Children: Language Input and Acquisition.* Cambridge: Cambridge University Press.

Culp, R., Watkins, R., Lawrence, H., Letts, D., Kelly, D. and Rice, M. (1991). Maltreated children's language and speech development: abused, neglected, and abused and neglected. *First Language,* 11, 377–90.

Curtiss, S. (1977). *Genie: A Psycholinguistic Study of a Modern-Day 'Wild Child'.* New York: Academic Press.

D'Odorico, L. and Jacob, V. (2006). Prosodic and lexical aspects of maternal input to late-talking toddlers. *International Journal of Language and Communication Disorders,* 41: 3, 293–311.

Dominey, P. F. and Dodane, C. (2004). Indeterminacy in language acquisition: the role of child directed speech and joint attention. *Journal of Neurolinguistics,* 17: 2–3, 121–45.

Eadie, P. A., Fey, M. E., Douglas, J. M. and Parsons, C. L. (2002). Profiles of grammatical morphology and sentence imitation in children with Specific Language Impairment and Down syndrome. *Journal of Speech, Language, and Hearing Research,* 45, 720–32.

Englund, K. and Behne, D. (2006). Changes in infant directed speech in the first six months. *Infant and Child Development,* 15: 2, 139–60.

Erbaugh, M. S. (1992). The acquisition of Mandarin. In D. I. Slobin (ed.), *The Crosslinguistic Study of Language Acquisition,* Vol. 3. Hillsdale, NJ: Erlbaum.

Farrar, M. J. (1992). Negative evidence and grammatical morpheme acquisition. *Developmental Psychology,* 28: 1, 90–8.

Ferguson, C. A. (1975). Toward a characterization of English foreigner talk. *Anthropological Linguistics,* 17, 1–14.

Ferguson, C. A. (1977). Baby talk as a simplified register. In C. E. Snow and C. A. Ferguson (eds), *Talking to Children: Language Input and Acquisition.* Cambridge: Cambridge University Press.

Ferguson, C. A., Peizer, D. B. and Weeks, T. E. (1973). Model-and-replica phonological grammar of a child's first words. *Lingua,* 31, 35–65.

Fernald, A. and Mazzie, C. (1991). Prosody and focus in speech to infants and adults. *Developmental Psychology,* 27, 209–21.

Fey, M. E. Long, S. H. and Finestack, L. H. (2003). Ten principles of grammar facilitation for children with Specific Language Impairments. *American Journal of Speech-Language Pathology* 12, 3–15.

Forrest, K. and Elbert, M. (2001). Treatment for phonologically disordered children with variable substitution patterns. *Clinical Linguistics and Phonetics,* 15: 1, 41–5.

Freed, B. (1980). Talking to foreigners versus talking to children: similarities and differences. In R. C. Scarcella and S. D. Krashen (eds), *Research in Second Language Acquisition.* Rowley, MA: Newbury House.

Gibson, E. and Wexler, K. (1994). Triggers. *Linguistic Inquiry,* 25, 407–54.

Gleitman, L. R., Newport, E. L. and Gleitman, H. (1984). The current status of the Motherese hypothesis. *Journal of Child Language,* 11, 43–79.

Goldin-Meadow, S. and Mylander, C. (1998). Spontaneous sign systems created by deaf children in two cultures. *Nature,* 391, 279–81.

Gordon, P. and Chafetz, J. (1990). Verb-based versus class-based accounts of actionality effects in children's comprehension of passives. *Cognition,* 36, 227–54.

Haggan, M. (2002). Self-reports and self-delusion regarding the use of Motherese: implications from Kuwaiti adults. *Language Sciences,* 24, 17–28.

Hamilton, M. (1999). Ethnography for classrooms: constructing a reflective curriculum for literacy. *Pedagogy, Culture and Society,* 7: 3, 429–44.

Harris, M. (1992). *Language Experience and Early Language Development: From Input to Uptake.* Hove: Lawrence Erlbaum.

Heath, S. B. (1983). *Ways with Words.* Cambridge: Cambridge University Press.

Hirsh-Pasek, K. and Treiman, R. (1982). Doggerel: motherese in a new context. *Journal of Child Language,* 9, 229–37.

Hirsh-Pasek, K., Treiman, R. and Schneiderman, M. (1984). Brown and Hanlon revisited: mothers' sensitivity to ungrammatical forms. *Journal of Child Language,* 11, 81–8.

Hoff-Ginsberg, E. (1985). Some contributions of mothers' speech to their children's syntactic growth. *Journal of Child Language,* 12: 2, 367–85.

Hornstein, N. (2005). Empiricism and rationalism as research strategies. In J. McGilvray (ed.), *The Cambridge Companion to Chomsky* (pp. 145–63). Cambridge: Cambridge University Press.

Jespersen, O. (1922). *Language: Its Nature, Development and Origin.* London: George Allen and Unwin.

Kuhl, P. K., Tsao, F. and Liu, H. (2003). Foreign language experience in infancy: effects of short term exposure and interaction on phonetic learning. *Proceedings of the National Academy of Sciences,* 100, 9096–101.

Lane, H. (1976). *The Wild Boy of Aveyron.* Cambridge, MA: Harvard University Press.

Lightfoot, D. (1989). The child's trigger experience: degree-0 learnability. *Behavioral and Brain Sciences,* 12, 321–75.

Lightfoot, D. (1991). *How to Set Parameters: Arguments from Language Change.* Cambridge, MA: MIT Press.

MacWhinney, B. and Snow, C. E. (1990). The child language data exchange system: an update. *Journal of Child Language,* 17, 457–72.

Mead, M. (1930). *Growing up in New Guinea: A Study of Adolescence and Sex in Primitive Societies.* Harmondsworth: Penguin.

Mitchell, R. W. (2001). Americans' talk to dogs: similarities and differences with talk to infants. *Research in Language and Social Interaction,* 34: 2, 183–210.

Mumme, D. L. and Fernald, A. (2003). The infant as onlooker: learning from emotional reactions observed in a television scenario. *Child Development,* 74, 221–37.

Murray, A., Johnson, J. and Peters, J. (1990). Finetuning of utterance length to preverbal infants: effects on later language development. *Journal of Child Language,* 17, 511–25.

Naigles, L. R. and Mayeux, L. (2000). Television as an incidental teacher. In D. Singer and J. Singer (eds), *Handbook of Children and the Media* (pp. 135–53). New York: Sage.

Nelson, K. E. (1977). Facilitating children's syntax acquisition. *Developmental Psychology,* 13, 101–7.

Nelson, K. E., Denninger, M. M., Bonvillian, J. D., Kaplan, B. J. and Baker, N. (1984). Maternal input adjustments and non-adjustments as related to children's linguistic advances and to language acquisition theories. In A. D. Pellegrini and T. D. Yawkey (eds), *The Development of Oral and Written Language in Social Contexts.* Norwood, NJ: Ablex.

Newport, E. L., Gleitman, H. and Gleitman, L. R. (1977). Mother, I'd rather do it myself: some effects and non-effects of maternal speech style. In C. E. Snow and C. A. Ferguson (eds), *Talking to Children.* Cambridge: Cambridge University Press.

Nicoladis, E. and Palmer, A. (2007). The role of type and token frequency in using past tense morphemes correctly. *Developmental Science,* 10: 2, 237–54.

Ochs, E. (1982). Talking to children in Western Samoa. *Language in Society,* 11, 77–104.

Owens, R. E. (2005). *Language Development: An Introduction* (6th edition). Boston: Pearson.

Pan, B., Feldman, H. and Snow, C. E. (1993). Parental speech to low-risk and at-risk children. Manuscript, Harvard Graduate School of Education.

Papousek, M. (2007). Communication in early infancy: an arena of intersubjective learning. *Infant Behavior and Development*, 30: 2, 258–66.

Patterson, J. L. (2002). Relationships of expressive vocabulary to frequency of reading and television experience among bilingual toddlers. *Applied Psycholinguistics*, 23, 493–508.

Phillips, J. R. (1973). Syntax and vocabulary of mothers' speech to young children: age and sex comparisons. *Child Development*, 44, 182–5.

Pinker, S. (1994). *The Language Instinct: The New Science of Language and Mind*. London: Penguin.

Pye, C. (1986). Quiché Mayan speech to children. *Journal of Child Language*, 13, 85–100.

Pye, C. (1992). The acquisition of K'iche' Maya. In D. I. Slobin (ed.), *The Crosslinguistic Study of Language Acquisition*, Vol. 3. Hillsdale, NJ: Erlbaum.

Ravid, D., Olshtain, E. and Ze'elon, R. (2003).Gradeschoolers' linguistic and pragmatic speech adaptation to native and non-native interlocution. *Journal of Pragmatics*, 35: 1, 71–99.

Rice, M. L., Huston, A. C., Truglio, R. and Wright, J. (1990). Words from *Sesame Street:* Learning vocabulary while viewing. *Developmental Psychology*, 26, 421–8.

Rice, M. L. and Woodsmall, L. (1988). Lessons from television: children's word learning when viewing. *Child Development*, 59, 420–9.

Rosenthal Rollins, P. and Snow, C. E. (1998). Shared attention and grammatical development in typical children and children with autism. *Journal of Child Language*, 25, 653–73.

Rowland, C. F., Pine, J. M., Lieven, E. V. M. and Theakston, A. L. (2003). Determinants of acquisition order in wh-questions: re-evaluating the role of caregiver speech. *Journal of Child Language*, 30: 3, 609–35.

Russo, T. and Volterra, V. (2005). Comment on 'Children creating core properties of language: Evidence from an emerging sign language in Nicaragua'. *Science*, 309: 573, 56.

Sachs, J., Bard, B. and Johnson, M. L. (1981). Language learning with restricted input: case studies of two hearing children of deaf parents. *Applied Psycholinguistics*, 2, 33–54.

Saxton, M. (1995). Negative evidence versus negative feedback: a study of corrective input in child language acquisition. Unpublished D.Phil. thesis, University of Oxford.

Saxton, M. (1997). The Contrast theory of negative input. *Journal of Child Language*, 24, 139–61.

Saxton, M. (2000). Negative evidence and negative feedback: immediate effects on the grammaticality of child speech. *First Language*, 20: 3, 221–52.

Saxton, M. (2005). 'Recast' in a new light: insights for clinical practice from typical language studies. *Child Language Teaching and Therapy*, 21: 1, 23–38.

Saxton, M. (2008). What's in a name? Coming to terms with the child's linguistic environment. *Journal of Child Language* 35(3): 677–686.

Saxton, M., Backley, P. and Gallaway, C. (2005). Negative input for grammatical errors: effects after a lag of 12 weeks. *Journal of Child Language*, 32, 643–72.

Saxton, M., Houston-Price, C. and Dawson, N. (2005). The Prompt hypothesis: clarification requests as corrective input for grammatical errors. *Applied Psycholinguistics*, 26: 3, 393–414.

Saxton, M., Kulcsar, B., Marshall, G. and Rupra, M. (1998). The longer-term effects of corrective input: an experimental approach. *Journal of Child Language*, 25, 701–21.

Scaife, M. and Bruner, J. (1975). The capacity for joint visual attention in infants. *Nature*, 253, 265–6.

Schmidt, C. L. and Lawson, K. R. (2002). Caregiver attention-focusing and children's attention-sharing behaviours as predictors of later verbal IQ in very low birthweight children. *Journal of Child Language* 14, 3–22.

Scholz, B. C. and Pullum, G. K. (2006). Irrational nativist exuberance. In R. J. Stainton (ed.), *Contemporary Debates in Cognitive Science*. Oxford: Blackwell.

Seitz, S. and Stewart, C. (1975). Imitations and expansions: some developmental: aspects of mother–child communication. *Developmental Psychology*, 11: 6, 763–8.

Senghas, A., Kita, S. and Ozyurek, A. (2004). Children creating core properties of language: evidence from an emerging sign language in Nicaragua. *Science*, 305: 5691, 1779–82.

Shady, M. and Gerken, L. (1999). Grammatical and caregiver cues in early sentence comprehension. *Journal of Child Language*, 26, 163–75.

Shatz, M. and Gelman, R. (1973). The development of communication skills: modifications in the speech of young children as a function of the listener. *Monographs of the Society for Research in Child Development*, Serial no. 5, 38.

Slobin, D. (1973). Cognitive prerequisites for the development of grammar. In C. A. Ferguson and D. I. Slobin (eds), *Studies of Child Language Development*. New York: Holt, Rinehart and Winston.

Snow, C. E. (1972). Mothers' speech to children learning language. *Child Development*, 43, 549–66.

Snow, C. E. (1979). The role of social interaction in language acquisition. In W.A. Collins (ed.), *Minnesota Symposia on Child Psychology*, Vol. 12 (pp. 157–82). Hillsdale, NJ: Lawrence Erlbaum.

Snow, C. E. (1995). Issues in the study of input: finetuning, universality, individual and developmental differences and necessary causes. In P. Fletcher and B. MacWhinney (eds), *The Handbook of Child Language*. Oxford: Basil Blackwell.

Snow, C. E., Arlman-Rupp, A., Hassing, Y., Jobse, J., Joosten, J. and Vorster, J. (1976). Mothers' speech in three social classes. *Journal of Psycholinguistic Research*, 5, 1–20.

Snyder, W. (2007). *Child Language: The Parametric Approach*. Oxford: Oxford University Press.

Sokolov, J. (1993). A local contingency analysis of the finetuning hypothesis. *Developmental Psychology*, 29, 1008–23.

Strapp, C. M. and Federico, A. (2000). Imitations and repetitions: what do children say following recasts? *First Language*, 20: 3, 273–90.

Swensen, L. D., Naigles, L. R. and Fein, D. (2007). Does maternal input affect the language of children with autism? In H. Caunt-Nolan, S. Kulatilake and I. Woo (eds), *Proceedings of the 30th Annual Boston University Conference on Language Development*. Somerville, MA: Cascadilla Press.

Tomasello, M. (2003). *Constructing A Language: A Usage-Based Theory of Language Acquisition*. Cambridge, MA: Harvard University Press.

Tomasello, M., Mannle, S. and Kruger, A. C. (1986). Linguistic environment of 1- to 2-year-old twins. *Developmental Psychology*, 22, 169–76.

Uchikoshi, Y. (2005). Narrative development in bilingual kindergartners: can *Arthur* help? *Developmental Psychology*, 41: 3, 464–78.

Vygotsky, L. S. (1978). *Mind in Society: The Development of Higher Psychological Processes*. Cambridge, MA: Harvard University Press.

Warren-Leubecker, A. and Bohannon, J. N. (1983). The effects of verbal feedback and listener type on the speech of preschool children. *Journal of Experimental Child Psychology*, 35, 540–8.

Warren-Leubecker, A. and Bohannon, J. N. (1984). Intonation patterns in child-directed speech – mother–father differences. *Child Development*, 55: 4, 1379–85.

Weppelman, T. L., Bostow, A. Schiffer, R., Elbert-Perez, E. and Newman, R. S. (2003). Children's use of the prosodic characteristics of infant-directed speech. *Language and Communication*, 23: 1, 63–80.

Young, M. W. (1979). *The Ethnography of Malinowski: The Trobriand Islands 1915–18*. London: Routledge and Kegan Paul.

4
universal grammar approaches to language acquisition

maria teresa guasti

introduction

How children succeed in acquiring language, without apparent effort and following similar milestones, at a time when dressing, and eating without getting dirty are still problems, has been a central question in generative linguistics (Chomsky, 1957, 1959, 1975; Guasti, 2002) since its inception. This chapter will provide an answer to this question by adopting the Universal Grammar (UG) approach to language acquisition which presumes that language is what makes us humans and distinguishes us from non-human animals. We acquire language because it is part and parcel of our nature.

This chapter begins by giving a flavour of the linguistic knowledge that underpins linguistic behaviour and examining the circumstances in which language is acquired. This leads to the observation of a discrepancy between the input (the primary linguistic data that the child hears) and the output (the child's competence): what has become known as the problem of 'the poverty of the stimulus'. It then presents evidence for output surpassing input in situations where children's competence is superior to their linguistic model and explores the source of the innovations that children introduce. It concludes by arguing that children are born with specific mechanisms and structures dedicated to the acquisition of language.

what does one know when one knows a language?

Work in generative linguistic theory has shown that there are limits on the form of a possible language, i.e. rules of language can take only certain forms and sentence meaning is dependent on specific syntactic configurations. Following are some examples of constraints on the form of rules:

(1) (a)   When did you say – that John went to the hospital —?
    (b)   When did you say – why John went to the hospital?
(2) (a)   I said it on Saturday
    (b)   He went on Friday

Despite their obvious surface similarities, the sentence in (1a) is ambiguous in a way that (1b) is not. The question in (1a) can be answered by indicating the time when you said something or the time when John was hospitalized; that is, 'when' can be interpreted in the two places indicated by the '—' and both (2a) and (2b) can be possible answers to (1a). By contrast, the question in (1b) can only be about the time at which you said something, that is, only (2a) is a possible answer.

While there are some complicating factors not considered here, the sentence in (1b) shows that one cannot (generally) form questions out of a subordinate clause introduced by a wh-element. (Such subordinate clauses are islands for extraction (Ross, 1983).) By contrast, one *can* make a question out of a subordinate clause of the kind in (1a), introduced by 'that'. Moreover, this constraint is not peculiar to English. In Italian, and in other languages, the counterparts of these kinds of sentences work in exactly the same way. Thus, it can be posited that it holds universally and is one of the *principles* that constrain the form of a possible language.

Consider another similar example, inspired by Moro (2006):

(3) (a)   I saw the goat that washed the cat hit the mouse
    (b)   Who did you see the goat [that washed the cat] hit —?
    (c)   *Who did you see the goat [that washed —] hit the mouse?

From the sentence in (3a), one can form the question in (3b), but not the question in (3c), although its meaning is understandable. One might try to appeal to a constraint on linear order, e.g. 'one can extract from the last position of the sentence, but not from within the sentence'. However, (1a) above clearly shows that extraction is possible from certain internal positions; and extraction from the last position of (4a) below yields an ungrammatical result.

(4) (a)   I saw the goat hit the mouse that washed the cat
    (b)   *Who did you see the goat hit the mouse [that washed —]?

We must conclude, therefore, that what controls possible extractions is not linear order but the underlying syntactic structure from which extractions are or are not permitted. One can extract from the main clause in (3b), but not from the relative clause in (3c) (where the relative clause is indicated by the brackets). As in the case of the subordinate clause introduced by a wh-element in (1b), the relative clauses in (3b) and in (4b) are islands for extraction in English, as well as in other languages.

As speakers of English (or of other languages), we know the facts in (1) through (4). Interestingly, children apparently also know them. They know that (1a) has two possible answers, but (1b) only one as illustrated by experiments reported in de Villiers et al. (1990) (See de Villiers and de Villiers, this volume). The key question is: How do children come to know this set of intricate facts? How do they manage to draw inferences about structure from the incoming sound stream?

Consider now the sentences in (5), taken from Guasti and Chierchia (1999/2000). They illustrate an example of a constraint on meaning rather than a constraint on form.

(5) (a)   We celebrate every child$_j$'s birthday the way he$_j$ likes best
    (b)   Every child$_j$'s birthday, we celebrate the way he$_j$ likes best
    (c)   *Every child$_j$'s birthday, he$_j$ celebrates with friends

The sentence in (5a) can mean that for every child x, we celebrate x's birthday the way x likes best, a reading in which the universally quantified phrase that is embedded within the direct object (every child's birthday) binds the pronoun.[1] The sentence in (5b) shows that the same reading remains possible when the object is dislocated to the left periphery of the clause (as for the birthday of every child x, we celebrate it the way this x likes best). In (5c), however, we see that this reading is no longer available. That is, (5c) cannot mean that as for the birthday of every child x, x celebrates x's own birthday with friends; equivalently, the quantifier in (5c) cannot bind the pronoun. The question is: Why?

To see why the facts in (5) are as they are, we have to assume that meaning is not computed on the surface structure. Assuming that movement is actually copying, the underlying structure of (5b) is (6), in which the dislocated NP leaves a copy in the canonical position indicated in boldface (and is not pronounced).

(6) Every child$_j$'s birthday, we celebrate **every child$_j$'s birthday** the way he$_j$ likes best.

The structure in (6) is also very similar to (5a) and it comes as no surprise that (5b) therefore has the same interpretation as (5a) (leaving aside the question of how scope is assigned to the quantifier, which is not relevant for our purposes here). This is tantamount to saying that meaning is computed not on the surface structure, but on the underlying structure: a structure in which surface movement has been 'undone'.

Once we accept the idea that the interpretation is computed on the basis of an underlying structure, in which what counts may not be overtly audible, we can see why (5c) is not acceptable on the bound interpretation of the pronoun interpretation, i.e. as meaning that as for the birthday of every child x, x celebrates x's own birthday with friends. Parallel to what we did for (5b), we assume that the dislocated NP left a copy in the canonical position, as in (7a) and that it is the copy that counts for computing meaning.

(7) (a) *Every child$_J$'s birthday, he$_J$ celebrates **every child$_J$'s birthday** with friends.

     (b) *He$_J$ celebrates with friends every child$_J$'s birthday

Under these assumptions, the interpretation indicated by the indexing is ruled out in (7a) as it is in (7b), in which the NP is pronounced in the canonical position. In both cases, we are faced with a violation of principle C of the binding theory (Chomsky, 1981), as a quantified expression (or more precisely the copy of the quantified expression) cannot be bound (by a pronoun). (Note that (7b) is perfectly acceptable, as is (5c), if it has the meaning that someone celebrates every child's birthday with friends.)

It should be clear from these examples that what counts for the interpretation is not the linear order. In all cases in (5) the quantified expression precedes the pronoun, but only in (5a) and (5b) can the pronoun be bound by the quantifier and give rise to the reading in which the quantified expression and the pronoun co-vary: for every child x, we celebrate x's birthday the way x likes best. What matters is the underlying hierarchical structure and the position elements occupy in this structure. Moreover, there is evidence from Italian that, at the age of 5, children can correctly interpret sentences, such as those in (5) (Guasti and Chierchia, 1999/2000). The question, then, is how do children figure out the syntactic structures from the strings of words and establish that some material must be interpreted in different positions from where it is heard? How do children come to have implicit access to a hierarchical structure, in which the surface order may be undone?

Before trying to answer this question, let us consider one last piece of 'hidden' knowledge that mature speakers of language possess. This has to do with the underlying logical structure on which truth is computed and from which inferences are drawn, since knowing the meaning of a sentence includes being able to recognize a series of inferences that can be drawn from that sentence. At the level of lexical items, knowing the meaning of 'John is a bachelor' requires knowing that John is male, adult and not married. Analogously, at the syntactic level, if one is speaking in Italy or about students of Italian, and one knows that (8a) is true, one will also know that (8b) is true.

(8) (a) Every student will bring oranges to the party
    (b) Every Italian student will bring oranges to the party

That is, if every student in the class will bring oranges to the party, then we can also be sure that every Italian student will bring oranges to the party. However from the truth of (8a), we cannot infer anything of the kind in (9), as every student may bring oranges from somewhere else than Sicily.

(9) Every student will bring Sicilian oranges to the party

One might suggest that what counts in licensing these kinds of inferences is adjacency to the quantifier 'every' since in (8) the inference concerns the noun directly adjacent to 'every' ('student', 'Italian student'), while in (9) it concerns the complement of the verb 'bring' ('oranges'). However, as in our previous examples, linear order is not what is involved. Consider the following examples:

(10) (a) No student will bring oranges to the party
     (b) No Italian student will bring oranges to the party
     (c) No student will bring Sicilian oranges to the party

If (10a) is true, then (10b) is also true, parallelling what we saw in (8). This fact seems to further support our previous conjecture. In this case, however, the inference from (10a) to (10c) also goes through. That is, if no student will bring oranges, then *a fortiori* no student will bring Sicilian oranges. This time our conjecture does not seem to be correct.
  Now consider (11):

(11) (a) Some students will bring oranges
     (b) Some Italian students will bring oranges
     (c) Some students will bring Sicilian oranges

This time neither the inference in (11b) nor the one in (11c) can be derived from (11a), inasmuch as (11a) could be verified by the existence of a French student bringing oranges from California. This failure suggests that what matters in licensing inferences is not whether the relevant noun is adjacent or not to the quantifier. As we will see, what matters is some abstract structure used to evaluate quantified sentences. Quantified sentences like (8a), (10a) and (11a) have the abstract structure in (12b) (Q = quantifier), where the NP is called the restrictor of the quantifier and the VP its nuclear scope:

(12) (a) Every/No/Some student will bring oranges
      (b) Q NP VP

Assuming that the NP and the VP denote sets of individuals (i.e. the set of students and the set of individuals who will bring oranges respectively), quantifiers express relations between these sets. 'Every' states that the set denoted by the NP is included in the set denoted by the VP (that is, (8a) is true when the set of students is a subset of the set of those who bring oranges). 'No' asserts that the set denoted by the NP and the set denoted by the VP are disjoint. 'Some' states that the set denoted by the NP and the set denoted by the VP have at least one member in common. From these very basic semantic relations it is possible to explain the inferential pattern: quantifiers such as 'every' license inferences from a set (the set of students) to its subsets (Italian students) only in the NP, (putting it technically, they are downward entailing in the restrictor), whereas quantifiers such as 'no' license such inferences in both the NP and the VP (i.e. they are downward entailing in both the restrictor and the nuclear scope); and quantifiers like 'some' do not license these kind of inferences, (i.e. they are not downward entailing). These facts constitute evidence that sentences have a logical structure that is not immediately recoverable from the surface structure. They raise the questions of how we recover this abstract structure allowing the making of certain inferences and not others; and whether children need to learn these facts or come to the language learning task already knowing them.

In summary, we have looked at three linguistic phenomena – two kinds of extraction and the derivation of certain kinds of inferences – that share a common feature: they are governed by rules that apply to an underlying abstract structure that is not revealed directly by the acoustic stream. As Chomsky (1959, p. 55, citing Lashley), suggested, the 'syntactic organization of an utterance is not something directly represented in any simple way in the physical structure of an utterance itself'. The question is: How do we come to know these intricate pieces of knowledge? And how does it happen that even young children, between 4 and 5 years, are sensitive to these logical properties? (See Gualmini and Crain, 2002, 2005; Han et al., 2007). Before answering this question, we turn our attention to some key features of the process of language acquisition.

how children acquire language

Children acquire language without specific instructions, without focused correction (see below), without being explicitly told whether a sequence of words is grammatical or not, and without being explicitly told what a sequence means or cannot mean. Moreover, this happens across widely varying circumstances. For example, Petitto (1996) showed that the same milestones characterize the acquisition of both spoken and sign languages, with oral and manual babbling emerging at 6–8 months (Petitto and Marentette, 1991); first words and signs at around 12 months (Meier and Newport, 1990; Lillo Martin, 1999; Petitto, 1988) and first combinations at around 24 months. Thus, the modality in which language is expressed, orally or manually, does not change the course of language acquisition.

Similarly, despite a smaller range of experience, blind children acquire language more or less at the same pace as sighted children and in the same way. Landau and Gleitman (1985) showed that the vocabulary of blind children is similar to that of sighted children and that blind children know the meaning of perception verbs such as 'see' and 'look' without sensory experience. They argue that this is possible because the meaning of verbs is gathered by inspecting the sentences in which verbs are used (e.g. the number of arguments, the way these arguments are expressed), a piece of information available to both sighted and blind children, plus observation of the extralinguistic contexts in which such sentences are used, information less available to blind subjects. These authors also showed that while blind children start to put words together a bit later than some sighted children, they are still within the range of normal development. Thus, even though blind and sighted children have different sensory experiences, their languages grow very similarly.

Variations in the language learning situations also exist among children without disabilities. In many cultures, children are exposed to the special register of motherese or child directed speech (CDS). [See

Saxton, this volume: SFC.] While this register has some similarities across cultures, the specific characteristics of CDS may vary from one culture to another (Ochs and Schieffelin, 1995), and in some cultures it is claimed that adults do not use a special register to address children (Schieffelin, 1979; Pye, 1986). However, even in cultures where CDS is employed, there is variation in the quantity and quality of this speech, and though CDS is assumed to make the task of language acquisition easier, it is possible that at some points in development, simplified CDS may actually hinder acquisition. Hoff and Naigles (2002), for example, have shown that the richer the input, the broader and more varied the children's lexicons. So a limited vocabulary may limit children's development.

In spite of the wide range of variation reviewed above, the major similarities in the development of language competence pose problems for an account of language acquisition without a nativist component.

the argument from the poverty of the stimulus

The facts about language shown in the examples in the previous sections are part of our knowledge of language and cannot be inferred from the input, as there is no sign in the input of what a sentence *cannot* mean or of what operations *cannot* be performed on it.

In addition to the facts considered in 1–13 above, consider the following example of 'hidden' or underlying knowledge which concerns rules regulating agreement between the subject and the inflected verb in a sentence such as (13).

(13) John has called Paul since yesterday

As with our earlier examples, generalizations based on linear order such as that in (14) cannot be correct as the examples in (15) make clear.

(14) The inflected verb agrees with the name on its left or adjacent to it

(15) (a)   John and Mary have called Paul since yesterday
      (b)   The sister of the twins has called Paul since yesterday

Rather, agreement is a structure-dependent relation, in this case holding between a phrase, the subject, and the inflection attached to the verb in a specifier-head configuration as in (16).

(16)

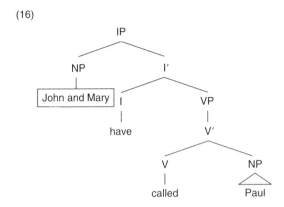

Even though the abstract structure of an utterance, as represented in (16), is not inferable in a simple way from the physical sequence of sounds, agreement is computed on it.

Interestingly, new brain imaging techniques are able to demonstrate that our brains respond differently to structure-dependent and structure-independent rules. Musso et al. (2003) taught adult subjects artificial languages. One language included rules that were linguistically possible; that is, they obeyed the constraint of structure dependency. The other artificial language contained rules that violated structure dependency and were framed in terms of fixed position in the string. Subjects were able to learn both kinds of rules and were able to establish whether a given sentence obeyed or did not obey the rules of the learned artificial language. However, only in the case of structure-dependent rules was there a significant increase in the activity in Broca's area, the area typically involved in syntactic processing. This finding suggests that Broca's area is particularly tuned to process strings that obey structure dependency. In other words, our brains recognize that there are different kinds of rules, and only those that obey structure dependency engage the area dedicated to language. As Moro (2006) claims, this result supports the hypothesis that acquisition of syntax is biologically determined.[2]

Another aspect of linguistic rules, explored by Matthei (1982) Roeper (1972), and Crain and Thornton (1998, p. 123),[3] demonstrates how words are combined hierarchically. When presented with Figure 4.1 and asked the sentence in (17),

(17) Show me the second black ball

you will point to the third ball in the row.

Figure 4.1   Show me the second black ball

Figure 4.2   Show me the second underlined black ball

This interpretation means that your brain has first applied a rule of adjectival modification that combines 'ball' and 'black' and formed a nominal unit. Then you have modified this new unit with the adjective 'second' to obtain [second [black ball]], a new nominal unit. If on the other hand your brain had first combined the two adjectives to give the unit [second black] (i.e. (a ball that is) both second and black) and then combined this unit with 'ball' to give [[second black] ball]], you would have indicated the second ball in the row.

Consider now Figure 4.2 and the sentence in (18):

(18) Show me the second underlined black ball

This time, you are likely to point to the fourth ball in the row. As in the previous case, the way words are combined is constrained. First, your brain modifies the noun 'ball' with the adjective 'black' to give [black ball]; then it applies the same rule to the result to yield [underlined [black ball]] and finally [second [underlined [black ball]]]. Any other possible combination would have elicited a different answer. These examples illustrate one of the key properties of linguistic rules: they are recursive. A recursive rule is one that applies to the results of its application. Again there is nothing in the string of sounds that alludes to this property.

These examples, together with those discussed in 1–12, illustrate one of the key observations in generative language acquisition research, known as the argument from the poverty of the stimulus (APS) (Chomsky, 1965, 1981). This argument is that we possess abstract knowledge of language, of the kind that we have illustrated, that cannot be inferred from the input. Specifically, the input is impoverished because it does not contain enough information about the nature of the underlying system. For example, as illustrated, the input does not specify that rules of language are structure dependent or recursive, and yet the way we respond to examples such as (17) and (18) shows that we (implicitly) possess this information. If we did not, we would not respond in the ways that we do.

A related component of the 'poverty of the stimulus argument' is that the knowledge we acquire outstrips the available information in the input (also called the primary linguistic data). The input is impoverished because children do not hear *only* well-formed utterances, but also fragments of utterances, sentences that include hesitation, that are incomplete or include slips of the tongue. Like trying to deduce the rules of a new game in which players are cheating, but where this is not marked in any way, ill-formed utterances should be a problem, leading the child to err in figuring out the properties of the language. Yet, this does not appear to be the case, as children make considerably fewer mistakes than would be expected if they relied solely on the input.

A further component of the APS argument is that children are not explicitly taught language and certainly are not taught what sentences *cannot* mean (i.e. which kinds of combinations are illegal in their language of exposure) and they are generally not corrected when they make grammatical mistakes. Yet, as speakers, we have clear intuitions about whether a given utterance is acceptable or not in our language, and can have a certain meaning or not. Thus, in spite of the fact that children are not explicitly taught language and do not receive negative evidence about what is not possible in their language(s) [but see Chapter 3, this volume: SFC], they come to have a fairly elaborate knowledge of the language of exposure.

To summarize, the linguistic output (our linguistic competence) outstrips the linguistic input or the input is impoverished; children are not explicitly taught language; and children have no access to what sentences do not mean. The conclusion is drawn, therefore, that to fill the discrepancy between input and output, one needs to postulate the existence of innate mechanisms and of an innate and fairly articulated structure dedicated to the acquisition of language (Chomsky, 1965, 1981).

There have been a number of criticisms levelled at the APS which can be addressed with evidence, not available at the time the argument was formulated. This evidence supports a nativist approach, and cannot be easily handled without recognizing a special status for the linguistic capacity of humans.

criticism of the argument from the poverty of the stimulus

Over the years, the argument from the poverty of the stimulus has been the object of lively debate in philosophical, linguistic and psychological circles (Quine, 1969; Putnam, 1967; Elman, 2004; Laurence and

Margolis, 2001). One feature of the proposal that has received heavy criticism is the claim that children are not corrected. The general observation is that adults do not generally correct children when they make phonological or grammatical mistakes and say such things as 'the bird got eated' (rather than eaten) or 'nobody don't like me' and, moreover, if they do, it is very unlikely that children learn from the corrections. Although it is acknowledged that children are not explicitly corrected, nevertheless it has been claimed that they receive some kind of feedback or indirect negative evidence, when they are mistaken (Farrar, 1992; Saxton, this volume). Adults are more likely to repeat grammatical utterances than ungrammatical ones (Hirsch-Pasek et al., 1984) and to ask for clarification when the utterance is incorrect (Demetras et al., 1986; Bohannon and Stanowicz, 1988). However, how consistent this sort of feedback is and how effective it is remains a controversial question (Marcus, 1993; Morgan and Travis, 1989). Morgan and Travis (1989), for example, have shown that the more frequent an error, the less the child is corrected, which would not seem to be an obvious way of eliminating it. Presumably, frequently noticed errors are also registered as resistant to change.

A more general objection to a nativist approach to language is based on findings showing that a statistical mechanism is available to 8-month-old infants which supports acquisition. [See Vihman, this volume: SFC.] Saffran et al. (1996) have shown that 8-month-old American babies can compute transition probabilities (TP) (or distributional regularities) between events, including linguistic events. They can track the probability that a syllable X will appear given syllable Y within a speech sequence. This ability is very important for segmenting speech into words, as the probability that two syllables co-occur is higher when these syllables belong to the same word than when they belong to different words. Other studies have shown that children are able to compute TP, not only with linguistic stimuli, but also with tones and with visual stimuli (Saffran et al., 1999; Fiser and Aslin, 2002).

When the findings of Saffran and colleagues were published (Saffran et al., 1996), they gave rise to much heated discussion, as they were taken to demonstrate that language acquisition was possible without an innate endowment. Saffran et al. argued that 'infants possess experience-dependent mechanisms that may be powerful enough to support not only word segmentation but also acquisition of other aspects of language' (p. 1928). However, these results have been overstated, since they suggest only that *some* aspects of language acquisition can be learned on the basis of a general purpose stochastic mechanism. They show neither that the *whole* process of language acquisition can be accomplished exclusively with such a mechanism, nor that this mechanism is the only mechanism necessary to explain acquisition.

Ironically, Chomsky suggested long ago (Chomsky, 1975, Chapter 5, fn. 18) that word segmentation was likely to be accomplished by looking at distributional regularities. Recently, it has been shown that humans actually have two mechanisms: a statistical mechanism that computes distributional regularities, and a mechanism that extracts rules (Marcus et al., 1999; Peña et al., 2002). Marcus et al. (1999) showed that 7-month-old babies familiarized with syllable sequences in an ABA or BAA pattern are able to induce the rules X__X or YXX and generalize them to sequences of unfamiliar syllables with the same structures. And in a study with adults, Peña et al. (2002) showed that, depending on the nature of the input, adults use one of two different mechanisms. If speech input includes subliminal pauses of 25 ms, adults use a mechanism that extracts regularities. If no pause is present, however, adults use a mechanism that computes statistical or transition probabilities but cannot extract regularities. Peña et al. thus suggest that while the mechanism that computes transition probabilities can segment the speech stream, it cannot be used to acquire linguistic rules. These must be learned using the regularity extracting mechanism, which is likely to be specifically designed for language.

In summary, we may conclude that language is a complex object and its acquisition requires, among other things, an ability to compute distributional regularities in the input and extract generalizations. However, this does not justify a belief that this is all we need to acquire language.

when the output surpasses the input: the case of sign languages

One key assumption of APS is that the input is underdetermined with respect to the output. Another is that the linguistic competence attained by children is superior to the linguistic competence displayed by the adults who provided the linguistic input. A dramatic illustration of this comes from the emergence of sign languages.

Singleton and Newport (2004) studied the language of a deaf child, Simon, who was exposed only to an inconsistent language model: the

American Sign Language (ASL) of his deaf parents, who learned it after the age of 15 years. Simon's teacher used a manual version of English, simultaneously articulated with spoken English, and Simon's classmates did not use ASL. In spite of such inconsistent and reduced input, Simon developed well-structured ASL that lacked many of the irregularities and errors present in his input. In several morphological domains, Simon's performance at age 7 was similar to that of his deaf age mates exposed to native ASL and was much more regular and error-free than that of his parents. It seems that Simon extracted the more frequent forms in the ASL produced by its parents and regularized them. Specifically he developed 'a morphological system with features organized in a contrastive fashion' (p. 399), i.e. he acquired a consistent form-meaning mapping out of an inconsistent one, regularizing the input and structuring it in ways that are typical of morphological rules in natural languages, suggesting an ability to enrich the input in highly specific ways.

A similar situation is provided by cases of spontaneously created home sign systems: rudimentary and idiosyncratic systems of gestures used by deaf children not exposed to a sign language to communicate with hearing members of the family or other deaf people. These systems are characterized by structural properties typical of natural languages. They have discrete elements, a vocabulary of gestures belonging to categories (e.g. nouns and verbs), which are combined in a consistent order that reveals a morphological structure. Moreover, these properties emerge gradually, following the same timetable that characterizes language acquisition in typically developing children exposed to a conventional model. Goldin-Meadow (1982) and Goldin-Meadow and Mylander (1984, 1998) showed that these deaf children started to produce single manual gestures, some iconic in nature, resembling words, at around 12 months. At around 24 months the children started to combine gestures in a structural organized way, something their mothers did rarely and inconsistently (Feldman et al., 1978).

Interestingly, sign combinations share properties across cultures. Zheng and Goldin-Meadow (2002) found that home sign systems in both China and the United States displayed the properties of ergative languages (such as Basque) in which the subject of transitive verbs is marked with the ergative case, while the subject of intransitive verbs is marked with absolutive case, the case also employed to mark the object of transitive verbs. Despite the fact that none of the ambient languages: English, Chinese, ASL or Chinese Sign Language are ergative languages, the home sign systems showed consistent features of ergative languages. They marked the subjects of transitive and intransitive verbs differently and the gestures expressing the subject of intransitive verbs and the object of transitive verbs were produced more frequently than the gestures expressing the subject of transitive verbs. This means that the subjects of transitive verbs were omitted more frequently than either the subjects of intransitive verbs or the objects of transitive verbs. Finally, the gestures expressing subjects of intransitive verbs and objects of transitive verbs were produced before the verb, while the subjects of transitive verbs could be freely placed either before or after the verb. Although the hearing mothers of these children possessed a vocabulary of gestures, they did not produce gestures as complex or as consistently structured as those of their children and certainly did not use the ergative pattern in their gestures.

While the creation of a home sign system did not occur from scratch (mothers used gestures), these findings indicate that it is the children who are responsible for the structural aspects of the home sign system. The syntactic properties that these systems display seem to come from constraints on the genetic endowment for language, as in the case of Simon. The development of these systems from a rather rudimentary and unstructured input suggests that language is resilient, as Goldin-Meadow (2003) puts it; it cannot help but emerge at the appropriate time and develop according to a maturational schedule.

While the spontaneous home sign gestural systems created by deaf children are not fully fledged languages, the change from a gestural system to a full grammatical language *has* been documented in the case of Nicaraguan Sign Language (NSL). Before 1977, deaf people in Nicaragua lived isolated in their families with little opportunity to meet. At that time they developed a system of home signs that varied from one household to another. In 1977, a centre for special education opened in Managua, and for the first time deaf students began sharing the gestural systems they used in their families. As these systems were different, the children had to create a mutually intelligible system based on the original home sign systems. In doing so, they created a pidgin with a lexicon and a rudimentary grammatical structure.

In the mid- to late 1980s, the first cohort of students were becoming adolescents and adults and a new cohort of children entered the school. This allowed intergenerational contacts between the two cohorts of subjects and created a language learning situation that promoted the creolization of the pidgin into Nicaraguan Sign Language, with its own system of signs, rules of combination and morphological contrasts (Senghas, 1995, 2003; Senghas and Coppola, 2001). The language signed by the second cohort included new grammatical structures, a consistent system of morphological inflections, classifiers and spatial modulation. For example, a sentence such as 'The woman pushed the man' is expressed by the first cohort of deaf students through a sequence of signs equivalent to WOMAN PUSHED MAN IS PUSHED (from Kegl et al., 1999); that is, they use a rule whereby each animate argument is followed by a verb (noun–verb noun–verb). The second cohort, however, uses spatial modulation to express the same sentence. First, the sign for WOMAN and the sign for MAN are signed in two positions of the signing space. Then, the sign corresponding to PUSH is signed moving from the position in which WOMAN was signed to the position where MAN was signed. Since such spatial modulations are present in the language of the second cohort, but not in the language of the first cohort, they could not have been learned from input. Moreover, spatial modulation is a feature typical of sign languages and is not present in spoken languages. Thus, the children of the second cohort could not have been influenced by the ambient language, Spanish.

According to Senghas 'the language abilities that children possess early in ontogenetic development enabled young signers to newly differentiate a contrast in form and apply that contrast systematically to a new contrast in meaning, thereby generating a form-function mapping not observed in the language of their adolescent model' (p. 527). The growth of NSL, like the case of Simon and of home sign, suggests that children have a special capacity to surpass their reduced model that adults have lost. Interestingly, in the case of NSL the innovations introduced by the second cohort of deaf students were not learned by those of the first cohort who were adolescents and adults when these innovations were introduced. They were too old to learn new aspects of language. Thus, it is only children that have a special gift for language, supporting the hypothesis that there is a sensitive or critical period for the acquisition of language.

The cases discussed in this section and in the previous ones also show that feedback has a limited role in the acquisition of language. In the Nicaraguan situation, signers of the pidgin could not provide feedback to the second cohort of children because they were not producing the structures their children were; and similarly Simon's parents were not in a position to correct their son, even indirectly. The fact that new communicative systems emerge and display the properties of known natural languages suggests that the form a new language can take is constrained. Similarly, the fact that our brains respond differently to rules that obey the form of natural language rules, (i.e. structure dependency) than to rules that do not suggests that we are set up biologically to expect linguistic rules to display certain forms.

The claim that there is an innate predisposition to acquire language, as shown by the fact that humans are unique among animals to have language, is relatively uncontroversial. However, differences of opinion exist over whether our innate capacity is domain specific or domain general. That is, do we have mechanisms and abilities specifically for language or are mechanisms and abilities operative in a range of cognitive domains enough to explain the course of language acquisition? The sets of facts discussed above provide support for Chomsky's original idea that there is not just a predisposition to acquire language, but a fairly structured system that guides the child in the acquisition of language and that shapes the form of possible natural languages. This system is dedicated to the acquisition and processing of language, although it is possible that general purpose mechanisms also contribute to language acquisition. Some evidence for this claim comes from a particular type of disorder called Specific Language Impairment (SLI).

when things go wrong: specific language impairments

As much as 7 per cent of pre-school age children (Tomblin et al., 1997) suffer from a range of specific language disorders in spite of having intelligence scores within the norm, and not displaying obvious neurological, sensory or emotional problems (Bishop, 1997; Leonard, 1997). Some have problems with sound perception, some with the lexicon, and others with grammatical (Van der Lely, 2005) or pragmatic aspects of language. Still others have a combination of linguistic difficulties. SLI may impact expressive or receptive abilities in various degrees that may change developmentally, with receptive disorders being generally the most resistant to intervention. Some language problems can be overcome or attenuated with age; and during the school years, they may be associated with dyslexia. There is evidence that SLI has a genetic origin, as it runs in families (Tomblin et al., 1997; Rice et al., 1998). Moreover, language disorders have a higher incidence among monozygotic (MZ) twins than among dizygotic (DZ) twins raised in the same household. As the environments of these twins are the same, the different incidence can be argued to be due to the genetics, which are identical for MZ twins, but not for DZ twins (Stromswold, 2001).

These data show that language can be selectively impaired, as, by definition, children with SLI do not have other cognitive impairments. In other words, these data are compatible with the idea that the language capacity is independent of other cognitive functions. Note that this does not preclude language difficulties impacting educational achievement. As some authors have noted (e.g. Leonard, 1997) the IQ of some children affected by language disorders may decrease with age. This is not surprising given that much of education, including reasoning and problem solving, is mediated through language.

the UG model of language acquisition

With the evidence of the previous sections in hand, we can now return to the question of where linguistic structure comes from if it is not present in the acoustic or signed stream. Chomsky's answer (1965, 1981) has always been that humans are biologically endowed with a Universal Grammar (UG), an innate structure that encodes the form of a possible human language and that assists the child during the acquisition of language. Thus, according to Chomsky, humans are not merely endowed with a predisposition to acquire language, but with specific mechanisms and structures that lead them to analyse the linguistic input in certain ways.

UG constrains children's conjectures about the form of linguistic rules: they must be structure dependent, as we have illustrated above. Children are biased not to even consider linear order rules because this is not the form linguistic rules can take. UG encodes constraints on the architecture of human language and in this respect it encodes properties that hold universally. In all languages, words and phrases are not put together randomly, but according to structure-dependent rules. This is a universal property of human languages and thus children expect to find an order in what they hear.

Not all properties of language are universal, clearly. Word orders, for example, vary from one language to another. In English the main order is SVO (subject verb object complements), while in Basque it is SOV. Similarly, all sentences have a subject and this is a universal property. However, Italian allows the clausal subject to remain unexpressed as in *'imparo'* (learn-1sg, 'I learn'), while English does not. These variations are encoded by parameters that can be expressed in terms of questions with binary answers, such as whether complements precede verbs; whether complements follow verbs; or whether the language allows a phonologically null subject. Children 'know' (unconsciously, of course) that there are certain parameters, because they are specified in UG. Their task is to determine the value of each parameter on the basis of what they hear. Clearly, having to figure out the properties of the ambient language by following the path traced by UG is much easier than having to figure out everything from scratch.

The arguments that led to the UG proposal in the 1960s are as powerful today as they were then, and new data have accumulated since showing that the output outstrips the input. However, it is important to bear in mind that 'none of the data [available today and in the future] is decisive in proving that a nativist approach to language acquisition is correct, but proof, in this area is an entirely misplaced standard', as Laurence and Margolis (2001) put it. We can only explore pieces of data that make the nativist hypothesis plausible.

conclusion

Children acquire language without being explicitly taught, in ways that are similar across cultures, regardless of the specific modality, manual or oral. There is no doubt that language is part of our biological make-up, and we acquire language in a short time and in similar manner in different environments because we are designed to do so. According to the nativist perspective, there exist specific structures and mechanisms dedicated to the process of language acquisition (in addition to mechanisms that are available for other learning tasks, e.g. observation of distributional regularities). Data making this hypothesis plausible come from specific impairments affecting only language, from cases in which the output surpasses the input, from the growth of new languages, such as NSL, and from linguistic analysis of the kind discussed at the beginning of this chapter.

Postulating the existence of a dedicated structure does not prevent one from accepting that language can recruit different kinds of mechanisms, some of which are specifically dedicated to language and some of which are not (Peña et al., 2002). The fact that children are endowed with such a structured capacity for language does not mean that the environment does not have a role: it does. Although some of the information that the child needs in order to acquire language comes from the genetic endowment, the input provides the raw materials to which the child can apply the guidelines offered by UG: one cannot make a cake without ingredients!

notes

1. A binds B if A is coindexed with B and c-commands B, where c-command is a structural relation that occurs when A is higher than B in a given configuration.

2. Strictly speaking, the finding that the brains of adults display hallmarks of specialization for linguistic rules does not imply that the brain of babies is set up in the same way. It may be possible that this specialization is the result of an interplay between innate abilities and experience. However, the finding is certainly compatible with a nativist perspective.
3. I owe this suggestion to Carlo Cecchetto.

references

Bishop, D. M. V. (1997). *Uncommon Understanding: Development and Disorders of Language Comprehension in Children*. Hove: Psychology Press.

Bohannon, N. and Stanowicz, L. (1988). The issue of negative evidence: adult response to children's language errors. *Developmental Psychology*, 24, 684–9.

Chomsky, N. (1957). *Aspects of the Theory of Syntax*. Cambridge, MA: MIT Press.

Chomsky, N. (1959). A review of B.F. Skinner's Verbal Behaviour. *Language*, 35, 26–58.

Chomsky, N. (1965). *Syntactic Structures*. The Hague: Mouton.

Chomsky, N. (1975). *The Logical Structure of Linguistic Theory*. New York: Plenum.

Chomsky, N. (1981). *Lectures on Government and Binding*. Dordrecht, NL: Foris.

Crain, S. and Thornton, R. (1998). *Investigations in Universal Grammar: A Guide to Experiments in the Acquisition of Syntax and Semantics*. Cambridge, MA: MIT Press.

De Villiers, J., Roeper, T. and Vainikka, A. (1990). The Acquisition of Long-Distance Rules. In L. Frazier and J. de Villiers (eds), *Language Processing and Language Acquisition*. Dordrecht, NL: Kluwer.

Demetras, M. J., Post, K. N. and Snow, C. E. (1986). Feedback to first language learners: the role of repetition and clarification questions. *Journal of Child Language*, 13, 275–92.

Elman, J. L. (2004). An alternative view of the mental lexicon. *Trends in Cognitive Science*, 7, 301–6.

Farrar, M. J. (1992). Negative evidence and grammatical morpheme acquisition. *Developmental Psychology*, 28, 90–8.

Feldman, H., Goldin-Meadow, S. and Gleitman, L. (1978). Beyond Herodotus: the creation of language by deprived deaf children. In A. Lock (ed.) *Action, Symbol and Gesture: The Emergence of Language*. New York: Academic Press.

Fiser, J. and Aslin, R. N. (2002). Statistical learning of higher-order temporal structure from visual shape sequences. *Journal of Experimental Psychology: Learning, Memory and Cognition*, 28, 458–67.

Goldin-Meadow, S. (1982). The resilience of recursion: a study of a communication system developed without a conventional language model. In E. Wanner and L. R. Gleitman (eds), *Language Acquisition: The State of the Art*. Cambridge: Cambridge University Press.

Goldin-Meadow, S. (2003). *The Resilience of Language*. New York: Psychology Press.

Goldin-Meadow, S. and Mylander, C. (1984). Gestural communication in deaf children: the effects and noneffects of parental input in early language development. *Monograph of the Society for Research in Child Development*, 49, 1–121.

Goldin-Meadow, S. and Mylander, C. (1998). Spontaneous sign systems created by children in two cultures. *Nature*, 391, 279–81.

Gualmini, A. and Crain. S. (2002). Why no child or adult must learn De Morgan's Laws. *Proceedings of the 26th Boston University Conference on Language Development*, Somerville, MA: Cascadilla Press.

Gualmini, A. and Crain, S. (2005). The structure of children's linguistic knowledge. *Linguistic Inquiry*, 36, 463–74.

Guasti, M. T. (2002). *Language Acquisition: The Growth of Grammar*. Cambridge, MA: MIT Press.

Guasti, M. T. and Chierchia, G. (1999/2000). Reconstruction in child language. *Language Acquisition*, 8, 129–70.

Han, C. H., Lidz, J. and Musolino, J. (2007). Verb-raising and grammar competition in Korean: evidence from negation and quantifier scope. *Linguistic Inquiry*, 38, 1–47.

Hirsch-Pasek, K., Treiman, R. and Schneidermann, M. (1984). Brown and Hanlon revisited: mother's sensitivity to ungrammatical forms. *Journal of Child Language*, 11, 81–8.

Hoff, E. and Naigles, L. (2002). How children use input to acquire a lexicon. *Child Development*, 73, 418–33.

Kegl, J., Senghas, A. and Coppola, M. (1999). Creation through contact: sign language emergence and sign language change in Nicaragua. In M. DeGraff (ed.), *Language Creation and Language Change: Creolization, Diachrony, and Development*. Cambridge, MA: MIT Press.

Landau, B. and Gleitman, L. R. (1985). *Language and Experience: Evidence from the Blind Child*. Cambridge, MA: Harvard University Press.

Laurence, S. and Margolis, E. (2001). The poverty of the stimulus argument. *British Journal of Philosophical Science*, 52, 217–76.

Leonard, L. (1997). *Children with Specific Language Impairment*. Cambridge, MA: MIT Press.

Lillo Martin, D. (1999). Modality effects and modularity in language acquisition: the acquisition of American sign language. In T. Bhatia and W. Ritchie (eds), *Handbook of Language Acquisition*. San Diego, CA: Academic Press.

Marcus, G. F. (1993). Negative evidence in language acquisition. *Cognition*, 46, 153–82.

Marcus, G. F., Vijayan, S., Rao, S. B. and Vishton, P. M. (1999). Rule learning in seven month-old infants. *Science*, 283, 77–80.

Matthei, E. H. (1982). The acquisition of prenominal modifiers. *Cognition*, 11, 301–32.

Meier, R. P. and Newport, E. L. (1990). Out of the hands of babes: on a possible sign advantage in language acquisition. *Language*, 66, 1–23.

Morgan, J. L. and Travis, L. (1989). Limits on negative information on language input. *Journal of Child Language*, 16, 531–52.

Moro, A. (2006). *I Confini di Babele*. Milano: Longanesi.

Musso, M., Moro, A., Glauche, V., Rjintjes, M., Reichenbach, J., Büchel, C. and Weiller, C. (2003). Broca's area and the language instinct. *Nature Neuroscience*, 6, 774–81.

Ochs, E. and Schieffelin, B. (1995). The impact of language socialization on grammatical development. In P. Fletcher and B. MacWhiney (eds), *The Handbook of Child Language*. New York: Blackwell.

Peña, M., Bonatti, L., Nespor, M. and Mehler, J. (2002). Signal driver computation in language processing. *Science*, 298, 604–7.
Petitto, L. A. (1988). Language in the pre-linguistic child. In F. Kessel (ed.), *Developmental of Language and Language Researchers: Essays in Honour of Roger Brown*. Hillsdale, NJ: Lawrence Erlbaum Associates.
Petitto, L. A. (1996). In the beginning: on the genetic and environmental factors that make early language acquisition possible. In M. Gopnik and S. Davis (eds), *The Biological Basis of Language*. Oxford: Oxford University Press.
Pettito, L. A. and Marentette, P. F. (1991). Babbling in the manual mode: evidence for the ontogeny of language. *Science*, 251, 1493–6.
Putnam, H. (1967). The innateness hypothesis and explanatory models in linguistics. *Synthese*, 17, 12–22.
Pye, C. (1986). The acquisition of K'iche' Mayan. In Slobin, D. *Crosslinguistic Studies of Language Acquisition*, Hillsdale, NJ: Lawrence Erlbaum.
Quine, W. V. O. (1969). Linguistics and Philosophy. In S. Hook (ed.) *Linguistics and Philosophy: A symposium*. New York: New York University Press.
Rice, M. L., Haney K. R. and Wexler, K. (1998). Family history of children with SLI who show extended optional infinitives. *Journal of Speech and Hearing Research*, 41, 419–32.
Roeper, T. (1972). Approaches to acquisition theory, using data from German children. Doctoral dissertation, Harvard University, Cambridge, MA.
Ross, J. R. (1983). *Inner Islands*. Cambridge, MA: MIT Press.
Saffran, J. R., Aslin, R. N. and Newport, E. L. (1996). Statistical learning by 8-month-old infants. *Science*, 274, 1926–8.
Saffran, J. R., Johnson, E. K., Aslin, R. N. and Newport, E. L. (1999). Statistical learning of tone sequences by human infants and adults. *Cognition*, 70, 27–52.
Schieffelin, B. (1979). Getting it together: an ethnographic approach to the study of the development of communicative competence. In E. Ochs and B. Schieffelin (eds), *Developmental Pragmatics*. New York: Academic Press.
Senghas, A. (1995). Children's contribution to the birth of Nicaraguan Sign Language. Tesi di dottorato, Massachusetts Institute of Technology. MIT Working Papers in Linguistics.
Senghas, A. (2003). Intergenerational influence and ontogenetic development in the emergence of spatial grammar in Nicaraguan Sign Language. *Cognitive Development*, 18, 511–31.
Senghas, A. and Coppola, M. (2001). Children creating language: how Nicaraguan sign language acquired a spatial grammar. *Psychological Science*, 12, 323–8.
Singleton, J. L. and Newport, E. L. (2004). When learners surpass their models: the acquisition of American Sign Language from inconsistent input. *Cognitive Psychology*, 49, 370–407.
Stromswold, K. (2001). The heritability of language: a review and metaanalysis of twin, adoption and linkage studies. *Language*, 77, 647–723.
Tomblin, J. B., Records, N. L., Buckwalter, P., Zhang, X., Smith, E. and O'Brien, M. (1997). Prevalence of SLI in kindergarten children. *Journal of Speech, Language, and Hearing Research*, 40, 1245–60.
Van der Lely, H. K. J. (2005). Domain-specific cognitive systems: insight from Grammatical specific language impairment. *Trends in Cognitive Sciences*, 9, 53–9.
Zheng, M. and Goldin-Meadow, S. (2002). Thought before language: how deaf and hearing children express motion events across cultures. *Cognition*, 85, 145–75.

5
second language acquisition

susan gass

introduction

The intent of this chapter is to provide a selective overview of current second language acquisition (SLA) research. I begin by presenting several approaches to SLA, including formal linguistics, sociolinguistics/socio-cultural theory and psycholinguistics. I then consider the roles of input, interaction, feedback and output as they relate to the acquisition of second language knowledge. The goal of this latter part is to show how this view of acquisition (the Input/Interaction/Output (IIO) approach) allows researchers to take into account a number of concepts which are necessary for understanding how second language learning takes place. In particular, I consider the role of attention as it relates to second language (L2) learning, particularly in the context of input, interaction, feedback and output. [See Vihman, Saxton and Peters, this volume for discussions of the role of attention in first language acquisition: SFC.]

the scope of the field of SLA

SLA research covers a variety of concepts and research areas. Historically, the discipline arose out of pedagogical concerns in language teaching (Lado, 1957; Corder, 1967), and early research in the field dealt primarily with grammatical knowledge (including phonology, morphology and syntax), how that knowledge developed over time and, particularly, how it might or might not depend on the first language of the learner. This emphasis gradually shifted and widened to include many other areas, such as learner characteristics (for example, motivation, attitudes, aptitude), language behaviour in context (for example, sociolinguistic and socio-cultural variables), information about learners' processing (for example, psycholinguistics, attention), and the variables of input, inter-action and output. Importantly, the discipline has seen a shift since its origins in the 1950s from primarily descriptive studies to highly theoretical current research that connects with many other disciplines.

Though there is not entire agreement on the scope of a theory of SLA, for the purposes of this chapter, I will take SLA to be the study of how second languages are learned. As such, it is the study of the acquisition of a non-primary language, i.e. the acquisition of a language beyond the native language. It is the study of how learners create a new language system with only limited exposure to a second language; what is learned and what is not learned; why most second language learners do not achieve the same degree of proficiency in a second language as they do in their native language; and why only some learners appear to achieve native-like proficiency in more than one language. Additionally, second language acquisition is concerned with the nature of the hypotheses (whether conscious or unconscious) that learners entertain regarding the rules of the second language. Are the rules like those of the native language? Are they like the rules of the language being learned? Are there patterns that are common to all learners regardless of the native language and regardless of the language being learned? Do the rules created by second language learners vary according to the context of use? As can be seen from these questions, the study of second language acquisition draws from and impacts many other areas of study, including linguistics, psychology, psycholinguistics, sociology, sociolinguistics, discourse analysis, conversational analysis and education (although it is not about pedagogy) (Gass and Selinker, 2008).

linguistics and SLA

Structural analyses were commonplace in the early days of SLA research; a central research interest being to determine to what extent learner-languages, also known as interlanguages, conformed to the universal constraints of so-called natural languages, or languages that have arisen naturally during the course of human history. The two main approaches to the study of language universals that have influenced the study of SLA are: Universal Grammar (UG) and typological approaches. Here I briefly describe SLA research within the framework of Universal Grammar, as this is the approach that has come to dominate linguistic approaches to SLA. (For a more complete description of linguistics and SLA, see Gass and Selinker, 2008; Mitchell and Myles, 2004).

Linguistic approaches are concerned with the products of learning, that is, what knowledge learners have about the language they are learning. The UG approach, in particular, begins from the question of learnability in first language acquisition. The observation and need to explain how languages are learned by children relatively quickly and uniformly without sufficient input leads to the assumption that there is something innate that provides 'help' in this task. [See, this volume, Saxton on input and Guasti on the UG approach to first language acquisition: SFC.] For second language researchers, the question is the extent to which UG can provide the same kind of help as it does for child first language learners. If Universal Grammar is 'the system of principles, conditions, and rules that are elements or properties of all human languages' (Chomsky, 1975, p. 29), then UG 'is taken to be a characterization of the child's prelinguistic state' (Chomsky, 1981, p. 7). The question in SLA, therefore, is what the *initial state* is for second language acquisition: What is the nature of the linguistic knowledge with which learners begin the second language acquisition process? And relatedly: What are early L2 grammars like?

There are two intersecting variables at the centre of the debate about the initial state in SLA: transfer (that is, the availability of the native language [NL] grammar) and access to UG (that is, the extent to which UG is available). According to White (2003, p. 60), the prevailing view is that 'UG is constant (that is, unchanged as a result of L1 acquisition); UG is distinct from the learner's L1 grammar; UG constrains the L2 learner's interlanguage grammars'. There is debate, however, as to whether the first language (L1) is the basis of the initial state (see Eubank, 1993/1994, 1996; Haznedar, 1997; Schwartz, 1998; Schwartz and Sprouse, 1996, 2000; Vainikka and Young-Scholten, 1994, 1996; Yuan, 1998) or whether the initial state is UG-based (Platzack, 1996; Epstein et al., 1998; Flynn, 1996; Flynn and Martohardjono, 1994). In addition to these more polarized views, other researchers consider various subcomponents of knowledge that may or may not be available to second language learners (for an overview, see White, 2003).

SLA and social context

In contrast to linguistics-based SLA research, sociolinguistics-based SLA research makes the assumption that numerous external variables (such as the specific task required of a learner, social status of the interlocutor, gender differences, and so forth) affect learner production. In other words, it sees learner production as in part dependent on external variables. There are three predominant directions taken in this broad area of SLA research: variation, social interaction, and speech acts and pragmatics.

variation

Variation refers to the differences in second language production based on factors such as interlocutor, prestige and context. Schmidt's (1977) research exemplifies the impact of social context on second language production. He investigated the pronunciation of the English sounds /θ/ as in *thing* and /ð/ as in *this* by two groups of Cairene Arabic speakers who differed in terms of their level of education: university students and working-class men. In colloquial Egyptian Arabic, there are lexical triplets with the sound /θ/ alternating with /s/ and with /t/, as in the three possible pronunciations of the word *third*: /θa:liθ/, /sa:lis/, /ta:lit/. Schmidt found that the university students produced the /θ/ variant some of the time, whereas the majority of the working-class group never pronounced words using the /θ/ variant, suggesting the prestige value (a marker of education) of that variant. This carried over into their English. The more educated group used a higher percentage of /θ/s in English than the less educated group, although for both groups there was variation that depended on how the data were elicited (from more formal elicitation to less formal elicitation). Thus, when considering particular learner-language forms, it is important to take into account the social context of learning.

social interactional approaches

Research that incorporates social context as an integral part of learning argues that language learning is linked to social and local ecology rather than being situated in an individual's cognition. Learning is anchored in the social practices that a learner engages in. Within the general area of social interactional approaches, two approaches dominate: Conversation analysis and socio-cultural theory.

In a conversation analysis approach, one examines the configuration of a speaker's orientation toward language. Markee (2000, pp. 3–4) describes conversation analysis as follows: '[Conversation analysis] represents one way of demonstrating how micro-moments of socially distributed cognition, instantiated in conversational behavior, contribute to observable changes in participants' states of knowing and using new language.' The example in (1) from Mondada and Pekarek Doehler (2004, p. 508) shows the orientation that a conversational analyst gives to a classroom conversation involving a language learner. It illustrates that there is 'more than one type of competence' (Mondada and Pekarek Doehler, 2004, p. 507) and that language learning involves 'deploying and developing a complex set of (social, cultural, or historical) competencies' (p. 507).

(1)

Text	Conversational Analysis Interpretation
[cette chaîne, This chain,	Line 17: B extends the activity away from the previous exercise that involved spelling to the spelling of a new set of words (*cette chaîne*). This move suggests a divergent orientation toward the closings of the sequence.
°chhhh:::::::° (.) Lorena une phrase avec ce[tte (trousse) *°chhhh:::::::° (.) Lorena a phrase with thi[s pencil case*	Line 18: Closing is repressed (by teacher) and new student is nominated.

[cette trousse est dans ma valise
[this pencil case is in my bag
B [( )]
P: *cette trousse est à moi*
   this pencil case is mine
24 J: ((cough))
25 K: *cette trousse est [[(0.3)*
   dans ma:] (0.9) ma sac
   this pencil case is [[(0.3)
   in my: (fem.)] (0.9) my
   (fem.) bag
	Lines 19–20: New student responds.
	
	Lines 22, 23 and 25: B overlaps, showing orientation toward task ending. Students P and K propose new phrase. Summary: Different students show different orientations toward task completedness.

As the authors note,

> [b]eing recognized as a good student presupposes putting to work not only one's linguistic competence, which focuses on academic content, but also one's socio-institutional competence. Being recognized as such involves the proper way of formulating content as well as the proper ways of participating in a specific instructional setting. In general terms, we can assume that this competence always combines with the way learners are socialized into the communities of practice in which they use the L2, whether as a student, an immigrant, or a professional person. (pp. 509–10)

Other approaches, notably the interactionist approach, discussed below, would analyse this conversation quite differently and would focus on a different aspect of the conversation, namely that part that illustrates language knowledge and not language socialization. In fact, below is a continuation of the conversation above that shows how this excerpt would have been treated in the interactionist approach which we introduce below (from Gass, 2004, p. 599).

(2)

25 K: *cette trousse est [[(0.3) dans ma:] (0.9) ma sac*	Line 25: K utters incorrect form (*ma*) rather than *mon*.
this pencil case is [[(0.3) in my: (fem.)] (0.9) my (fem.) bag	Long pause suggests that student may be aware of the incorrectness of the adjective or at least shows that this student knows that this is a problem area.
°27. *T: mon;°*	Line 27: Teacher corrects form, in essence confirming for the student what was already a problem.
° my:;° (masc.)	
28 *K: mon sac*	Lines 28–29: Student immediately demonstrates uptake which is acknowledged by teacher.
my bag	
29 *T: sac.*	
bag	

This excerpt shows only one instance of language learning or at least evidence of recognition of a problem area. The important point is that conversation analysis:

> attempts to explicate in emic terms the conversational practices that speakers orient to (i.e., the rules of talk they deploy for each other and, by extension, for analysts) by 'unpacking the structure of either single cases or collections of talk-in-interaction. Such cases provide the primary evidence for the asserted existence of particular conversational mechanisms identified by analysts. In short, a case is only convincing to the extent that it is directly motivated by the conversational data presented for analysis. (Markee, 2000, p. 26)

In other words, attempting to provide motives for a particular speech event or to claim learning opportunities from the data without direct evidence from the data is not part of conversation analysis methodology. It is, however, part of an interactionist approach, to which we return below.

A second perspective within the social-interactionist framework is known as socio-cultural theory (Lantolf, 2000; Lantolf and Thorne, 2006, 2007). Similar to conversation analysis, socio-cultural theory is concerned with situated language, but unlike conversation analysis, its concern is with situated language as it relates to internal processes. Concepts unique to this approach within SLA, are 'mediation/regulation', 'internalization' and 'the zone of proximal development'. Mediation assumes that human activity (including cognitive activity) is mediated by symbolic artefacts (higher-level cultural tools) such as language and literacy and by material artefacts. These artefacts mediate the relationship between humans and the social and material world around us. So, just as we have developed tools to facilitate tasks such as weaving or growing food, we have developed symbol systems such as language as tools to mediate psychological activity and to control psychological processes. Language allows us to connect to our environment, attend to specific things, to plan and to think rationally. It gives humans the power to go beyond the immediate environment and to think about and talk about events and objects that are far-removed both physically and temporally.

Internalization is the process which allows us to move the relationship between an individual and his/her environment to later performance. Imitation is one means of internalization, and can be either immediate and intentional or delayed. This occurs, for example, through private speech, which has been observed in L2 classrooms (see Ohta, 2001; Lantolf and Yáñez, 2003). The items focused on by learners in these imitation/private speech situations are controlled by the learner and not necessarily by a teacher's agenda. An example from an L2 Japanese classroom (Ohta, 2001, p. 59) is given in (3) below.

(3)
T: *kon shuumatsu hima desu ka? Hyun-san*
     Hyun, are you free this weekend?
H: *Um (..) iie (.) um (.) uh:: (.) hima- (.) hima: (.) hima nai,*
     Um (.) no (.) um (.) uh:: (.) free-(.) free: (.) free-NEG,
     (negator 'ni' is incorrect.))
T: *Hima ja ^ arimasen*
     You're not free ((T uses the correct negative form))
H: *Oh ja arim[asen =*
     Oh not free
C: *[°°^ arimasen°°*
     °°not free°°
T: *= Hima ja arimasen (.) ii desu ne (.) Eh:to ja S-san Kon shuumatsu hima desu ka?*
     = You're not free (.) well done (.) Uh so S, are you free this weekend?
Key: °°signifies whispering

Ohta points out that Candace (C), who is not being addressed by the teacher, nonetheless participates in this question and answer session. As Ohta notes,

> Although Candace [C] is not called on during this particular oral practice session, she is engaged as a peripheral participant in the interaction. The results of this engagement are evident later in the class when she uses the form correctly in peer interaction, as well as when, in subsequent teacher-fronted practice, she covertly corrects classmates who use the wrong form. (p. 59)

The view of imitation within socio-cultural theory is different from what is normally considered as mindless repetition. Rather, within this framework, 'it involves goal directed cognitive activity that can result in transformations of the original model' (Lantolf and Thorne, 2006, p. 207). Imitation in this view can occur immediately, as in the example below, or be delayed.

Example (4) is from Saville-Troike (1988, p. 584):

(4)
Teacher: *You guys go brush your teeth. And wipe your hands on the towel.*
Child: *Wipe your hand. Wipe your teeth.*

In discussing this example, Lantolf and Thorne (2007) point out the self-directive nature of the imitative pattern, noting in particular the extension of 'wipe' to 'teeth', a non-English pattern.

The zone of proximal development was defined by Vygotsky (1978) as:

> the distance between the actual developmental level as determined by independent problem solving and the level of potential development as determined through problem solving under adult guidance or in collaboration with more capable peers. (p. 86)

In other words, learning results from interpersonal activity which forms the basis of individual functioning. This clearly embodies the social nature of learning and underscores the importance of collaborative learning as it shapes what is learned.

In sum, under social interactional approaches human cognition results from the full context (historical, social, material, cultural) in which experiences take place. Thus, the experiences we have and the interactions we engage in are crucial in the development of cognition. Language is a tool (a symbolic artefact) that mediates between individuals and their environment.

interlanguage speech acts and pragmatics

A great deal of work has been conducted looking at L2 *speech acts* such as complaining, thanking, apologizing, refusing, requesting and inviting. All languages have the means of performing speech acts such as these, but the *form* used in specific speech acts varies from culture to culture and language to language. This is often a source of miscommunication and misunderstanding in second language performance. Thus, the study of second language speech acts is concerned with the linguistic possibilities available in languages for speech act realization and the effect of cross-cultural differences on both second language performance and the interpretation by native speakers of second language speech acts. In learning a second language, first language pragmatic norms are often used without recognition of the force of those norms by either the speaker or the listener (see Kasper and Rose, 2002). When breakdowns occur, they are frequently disruptive because native speakers attribute not linguistic causes to the breakdown, but personality (individual or cultural) causes. An example of such miscommunication is given in (5) below (from Goldschmidt, 1996, p. 255).

(5)
[NNS = non-native speaker; NS = native speaker]
NNS: *I have a favor to ask you.*
NS: *Sure, what can I do for you?*
NNS: *You need to write a recommendation for me.*

In this example, the non-native speaker's failure to use the appropriate language for asking a favour could well lead the native speaker to interpret the NNS's request as rude and inappropriate.

Second language pragmatics is perhaps one of the most difficult areas for learners because they are generally unaware of this aspect of language and may be equally unaware of the negative perceptions that native speakers may have as a result of their pragmatic errors. Miscommunication resulting from NS perceptions of relatively proficient NNSs is often serious in terms of interpersonal relations because the source of the difficulty is more likely to be attributed to a defect in a person (or a culture) (for example, Americans are insincere, Israelis are rude, Japanese are indirect), than to a NNS's inability to map the correct linguistic form onto pragmatic intentions. Without a shared back-ground, linguistic system, and specific beliefs, 'when one interlocutor confidently [but inaccurately] interprets another's utterance, it is likely that participants will run into immediate problems because they do not share a common discourse space' (Gass and Varonis, 1985a, p. 341).

psycholinguistic SLA research

Psycholinguistic SLA research addresses questions of processing rather than the structure of linguistic products (oral or written). As with the other areas discussed, there are numerous ways of approaching SLA psycholinguistic research. Here, I focus on a few of these areas: usage-based accounts, competition model, processing approaches and connectionism/emergentism.

usage-based accounts

In this approach to language learning, also referred to as construct-ivist approaches, the emphasis is on usage. Learning does not rely on an innate module, but rather learning takes place based on the extraction of regularities from the input. Learning takes place as these regularities or patterns are used over and over again and are therefore strengthened. Frequency accounts (N. Ellis, 2002) are an example. In frequency accounts of second language acquisition, one relies on the assumption that '[h]umans are sensitive to the frequencies of events in their experience' (p. 145). The approach is exemplar-based in that it is the examples that are present in the input that form the basis of complex patterns and from which regularities emerge. N. Ellis (2002, p. 144) proposes that 'comprehension is determined by the listeners' vast amount of statistical information about the behavior of lexical items in their language…' In other words, language is not driven by an innate faculty; rather, the complex linguistic environment provides the information from which learners abstract regularities. [See Vihman and Peters, this volume for similar approaches to first language acqui-sition and Kuiper et al. for the role of frequency in SLA: SFC.]

competition model

Assuming aspects of language are sensitive to frequency of usage has implications for how one conceives of grammar. The representation of language, in this view, relies on the notion of variable strengths that reflect the frequency of the input and the connections between parts of language. One example of such an approach is the competition model.

The basis for the competition model is work by Bates and MacWhinney (1982), with more recent research (for example, MacWhinney, 2002, 2004) expanding on the underlying concepts. The Bates and MacWhinney model assumes that form and function cannot be separated. According to MacWhinney et al. (1984, p. 128), 'the forms of natural languages are created, governed, constrained, acquired and used in the service of communicative functions'.

The competition model assumes that speakers must have a way to determine relationships among elements in a sentence. Language processing involves competition among various cues, each of which contributes to a different resolution in sentence interpretation. Although the range of cues is universal (that is, the limits on the kinds of cues one uses are universally imposed), there is language-specific instantiation of cues and language-specific strength assigned to cues. From a second language perspective, the question is: how do learners acquire new cues (for example, case-marking if their native language does not have overt case markings) and how do learners modify cue strength (for example, word order is a major cue in English, but is less important in other languages, such as Italian).

One possibility is that in L2 sentence interpretation, the learner's initial hypothesis is consistent with sentence interpretation in the NL. However, there may be universal tendencies toward the heavy use of particular cues. One finding is that, under certain circumstances, a meaning-based comprehension strategy takes precedence over a grammar-based one. For example, English speakers learning Italian (Gass, 1987) and English speakers learning Japanese (a language that relies on the pragmatics of the situation for sentence interpretation, as well as on case-marking and lexico-semantic information) (Sasaki, 1994) readily drop their strong use of word-order cues and adopt meaning-based cues as a major cue in interpreting Italian and Japanese sentences. On the other hand, Italian and Japanese speakers learning English maintain their native language meaning-based cues as primary, not readily adopting word order as a major interpretation cue.

Although the tendency of learners to adopt a meaning-based strategy as opposed to a grammar-based one is strong, there is also ample evidence that learners first look for correspondences in their NL as their initial hypothesis. Only when that appears to fail (that is, when learners become aware of the apparent incongruity between L1 and L2 strategies) do they adopt what might be viewed as a universal prepotency: that of using meaning to interpret sentences (Gass, 1987; Sasaki, 1994). The strong use of animacy/semantic information, however, is not always straightforward (Liu et al., 1992). Sasaki and MacWhinney (2006), in their review of the competition model, suggest an interplay between semantic information and instances where there is congruence/incongruence between L1 and L2 systems.

In sum, it is through the frequency of exposure that learners can sort out the complexities of language by recognizing regularities and through the demands of use. Form-function mappings are dependent on the reliability/frequency of the input. That is, the more reliable a cue (for example, word order in English), the easier (and faster) it is to learn. When multiple cues compete, learning will take longer.

processing approaches

Processing approaches to SLA are concerned with the mechanisms and capacities of the human brain and how they operate within the context of second language learning. For example, Processability Theory (Pienemann, 2007) assumes that both production and comprehension of second language forms take place only to the extent that they can be handled by the linguistic processor. Thus, the focus is on how the processor shapes and constrains developmental paths. One area that has been studied extensively is the acquisition of question formation (Pienemann and Johnston, 1987) and the processing mechanisms that constrain movement from one stage to the next (Clahsen, 1984).

Processability Theory appeals to a Processability Hierarchy which governs that way the processor checks on the matches of grammatical information within an utterance. So, hearing a sentence such as 'The girls plays in the park', the processor checks to see if there is an appropriate match (plurality in this example). Before matching can work, however, learners have procedures for putting together parts of sentences (for example, *the* and *girls*) and procedures for comparing relevant grammatical information (for example, in a language in which there is no subject–verb agreement, such a matching procedure is not relevant). Lack of agreement would suggest that the learner has not yet developed appropriate procedures for matching grammatical information. Pienemann (1998) suggests a hierarchy relevant to the ordering of procedures, as follows:

1. no procedure (for example, single word utterances)
2. category procedure (for example, adding a plural morpheme to a noun)
3. noun phrase procedure (for example, matching gender as in *la casa* [the house] where both article and noun are feminine)

4. verb phrase procedure (for example, movement of elements within a verb phrase)
5. sentence procedure (for example, subject–verb agreement)
6. subordinate clause procedure (e.g. use of a particular tense based on something in the main clause).

This hierarchy is implicational in that each procedure is a prerequisite for the next. Even though these are universal procedures, there is some leeway for learners to create individual solutions to a processing limitation. The principles appear to be invariant; what is less understood are the language-specific facts representing a range of languages. (For an example of how one determines relevant procedures for a language, see Kawaguchi, 2005.)

connectionism/emergentism

Connectionism is a cover term that includes a number of network architectures. The best known of these is parallel distributed processing (PDP). At the heart of PDP is a neural network that is generally biologically inspired in nature. The network consists of nodes that are connected by pathways which are strengthened or weakened through activation or use. The more often an association is made, the stronger that association becomes. New associations are formed and new links are made between larger and larger units until complexes of networks are formed.

In the connectionist approach, learning is seen as simple instance learning which proceeds based on input alone. The resultant knowledge is seen as a network of interconnected exemplars and patterns, rather than abstract rules. Thus, even though language use appears to be rule-like, it does not necessarily mean that it is rule-governed (N. Ellis, 1998), and the connectionist approach argues that it is not; in either first language or second language. Even though connectionist approaches to learning have been around for a number of years, only recently has research within a second language context begun to take place (see Broeder and Plunkett, 1994 for a review of studies). One interesting suggestion (Sokolik, 1990) is that with age, learners are less able to establish connectionist patterns.

Emergentist approaches (N. Ellis and Larsen-Freeman, 2006; MacWhinney, 2006) take as an assumption that:

Language is a complex adaptive system. It comprises the ecological interactions of many players: people who want to communicate and a world to be talked about. It operates across many different levels (neurons, brains, and bodies; phonemes, morphemes, lexemes, constructions, interactions, and discourses), different human conglomerations (individuals, social groups, networks, and cultures), and different timescales (evolutionary, epigenetic, ontogenetic, interactional, neuro-synchronic, diachronic). As a complex system, its systematicities are emergent following adaptive, Darwinian principles. (N. Ellis and Larsen-Freeman, 2006, p. 576)

Within an emergentist perspective, language is dynamic and language learning reflects this dynamism. It can therefore account for the many ways that groups and/or individuals deal with a new language system. It is a traditional way of conceptualizing language that appears to be compatible with a number of approaches including connectionism, chaos theory (Larsen-Freeman, 1997), and complexity theory to name a few. Its usefulness, as noted by Meara (2006), Ke and Holland (2006), Mellow (2006) and Cameron and Deignan (2006), will be dependent on ever-increasing sophistication in computer-modelling and increased corpora of spoken and written data.

interaction approach

Finally, let's turn to the Interaction Approach. Gass and Mackey (2006, 2007) note that this approach has changed over the years from its initial moniker of Interaction *Hypothesis* (for example, Gass, 2003; Long, 1996) and currently incorporates notions of a *model* (Ramírez, 2005; Byrnes, 2005; Block, 2003). In fact, Jordan (2005) points out that the Interaction Hypothesis may be moving toward a *theory* and that it is an example of how 'an originally well-formulated hypothesis is upgraded in the light of criticism and developments in the field' (p. 220). At what point something is or is not a theory or becomes or does not become a theory is not my concern in this chapter. What I do claim, however, is that the Interaction Approach is able to account for some (but not all) of second language acquisition by incorporating concepts and findings from some of the disciplinary approaches discussed in earlier sections of this chapter. In this section, I deal with the main concepts of the Interaction Approach and attempt to provide an overall explanation of how interaction is an integral part of acquisition.

input

Input, simply put, is the language that a learner is exposed to through reading, listening or watching (in the case of learners who are exposed to a sign language). Clearly input is a necessary part of acquisition, but its significance is not uniform across all theories or approaches to SLA. [See Saxton and Guasti, this volume, for discussion of input in relation to first language acquisition and Kuiper et al. for input in SLA: SFC.]

Within the framework of UG, input serves to trigger the innate system, and the study of what type or how much input is needed is not a matter of serious investigation. In this approach, there are parts of an L2 that learners come to know without input – namely, universal constraints. Input is needed to trigger language-specific information related to universals, but universal constraints come 'with no charge', that is, no input is needed. On the other hand, a usage-based account is clearly dependent solely on input; the learner uses exemplars to create abstractions and the exemplars are found in the input. Input serves as the *positive evidence* necessary for making linguistic generalizations, where positive evidence refers to the language that learners are exposed to.

Early studies of SLA focused on the nature of the input recognizing that, like the child directed speech addressed to first language learners (see Saxton, this volume: SFC], the input addressed to non-native speakers (NNS) of a language was not the same as language addressed to native speakers. Sometimes these differences are obvious as in example (6) below from Ferguson (1971):

(6)
NS to NNS: *Mi ver soldado*
             Me to see soldier
             'I see the soldier'
             (standard Spanish 'yo veo al soldado' [I see (1-sg.) to the soldier]

and at times they are more subtle, as in Example (7) below, in which the native speaker elaborates a response to a non-native speaker in a way that she does not when addressing a native speaker (Gass and Varonis, 1985b; emphasis in original):

(7)
NNS: *How have increasing food costs changed your eating habits?*
NS: *Um, I maybe I cut down SOME.*
NNS: *Pardon me?*
NS: *I cut down SOME ON EATING.*

This exchange includes an indication of a lack of understanding by the non-native speaker when she said *Pardon me?* At this point, the native speaker (NS) replies by elaborating upon her original response and by changing *some*, to a full, elaborated phrase, *some on eating*.

Regardless of the perspective that one takes, it is important to understand precisely the nature of the input if one is to determine how a learner uses that information as she/he builds a second language system.

interaction/feedback

Conversational interactions form the basis of the interaction approach. The idea is that conversational interactions are the context in which information is provided to a learner that a problem may exist. In other words they can provide learners with *negative evidence*. [See Saxton and Guasti, this volume: SFC.] What happens following the provision of such negative evidence (feedback) often depends on the degree of explicitness and is learner-specific. Two examples are given below, one (8) that involves explicit correction and the other (9) indirect correction. Both are considered negative evidence. The relevant utterances are indicated by arrows.

(8) Example of explicit correction (from Loewen and Philp, 2006, p. 537)
Student (S):   *uh didn't work well (.) it must be rip = ded*
Teacher (T):   *so you need a noun now*   ⇦
        S: *it must be rip = ded*
        T: *it must be a rip off*

(9) Two examples of implicit correction ([a] Loewen and Philp, 2006, p. 538; [b] Mackey, 2006, p. 413)
a.   S: *to her is good thing (.) to her is good thing*
     T: *yeah for her it's a good thing*   ⇦
     S: *because he got a lot of money there*
b.   S: *He have many spot in he have one*
     T: *Huh? One? Or many what? Quick*   ⇦

Recasts are one form of feedback common in interactions with non-proficient non-native speakers. Nicholas et al. (2001) suggest recasts are: 'utterances that repeat a learner's incorrect utterance, making only the changes necessary to produce a correct utterance, without changing the meaning' (p. 733). Recasts provide learners with linguistically more target-like reformulations of their own utterances and, importantly, are both temporally juxtaposed to an incorrect utterance and reflect the same semantic information as the original utterance. An example was given above where the student says *to her is good thing* and the teacher reformulates this phrase with correct English *for her it's a good thing.* A great deal of recent research has focused on the function of recasts (see Long, 2007; Saxton, 2005 and this volume).

Recasts are hypothesized to serve learning by contrasting an incorrect (learner) utterance with a correct one (fluent L2 speaker) (see Saxton, 1997, 2005, this volume). But there are many different forms that recasts can take and, as a result, their function is controversial. For example, the complexity of recasts varies. In (10) below, for example, the recast responds to a single error. In (11) it responds to multiple errors: one with the preposition and a pronunciation error.

(10) From Philp (2003).
NNS: *Why he is very unhappy?*
NS: *Why is he very unhappy?*
NNS: *Yeah why is very unhappy.*

(11) From Mackey et al. (2003).
NNS: *And in the er kitchen er cupboard no on shef.*
NS: *On the shelf. I have it on the shelf.*
NNS: *in the shelf, yes OK.*

In (12) a reformulation is expressed with rising intonation accompanied by the addition of the auxiliary and the correction of verbal morphology.

(12) From Philp (1999)
NNS: *What doctor say?*
NS: *What is the doctor saying?*

Clearly, in (12), as opposed to the first example in (9), the rising intonation focuses the learners' attention on the fact that there is a problem. In (9) the conversation simply continues and it is likely that the learner was unaware of a problem.

The important point to note is that recasts, like other forms of conversational interaction, may or may not be perceived as corrective regardless of the speaker's intent. Their effect on acquisition is therefore questionable (see recent reviews of recasts in the second language literature, Nicholas et al., 2001; Long, 2007; R. Ellis and Sheen, 2006). There have been a number of empirical studies focused specifically on the effectiveness of recasts, but the results are mixed (see Lyster and Ranta, 1997; Lyster, 1998, 2004; Ammar and Spada, 2006; Ellis et al., 2006;

Leeman, 2003; Long, 2007; McDonough, 2007; R. Ellis and Sheen, 2006; Ishida, 2004; Han, 2002; Iwashita, 2003; Mackey and Philp, 1998; McDonough and Mackey, 2006).

In addition to recasts, *negotiation of meaning* is frequent in conversations with NNSs. Included in this category are confirmation checks, clarification requests, and comprehension checks. In other words, these are parts of conversation in which the focus is on seeking some sort of clarification or making sure that a message has been understood. Examples are given below. Confirmation checks attempt to ensure that a partner's message has been understood.

(13) Confirmation check (from Varonis and Gass, 1985)
NNS1: *When can you go to visit me?*
NNS2: *Visit?*   ⇐

A clarification request is an expression that indicates that something has not been understood.

(14) Clarification request (from Gass et al., 2005)
NNS 1: *¿Qué es importante a ella?*
        What is important to her?
NNS 2: *¿Cómo?*   ⇐
        What?
NNS 1: *¿Qué es importante a la amiga? ¿Es solamente el costo?*
        What is important to the friend? Is it just the cost?

A comprehension check is an attempt to ensure that one's partner has correctly understood what a speaker just said.

(15) Comprehension check (from Gass et al., 2005)
NNS 1: *La avenida siete va en una dirección hacia el norte desde la calle*
        siete hasta la calle ocho. ¿Quieres que repita?   ⇐
        Avenue Seven goes in one direction towards the north from Street Seven to Street Eight. Do you want me to repeat?
NNS 2: *Por favor.*
        Please.
NNS 1: *La avenida seven, uh siete, va en una dirección hacia el norte*
        desde la calle siete hasta la calle ocho.
        Avenue Seven, uh Seven, goes in one direction towards the north from Street Seven to Street Eight.

One difficulty in dealing with both negotiations and recasts, but particularly the latter, is that their effectiveness is often measured by the presence or absence of a confirming utterance, often referred to as *uptake*. In example (16) below, the NNS is describing something in a picture to the NS, and after some back-and-forth negotiation about the Italian word for 'cups', the learner finally gets the correct form (feminine plural). However, as becomes clear, the repetition of the correct form may have been only repetition and did not represent learning.

(16) Morphosyntactic feedback (from Mackey et al., 2000)
NNS: *C'è due tazzi.*
        There is two cups (m. pl.).
INT: *Due tazz-come?*
        Two cup—what?
NNS: *Tazzi, dove si puó mettere té, come se dice questo?*
        Cups (m. pl.), where one can put tea, how do you say this?
INT: *Tazze?*
        Cups (f. pl.)?
NNS: *OK, tazze.*
        OK, cups (f. pl).

The possibility of immediate responses being simply 'mimicking or repeating without true understanding' (Gass, 2003, p. 236), rather than true uptake, is reflected in mixed results in studies of efficacy. For example, Mackey and Philp (1998) found that an immediate response by a learner was not necessarily related to development, whereas Nabei and Swain (2002) and Lyster (2004) found the reverse. Further, there are often delayed effects from interactions. In fact, Mackey and Philp (1998) suggested that uptake may be the wrong measure to use in determining effectiveness. They make the point (see Gass, 1997; Gass and Varonis, 1994; Lightbown, 1998) that if one is to consider effectiveness (that is, development/acquisition), then one should more appropriately measure delayed effects. This was also noted in the discussion earlier in relation to socio-cultural theory

When looking at how learners themselves perceive corrective feedback, the effectiveness of such feedback is again called into question. In a study by Mackey et al. (2000), data were collected from ten learners of English as a second language and seven learners of Italian as a foreign language. The study explored learners' perceptions about feedback provided to them through task-based dyadic interaction. In the interactions, learners received feedback focused on a range of morphosyntactic, lexical and phonological forms. After completing the tasks, learners watched videotapes of their previous interactions and were asked to introspect about their thoughts at the time the original interactions were in progress. Example (16) above was followed by a reflection on the interaction by the NNS. From the reflective comment, given in (17) below, it is clear that the intended correction on the form of the word *tazzi* was not perceived as corrective at all. Rather, what she was focused on was the word itself and not the morphological form.

(17) Reflective comment following (16) above
    Recall: I wasn't sure if I learned the proper word at the begin-
             ning.

This does not mean that feedback is never interpreted as it was intended, as the following example shows.

(18) Lexical feedback correctly perceived (from Mackey et al., 2000)
    NNS: *There is a library.*
    NS: *A what?*
    NNS: *A place where you put books.*
    NS: *A bookshelf?*
    NNS: *Bok?*
    NS: *Shelf.*
    NNS: *Bookshelf.*
    Recall: That's not a good word she was thinking about library
             like we have here on campus, yeah.

What Mackey et al. found was that lexical (16), semantic and phono-logical feedback were highly correlated between provider and receiver, but that morphosyntax was not.

Figure 5.1 represents a model of the role of negative evidence and schematizes the way learners might utilize interaction to focus on input and make adjustments in their L2 linguistic system.

This figure is to be interpreted as suggesting that negative evidence, occurring through interaction, puts learners in a position to notice their errors. The correct form may or may not be present in the input (for example, through a recast). On the basis of initial input, learn-ers may create a hypothesis and then need to search the input (for example, wait for more exemplars, look in a grammar book, look up a word in a dictionary, ask a NS) for confirmatory evidence. There are times, however, when learners may not come up with a hypothesis and

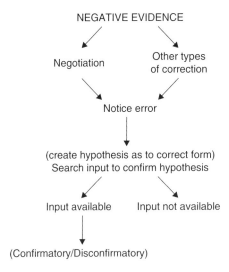

NEGATIVE EVIDENCE

Negotiation   Other types
                   of correction

Notice error

(create hypothesis as to correct form)
Search input to confirm hypothesis

Input available   Input not available

(Confirmatory/Disconfirmatory)

Figure 5.1 A model of the role of negative evidence

will in that case seek out exemplars in the input as part of hypothesis creation.

output

Another concept within the IIO framework is *output*. In its simplest form, output refers to language production. Thus, anything a learner produces in speech/writing, or signing in the case of non-hearing learners, is considered output. Swain (1985) emphasized the importance of output in learning and formulated the *output hypothesis* (see also Swain, 1995, 2005) on the basis of her work with Canadian immersion programs where she noted that even after many years children were unable to achieve native-like performance, primarily due to their lack of language use. The importance of output, in her original formulation, was to allow learners to use syntactic structures.

Unlike in language production, when listening, one can comprehend utterances using semantic and real world knowledge rather than syntax. For example, if one hears the words *dog, bit, boy*, one can assume that it is a dog that bit a boy rather than the other way around. This is so without knowing anything about word order possibilities in English. On the other hand, to express that same meaning, one has to know that subjects precede verbs and that objects follow verbs in English. Swain claims that language production forces learners to move from comprehension (semantic use of language) to syntactic use of language. An important part of this process is feedback, which is provided following production. This is referred to as *pushed output* and is exemplified in (19) below.

> (19) Pushed output (from McDonough and Mackey, 2006).
> NNS: *Why he hit the deer?*
> NS: *why did he hit the deer? He was driving home and the deer ran out in front of his car.*
> NNS: *What did he do after that?*

In (19), following an incorrect question, the learner receives feedback through a recast and appears to incorporate that new information producing a correct question in her next turn. Feedback, however, is often more subtle, and is perhaps better referred to as *nudged output*, because it represents a gentle push. An example of nudged output is given in (20):

> (20) Nudged output (from McDonough, 2005)
> NNS: *what happen for the boat?*
> NS: *what?*
> NNS: *what's wrong with the boat?*

In this example, the correct form is not provided, but the learner is alerted to a problem by the NS's lack of comprehension. The general point is that producing language is an essential part of the learning process (R. Ellis and He, 1999; McDonough, 2005; McDonough and Mackey, 2006; Muranoi, 2000; Shehadeh, 2002). As noted earlier, it pushes learners to produce more target-like utterances; but through feedback, it also affords them the opportunity to test hypotheses (see Gass, 1997). This use of language became apparent in the work of Mackey et al. (2000). When learners were reflecting on their interactions by watching a videotape of the interaction, they often provided retrospective comments that suggest that they were using language to gauge the reaction of an interlocutor. This is indicated in (21).

> (21) (from Mackey et al., 2000) (INT = interviewer)
> NNS: *poi un bicchiere*
>   then a glass
> INT: *un che, come?*
>   A what, what?

NNS: *bicchiere*
        glass
Recall: I was drawing a blank. Then I thought of a vase but then
I thought that since there was no flowers, maybe it was just a big
glass. So, then I thought I'll say it and see. Then, when she said *'come'*
(what?), I knew that it was completely wrong.

In this instance, the learner wasn't sure what word to use and said
'I'll say it and see' and waited for the response to see if she was right
or not.

To sum up, there is a substantial body of evidence documenting the
relationship between interaction and learning (see Mackey and Gass,
2006 for an overview). What is necessary is an understanding of the
mechanism(s) that mediate(s) between interaction and learning. In recent
years, the focus has been on the concept of attention as that mediating
factor; an idea to which we now turn. [See also Vihman, Saxton and
Peters, this volume, on the role of attention in first language: SFC.]

attention

The IIO model integrates linguistic information, sociolinguistic information and psycholinguistic information in accounting for SLA.
The role of attention as a mediating factor in SLA is schematized in
Figure 5.2. The argument is that, through interaction, a learner's attention is focused on a particular problem in his/her language. At times,
the feedback itself provides a partial answer to the nature of the problem and also provides information as to correct forms, as is the case
with recasts.

As Long (1996) points out, '... *negotiation for meaning*, and especially
negotiation work that triggers *interactional* adjustments by the NS or
more competent interlocutor, facilitates acquisition because it connects
input, internal learner capacities, particularly selective attention, and
output in productive ways' (pp. 451–2). In other words, selective attention, triggered by interaction, mediates between what the learner knows
and what she or he perceives to be part of the target language. Thus,
interaction highlights a gap in knowledge, often referred to as noticing
the gap, and at times the correct form is even provided, as, for example,
in the case of recasts.

An underlying assumption in this model is that for learning to
take place, there has to be some awareness that there is something to
be learned. This can come as the learner notices a gap made salient
through interaction. Or, it can come about through listening, reading

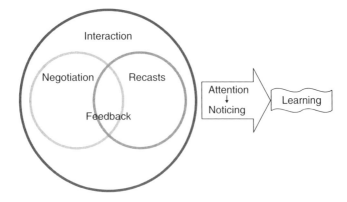

Figure 5.2   A schematic representation of the relationship between interaction and learning

Source: Adapted from 'Input, Interaction and Output: An Overview' by S. Gass and A. Mackey. In Z. Dörnyei and K. Bardovi-Harlig. *AILA Review,* 2006. With kind permission by John Benjamins Publishing Company, Amsterdam/Philadelphia. (www.benjamins.com)

or viewing (in the case of sign language) and a recognition through his/her own resources that there is a gap in knowledge. In either case, attention is crucial as a mechanism that allows learners to focus on some aspects of language and not on others. Clearly learners cannot process the input in its entirety, and attention serves as the mechanism that allows some input to be foregrounded and other input to be backgrounded. As Gass et al. (2003) point out, 'language processing is like other kinds of processing: Humans are constantly exposed to and often overwhelmed by various sorts of external stimuli and are able, through attentional devices, to "tune in" some stimuli and "tune out" others' (p. 498).

Attention has been the object of discussion for a number of years (Schmidt, 1990, 2001; Tomlin and Villa, 1994). Schmidt makes the argument that attention is necessary for learning. Robinson (1995, 2003) relates attention to working memory arguing that only input that is encoded in working memory can become part of long-term memory, or what we might refer to as language knowledge. The IIO model, with attention as a mechanism that serves as part of its explanatory foundation, complements a number of perspectives discussed in this chapter. It is agnostic as to whether learners do or do not have 'help' in the form of UG or whether learners learn through exposure to multiple exemplars. What it does claim is that input is crucial, but is not explicit as to how precisely that input feeds into a learning system.

conclusion

This chapter has attempted to provide a brief overview of SLA research highlighting some of the main research areas. Space limitations have precluded coverage of other research areas that focus on variation between individual learners, for example in terms of working memory capacity, aptitude and motivation. A complete understanding of how humans come to know a second or even a third or fourth language also entails a broader view than could be covered in this chapter. However, I have selected those areas that have impacted the study of SLA to the greatest extent and I have presented a view of L2 acquisition that puts language use as central.

references

Ammar, A. and Spada, N. (2006). One size fits all? Recasts, prompts and L2 learning. *Studies in Second Language Acquisition,* 28, 543–74.

Bates, E. and MacWhinney, B. (1982). Functionalist approach to grammar. In E. Warmer and L. Gleitman (eds), *Language Acquisition: The State of the Art* (pp. 173–218). New York: Cambridge University Press.

Block, D. (2003). *The Social Turn in Second Language Acquisition.* Edinburgh: Edinburgh University Press.

Broeder, P. and Plunkett, K. (1994). Connectionism and second language acquisition. In N. Ellis (ed.), *Implicit and Explicit Learning of Languages* (pp. 421–53). San Diego, CA: Academic Press.

Byrnes, H. (2005). Review of task-based language learning and teaching. *The Modern Language Journal,* 89, 297–8.

Cameron, L. and Deignan, A. (2006). The emergence of metaphor in discourse. *Applied Linguistics,* 27, 671–90.

Chomsky, N. (1975). *Reflections on Language.* New York: Pantheon.

Chomsky, N. (1981). *Lectures on Government and Binding.* Dordrecht, the Netherlands: Foris.

Clahsen, H. (1984). The acquisition of German word order: a test case for cognitive approaches to L2 development. In R. Andersen (ed.), *Second Languages: A Crosslinguistic Perspective* (pp. 219–42). Rowley, MA: Newbury House.

Corder, S. P. (1967). The significance of learners' errors. *International Review of Applied Linguistics,* 5, 161–70.

Ellis, N. (1998). Emergentism, connectionism and language learning. *Language Learning,* 48, 631–64.

Ellis, N. (2002). Frequency effects in language processing. *Studies in Second Language Acquisition,* 24, 143–88.

Ellis, N. and Larsen-Freeman, D. (2006). Language emergence: implications for applied linguistics – introduction to the special issue. *Applied Linguistics,* 27, 558–89.

Ellis, R. and He, X. (1999). The roles of modified input and output in the incidental acquisition of word meanings. *Studies in Second Language Acquisition,* 21, 285–301.

Ellis, R., Loewen, S. and Erlam, R. (2006). Implicit and explicit corrective feedback and the acquisition of L2 grammar. *Studies in Second Language Acquisition*, 28, 339–68.

Ellis, R. and Sheen, Y. (2006). Reexamining the role of recasts in second language acquisition. *Studies in Second Language Acquisition*, 28, 575–600.

Epstein, S., Flynn, S. and Martohardjono, G. (1998). The strong continuity hypothesis in adult L2 acquisition of functional categories. In S. Flynn, G. Martohardjono and W. O'Neil (eds), *The Generative Study of Second Language Acquisition* (pp. 61–77). Mahwah, NJ: Lawrence Erlbaum Associates.

Eubank, L. (1993/1994). On the transfer of parametric values in L2 development. *Language Acquisition*, 3, 183–208.

Eubank, L. (1996). Negation in early German-English interlanguage: more valueless features in the L2 initial state. *Second Language Research*, 12, 73–106.

Ferguson, C. (1971). Absence of copula and the notion of simplicity: a study of normal speech, baby talk, foreigner talk and pidgins. In D. Hymes (ed.), *Pidginization and Creolization of Languages* (pp. 141–50). Cambridge: Cambridge University Press.

Flynn, S. (1996). A parameter-setting approach to second language acquisition. In W. Ritchie and T. Bhatia (eds), *Handbook of Second Language Acquisition* (pp. 121–58). San Diego, CA: Academic Press.

Flynn, S. and Martohardjono, G. (1994). Mapping from the initial state to the final state: The separation of universal principles and language–specific principles. In B. Lust, M. Suner and J. Whiteman (eds), *Syntactic Theory and First Language Acquisition: Cross-linguistic perspectives. Vol. 1. Heads, Projections and Learnability* (pp. 319–35). Hillsdale, NJ: Lawrence Erlbaum Associates.

Gass, S. (1987). The resolution of conflicts among competing systems: a bidirectional perspective. *Applied Psycholinguistics*, 8, 329–50.

Gass, S. (1997). *Input, Interaction and the Second Language Learner*. Mahwah, NJ: Lawrence Erlbaum Associates.

Gass, S. (2003). Input and interaction. In C. Doughty and M. Long (eds), *Handbook of Second Language Acquisition* (pp. 224–55). Oxford: Blackwell.

Gass, S. (2004). Conversation analysis and input-interaction. *The Modern Language Journal*, 88, 597–602.

Gass, S. and Mackey, A. (2006). Input, interaction, and output: an overview. In K. Bardovi-Harlig and Z. Dörnyei (eds), *AILA Review (19): Themes in SLA Research* (pp. 3–17). Amsterdam: John Benjamins Publishers.

Gass, S. and Mackey, A. (2007). Input, interaction and output in second language acquisiton. In J. Williams and B. VanPatten (eds), *Theories in Second Language Acquisition*. Mahwah, NJ: Lawrence Erlbaum Associates.

Gass, S., Mackey, A. and Ross-Feldman, L. (2005). Task-based interactions in classroom and laboratory settings. *Language Learning*, 55, 575–611.

Gass, S. and Selinker, L. (2008). *Second Language Acquisition: An introductory course*. Third edition. Mahwah, NJ: Lawrence Erlbaum Associates.

Gass, S., Svetics, I. and Lemelin, S. (2003). Differential effects of attention. *Language Learning*, 53, 497–545.

Gass, S. and Varonis, E. (1985a). Miscommunication in native/non-native conversation. *Language in Society*, 14, 327–43.

Gass, S. and Varonis, E. (1985b). Variation in native speaker speech modification to non-native speakers. *Studies in Second Language Acquisition*, 7, 37–57.

Gass, S. and Varonis, E. (1994). Input, interaction and second language production. *Studies in Second Language Acquisition*, 16, 283–302.

Goldschmidt, M. (1996). From the addressee's perspective: imposition in favor-asking. In S. Gass and J. Neu (eds), *Speech Acts across Cultures* (pp. 241–56). Berlin: Mouton de Gruyter.

Han, Z. (2002). A study of the impact of recasts on tense consistency in L2 output. *TESOL Quarterly*, 36, 543–72.

Haznedar, B. (1997). L2 acquisition by a Turkish-speaking child: evidence for L1 influence. In E. Hughes, M. Hughes and A. Greenhill (eds), *Proceedings of the 21st Annual Boston University Conference on Language Development* (pp. 245–56). Somerville, MA: Cascadilla Press.

Ishida, M. (2004). Effects of recasts on the acquisition of the aspectual form -*te i-(ru)* by learners of Japanese as a foreign language. *Language Learning*, 54, 311–94.

Iwashita, N. (2003). Negative feedback and positive evidence in task-based interaction. *Studies in Second Language Acquisition*, 25, 1–36.

Jordan, G. (2005). *Theory Construction in Second Language Acquisition*. Amsterdam: John Benjamins.

Kasper, G. and Rose, K. (2002). *Pragmatic Development in a Second Language*. Oxford: Blackwell.

Kawaguchi, S. (2005). Argument structure and syntactic development in Japanese as a second language. In M. Pienemann (ed.), *Cross-linguistic Aspects of Processability Theory* (pp. 253–98). Amsterdam: John Benjamins.

Ke, J. and Holland, J. H. (2006). Language origin from an emergentist perspective. *Applied Linguistics*, 27, 691–716.

Lado, R. (1957). *Linguistics across Cultures*. Ann Arbor: University of Michigan Press.

Lantolf, J. (ed.). (2000). *Sociocultural Theory and Second Language Learning*. Oxford: Oxford University Press.

Lantolf, J. and Thorne, S. (2006). *Sociocultural Theory and the Genesis of Second Language Development*. Oxford: Oxford University Press.

Lantolf, J. and Thorne, S. (2007). Sociocultural theory and second language learning. In B. VanPatten and J. Williams (eds), *Theories in Second Language Acquisition* (pp. 201–24). Mahwah, NJ: Lawrence Erlbaum Associates.

Lantolf, J. and Yáñez, C. (2003). Talking yourself into Spanish: intrapersonal communication and second language learning. *Hispania*, 86, 97–109.

Larsen-Freeman, D. (1997). Chaos/Complexity science and second language acquisition. *Applied Linguistics*, 18, 141–65.

Leeman, J. (2003). Recasts and second language development: beyond negative evidence. *Studies in Second Language Acquisition*, 25, 37–63.

Lightbown, P. (1998). The importance of timing in focus on form. In C. Doughty and J. Williams (eds), *Focus on Form in Classroom Second Language Acquisition* (pp. 114–38). Cambridge: Cambridge University Press.

Liu, H., Bates, E. and Li, P. (1992). Sentence interpretation in bilingual speakers of English and Chinese. *Applied Psycholinguistics*, 13, 451–84.

Loewen, S. and Philp, J. (2006). Recasts in the adult English L2 classroom: characteristics, explicitness, and effectiveness. *The Modern Language Journal*, 90, 536–56.

Long, M. (1996). The role of the linguistic environment in second language acquisition. In W. C. Ritchie and T. K. Bhatia (eds), *Handbook of Language Acquisition,* Vol. 2 (pp. 413–68). New York: Academic Press.

Long, M. (2007). *Problems in SLA.* Mahwah, NJ: Lawrence Erlbaum Associates.

Lyster, R. (1998). Recasts, repetition, and ambiguity in L2 classroom discourse. *Studies in Second Language Acquisition,* 20, 51–81.

Lyster, R. (2004). Differential effects of prompts and recasts in form-focused instruction. *Studies in Second Language Acquisition,* 26, 399–432.

Lyster, R. and Ranta, L. (1997). Corrective feedback and learner uptake: negotiation of form in communicative classrooms. *Studies in Second Language Acquisition,* 20, 37–66.

Mackey, A. (2006). Feedback, noticing and instructed second language learning. *Applied Linguistics,* 27, 405–30.

Mackey, A. and Gass, S. (2006). Introduction to special issue – interaction research: extending the methodological boundaries. *Studies in Second Language Acquisition,* 28, 169–78.

Mackey, A., Gass, S. and McDonough, K. (2000). How do learners perceive interactional feedback? *Studies in Second Language Acquisition,* 22, 471–97.

Mackey, A., Oliver, R. and Leeman, J. (2003). Interactional input and the incorporation of feedback: an exploration of NS–NNS and NNS–NNS adult and child dyads. *Language Learning,* 53, 35–66.

Mackey, A. and Philp, J. (1998). Conversational interaction and second language development: recasts, responses, and red herrings? *The Modern Language Journal,* 82, 338–56.

MacWhinney, B. (2002). Extending the competition model. In R. Heredia and J. Altarriba (eds), *Bilingual Sentence Processing.* New York: Elsevier.

MacWhinney, B. (2004). A unified model of language acquisition. In J. Kroll and A. De Groot (eds), *Handbook of Bilingualism: Psycholinguistic Approaches.* Oxford: Oxford University Press.

MacWhinney, B. (2006). Emergentism – use often and with care. *Applied Linguistics,* 27, 729–40.

MacWhinney, B., Bates, E. and Kliegl, R. (1984). Cue validity and sentence interpretation in English, German, and Italian. *Journal of Verbal Learning and Behavior,* 23, 127–50.

Markee, N. (2000). *Conversation Analysis.* Mahwah, NJ: Lawrence Erlbaum Associates.

McDonough, K. (2005). Identifying the impact of negative feedback and learners' responses on ESL question development. *Studies in Second Language Acquisition,* 27, 79–103.

McDonough, K. (2007). Interactional feedback and the emergence of simple past activity verbs in L2 English. In A. Mackey (ed.), *Conversational Interaction in Second Language Acquisition: A Collection of Empirical Studies.* (pp. 323–38). Oxford: Oxford University Press.

McDonough, K. and Mackey, A. (2006). Responses to recasts: repetitions, primed production, and linguistic development. *Language Learning,* 56, 693–720.

Meara, P. (2006). Emergent properties of multilingual lexicons. *Applied Linguistics,* 27, 620–44.

Mellow, J. D. (2006). The emergence of second language syntax: a case study of the acquisition of relative clauses. *Applied Linguistics*, 27, 645–70.

Mitchell, R. and Myles, F. (2004). *Second Language Learning Theories*, 2nd edition. London: Arnold.

Mondada, L. and Pekarek Doehler, S. (2004). Second language acquisition as situated practice: task accomplishment in the French second language classroom. *The Modern Language Journal*, 88, 501–18.

Muranoi, H. (2000). Focus on form through interactional enhancement: integrating formal instruction with a communicative task in EFL classrooms. *Language Learning*, 50, 617–73.

Nabei, T. and Swain, M. (2002). Learner awareness of recasts in classroom interaction: a case study of an adult EFL student's second language learning. *Language Awareness*, 11, 43–63.

Nicholas, H., Lightbown, P. and Spada, N. (2001). Recasts as feedback to language learners. *Language Learning*, 51, 719–58.

Ohta, A. (2001). *Second Language Acquisition Processes in the Classroom: Learning Japanese*. Mahwah, NJ: Lawrence Erlbaum Associates.

Philp, J. (1999). Interaction, noticing and second language acquisition: an examination of learners' noticing of recasts in task–based interaction. Unpublished doctoral dissertation, University of Tasmania, Australia.

Philp, J. (2003). Constraints on 'noticing the gap': nonnative speakers' noticing of recasts in NS–NNS interaction. *Studies in Second Language Acquisition*, 25, 99–126.

Pienemann, M. (1998). Language processing and second language development: processability theory. Amsterdam: John Benjamins.

Pienemann, M. (2007). Processability theory. In B. VanPatten and J. Williams (eds), *Theories in Second Language Acquisition* (pp. 137–54). Mahwah, NJ: Lawrence Erlbaum Associates.

Pienemann, M. and Johnston, M. (1987). Factors influencing the development of language proficiency. In D. Nunan (ed.), *Applying Second Language Acquisition Research* (pp. 45–141). Adelaide, Australia: National Curriculum Resource Centre, AMEP.

Platzack, C. (1996). The initial hypothesis of syntax: a minimalist perspective on language acquisition and attrition. In H. Clahsen (ed.), *Generative Perspectives on Language Acquisition: Empirical findings, Theoretical Considerations, Crosslinguistic Comparisons* (pp. 369–414). Amsterdam: John Benjamins.

Ramírez, A. G. (2005). Review of the social turn in second language acquisition. *The Modern Language Journal*, 89, 292–3.

Robinson, P. (1995). Attention, memory and the 'noticing' hypothesis. *Language Learning*, 45, 283–331.

Robinson, P. (2003). Attention and memory in SLA. In C. Doughty and M. Long (eds *Handbook of Second Language Acquisition* (pp. 631–78). Oxford: Blackwell.

Sasaki, Y. (1994). Paths of processing strategy transfers in learning Japanese and English as foreign languages: a competition model approach. *Studies in Second Language Acquisition*, 16, 43–72.

Sasaki, Y. and MacWhinney, B. (2006). The competition model. In M. Nakayama, R. Mazuka and Y. Shirai (eds), *Handbook of East Asian*

Psycholinguistics: Volume 2, Japanese (pp. 307–14). Cambridge: Cambridge University Press.

Saville-Troike, M. (1988). Private speech: evidence for second language learning strategies during the 'silent period'. *Journal of Child Language*, 15, 567–90.

Saxton, M. (1997). The contrast theory of negative input. *Journal of Child Language*, 24, 139–61.

Saxton, M. (2005). 'Recast' in a new light: insights for practice from typical language studies. *Child Language Teaching and Therapy*, 21, 23–38.

Schmidt, R. (1977). Sociolinguistic variation and language transfer in phonology. *Working Papers on Bilingualism*, 12, 79–95.

Schmidt, R. (1990). The role of consciousness in second language learning. *Applied Linguistics*, 11, 129–58.

Schmidt, R. (2001). Attention. In P. Robinson (ed.), *Cognition and Second Language Instruction* (pp. 3–32). Cambridge: Cambridge University Press.

Schwartz, B. (1998). On two hypotheses of 'transfer' in L2A: minimal trees and absolute influence. In S. Flynn, G. Martohardjono and W. O'Neil (eds), *The Generative Study of Second Language Acquisition* (pp. 35–59). Mahwah, NJ: Lawrence Erlbaum Associates.

Schwartz, B. and Sprouse, R. (1996). L2 cognitive states and the full transfer/full access model. *Second Language Research*, 12, 40–72.

Schwartz, B. and Sprouse, R. (2000). When syntactic theories evolve: consequences for L2 acquisition research. In J. Archibald (ed.), *Second Language Acquisition and Linguistic Theory* (pp. 156–86). Oxford: Basil Blackwell.

Shehadeh, A. (2002). Comprehensible output, from occurrence to acquisition: an agenda for acquisitional research. *Language Learning*, 52, 597–647.

Sokolik, M. (1990). Learning without rules: PDP and a resolution of the adult language learning paradox. *TESOL Quarterly*, 24, 685–96.

Swain, M. (1985). Communicative competence: some roles of comprehensible input and comprehensible output in its development. In S. Gass and C. Madden (eds), *Input in Second Language Acquisition* (pp. 235–53). Rowley, MA: Newbury House.

Swain, M. (1995). Three functions of output in second language learning. In G. Cook and B. Seidlhofer (eds), *Principle and Practice in Applied Linguistics* (pp. 125–44). Oxford: Oxford University Press.

Swain, M. (2005). The output hypothesis: theory and research. In E. Hinkel (ed.), *Handbook on Research in Second Language Teaching and Learning* (pp. 471–84). Mahwah, NJ: Lawrence Erlbaum.

Tomlin, R. and Villa, V. (1994). Attention in cognitive science and second language acquisition. *Studies in Second Language Acquisition*, 16, 183–203.

Vainikka, M. and Young–Scholten, M. (1994). Direct access to X'-theory: evidence from Korean and Turkish adults learning German. In T. Hoekstra and B. Schwartz (eds), *Language Acquisition Studies in Generative Grammar* (pp. 265–316). Amsterdam: John Benjamins.

Vainikka, M., and Young–Scholten, M. (1996). The early stages of adult L2 syntax: additional evidence from Romance speakers. *Second Language Research*, 12, 140–76.

Varonis, E. and Gass, S. (1985). Non-native/non-native conversations: a model for negotiation of meaning. *Applied Linguistics*, 6, 71–90.

Vygotsky, L. (1978). *Mind in Society: The development of Higher Psychological Processes* (ed. by M. Cole, V. John-Steiner, S. Scribner and E. Souberman). Cambridge, MA: Harvard University Press.

White, L. (2003). *Second Language Acquisition and Universal Grammar.* Cambridge: Cambridge University Press.

Yuan, B. (1998). Interpretation of binding and orientation of the Chinese reflexive *ziji* by English and Japanese speakers. *Second Language Research*, 14, 324–40.

part 2.
windows on language acquisition

6
language and the many faces of emotion

judy s. reilly

introduction

From the early parental diaries of the 1920s to recent studies of the neural bases of language using functional brain imaging, enormous progress has been made in our understanding of the language acquisition process both across languages and cultures, as well as in typical and atypically developing children. However, language does not develop in a vacuum. Not only are there basic neural and social requirements for language to be acquired, but every utterance is produced and interpreted in an emotional context. As adults we consider our primary communicative system to be language, but we use emotional cues to help interpret utterances; and in producing speech, we exploit emotional expression to enhance, supplement or even, in the case of sarcasm or irony, to contradict the content of our messages. Moreover, we can convey this emotional colouring paralinguistically using intonation, voice quality or facial expression; or we can shade our utterances lexically using emotion words. Developmentally, long before children ever utter their first words, they are already competent affective communicators. The onset of productive language at about 12 months represents a developmental challenge for the child: how to integrate these two communicative systems. In this chapter, we will look at the intersection of language and emotion and their development in four different contexts drawing on 20 years of research. Each of the four acts in this unfolding story focuses on a different population of children at different developmental stages, from infancy through school age, to elucidate different aspects of the developmental relations between language and emotion. By chronicling the development of the behavioural, or functional, relations of these two communicative systems, we begin to understand their underlying neural substrates.

143

act 1: infancy, the brain and first words

Our opening question concerns the neural underpinnings for language and emotion. From recent studies of brain development (e.g. Stiles, 2008), it is clear that from early in gestation, the developing brain is constantly evolving, responding to environmental influences from its first moments. Nonetheless, constraints on development are also evident, with some structures being privileged to assume particular behavioural functions. The issue for discussion here is the degree to which specific areas of the brain might be privileged from the outset, for the two communicative systems, language and emotion. To address this issue, we will look at the initial stages of language and emotional development in children with perinatal stroke (PS). These rare children (1 in 4,000: Lynch and Nelson, 2001) suffered a stroke just before birth, during the birth process, or in the first four weeks of life. The strokes were focal and unilateral, that is affecting only one hemisphere of the brain, and they have been verified by CT or MRI scans. By tracing the emergence of language and emotional expression in these children we can investigate both the degree to which the brain is 'pre-wired' for particular systems, in this case language and emotion, and also, the degree to which the developing brain can respond flexibly to this early insult. To contextualize these studies, we begin with a brief overview of the adult brain organization for language and emotion, and then of the development of emotional expression in typically developing children. We then discuss our studies on language and emotional development from children with perinatal stroke.

the neural substrates for language and emotion

Much of what we know regarding the brain bases of behavioural systems stem from studies of adults who have suffered strokes later in life. Such studies have found consistent links between behavioural profiles or deficits, and the site of the lesion. More recently, functional imaging studies have broadly confirmed these original neuropsychological findings. For more than 95 per cent of adults, language is mediated by the left hemisphere of the brain (Rasmussen and Milner, 1977) and adults with lesions to the left hemisphere are often aphasic, that is, demonstrate problems with processing language (Goodglass, 1993). Broadly, those with lesions in the left frontal areas of the brain demonstrate problems with language production (Broca's aphasia) and those with lesions to the left temporal lobe are more likely to suffer comprehension problems (Wernicke's aphasia). Studies in numerous languages, including sign language (Poizner et al., 1987) have confirmed these profiles, first identified by Paul Broca and Carl Wernicke in the mid-1800s.

With respect to the neural substrates of emotion, the vast majority of adult lesion studies suggest that the right hemisphere, especially fronto-parietal regions play a critical role in emotional processing (Adolphs, 2003; Blonder et al., 1991; Borod, 1993, 2000; Damasio et al., 2003). Studies using structural and functional imaging have largely confirmed this view (Adolphs et al., 2000). Thus, emotion processing, in contrast to language processing, is predominantly in the right hemisphere of the brain; although some aspects of prosody also recruit the left hemisphere (Pell, 2006; Friederici and Alter, 2004).

emotional development in typically developing children

In his seminal work, *A First Language*, Roger Brown (1973) noted that affective expression seemed to play an important role in adults' talk to infants and toddlers. Subsequent studies of motherese and child directed speech (CDS) have shown that the contours of 'motherese' consistently reflect meaningful affective patterns, such as approval or prohibition (Fernald, 1992, 1993); moreover, infants as young as 4 months of age respond accordingly (Fernald, 1993). Looking at prosody from a linguistic perspective, others (e.g. Jusczyk, 1997) have shown that infants use prosodic cues to segment the speech stream. Therefore, before infants are responding to, or producing their first words, prosody serves as a bridge to both formal and content aspects of language. (See Peters, this volume: SFC)

The face, like the voice, also represents a powerful channel for emotional communication. More than a century after Darwin's writings from the 1860s, the cross-cultural studies of Izard (1971) and Ekman (1972) demonstrated the universality of specific facial configurations for particular emotions. These results led developmental psychologists to investigate the emergence of such expressions. Studies of early facial expressions showed that newborns use a canonical cry-face, and by 3 to 4 months babies can use smiles and cries instrumentally; they respond with a canonical angry face to frustrating situations beginning about 7 months (Stenberg and Campos, 1990) and also show surprise at incongruities. Similarly, perception studies have shown that by 6 to 7 months infants can generalize facial expressions across models (Nelson, 1987; Nelson and de Haan, 1997) and show categorical perception for at least one emotional distinction: Happy-Fear (de Haan, 2001) providing evidence for a negative/positive bifurcation of the emotional spectrum (Nelson and de Haan, 1997). Researchers using event-related potentials (ERPs) have confirmed these findings offering neurologically based evidence for the gradual differentiation of emotion categories (see de Haan, 2001 for a review) as well as a right hemisphere bias for faces from about 4 months of age (deSchonen and Mathivet, 1990). Thus, by their first birthday, as they produce their first words, infants are fluent emotional communicators.

language development in children with perinatal stroke

Studies of children with perinatal focal lesions document early deficits, but deficits that are more subtle than those of adults with comparable lesions (Basser, 1962; Bates et al., 1997; Eisele and Aram, 1995; Lenneberg, 1967; Vargha-Khadem et al., 1994; Vicari et al., 2000). The various groups studying early language in children with PS have all noted initial delay in the emergence of language. Interestingly, children in the PS group with *either right or left* hemisphere lesions are delayed in the major linguistic milestones: phonology (Marchman et al., 1991), first words and the onset of syntax (Bates et al., 1997; Eisele and Aram, 1995; Feldman et al., 1992; Feldman, 1994) and narrative abilities (Reilly et al., 1998; Reilly et al., 2004). Overall, their language acquisition profiles are iterative, characterized by initial delay and subsequent development with each new linguistic challenge. Importantly, spontaneous language in the PS group (with either right *or* left hemisphere injury) is in the (low) normal range by about age seven (see Reilly et al., 2008).

What can the initial stages of language development tell us about how the infant's brain is organized for language? Bates and colleagues (Bates et al., 1997) used the MacArthur Communicative Inventory (MCDI) (Fenson et al., 1993), a parental report form, to chronicle early language development in a group of 40 PS children aged 8 to 30 months. They found overall delay in the PS group as a whole, for both comprehension and production of first words. In the context of this broad delay, site specific deficits were identified: between 10 and 17 months, children with early injury to right posterior regions demonstrated greater delays in word *comprehension* than the rest of the PS group; but between 19 and 31 months, children with left temporal damage showed the greatest delays for *productive* vocabulary.

Bates et al. (1997) also collected naturalistic language samples from parent–child play sessions from 30 children with PS and a control group (19 to 44 months of age). Consistent with the parental report data, they found that those with left <u>temporal</u> lesions produced shorter utterances than children with injury to other brain regions. According to the adult model, we would have expected those with left <u>frontal</u> injury to be most compromised in production. As such, their findings did not mirror the typical adult profile of deficits in comprehension after left temporal injury, but rather a production deficit in those with left temporal lesions. In these children, the specific patterns of language deficit differ by lesion side and site, but the deficits *do not map* straightforwardly onto the typical adult profiles. These findings on the early stages of language emergence and development suggest that, in contrast to maintaining language (as in the adult brain), to acquire a language, both hemispheres are recruited.

emotional expression in children with perinatal stroke

From the language studies of children with early lesions, we might conclude that the developing brain is not pre-specified for language, and even that the developing brain is equipotential for language. Since these children go on to perform in the normal range by about age 7, irrespective of lesion site, the findings are consistent with the idea that either hemisphere is capable of assuming language functions. Given this enormous neuroplasticity for language, we might then expect a similar flexibility for the development of emotional expression in these infants. To evaluate emotional expression in infants and toddlers with PS, we used videotaped recordings of free-play situations with mothers and their infants (Reilly et al., 1995). Our sample included 24 infants (aged 6 to 22 months), six with right perinatal stroke (RPS) and six with left perinatal stroke (LPS), and 12 age- and gender-matched controls.

Using criteria from the Facial Action Coding System (FACS) (Ekman and Friesen, 1978), we looked at the frequency with which infants and toddlers responded with positive facial expressions (smiles) to their mothers' bids for interaction. While all the children, both those with left posterior injury and controls, smiled easily and often, this was in marked contrast to those with right posterior injury who smiled infrequently, as depicted in Figure 6.1. Moreover, those with lesions to the right hemisphere also produced more negative affect than either those with left hemisphere injury or controls.

These cross-sectional profiles were confirmed by longitudinal case studies (Reilly et al., 1995). Together these findings suggest that the right hemisphere plays a significant role in emotional expression from at least the middle of the first year of life; moreover, unlike the situation with language, the early deficits *are* similar to the adult pattern. These data also suggest that valence (positive/negative) is a significant factor in the organization of emotions. The finding of differential right hemisphere involvement in emotional production dovetails nicely with infant perception data. That is, data from typically developing infants

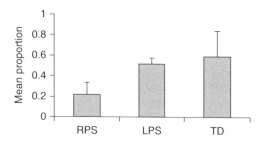

Figure 6.1   Proportion of smiles

show a right hemisphere bias for face perception in infants from 4 to 9 months (de Schonen and Mathivet, 1990).

It is tempting to conclude that the impact on emotional expression of right hemisphere damage reflects a visual processing deficit since studies from Stiles and her colleagues (e.g. Stiles et al., 2006) have shown that in visuo-spatial tasks, children with RPS display an integrative deficit similar to adults with acquired lesions. However, our data from a larger sample of 21 pre-linguistic infants with PS (aged 9 to 16 months) suggest that this profile is also reflected in their vocalizations (Reilly et al., in preparation): children with right hemisphere injury produce fewer positive and more negative vocalizations in free play than either those with left hemisphere injury or the typically developing infants. Thus, the findings for the early role of the right hemisphere in the production of positive facial expression are not due solely to a visuo-spatial impairment, but rather are reflective of a more general emotion profile that broadly mirrors that of adults with brain injury (cf. Blonder et al., 1991; Borod, 2000; Adolphs, 2003; Damasio et al., 2003).

Comparing profiles for the emergence of language and emotion in children with perinatal stroke, we see two very different patterns: for language, there is initial delay regardless of lesion site, suggesting that unlike the profile for adults, language is not lateralized to the left hemisphere early on in development, but rather is initially distributed bilaterally. Neuropsychological (Mills et al., 1997) and recent functional imaging data from typically developing toddlers (Redcay et al., 2008) support this thesis. In contrast, the pattern of behaviour in the development of emotional expression in the PS group is much more similar to that of adults with acquired strokes: similar to their adult counterparts, children with right hemisphere injury demonstrate atypical emotional responsivity. In contrast to the neural bases of language, such findings suggest that the neural substrates of emotion are laid down very early in development. What might explain these striking differences in the early neural localization of function? One possibility is evolutionary: emotion is an old system drawing on both cortical and subcortical structures. Approach/avoidance, a primary basis for emotional responses, is present across species. Language, however, is the sole province of humans, and thus a late developing system; it may well be, as Elizabeth Bates was wont to say, 'a new system made up of old parts'.

act 2: from communication to grammar: first signs to syntax

Our second act focuses on a group of typically developing deaf children of deaf parents who are acquiring American Sign Language (ASL) as their first language. In ASL, as with other signed languages, facial expression serves not only to convey emotion, as it does with hearing people, but specific facial behaviours also constitute aspects of the grammar of ASL. That is, certain specific constellations of facial behaviours are the morphological markers for a range of grammatical structures, including wh- and yes–no questions, relative clauses and conditional clauses. Other facial behaviours, which can be described as non-manual adverbs, co-occur with manually signed predicates to modify the meaning of the verb. Consider, for example, the ASL sentence in (1):

(1) OFFICE, MAN DRIVE   'The man drives to the office'

We can modify the predicate DRIVE with a co-occurring non-manual or facial adverb which modulates the meaning of the verb:

(2)   _____mm
       OFFICE, MAN DRIVE   'The man drives happily to the office'

Or we can use a different non-manual adverb with the same predicate.

(3)   _____th[1]
       OFFICE, MAN DRIVE   'The man drives carelessly to the office'

The fact that facial expression in ASL is multifunctional, serving both affective and grammatical roles, provides a unique context for addressing the developmental relations between emotion and language. As noted above, by their first birthday, both deaf and hearing infants employ facial expressions both to express and to interpret emotional states (Campos et al., 1983; Hiatt et al., 1979; Nelson, 1987; Reilly et al., 1986/1990; Stenberg and Campos, 1990; Marschark and Clark, 1993). However, as productive language emerges, at about 12 months, infants acquiring ASL face an unusual challenge: they must learn to use faces linguistically as well. How do toddlers make this transition from using faces affectively to using them both linguistically and emotionally as well? One obvious route to the acquisition of grammatical facial signals would be for the child to extend and generalize pre-linguistic affective communicative abilities to appropriate linguistic contexts. This would imply one global system of facial expression that serves both linguistic and affective functions. Alternatively, children might 'ignore' the similarities in the emotional and linguistic signals and treat the grammatical facial signals as a separate system, i.e. as information to be analysed independently, within the context of acquiring a linguistic system. In sum, because facial expression in ASL is multifunctional, serving both affective and linguistic purposes, its development serves as a unique context to address issues bearing on the relationship of language to other symbolic systems, in this case affect.

Over the past 25 years we have studied the development of non-manual morphology and its relation to affect in over 100 deaf children acquiring ASL (for a review, see Reilly, 2006); contexts of inquiry range from one-sign utterances to complex syntax, e.g. the acquisition of conditional sentence morphology, to the use of facial expression in signed narratives. Whereas our focus in Act 1 was the emergence of language and affect, here we present data on the transition from first signs to grammar.

facial expression at the one-sign stage

Our initial studies began with a search for the first facial behaviours used in conjunction with manual signs, and the earliest examples we observed occurred in children around 18 months of age (Reilly et al., 1986/1990). In such instances, children accompanied single sign utterances of emotion signs with the appropriate emotional facial expression, as is typical in the adult model. Utterances at this stage were generally single sign productions, as in the following examples:

(4)   _____smile
               HAPPY

(5)   ____furrow brow
             MAD
(6)   ____lip pout
             CRY

Just as in adult signing, when the children were first producing emotional signs, they typically appeared with the appropriate facial expression. Given that the emotional facial expression and the sign for the emotion both convey similar content, it is possible that information from the emotional facial expression has simply transferred to the linguistic context. Another possibility is that the child is just expressing her own feelings. Looking more broadly across the naturalistic data of these children's one-sign productions, we found other single sign utterances, not emotion signs, and these too were accompanied by facial behaviours:

(7) (age 2;3) _____mm (AU 15 + 22)[2]
                VACATION
(8) (age 2;0) ____furrowed brow (AU 4)
                WHAT
(9) (age 2;3) _____sh (AU 18 + 22)
                SHARE

In this last example, the child pursed her lips to mimic the 'sh' shape of the initial sound of the word *share* even though she does not know or use the English word for *share*. (Both hearing and deaf adults may co-articulate the initial sound of the word as they produce a sign.) These examples (examples 7–9) suggest that the child had analysed the manual and non-manual signals together as whole packages, and that these single sign utterances co-occurring with facial behaviours represent unanalysed 'amalgams' or 'gestalts' similar to those noted in the spoken language acquisition literature (e.g. MacWhinney, 1975; Peters, this volume) in which children regularly produce multi-morphemic utterances without having mastered the individual components.

After this initial stage of combined emotional and linguistic expression, children moved to a stage where they produced emotional signs with blank faces, suggesting they had separated the two channels: the hands serve language and the face is reserved for emotional functions. Further evidence for the separation and analysis of the two channels stems from examples of utterances such as the following where the child first pouted, then with a neutral face, signed CRY, and then re-assumed a pouting face.

(10) (age 2;3)
　　　　　＿＿＿＿lip pout ＿＿＿＿＿lip pout
　　　　　　　　　CRY

In this case, the child has separated the two systems, and the non-manual emotional expression and manual linguistic signals are distinct.

emotion and language in syntax: the case of wh-questions

In addition to wh-signs, such as HOW, WHERE, WHY and WHAT, wh-questions in ASL are also signalled with an obligatory co-occurring fur-rowed brow and head tilt (AU 4 + 57). The timing of these facial/head behaviours is critical (Baker-Shenk, 1983): they begin milliseconds prior to the initiation of the manually signed string and terminate just prior to the manually signed questions as in example (11).

(11) ＿＿＿＿＿＿＿＿＿＿＿＿4 + 57 [brow furrow + head forward]
　　　　　WHERE DOG WHERE 'Where is the dog?'

Interestingly, the wh-question non-manual morphology, a furrowed brow (AU4), can also convey anger or distress in ASL, and it also sig-nifies puzzlement for both hearing and deaf people. For example, if I am up in front of a class delivering a lecture and a student furrows her brow, I interpret this affective, non-linguistic signal as a lack of com-prehension or puzzlement. Both deaf and hearing infants and toddlers use the furrowed brow to convey distress from their earliest days. The question is: Will deaf toddlers recruit this pre-linguistic affective/com-municative knowledge to bootstrap them into language by applying it directly to wh-questions?

Our research suggests toddlers use wh-signs before they produce sentences, and as example (8) above demonstrates, many of the early single sign questions are produced with the obligatory furrowed brow. In fact, before the age of 2 or so, children's questions were fre-quently accompanied by aspects of the adult non-manual behaviour, similar to other one-sign utterances, (Reilly et al., 1986/90; Reilly and McIntire, 1991). However, the timing, scope and individual non-manual components often did not match those of the adult model as in the following which show partial use of the required non-manual constituents:

   (12)   Child (1;6)
            _____ 4 [brow furrow] (omitted: head tilt)
            'WHAT'

   (13)   Child (1;9)
            _____ 51<>52_ [headshake] (omitted: brow furrow 1 head tilt)
            WHERE MELON
            'Where's the melon?'

As the children began producing multi-signed utterances in the naturalistic videotaped data, at about age 2;0 to 2;6, we found that children's productive discourse frequently included wh-questions. Other studies, using the MacArthur Communicative Development Inventory for ASL (Anderson and Reilly, 2002), matched these results and showed that by the time children had vocabularies of 100 signs (on average by age 16 to 19 months), the sign WHERE was in their vocabulary; and by 2;0 the vast majority of the children also used the wh-signs, WHO, WHAT and WHICH. Interestingly, in the naturalistic data, when we coded the facial behaviours co-occurring with their multi-signed questions, we found that in the majority of cases, their faces were neutral; that is, they omitted the obligatory non-manual behaviours, as in (14):

   (14)   Child (2;3) WHERE 'WHAT'
             'Where is it?'

From the data summarized in Figure 6.2, we can see that before age 4, the majority of children's wh-questions lack the appropriate facial morphology, although they do use some aspects of the adult non-manual behaviours.

It is not until they approach age 5 that children produce the manually signed wh-questions with the required facial behaviours; and when they do, the facial behaviours first have scope only over the wh-signs, rather than the entire wh-question. (For more detail see Reilly and McIntire, 1991 and for complementary data and discussion, Lillo-Martin, 1996/2000.)

We can conclude that the pattern of acquisition for the non-manual morphology of wh-questions includes the following:

1. At the single sign stage, wh-signs co-occur with the communicative brow furrow, signalling distress or puzzlement.

2. As children move into syntax, wh-questions are signalled with a manual wh-sign, and the non-manual facial morphology is by and large omitted.
3. It is not until about kindergarten that the child has acquired the non-manual morphology and uses it appropriately with accurate scope and timing.

In response to our initial questions, we can say that the child does not recruit her pre-linguistic affective/communicative abilities to signal wh-questions. Rather, as she enters the multi-sign stage, she approaches questions with a lexical strategy, using manual wh-signs to signal questions. Even when she begins to use the non-manual marker, its scope is limited to the wh-sign, confirming the strength of this lexical, manual approach. This pattern of acquisition: a gestalt of hands and faces together, then bare manually signed multi-sign strings, and finally the emergence of non-manual morphology co-occurring with the manually signed structure, is similar to the pattern we have found for emotion signs as well as for the acquisition of negation (Anderson and Reilly, 1998a), non-manual adverbials (Anderson and Reilly, 1998b) and conditional clauses (Reilly et al., 1990). In every instance, once children are producing multi-signed utterances, they first signal the structures that require non-manual markers with only manual lexical signs. Thus, rather than directly recruiting what appear to be pertinent affective/communicative behaviours, the bound non-manual morphology is acquired slowly and secondarily to the lexical markers; a pattern seen

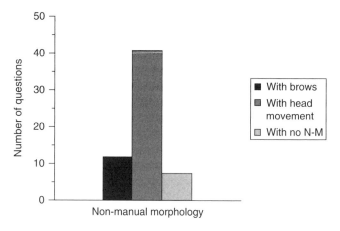

Figure 6.2   Non-manual morphology in wh-questions from 3-year olds

in spoken language acquisition as well. It appears that after the two-sign stage, that is, the onset of syntax, children no longer have access to affective/communicative behaviours to scaffold their acquisition of non-manual morphology.

act 3: integrating language and emotion in narratives

By the time they reach the age of 4 or 5, both hearing and deaf children have mastered the majority of the morphological and syntactic structures of their language (Slobin, 1985, 1992, 1995). After age 5, language development entails learning to recruit, successfully and flexibly, particular linguistic structures appropriately for various discourse contexts. Narratives or stories represent a common discourse genre in children's lives, and even children as young as age 2 have some notion of 'a story' (Appleby, 1978). Moreover, as Labov and Waletzsky observed (1967), narratives include two distinct aspects: the *referential function* that supplies information about the characters and events in the story, and the *evaluative function* which reflects the narrator's perspective regarding the significance of those events, including their emotional perspective. Given this combination of functions, stories present a perfect context to investigate the developing relations of language and affect.

Along with other researchers around the world (cf. Berman and Slobin, 1994), we have used Mercer Mayer's wordless picture book, *Frog, where are you?* (1969) to elicit spoken stories from pre-school and school-age children. Reilly (1992) began this research by asking typically developing children in two age groups – 3 to 4 years and 7 to 8 years – to look through the frog story picture book and then retell the story to an unfamiliar adult. Not surprisingly, the 7–8-year-olds told longer and more complete stories than the pre-schoolers, with the stories of the younger children often reflecting a linear construction from which critical structural elements were missing. However, the younger group used significantly more paralinguistic affective expression than the 7- and 8-year-olds, as seen in Figure 6.3. Specifically, prosodic modulations (stress, pitch changes and vowel lengthening), rather than facial expression or gesture, are far and away the preferred affective signal of the pre-schoolers.

We wondered whether the structurally more complex, but affectively bland stories of the 7- and 8-year-olds might have been the product of 'school socialization'. To test this possibility, we asked another group of 7- and 8-year-olds, and also a group of 10- and 11-year-olds to tell the frog story to a 3-year-old, and we asked them 'to make the story really interesting'. We found that two children in the middle group slightly raised the pitch of their voice, but overall the 7- and 8-year-olds still told coherent, complete, but emotionally flat stories, consistent with the first group of this age. In contrast, the 10–11-year-old group told complete and coherent stories that were *also* affectively expressive, as depicted in Figure 6.4.

Taken together, Figures 6.3 and 6.4 suggest a U-shaped curve in the use of affective prosody across the three groups, with both pre-school-ers and the older group using a great deal of affective expression and the middle group using little. However, on closer inspection, this initial similarity between the oldest and youngest group appears to be more apparent than real.

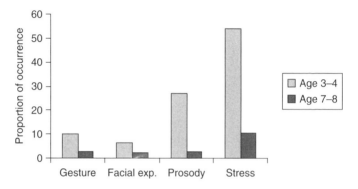

Figure 6.3   Use of paralinguistic affective expression in story telling

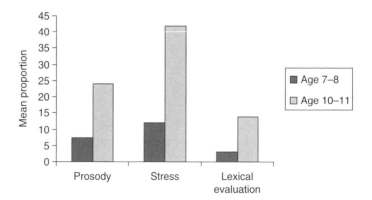

Figure 6.4   Evaluation in stories told to a pre-schooler

Recall that the stories from the youngest children are structurally impoverished; they often omit events, even though the book is in front of them. More than half the 3-year-olds did not infer that the boy was looking for his frog! This suggests that telling the story is cognitively challenging for this age group. Moreover, if we look more closely at how the youngest and oldest groups used prosody, we find some consistent differences. For example, in the youngest group, we find a singsong rhythm that may help propel the child through the process of telling the story, and/or serve as a type of persistent genre marking indicating that the child is participating in the activity of storytelling. Given the structural immaturity of the stories of these youngest children, we suggest that they are recruiting their well-developed affective expressive abilities as a sort of 'glue', or scaffold to help them through this cognitively and linguistically challenging task.

In contrast, the high frequency of affective expression in the stories from the older group implies a fluency and flexibility in storytelling style. The 10- and 11-year-olds tell complete and coherent stories, and within individual utterances, their prosody follows the adult syntactic model. The increased affect serves to entice and captivate their preschool listener. This is evident from their leaning forward, posing questions, e.g. 'And what do you think happens next, Jenny?' to attract and maintain the attention of their 3-year-old audience. Moreover, in addition to their increased use of paralinguistic affective devices, the oldest group also includes more evaluative comments than do the 7- and 8-year-olds, linguistically incorporating affect into their stories as well. In sum, whereas the pre-schoolers rely on a developmentally earlier system, affective expression, to bind their stories together, 10-year-olds use affect to enhance and supplement their already complex and coherent narratives.

act 4: a genetic basis of sociability: lexical evaluation in narratives from children with williams syndrome

Williams syndrome (WS) is a rare genetically based disorder resulting from a deletion of one copy of about 20 genes on chromosome 7, including Elastin, Lim1kinase, Syntaxin1a, among others (Ewart et al.,1993; Frangiskakis et al., 1996; Botta et al., 1999; Korenberg et al., 2000). This deletion results in a distinctive medical, psychological, neuropsychological and neuroanatomical profile. For example, children with WS have a particular facial dysmorphology, and they often suffer from cardiac problems. Cognitively, children with Williams present an unusual profile: they are mildly to moderately retarded with IQs ranging from 50 to 70, but unlike children with other neurodevelopmental disorders (such as Down syndrome), their neurocognitive profile is markedly uneven: They have very poor visuo-spatial skills, but good face processing; similarly while numerical abilities and problem solving are a challenge, language, though delayed, is a relative strength. From an affect point of view, children with Williams syndrome are extremely friendly and highly social, even though they have problems making friends. Recruiting their stronger systems, face processing, language and affect, individuals with WS are known to charm, flatter and socialize with any available adult. Our focus in this fourth Act is on the interface of these systems in this unusual population again using narratives as a context of inquiry.

Returning to Labov's concept of evaluation in narratives, that is, those aspects of the story that reflect the narrator's perspective on characters or events in the plot, we have elaborated his initial characterization to include both paralinguistic expression, as discussed above, and also lexically encoded evaluation and its development (Reilly et al., 1990; Bamberg and DamradFrye, 1991; Bamberg and Reilly, 1996; Losh et al., 2000; Reilly, 1992; Reilly, et al., 1998; Reilly et al., 2004). Lexically encoded evaluation includes such categories as the following, with examples taken from typical children's retellings of the frog story:

1) attributing emotional or mental states to characters (*When he found the jar empty, he was sad*);
2) hedges, conveying differing levels of certainty (*Well, maybe the frog was in the hole*);
3) attributing motivation or causality;
4) using character speech (*And he called, 'Frooooooogie, where are you?'*);
5) sound effects (*He fell in the water, kersplash!!!*);
6) intensifiers or emphatics (*Oh, look at the little bitty tiny baby frogs*);
7) 'audience hookers', that is, devices to attract or maintain audience attention, e.g. exclamations, rhetorical questions (*Now where could that little frog be?*).

We wondered how similar frog story retellings by children with WS would be to those of typically developing children, so we asked a group of children aged 5 to 10 years with WS to look through the frog story and then tell the story to an experimenter (Losh et al., 2000). When compared with a control group of typically developing children, the results showed that the language used by children with WS consisted of short syntactically simpler sentences containing a significantly greater number of morphological errors (see Figure 6.5).

In fact, comparing their stories to those of age-matched children with language impairment (LI) (Reilly et al., 2004), the morphosyntactic performance of the WS group is comparable to those with LI, who are not cognitively delayed. With respect to narrative structure, the group with WS also had impoverished stories compared to those with LI.

However, if we focus on the *use* of language for evaluation by the children with WS, especially social evaluation (emotion words, sound effects, emphatics, character speech, intensifiers and questions), we find that at every age, children with WS use significantly more evaluation than typically developing children, as is evident in Figure 6.6. These children appeared, in fact, excessively social.

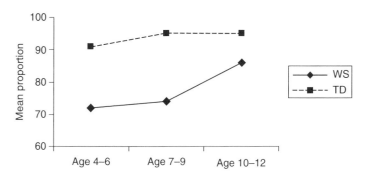

Figure 6.5   Morphosyntax in narratives of children with WS (Proportion of grammatical clauses)

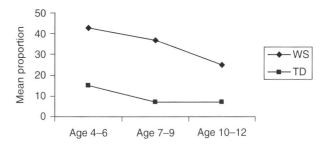

Figure 6.6   Social evaluation in narratives from children with WS (Frequency of social evaluation in narratives)

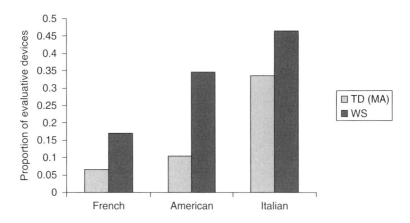

Figure 6.7   Use of social evaluation in narratives across cultures in WS

Even while children with WS struggle with the morphosyntax of English, they nevertheless exceed their age-matched TD controls in the use of social evaluative language at each time point studied. In the face of a restricted command of English, as soon as a child with WS can recount a story, or even just describe the pictures, she frequently recruits evaluative devices, effectively using language for social purposes. Thus, in the WS group, there appears to be a dissociation between the proficiency with linguistic structure (syntax) and affective use of language (evaluation).

The studies described to this point were restricted to American and Canadian English-speaking children. More recently we have had the opportunity to also look at evaluation in frog stories from French and Italian children with Williams syndrome (Reilly et al., 2005). As can be seen in Figure 6.7, excessively expressive social use of language by children with WS is also apparent across different cultures. Although culture plays a role in how children learn to use language for social purposes, in each of the three communities studied, the children with Williams far outstripped their controls in the use of evaluation in narratives.

finale: the many faces of emotion

Our goal in this chapter has been to better understand the developing relations between language and emotion from infancy through school age. We began our story during the first year of life, focusing on the brain bases for both language and emotion through the lens of infants and toddlers who have suffered perinatal stroke. In the case of emotional expression, in both the face and the voice, the profile displayed by the children with PS broadly mapped onto that of adult stroke patients. The children with left hemisphere injury, like controls, smiled and gurgled easily; those children with right hemisphere injury displayed a very different pattern of emotional responsivity. In contrast, the developmental trajectory for language in children with PS did not map onto that of the adult neuropsychological model: language onset in children with *either right or left* hemisphere injury is initially delayed. Site specific profiles do emerge, but they are unlike those of adults, and such differences resolve by age 5, at least in spontaneous conversation. By mid-elementary school, the language of the PS group is in the normal range, regardless of lesion site. Together these data suggest that the neural bases for emotion are present from early in the first year of life while those for language are initially bi-laterally distributed and only later in development become lateralized to the left hemisphere adult language areas. Moreover, the children's rapid progress reflects the brain's remarkable neuroplasticity for acquiring language.

The second act focused on deaf children acquiring the non-manual grammar of ASL as a means to elucidate the transition from affective communication to language. Initially, when infants are signing one sign at a time, the manual signs are accompanied by the pertinent facial behaviour. However, with the onset of syntax, toddlers no longer use the relevant facial expressions and their multi-signed constructions lack the required facial morphology. Subsequently, the non-manual morphology begins to accompany the manually signed utterance in a gradual and patterned manner.

Our third act concerned narratives by typically developing hearing children as another avenue to explore relations between language and emotional expression. We saw that the pre-schoolers told prosodically rich, but structurally impoverished stories, while those of the 8-year-old group were structurally complete and coherent, but affectively flat, even when their audience was a 3-year-old. On the other hand, similar to the pre-schoolers, and unlike the middle group, the 10-year-olds told coherent stories that were affectively rich, both paralinguistically and lexically. Whereas the youngest group used affective prosody to scaffold their storytelling, the older group used it to enrich already coherent narratives.

The fourth and final act looked at narratives from school-age children with Williams syndrome where we saw an abundant use of lexical and prosodic evaluation, even while the stories themselves were impoverished and sentences error-full, suggesting a dissociation between morphosyntactic proficiency and the use of language for social purposes.

These four sets of studies demonstrate that the relationships between affect and language differ according to the task at hand and the developmental period of inquiry. In infancy, affect scaffolds language as infants use prosody to discover both the content and the formal boundaries of speech. Similarly, at the one-sign stage of ASL, emotional facial expressions such as furrowed brows that are semantically parallel to wh-question signs serve as a bridge to those signs and appear to help toddlers penetrate the meaning of wh-questions. A few years later, preschoolers use exuberant prosody to propel them through the otherwise much more challenging task of telling a story. And children with Williams syndrome make use of lexically encoded affect to attract and maintain social connections in spite of their struggle to master the morphosyntax of English.

In striking contrast to these supportive, scaffolding relationships between language and affect, there is evidence that at certain stages, language and affect are cut off from each other. As deaf children acquiring ASL begin to produce multi-signed utterances, the developing linguistic system appears to lose free access to communicative/affective behaviours, even when they are semantically and formally homologous. Thus, rather than directly recruiting their pre-linguistic affective skills and knowledge, they *ignore* the relevant emotional facial expressions. How might we explain this shift in the relationships between emotional expression and language?

At the beginning of this chapter, we noted that emotional expression was mediated by the right hemisphere of the brain from early in infancy, but that language functioning was distributed across both hemispheres. In a study of typically developing toddlers at two time points early in language development, Mills et al. (1997) used ERPs to investigate the neurophysiology of early language. She found that in the younger group (average 13 months of age) broad areas of both the left and right hemisphere of the brain were activated in the baby's response to familiar words. As children approached their second birthday (average age of 20 months), however, the response to known words was qualitatively different: only the left hemisphere was activated and the area was significantly more circumscribed. If we apply these findings to the acquisition of ASL, we can propose that, in infancy, facial expression is mediated by the right hemisphere. With the onset of syntax at about 20 months, the behavioural changes in the use of facial expression accompanying manually signed utterances imply a reorganization and bifurcation and lateralization, such that the systems for language and affect are no longer mapped onto the same, bilateral, areas of the brain. The ERP and behavioural data together raise the possibility that we are witnessing the ontogenetic (and phylogenetic) evolution of brain specialization for language.

Finally, if it is correct that facial expression for affective purposes is mediated by the right hemisphere, whereas those facial behaviours functioning as non-manual morphology is controlled by the left hemisphere, then ASL signers who have suffered strokes should pattern like speakers of oral language. We have been able to put this hypothesis to the test in two adult lifelong signers who had suffered strokes later in life. We coded the use of facial behaviours in spontaneous conversation both in contexts in which one would anticipate emotion, e.g. when discussing the hospital visits, and in those linguistic contexts where non-manual behaviours were required. The first patient, SM had a large right hemisphere lesion including most of the territory of the middle cerebral artery with subcortical involvement and the second patient, G, had a left frontal lesion.

As can be seen in Figure 6.8, SM uses appropriate facial behaviours for grammar, but uses little emotional facial expression. In contrast, G employs abundant emotional facial expression, but lacks the required grammatical facial behaviours. This double dissociation parallels the children's behavioural shift at the onset of syntax. Thus the acquisition

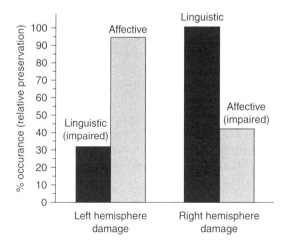

Figure 6.8　Facial expression in free conversation from deaf adults with unilateral stroke

of non-manual morphology in deaf children has provided a unique opportunity to systematically track the reorganization of presumably innate behaviours for linguistic purposes.

In conclusion, by looking at children from different groups and at different developmental stages, we have seen that children rely on affective expression to bolster and supplement their linguistic performance at multiple time points and in a variety of contexts. However, once such behaviours begin to be processed as part of the language system itself, i.e. once the process of lateralization has begun, the status of those behaviours change, and they lose their easy accessibility. The remarkable acquisition of language in children with perinatal stroke speaks to the remarkable neuroplasticity of the brain for language. That ASL uses facial expression for grammar confirms the flexibility of language to adapt as a system. At the same time, we have witnessed a rigidity in its inability to recruit relevant pre-linguistic knowledge.

notes

1. Conventions for transcribing signs.
2. FACS coding: AU.

references

Appleby, A. (1978). *The Child's Concept of Story*. Chicago: University of Chicago Press.

Adolphs, R. (2003). Cognitive neuroscience of human social behaviour. *Nature Reviews Neuroscience*, 4: 3, 165–78.

Adolphs, R., Damasio, H., Tranel, D., Cooper, G. and Damasio, A. R. (2000). A role for somatosensory cortices in the visual recognition of emotion as revealed by three-dimensional lesion mapping. *The Journal of Neuroscience*, 20: 7, 2683–90.

Anderson, D. and J. S. Reilly (1998a). The puzzle of negation: how children move from communicative to grammatical negation in ASL. *Applied Psycholinguistics*, 18, 411–29.

Anderson, D. and J. S. Reilly (1998b). PAH! The acquisition of non-manual adverbials in ASL. *International Journal of Sign Linguistics*, 1, 117–42.

Anderson, D. and Reilly, J. S. (2002). The MacArthur communicative development inventory for American sign language: the normative data. *Deaf Studies and Deaf Education*, 7, 83–106.

Baker-Shenk, C. (1983). A microanalysis of the non-manual components of questions in American Sign Language. Unpublished Ph.D. dissertation, University of California, Berkeley.

Bamberg, M. and Damrad-Frye, R. (1991). On the ability to provide evaluative comments: further explorations of children's narrative competencies. *Journal of Child Language*, 18, 689–710.

Bamberg, M. and Reilly, J. (1996). Emotion, narrative and affect: how children discover the relationship between what to say and how to say it. In D. Slobin, J. Gerhardt, A. Kyratzis and J. Guo (eds), *In Interaction, Social Context, and Language. Essays in Honor of Susan Ervin-Tripp*. Hillsdale, NJ: Lawrence Erlbaum.

Basser, L. S. (1962). Hemiplegia of early onset and the faculty of speech with special reference to the effects of hemispherectomy. *Brain*, 85, 427–60.

Bates, E., Thal, D., Trauner, D., Fenson, J., Aram, D., Eisele, J. and Nass, R. (1997). From first words to grammar in children with focal brain injury. In D. Thal and J. Reilly (eds), special issue on origins of communication disorders. *Developmental Neuropsychology*, 13: 3, 275–343.

Berman, R. and Slobin, D. (1994). *Relating Events in Narrative: A Cross-Linguistic Developmental Study*. Hillsdale, NJ: Lawrence Erlbaum.

Blonder, L. X., Bowers, D. and Heilman, K. M. (1991). The role of the right hemisphere in emotional communication. *Brain*, 114: 3, 1115–27.

Borod, J. C. (1993). Cerebral mechanisms underlying facial, prosodic, and lexical emotional expression: a review of neuropsychological studies and methodological issues. *Neuropsychology*, 4, 445–63.

Borod, J. C. (2000). *The Neuropsychology of Emotion*. New York: Oxford University Press.

Botta, A., Novelli, G., Mari, A., Novelli, A., Sabani, M., Korenberg, J., Osborne, L. R., Digilio, M. C., Giannotti, A. and Dallapiccola, B. (1999). Detection of an atypical 7q11.23 deletion in Williams syndrome patients which does not include the STX1A and FZD3 genes. *Journal of Medical Genetics*, 36, 478–80.

Brown, R. (1973). *A First Language*. Cambridge, MA: Harvard University Press.

Campos, J., Barret, K. C., Lamb, M. E., Goldsmith, H. H. and Stenberg, C. (1983). Socioemotional development. In P. Mussen (ed.), *Handbook of Child Psychology, Vol. II*, M. Haith and J. Campos (eds), *Infancy and Development: Psychobiology*. New York: Wiley Press.

Damasio, A. R., Adolphs, R. and Damasio, H. (2003). The contributions of the lesion method to the functional neuroanatomy of emotion. In R. J. Davidson, K. R. Scherer and H. H. Goldsmith (eds), *Handbook of Affective Sciences* (pp. 66–92). Oxford: Oxford University Press.

de Haan, M. (2001). The neuropsychology of face processing during infancy and childhood. In C. A. Nelson and M. Luciana (eds), *Handbook of Developmental Cognitive Neuroscience* (pp. 3831–98). Cambridge, MA: MIT Press.

de Schonen, S. and Mathivet, E. (1990). Hemispheric asymmetry in a face discrimination task in infants. *Child Development*, 61, 1192–205.

Eisele, J. and Aram, D. (1995). Lexical and grammatical development in children with early hemisphere damage: a cross-sectional view from birth to adolescence. In P. Fletcher and B. MacWhinney (eds), *The Handbook for Child Language* (pp. 664–89). Oxford: Basil Blackwell.

Ekman, P. (1972). Universal and cultural differences in facial expressions of emotion. In J. K. Cole (ed.), *Nebraska Symposium on Motivation 1971*. Lincoln, NE: University of Nebraska Press.

Ekman, P. and Friesen, W. (1978). *Facial Action Coding System*. Palo Alto, CA: Consulting Psychologists Press.

Ewart, A. K., Morris, C. A., Atkinson, D., Jin, W., Sternes, K., Spallone, P., Stock, A. D., Leppert, M. and Keating, M. T. (1993). Hemizygosity at the elastin locus in a developmental disorder, Williams syndrome. *Nature Genetics*, 5, 11–6.

Feldman, H. M. (1994). Language development after early brain injury: a replication study. In H. Tager-Flusberg (ed.), *Constraints on Language Acquisition: Studies of Atypical Children* (pp. 75–90). Hillsdale, NJ: Lawrence Erlbaum Associates.

Feldman, H. M., Holland, A. L., Kemp, S. S. and Janosky, J. E. (1992). Language development after unilateral brain injury. *Brain and Language*, 42, 89–102.

Fenson, L. D. P., Reznick, J. S., Thal, D., Bates, E., Hartung, J., Pethick, S. and Reilly, J. (1993). *MacArthur Communicative Development Inventories: User's Guide and Technical Manual*. San Diego California: Singular Publishing Group.

Fernald, A. (1992). Human maternal vocalizations to infants as biologically relevant signals: an evolutionary perspective. In J. H. Barlow, L. Cosmides and J. Tooby (eds), *The Adapted Mind: Evolutionary Psychology and the Generation of Culture* (pp. 391–428), New York: Oxford University Press.

Fernald, A. (1993). Approval and disapproval: infant responsiveness to vocal affect in familiar and unfamiliar languages. *Child Development*, 64, 657–74.

Frangiskakis J. M., Ewart A. K., Morris, C. A., Mervis, C. B., Bertrand, J., Robinson, B. F., Klein, B. P., Ensing, G. J., Everett, L. A. and Green, E. D. (1996) LIM-Kinase-1 hemizygosity implicated in impaired visuospatial constructive cognition. *Cell*, 86, 59–69.

Friederici, A. D. and Alter, K. (2004). Lateralization of auditory language functions: a dynamic dual pathway model. *Brain Lang*, 89: 2, 267–76.

Goodglass, H. (1993). *Understanding Aphasia*. San Diego: Academic Press, Inc.

Hiatt, S., Campos, J. and Emde, R. (1979). Facial patterning and infant emotional expression: happiness, surprise and fear. *Child Development*, 50, 1020–35.

Izard, C. R. (1971). *The Face of Emotion*. New York: Appleton-Century-Crofts.

Jusczyk, P. W. (1997). *The Discovery of Spoken Language*. Cambridge, MA: MIT Press.

Korenberg, J. R., Chen, X.-N., Hirota, H., Lai, Z., Bellugi, U., Burian, D., Roe, B. and Matsuoka, R. (2000). VI. Genome structure and cognitive map of Williams syndrome. *Journal of Cognitive Neuroscience, 12, Supplement 1*, 89–107.

Labov, W. and Waletzky, J. (1967). Narrative analysis: oral versions of personal experience. In J. Helm (ed.), *Essays on the Verbal and Visual Arts* (pp. 251–63), reprinted in 1997.

Lenneberg, E. H. (1967). *Biological Foundations of Language*. New York: John Wiley Publishers.

Lillo-Martin, D. (2000). (LSA Annual Meeting., Jan. 1996, San Diego, CA, US.) Early and late in language acquisition: Aspects of the syntax and acquisition of wh-questions in American Sign Language. In K. Emmorey and H. Lane (eds), *The Signs of Language Revisited: An Anthology to Honor Ursula Bellugi and Edward Klima*. Mahwah, NJ: Lawrence Erlbaum Associates.

Losh, M., Bellugi, U. Reilly, J. and Anderson, D. (2000). Narrative as a social engagement device: the excessive use of evaluation in narratives from children with Williams syndrome. *Narrative Inquiry,* 10: 2, 265–90.

Lynch, J. K. and Nelson, K. B. (2001). Epidemiology of perinatal stroke. *Current Opinion in Pediatrics*, 13, 499–505.

MacWhinney, B. (1975). Rules, rote, and analogy in morphological formations by Hungarian children. *Journal of Child Language,* 2: 1, 65–77.

Marchman, V. A., Miller, R. and Bates, E. A. (1991). Babble and first words in children with focal brain injury. *Applied Psycholinguistics*, 12, 1–22.

Marschark, M. and Clark, D. (1993). *Psychological Perspectives on Deafness*. Hillsdale, NJ: Lawrence Erlbaum Associates.

Mayer, M. (1969). *Frog, Where Are You?* New York: Dial Books for Young Readers.

Mills, D. L., Coffey-Corina, S. A. and Neville, H. J. (1997). Language comprehension and cerebral specialization from 13–20 months. *Developmental Neuropsychology* 13: 3, 397–445.

Nelson, C. A. (1987). The recognition of facial expressions in the first two years of life: mechanisms of development. *Child Development* 58, 890–909.

Nelson, C. A. and de Haan, M. (1997). A neurobehavioral approach to the recognition of facial expressions in infancy. In J. A. Russell and J. M. Fernandez-Dols (eds), *The Psychology of Facial Expression* (pp. 176–204). New York: Cambridge University Press.

Pell, M. D. (2006). Cerebral mechanisms for understanding emotional prosody in speech. *Brain Language*, 96: 2, 221–34.

Poizner, H., Klima, E. and Bellugi, U. (1987). *What the Hands Reveal about the Brain*. Cambridge: Cambridge University Press.

Rasmussen, T. and Milner, B. (1977). The role of early left brain injury in determining lateralization of cerebral speech functions. *Annals of the New York Academy of Sciences*, 299, 355–69.

Redcay, E. Haist, F. and Courchesne, E. (2008) Functional neuroimaging of speech perception during a pivotal period in language acquisition. *Developmental Science*, 11: 2, 237–52.

Reilly, J. S. (1992). How to tell a good story: the intersection of language and affect in children's narratives. *Journal of Narrative and Life History*, 2: 4, 355–77.

Reilly, J. S. (2006). How faces come to serve grammar: the development of non-manual morphology in ASL. In B. Schick, M. Marschark and P. Spencer (eds), *Advances in the Development of Sign Language by Deaf Children* (pp. 262–90). Oxford: Oxford University Press.

Reilly, J. S., Anderson, D. and Martinez, R. (in preparation). Pre-linguistic vocalizations in infants with early focal brain injury.

Reilly, J. S., Bates, E. and Marchman, V. (1998). Narrative discourse in children with early focal brain injury. *Brain and Language*, 61: 3, 335–75.

Reilly, J. S., Bernicot, J., Vicari, S., Lacroix, A. and Bellugi, U. (2005). Narratives in children with Williams Syndrome: a cross linguistic perspective. In D. Ravid and H. Bat-Zeev Shyldkrot (eds), *Perspectives on Language and Language Development: Essays in honor of Ruth A. Berman* (pp. 303–12). Dordrecht, the Netherlands: Kluwer.

Reilly, J. S., Klima, E. and Bellugi, U. (1990). Once more with feeling: affect and language in atypical populations. In D. Cicchetti (ed.), *Development and Psychopathology*. Cambridge, MA: Cambridge University Press.

Reilly, J. S., Levine, S., Nass, R. and Stiles, J. (2008). Brain plasticity: evidence from children with prenatal brain injury. In J. Reed and J. Warner-Rogers (eds), *Child Neuropsychology: Concepts, Theory and Practice* (pp. 58–91). Wiley-Blackwell.

Reilly, J. S., Losh, M. Bellugi, U. and Wulfeck, B. (2004). Frog, where are you? Narratives in children with specific language impairment, early focal brain injury and Williams Syndrome, *Brain and Language*, 88: 2, 229–47.

Reilly, J. S. and McIntire, M. L. (1991). WHERE SHOE: The acquisition of wh-questions in ASL. *Papers and Reports in Child Language Development*. 30, 1–8.

Reilly, J. S., McIntire, M. L. and Bellugi, U. (1986/1990). Faces: the relationship of language and affect. In V. Volterra and C. Erting (eds), *From Gesture to Language in Deaf and Hearing Children*. New York: Springer-Verlag; Washington DC: Gallaudet.

Reilly, J. S., Stiles, J., Larsen, J. and D. Trauner. (1995). Affective Facial Expression in Infants with Focal Brain Damage. *Neuropsychologia, 33*, 1, 83–99.

Slobin, D. I. (1985, 1992, 1995). *Crosslinguistic Studies of Language Acquisition*. Vols. 1, 3, 4. Hillsdale, NJ: Lawrence Erlbaum Associates.

Stenberg, C. R. and Campos, J. J. (1990). The development of anger expressions in infancy. In N. Stein, B. Leventhal and T. Trabasso (eds), *Psychological and Biological Approaches to Emotion* (pp. 247–82). Hillsdale, New Jersey: Lawrence Erlbaum Associates.

Stiles, J. (2008). *The Fundamentals of Brain Development: Implications for Social and Cognitive Development*. Cambridge, MA: Harvard University Press.

Stiles, J., Paul, B. and Hesselink, J. (2006). Spatial cognitive development following early focal brain injury: Evidence for adaptive change in brain and cognition. In Y. Munakata (ed.), *Processes of Change in Brain and Cognitive Development* (pp. 533–60). New York: Oxford University Press.

Vargha-Khadem, F., Isaacs, E. and Muter, V. (1994). A review of cognitive outcome after unilateral lesions sustained during childhood. *Journal of Child Neurology, 9*, Supplement 2, 67–73.

Vicari, S., Albertoni, A., Chilosi, A. M., Cipriani, P., Cioni, G. and Bates, E. (2000). Plasticity and reorganization during language development in children with early brain injury. *Cortex, 36*: 1, 31–46.

7

complements enable representation of the contents of false beliefs: the evolution of a theory of theory of mind

jill g. de villiers and peter a. de villiers

introduction

In 1995 we proposed that certain aspects of grammatical development may be necessary for children to achieve understanding of other people's false beliefs (J. de Villiers, 1995; de Villiers and de Villiers, 2000). In this chapter we review the theory on which the proposal was built, how the proposal itself has been modified over the years, and the empirical work that has addressed it. One of the risks of putting forth a strong proposal is that it will be wrong, but falsifiability is exactly its strength. At a certain point in the history of an idea, it can suffocate under the number of auxiliary hypotheses that must be marshalled to maintain it in the face of contradictory data. On the other hand, that is also the process whereby an idea gets theoretically refined. Deciding which is true in this case is the reader's choice.

Our argument is part of a more general claim that certain kinds of thinking are irrevocably tied to language because of the properties of recursion, negation, conditional, conjunction etc. that language has and that non-propositional representational systems (e.g. images) do not have (Fodor, 1975). Specifically, language is particularly well suited to the thinking humans do around propositional attitudes: understanding others' desires, beliefs, knowledge states, emotions, and so forth (Segal, 1998; see also Collins, 2000). In light of these observations, we proposed that a child must recruit the language faculty in reasoning about propositional attitudes, specifically the false beliefs of others (J. de Villiers,

1995; de Villiers and de Villiers, 2000) because it relies on structures that are able simultaneously to represent the truth in someone else's mind and attribute it only to that person. This kind of representation is seen in the complement clause under a mental state verb:

(1) Bill thought *that Miranda left* (where Miranda did not in fact leave).

The complement clause ('that Miranda left') captures the world in Bill's mind and marks it as belonging to Bill, not to the speaker. A child possessed of such a structure can then use it to support long chains of reasoning, such as to predict what Bill will do next:

(2) Bill thought that Miranda left so he will chase after her.

to explain what Bill did:

(3) Bill thought that Miranda left so he tried to call her cell phone.

and to account for other mental states:

(4) Bill thought that Miranda left so he was depressed.

The complement clause represents the basis of the reasoning, and it is centred on a *false* proposition: *that Miranda left* which must be *attributed* to someone other than the speaker in order for the reasoning to proceed.

In refining the initial idea of attribution, J. de Villiers (2001, 2005) has proposed a Point of View feature, handed down from the matrix verb to its complement and affecting everything in the scope of the complement, including the noun phrases. This allows sentences like:

(5) Bill thought that *the most beautiful woman in the world* left (whereas we think Miranda is plain).

In essence, then, the claim is that once the child has the grammatical machinery in place to represent a false complement, then this opens up the possibility of false belief reasoning. Before the possession of the appropriate grammatical machinery and key vocabulary (such as the mental state verbs, 'believe', 'think', etc.), children may have a range of important understandings of both their own and other people's mental states, but the explicit understanding of the content of false beliefs is not possible.

The next step in the development of the approach was to explore how the idea that learning complements allows reasoning about false beliefs could be tested empirically, and this required the satisfactory operationalization of the constructs of both *complementation* and *false belief understanding*.

complement comprehension

The focus on *complementation* grew out of work on *long distance* wh-questions, namely questions that attach to the lower verb in a two-clause sentence such as 'When did the boy say he fell', where the answer is about when he *fell* not about when he spoke about it (de Villiers et al., 1990). Consider the following context:

(6) This boy loves climbing trees. One afternoon he fell from a tree. He got up and went home. That night when he had a bath he noticed a big bruise on his arm and he said to his dad, 'I must have hurt myself this afternoon'.

(7) When did the boy say he fell?

The question in (7) has two possible answers depending on whether the interpretation is when the boy *said* it (at night, at bath time) or when he said he *fell* (that afternoon). By posing this, as well as alternate questions that disallow the long distance ('when he did it') reading and only allow the 'when he said it' reading, such as (8):

(8) When did the boy say how he fell?

we determined that young children have grammars that both permit long distance ('When he did it') readings and appropriately block them in the case of a syntactic barrier (the 'how') (Chomsky, 1986). However, children responded in some unexpected ways. For example, they might answer (8) with 'by falling out of the tree'. That is an answer to the medial 'how', not the initial 'when'. This was particularly prevalent with a medial 'what' as in (9):

(9) How did the mother say what she baked?

The children would frequently answer 'cake', i.e. answering the medial 'what'.

Following on from a suggestion (Juan Urriagereka, pc) that we might test whether the 'what' was restricted to the lower verb by changing the situation so that what the mother actually baked was not what she said she baked, we added the sentence in (10):

(10) What did the mother say she baked?

fully anticipating that every child would answer that one accurately. We were thus puzzled when 3-year-olds answered with what she *actually* baked, rather than what she said she baked. Since this was incompatible with our explanation for the children's adeptness with long distance movement, the easy solution was to write it off as a problem in cognitive 'theory of mind', not in the grammar itself.

The issue of whether the responses were cognitively or linguistically motivated was a key question in our understanding of the phenomenon. So, to explore this further, we examined the understanding of false belief in oral deaf children whose non-verbal cognitive development was typically developing, but whose language development was delayed. Using theory of mind tests that were not dependent on language, we showed that oral deaf children with delayed language were also several years delayed on non-verbal and verbal theory of mind false belief tasks (Gale et al., 1996). Noting that in a study of typically developing children, the ability to succeed on the 'memory for complements' task shown in (10) seemed to precede the ability to do false belief tasks (de Villiers and Pyers, 1997, 2002), we embarked on a large study of the language and theory of mind understandings of 180 oral and signing deaf children designed to tease out the precise relationship between false beliefs and linguistic development (P. de Villiers, 2005; Schick et al., 2007).

The groups in this new study included oral deaf children with language delays; signing deaf children with hearing parents who were acquiring ASL, but with some delay; and signing deaf children with deaf parents who were exposed to ASL at birth and so acquired language on a normal timetable. We included multiple measures of false belief reasoning, both verbal and largely non-verbal. We used a variety of language measures, but at the heart was the test of 'memory for complements' (illustrated in (10) above) used by de Villiers and Pyers, in spoken form for the oral deaf children and translated into ASL for the signing children. The results showed the same predictive relationship between false complement comprehension and false belief reasoning for both the oral deaf children and the ASL children, and the relationship was found for low-verbal analogues of the traditional verbal tasks as well as for the most verbal tasks. So we were confident that the relationship was not an artefact of the language of the false belief tasks themselves. As expected, other language measures, such as mental state verb vocabulary, contributed to the variance in false belief understanding, especially for the verbal tasks.

the challenges

Despite philosophical support for our hypothesis (Collins, 2000; Segal, 1998), numerous questions remained around the operationalization of the essential construct 'mastery of complements'. One question concerned whether complements are universal, which they need to be if they are the *only* trigger for the fundamentally human ability to entertain false beliefs. Or, we wondered, could other devices such as the ASL postural markers of 'role shift' used to indicate whose point of view a proposition has, also mark a proposition as attributed to another person, and therefore function in the same way as complements in other languages? What about languages with *evidential* markings, that is, morphemes that indicate the source of a belief? Could that be a viable alternative to using complementation to learn about other's belief and knowledge states? What about languages such as Chinese, which have very bare complements without complementizers? How does a Chinese child proceed to recognize the structure? Perhaps the most central question was whether it is semantics or syntax that matters here. Why consider it *grammar*?

Beyond that, there were questions about the operationalization of false belief reasoning: How could infants or younger children succeed on apparent false belief tasks in the absence of language (Onishi and Baillargeon, 2005; Southgate et al., 2007)? And how could persons with severe aphasia succeed on false belief tasks (Varley and Siegal, 2000; Varley, Siegal and Want, 2001).

the 'complement' construct

Linguistic authorities do not agree on whether all languages have complements. Wierzbicka (1992) is confident of a positive answer, but Baker (cited in Carruthers, 2007) hesitates, because some Aboriginal languages (Evans, 1999) seem to have something that more resembles an embedded noun phrase: as if the English sentence in (1) were something like (11):

(11)   Bill had the thought that Miranda left.

Dan Everett has even claimed that the Pirãha, a small tribe in the Brazilian Amazon has no complex embedded structures at all (Everett,

2005), which if true (but see Nevins et al., 2007; Wierzbicka, 2005), would predict significant difficulties in false belief reasoning, even in Pirāha adulthood (a hypothesis that remains to be tested).

Even if some languages lack complements, it could still be that other devices serve the same purpose with respect to the child's developing theory of mind capacities. For example, perhaps a structure equivalent to:

(12)   According to Bill, Miranda left.

might have the right property of attributing a view to an individual and distinguishing it from reality. No one has studied whether these devices might subserve the development of false belief reasoning. To compare them, we need to better understand the nature of complements.

verb types

First of all, we find that complements only occur under certain verbs of communication and mental state (Gleitman, 1990; Fisher et al., 1991) as in (13):

(13)   Bill said/thought/forgot/murmured that Miranda left.

and have a different distribution from verbs for *direct* speech, which are more limited:

(14)   Bill said/thought/murmured/*forgot, 'Miranda left!'

and have other less formal devices:

(15)   Bill was/like/goes, 'Miranda left.'

We can note, too, that postural role shift in ASL, and voice or pitch changes in spoken languages only occur in direct and not indirect speech reports. Moreover, in contrast to the limitations on complements, any verb or verb phrase can take an *adjunct*:

(16)   Bill fell/whistled/sneezed/ broke the window/ then Miranda left.

truth

Despite the differences noted above for complements and direct speech reports, both can be false independently of the truth of the matrix sentence as (17) to (19) show. Suppose Miranda is still present:

(17)   Bill said that Miranda left.

(18)   Bill said: 'Miranda left!'

(19)   *Bill was sad because Miranda left.

As (16) and (19) show, this is not true of adjunct clauses. At the same time, 'According to X' has the right properties, as shown in (12).

reference

Neither complements nor direct speech allow the use of terms that are not known by the subject of the sentence even though they are known to the speaker, i.e. that designation must be known to the subject. This phenomenon, known as *referential opacity*, is a complex matter, as it varies with (at least) the definiteness of the noun phrase. Consider a domestic dispute where Peter has shovelled a mass of papers, which is in fact Jill's grant proposal, off the kitchen table into the rubbish bin. We can say (20):

(20) Peter knew he put a mass of papers in the bin.

But it is not fair to say (21):

(21)   Peter knew he put Jill's grant proposal in the bin.

The indirect speech report seems to vary with the definiteness:

(22)   ?Peter said that he put Jill's grant proposal in the bin.

(23)   *Peter said that he put a grant proposal in the bin.

But the direct speech report would not pass muster as evidence in a divorce court:

(24)   *Peter said, 'I put Jill's grant proposal in the bin.'

Notice this same property, namely an agreement between the term used inside the complement with the point of view of the speaker, allows us to express delusions, not just different terms for the same thing:

(25)   Peter thought he was the King of France.

In contrast, in adjuncts, as in ordinary clauses, any nominals agreed on and known by the speaker can be used:

(26)   Peter left after he put Jill's grant proposal in the bin.

but obviously, not false designations:

(27)   *I went for coffee then I met the King of France.

Again, 'according to' has the right properties:

(28)   According to Peter, he's the King of France.

wh-movement

Complements allow wh-extraction:

(29)   Bill said he saw Miranda.
            Who did Bill say he saw?

Direct speech does not:

(30)   Bill said: 'I saw Miranda!'
            *Who did Bill say 'I saw'?

Neither do adjuncts:

(31)   Bill sneezed then he saw Miranda.
            *Who did Bill sneeze then he saw?

We return later in the chapter to the point that wh-movement is thus a neat diagnostic of complementation in some languages.

recursion

Complements allow specific kinds of recursion (Roeper, 2007; Hollebrandse and Roeper, 2007). One can say:

(32)   Jane believed that Bill thought that Miranda left.

In fact, complements are as recursive as propositional attitudes themselves can be. But do alternative devices work the same way? For example, could discourse not carry the same second-order meaning as the embedded complement? Look at the following:

(33) Miranda left.

Bill thought that.

Jane believed that.

Our tests of English speakers reveal that they cannot easily get the meaning of (32) from (33) (Hollebrandse et al., 2007). Notice also that the whole discourse begins with an assumed true statement, so how could one then represent a false belief? In other languages with devices other than complements, is it possible to say the equivalent of this:

(34) According to Jane, according to Bill, Miranda left.

English speakers have difficulty with this recursion, but it remains a possibility that speakers of other languages use such a structure for recursive beliefs.

summary of the special nature of complements

This by no means exhausts the interesting syntactic properties of complements, direct speech and adjuncts, but we can conclude that:

a) Complements and adjuncts, but not direct speech, *subordinate* certain features to the matrix verb (e.g. tense, pronouns and spatial deictic terms). Complements but not adjuncts allow wh-movement. In addition we can notice that this is so precisely when there is a point of view on the complement that is other than the speaker's (see de Villiers et al., in press). It does not occur with factive complements whose truth is presupposed:

(35) Bill forgot/knew/was glad that he saw Miranda.
        *Who did Bill forget/know/was Bill glad that he saw?

This property gives the 'memory for complements' task its nice distinction, but it will not necessarily work in a non-wh-movement language.

b) Complements and direct speech reports (and perhaps phrases like 'According to') introduce a Point of View on the clause that makes it possible to have: i) the truth of the lower clause relative to the Point of View of the subject, and ii) the designation of objects in the scope of the lower clause relative to the subject.

c) Complements are recursive, therefore they can represent all the rich array of complex propositional attitudes.

Considering this array of properties, and recognizing that there is ongoing theoretical work focused on other linguistic devices that might have these properties (Joshi, 2007; Roeper, 2007; Hollebrandse and Roeper, 2007), we can suggest that the feature that seems to matter most for at least an initial representational theory of mind is one concerning Point of View, because it allows the representation of a *false* saying or belief, and marks it as *attributed* to another individual. However, recognizing point of view devices is not easy. In some languages (e.g. Tibetan, Chinese) the distinction between indirect and direct speech reports is very hard to make, because there are no pronouns, or tense, or other signs of subordination, and no wh-movement. In speech, the only clue would be voice, pitch or postural changes to indicate a new speaker. In languages *with* wh-movement, the movement property is the most useful guide to the adjunct/complement distinction. However in non-wh-movement languages, the only clue to that difference may be a two-proposition (basically two-verb) sentence, with a matrix communication or mental verb, in the absence of a lexical connective such as *after, before, then*. As we shall see below, that is not *quite* enough to get Point of View.

empirical evidence on complements and false beliefs

typical development

The finding that mastery by learners of complements, indexed by the memory for complements task, correlates with false belief reasoning has been documented now in several different languages, and discounted in one. It has been confirmed for English (J. de Villiers, 2005, 2007), German (Perner et al., 2003), Danish (Jensen-Lopez, 2005) and ASL (Schick et al., 2007), all languages in which there is wh-movement. (No one has yet tested postural role shift in sign language as an alternative way to mark Point of View in theory of mind development.) Kyuchukov (2006) found the same result in bilingual Turkish-Bulgarian and Romani-Bulgarian children, and we have confirmed it for Tibetan (de Villiers et al., 2007), even though this is a language with no wh-movement. Notably, Tibetan does have evidentials, but we found that evidential marking by the children was unrelated to false belief mastery.

Others have tried operationalizing the construct of complement mastery in language production paradigms rather than comprehension paradigms of the kind we have developed. Aksu-Koc et al. (2005) found that production of complements predicted false belief reasoning in Turkish better than evidentials did. In the special case of the newly evolving Nicaraguan Sign Language, it proved impossible for Pyers (2004) to ask the necessary wh-questions without imposing some grammar on the subjects. But by using an elicitation task to get subjects to describe such things as mistakes, Pyers found those signers who had propositional contents with mental state verbs were able to do false belief reasoning (in a non-verbal test), but those signers who did not, failed them even as adults.

The exceptional case so far is that of children learning Cantonese (Cheung et al., 2004; Cheung, 2006; Tardif et al., 2007), a language in which the surface markers of complementation are virtually non-existent and there is no wh-movement. In a recent paper, Tardif et al. (2007) reported a large longitudinal study of children learning Cantonese in Hong Kong, and though she found significant correlations between complement comprehension on the de Villiers and Pyers 'memory for complements' task and false belief understanding, overall the children were abysmally poor at the complement comprehension test, even at age 6; results partially echoed by Cheung et al. (2004). Because Cantonese has a verb that means 'to think falsely' (found also in Turkish), Tardif argues that perhaps the children take a different route, using some of the lexical information provided by that verb to compensate for the inadequate clues from complementation structures. We return below to questions about a language lean in syntactic markers of complementation.

delayed development

In the case of children with delayed language, the results are clearer because the time course is extended and the variability is more striking. Schick et al. (2007) demonstrated that one of the highest predictors of false belief reasoning in language-delayed deaf children is their understanding of complements, tested in either ASL or spoken English. This was true whether or not the children were late learners of ASL, or delayed because they were learning oral English. Other measures of syntax were not as significant, though vocabulary seemed to play a secondary role in the verbal tasks. P. de Villiers et al. (2003) found that in a large sample of over 1,000 children aged 4 to 9, 350 of them with SLI, a single item of complement understanding was a strong predictor of performance on a false belief explanation task in a narrative context, independent of the children's communicative role taking skills and other general language measures. And Tager-Flusberg and Joseph (2005), in a longitudinal study of children with autism, showed that mastery of complement comprehension with verbs of communication was the strongest predictor of any changes over the period of a year in the children's false belief performance.

training studies

Perhaps the most striking results emerge from two training studies aimed at teaching children the necessary language to see if they improved on false belief performance (Hale and Tager-Flusberg, 2003; Lohmann and Tomasello, 2003). Hale and Tager-Flusberg (2003) selected 3-year-old children who failed on both memory for complements and false belief reasoning tasks. They then provided three different types of training: explicit training in false belief reasoning; training in understanding relative clauses; and training in understanding false complement clauses with verbs of communication. When tested three weeks later, the children all showed significant improvements on the tasks on which they were trained, but in addition, the group trained on the complement clauses with communication verbs also showed significant growth in their reasoning about false beliefs. In fact their improvement on false belief reasoning tasks was equivalent to that of the group explicitly trained on those tasks. Training on relative clauses, another complex embedded grammatical structure, showed no transfer to false belief reasoning.

Lohmann and Tomasello (2003) also selected children who failed false belief reasoning. However, these children's scores on the complement comprehension task averaged 2.4/4, so it is possible that some of them already had some command of complementation before training. Between 24 and 30 children were assigned to each of five training conditions. These were: (1) training about deceptive objects with mental state verbs and false complement clauses; (2) training about deceptive objects with communication verbs and false complement clauses; (3) exposure to discourse about the deceptive objects but that did not use either mental state verbs or complements (the 'discourse only' condition); (4) exposure to deceptive objects with the command to 'look!' that highlighted their deceptive features, but without accompanying discourse about them; and (5) training on false complement clauses without any clear reference to the deceptive features of the objects. The strongest training effects were found for conditions (1) and (2). The children in condition (4) showed no training effect at all. Children in the remaining two training conditions ((5) and (3)), showed an intermediate level of growth on false belief reasoning after training. In discussing these results, Harris (2005) interprets the fact that condition (3) group showed some improvement on false belief tasks as decisive counter-evidence to the claim that mastery of complements is prerequisite for false belief reasoning. However, the gains were quite small compared to condition (2): On the false belief task at post-test, the condition (3) children got 40 per cent of the questions correct (less than chance) compared to 75 per cent correct in condition (2). The evidence suggests that test–retest improvement alone might account for the improvement under condition (3). So overall, one cannot tell whether any child at the end of the study succeeded in passing the false belief tasks without 'knowing' complements, the litmus test for disproving the complement hypothesis as we have proposed it. (Notice that such training studies could easily fail to find any effect even if the complement theory were correct, because the prediction is that mastery of complements *opens the doors to* false belief reasoning, but it does not say that false belief reasoning will inevitably follow.) It seems counterintuitive that complements can be taught in a couple of sessions. However, they clearly can if the children are right on the cusp of mastering the structure in any case. No one would expect 2-year-olds to learn them in a training study. This fact raises two problems for training studies: they can fail to show anything because the children don't show any training effect at all, or because all the children show enough growth in the interim between pre-test and post-test to swamp any differential effects of specific training conditions.

semantics versus syntax

Though Perner et al. (2003) found a sizeable correlation between complements and false belief reasoning, the main conclusion of that study was to cast doubt on the complement hypothesis. In German (as in French and Danish), the complement clause under a verb of desire (35) has the same superficial form as the complement under a verb of mental state such as *think* (36):

(35)   Mutter will, dass Andreas ins Bett geht.
       [Mom wants that Andy goes to bed].

(36) Mutter glaubt dass Andreas ins Bett geht.
      [Mom thinks that Andy goes to bed].

Perner et al. showed that despite the similarity in structure, German children achieve understanding of them at quite different times. That is, children understand the *want* questions well before they understand the *think* questions, and only the latter connect to false belief reasoning. On these grounds, Perner et al. argue that the change is really conceptual, not linguistic, and children just master *desire* before *belief*. If this is true then the memory for complements task could be interpreted merely as a slightly *easier* false belief task, an idea proposed in Ruffman et al. (2003). For these theorists, even with the verb *say* instead of *think*, the task taps theory of mind itself, not anything about syntax. As we shall see below, Perner has good reason for believing in the primacy of conceptual understanding before language. On the other hand, we find the data from deaf children showing their poor performance on non-verbal theory of mind tasks hard to reconcile with the conceptual primacy argument.

It is important to unpack the data on *want* versus *think*. Certainly, understanding desire comes before understanding beliefs, and understanding desire seems to have no obvious linguistic prerequisites. Deaf children with language delay and SLI children are *not* delayed in understanding desire, nor using terms for it (P. de Villiers, 2005). However, English, unlike German, has different complement structures for 'want' than for 'think': 'want' uses an infinitival complement:

(37) John wants her to go to bed.

while 'think' uses a tensed clause complement:

(38) John thinks she went to bed.

It is transparent in English that the clauses have a radically different semantics: there is no 'truth' index on the clause under *want*. It is an event that has yet to occur: it is an *irrealis* clause. Tensed clauses, on the other hand, are *realis*; that is, their truth can be evaluated (did she go to bed or didn't she?). Notice, however, that modals can carry irrealis properties, as in:

(39) John thinks that she should go to bed.

creating a complement clause that, like 'want' clauses also has no evaluable truth. J. de Villiers (2005) showed that children aged 3 to 4 not only found *want* clauses easier, but they also clearly differentiated between *think did* and *think should*, and found the latter as easy as *want*. Only *think did* was connected to false belief understanding. This means that the notion of 'complements' must be refined to mean *realis tensed complements*, a concept as available in German as in English.

That the realis/irrealis distinction is important in children's interpretation of complements is not surprising given their importance in grammars of the world's languages (Bickerton, 1984) and the fact that this and other distinguishing features of complements may be either overt or covert in a given language (Felser, 1999). While some may try to argue that the realis requirement means that the concept of 'complement' has become entirely *semantic*, not syntactic at all, we have nothing particularly at stake in agreeing that Point of View is fundamentally semantic, and that the only kind of complements that matter is the subtype *realis* that capture truth in another's mind.

So, if realis complements permit thinking about false beliefs, how do children recognize the expressive power of the structures? We have argued that it is verbs of *communication* that pave the way, because they allow overt comparison of what someone said and what was true:

(40) Bill: 'Miranda left!' (but we know she didn't)
      Fred: 'Bill says Miranda left!'

Children must experience circumstances, in all languages, in which this kind of discourse occurs, and in which (crucially) no one corrects Fred. That is, it is no use for the child just to witness people saying false things. The *event of a person saying something false* must be encoded to reveal the embedding that language makes possible. Once the grammar for expressing this is made apparent with verbs of communication, then the child has the linguistic representation ready to follow the discourse:

(41) Bill, looking morosely out of the window.
      (Miranda is present but out of Bill's sight)
      Fred: 'Bill thinks Miranda left!'

To the extent that the notion of 'complement' varies cross-linguistically, it becomes even more necessary that there be a route to discovery of the right form via verbs of communication.

The puzzle remains, however, as to why the Cantonese children would be so poor at the memory for complements task. Recently, we have suggested it is related to a general locality constraint (Chomsky, 2005) which encourages all children to answer the wh-question in a two-clause structure with respect only to the lower clause (de Villiers et al., submitted). Children learning Cantonese, which has no overt wh-movement, will have a harder time recovering from this 'error' because there are no overt clues that the wh–word must be interpreted as having scope over the whole structure. The wh-question task may not then be the best test of their understanding of complements in Cantonese. Perhaps a yes/no question such as (48) would work better to measure complement mastery than a wh-question in a language with no wh-movement:

(48)   Woman say bought apple?

This experiment remains to be done.

the construct 'false belief reasoning'

How should we assess whether a child is capable of recognizing another's false belief state? There has been much discussion about the nature of the tasks, with critics arguing that many (unseen object displacement, unexpected contents) are far too *unnatural* (Nelson, 2005). Others have suggested that they demand more of the child than simply recognition of another's false belief. In particular, it is suggested that they involve other performance demands, such as resisting an impulse to answer with reality, or working memory demands, both of which tap executive function, and we know that the components of executive function represent another set of cognitive skills that are mastered just around the time that children pass the false belief tests (Carlson and Moses, 2001; Moses, 2001).

However, our recent findings from language-delayed deaf children demonstrate that it is the language of the children rather than their executive functioning that is the proximal predictor of their performance on false belief reasoning tasks. P. de Villiers (2005) and de Villiers et al. (2007) showed that language delayed orally taught deaf children who still fail false belief tasks are not at all impaired in executive function skills such as non-verbal working memory, inhibitory control, and conditional rule following; each of which has been implicated in hearing pre-schoolers' theory of mind development. Furthermore, the deaf children's performance on both the standard high-verbal false belief reasoning tasks and on low-verbal analogues of those tasks (Schick et al., 2007; Woolfe et al., 2002) was predicted by their language, not by their executive functioning. The strongest predictor of the children's false belief reasoning was their processing of false complement clauses with the verb 'say' on the memory for complements task (replicating Schick et al., 2007).

Nevertheless, theorists such as Leslie (1994) and Fodor (1992) argue that the child's concept of false belief is there from very early in childhood, and it is the other cognitive and linguistic skills that must catch up before children can pass false belief reasoning tasks. These theorists are encouraged by Onishi and Baillargeon's (2005) surprising results that even 17-month-olds can recognize another person's false belief when that recognition is measured by looking time in a violation of expectancies paradigm. In this study, toddlers first habituated to a stranger who reached into one of two containers to retrieve an object that moved (on its own) into that container. In carefully arranged conditions, the object subsequently changed positions while the person was not looking but the toddler was. Toddlers' looking time was measured to two different outcomes: one in which the person reached into the wrong container, and one in which the person reached into the right container. The 17-month-olds looked a second or so longer (statistically significant) when the person reached into the right container when they could not have 'known' the object was there. The control condition was the 'true belief' case where the person saw the object move and then reached into the right container.

Onishi and Baillargeon maintain that these very young children have an understanding of the adult's false belief state as indexed by their looking time. Their expectations are violated when the person searches in the container to which the object was moved without them seeing the relocation. Notice that the behavioural demand of this task is minimal: the subjects did not have to do anything but watch. The young children do not have to make any explicit decision about what the adult believes or where they will look. Does this represent the golden age of understanding before task demands cloud the picture?

Clements and Perner (1994) were the first to try minimizing response demands, studying children aged 2;5 to 4;6, in a task involving looking *direction*, rather than looking *time*. In a verbal false belief reasoning task they first told the children a rather complex story about a mouse who hides his cheese in a box in front of one of two entrances to his burrow. Then while he is away, his cheese is moved to a box in front of the other entrance by a wily cat. Instead of (in fact before) the standard false belief question, 'Where will the mouse look for his cheese?', the experimenters said 'Look, look, the mouse is coming! I wonder where he will look for his cheese?' and measured the direction in which the children looked: to the mouse-hole beside the old or the new location of the cheese. Clements and Perner report that at 2;11, but *not* before, children looked more often at the location where a mouse-with-false-belief would emerge, i.e. near the old location where they had put the cheese. However, when those children were subsequently asked the standard question, and had to explicitly indicate where the mouse would first look for the cheese, they failed in the classic way of choosing the new location where the cheese would be found. A true belief condition in which the mouse stayed out of his burrow and watched the movement of the cheese provided a necessary control against the children simply having a preference for seeing the mouse emerge where he last exited the scene. Clements and Perner conclude that just before children can explicitly use their knowledge about false beliefs to make judgements and predict actions, they have an implicit understanding of false beliefs (see also Dienes and Perner, 1999). That understanding is sufficient to influence eye gaze and attention, but not sufficient for explicit reasoning about the situation, i.e. making a decision.

Perner and Ruffman (2005), in response to Onishi and Baillargeon (2005), argue that their own 1994 task is an appropriate operationalization of 'implicit' false belief, but that the younger children in Onishi and Baiilargeon's study might in fact be responding on the basis of more primitive event cues. They argue that the toddlers may simply have formed a lower-level stimulus association between character + location + object, and when any of those associations was new, there was increased gaze time to process the new combination. In contrast, they argue that in their own paradigm the children have a precursor of real false belief representation, but it is yet implicit and not sufficient to drive the explicit reasoning demanded of the standard question. Dienes and Perner (1999) consider several such cases in psychology in which 'implicit' precedes 'explicit' understanding of a concept.

Recently, however, Southgate et al. (2007) have replicated the findings of Clements and Perner with 24-month-olds by removing any language from the cues provided to the child. Instead of saying, 'I wonder where the mouse will look?', the child is confronted only with a nonverbal scene. The measure taken is the direction of eye gaze to the location where a person will go premised on a false belief. They found that the 2-year-olds expect the person to look in the place where that person last saw the object. That is, at a minimum, 2-year-olds seem to predict (as indexed by eye gaze) that a person who was not watching will maintain their earlier goal orientation, i.e. cannot update it. This is the foundation of the unseen displacement task. But why then does explicit 'deciding' where the person will look take two more years?

In a study of both children and primates, Povinelli and Vonk (2004) argued that in order to develop a sophisticated understanding of others, any creature must observe behaviour and arrive at generalizations across that behaviour. For example, they might deduce that '[a] person seeking an object generally goes back to where they left an object'. Notice there is no mention here of mental state. Rather it demands a kind of social cognition without reference to mental states which Povinelli and Vonk demonstrated is achievable even by chimpanzees. The usual tests of false belief with children go beyond this kind of social cognition. However, the unseen displacement task *may* be one demanding only the primitive kind of social cognition, especially if it is stripped to the level of an eye gaze response. That is, children could be operating with a rule such as 'People who seek an object will go to where it *is*', or even 'People who seek an object go to where they last *put* it', which is the ubiquitous answer 4-year-old children give when asked why the subject returns to the wrong location. In some versions of the task, someone else is placing the object, in which case they need: 'People who seek an object go to where they last *saw* it', which would seem to entail minimally tracking where someone was watching. But all these versions are less sophisticated than: 'People who seek an object go to where they *believe* it to be', which involves true mental state social cognition.

The findings of Southgate et al. (2007) and Clements and Perner (1994) with toddlers are at variance with our own work using low or non-verbal tasks that require a *decision* on the part of the subject. We used a version of Povinelli's hide-and-seek task with typical-hearing and deaf individuals who must reason that a person who has not seen where a sticker was hidden, is in no position to point to the right location to find it; whereas a person who watched it hidden is likely to give good advice on where to find it. Ten trials are given, with different people serving the clearly marked roles of 'knower' and 'ignorant-guesser'. We found it was not until 4;6 that hearing children can pass this task, around the same time as they can handle standard verbal tasks (P. de Villiers and Pyers, 2001; Gale et al., 1996). Moreover, whereas one might expect that deaf children who are older, and more socially adept, could succeed on this low-verbal task long before they could handle the verbal tests, we found language-delayed signing and oral deaf children continue to fail the task until they can pass the standard verbal tasks (P. de Villiers, 2005; Schick et al., 2007). In fact, the best predictor of when they pass it is when they have enough language, namely, command of complementation. Why then is this task so hard, if all the conceptual components – implicit theory of mind, working memory and inhibitory control – are squarely in place? We cannot offer a satisfactory explanation except to invoke yet another requirement: language.

In an important series of studies, Jennie Pyers (2004) conducted extensive tests of non-verbal and low-verbal false belief reasoning in the special deaf population residing in Nicaragua, who have learned an emerging Creole Nicaraguan Sign Language since beginning school there at the school for the deaf. The older individuals in the deaf community have a more incomplete sign language (that emerged early in the evolution of NSL) that seems to lack mental verbs with complementation. Those same individuals failed non-verbal tests of false belief understanding in Pyers' studies, even though they were adults aged 24–36 years at the time of testing. Younger deaf signers of NSL who had a more complex sign language passed all of the same tests. These tasks involved making explicit decisions about the actions and emotional responses of the characters with the false beliefs and thus made demands on working memory and inhibitory control, but not beyond the level one would expect of adults in any case. Pyers found that the best predictor of the Nicaraguan signers' success on the false belief tasks was their language status, i.e. whether they had learned the incomplete or the more elaborated NSL.

Finally, some recent work with typical adults sheds important light on the developmental evidence. We have explored whether they can do non-verbal reasoning about false beliefs while simultaneously engaged in a language task (Newton and de Villiers, 2007). Subjects watched video scenarios similar to the Clements and Perner story (acted out by students dressed in animal costumes), in which some cheese was moved by a cat to a new location while a mouse character was out of sight. When the mouse re-emerged, the subjects had to choose which of two video clips was the appropriate ending to the video: one in which the character went to the place he falsely believed the object was, or where the object now was? Subjects practised with a video with clear 'causal' endings ('what will happen next?') to show they understood the very limited task demand of tapping on a coloured block next to the video they chose. The adult subjects had to do one of two things when they saw the movie: either follow varied rhythmic tapping by repeating it with a drumstick, or repeat (shadow) a voice telling a story unconnected to the video. As in Clements and Perner, a video of a true belief scenario in which the mouse watched the change in location of the cheese served as a control condition.

The results were startling: adults behave like 3-year-olds when they try to do the false belief task while engaged in verbal shadowing. That is, they choose the video ending where the mouse goes to the box where the cheese really is, ignoring the character's false belief. However, they are perfectly fine in choosing the right ending if they are shadowing rhythmic tapping – a non-language task. The effect does not seem to be simply one of attention because a different set of subjects was given a fairly complex control task on face perception that did not involve beliefs, and the two interference tasks proved equal in their disruption of reaction time on this third task, suggesting that the language faculty is crucially engaged when explicit reasoning on false beliefs is called for.

How can these various results be reconciled? Carruthers (2007), who believes executive function is crucially involved invokes a distinction between fast, automatic and unconscious processing (System 1) and slow, reflective decision-making that might call upon self-generated internal responses such as inner speech or visual imagery (System 2). Carruthers, like Leslie, believes that theory of mind (ToM) is an innate module, so the infant is capable of processing a situation involving a character's false belief using an innate System 1 module. However, in making decisions, other factors come into play, such as a pull towards reality responses (where is the cake?). The child develops (in System 2) enough resources to resist these competing impulses and arrive at a decision (pointing, talking, choosing an ending) based on the character's false belief, i.e. to consolidate the right answer generated by the early System 1 model. These resources include self-generated language. For Carruthers, the significant piece is the *control* rather than the *representational* function of language. However, this still does not account for the data from adult Nicaraguan signers with the non-complementation version of NSL, who surely have control functions but perhaps not yet representational sufficiency in their language.

In summation, the data on alternative ways of tapping false belief recognition are highly ambiguous. On the strong version of the language determinism thesis, no one should be able to *recognize* a false belief in another without an appropriate (and for us, linguistically based) representational system. But the measures of recognition that we have counted have entailed an explicit response: a choice, a decision, a prediction. It could be that recognition could be established at some fundamental, implicit level of 'expectancy' or 'surprise', but no further higher decision might be able to follow from it. An argument of this sort about infants' looking time has been made in other areas of cognitive development by Rachel Keen (2003). Much has been made in the past ten years of research on the conceptual capacities of infants of differences in looking time, with the concept being 'registered' by the infants not available to other means of assessment for months thereafter. Is looking time the *leading edge* of concept formation, or does the concept get built out of *lower-level stimulus expectancies* to which eye gaze is sensitive? Any time a decision must be made, however non-verbal, and however simple a response, it looks as if false beliefs are not 'understood' until later.

Yet the gap between infants' and pre-schoolers' false belief understanding is not *merely* a function of performance limitations based on e.g. working memory or inhibitory control skills, as our data on the deaf reveal. Some critics of the complement theory (e.g. Harris, 2005; Woolfe et al., 2002) argue that deaf children, like hearing children, have to acquire the complete theory of mind from the discourse in the culture, and it is lack of access to the appropriate *information* about the theory in language and conversation that slows the deaf child's success. For these theorists, language is primarily about conveying the theory, not about a representational system for thinking online. But hearing adults have it all: they have a fully developed concept of false belief, and they have the memory and inhibitory skills, so why do they apparently need to recruit the language faculty to reason about false beliefs in a non-verbal video task? And when they do, is it the representation or control functions of language that they need?

conclusion

Exploring the relationships between theory of mind and language development remains a vibrant area of research. From the perspective of the linguistic determinism thesis that we have proposed, a number of questions remain unresolved. To begin with, we are not sure if complementation is universal across all languages; and even if it is, we are not sure how many different paths the child can take to recognize it. We are not sure that verbs of communication can serve the same bootstrapping role in every language for the later understanding of mental state verbs. Indeed in some languages, verbs of communication may be all one has to express mental states. We have reason to doubt that the wh-test for complementation is the best index for representing the grammar of complements across languages, especially in languages with no wh-movement such as Chinese. And it is not clear whether the standard or even low-verbal false belief tasks tap 'pure' false belief recognition, or whether they involve extra task performance demands. In the end, we do not know if what we are seeing at 4 years of age is just a relation between explicit complement understanding and explicit false belief reasoning, with the real developmental action taking place much earlier in either or both domains. Moreover, even if all these debates were settled in favour of the claims we make, there are still methodological concerns to be addressed around appropriate measurements and statistical approaches for determining a contingency relationship between the variables, not just correlation. Finally, even if the finding of a contingency was proven beyond doubt, the story would still leave ample room for the role of maternal speech, discourse and mental verb learning to play significant roles in the preparation of the child for mental state understanding and reasoning.

The theory that the mastery of tensed complement clauses provides children with a new means of representation of the propositional contents of false beliefs has undergone considerable evolution since it was first proposed. It has motivated interesting ongoing cross-linguistic research (Tardif et al., 2007; Kyuchukov, 2006), important studies of special populations of children with language delay (e.g. deaf or SLI or autistic children (de Villiers et al., 2003; Peterson and Siegal, 1999; Schick et al., 2007; Tager-Flusberg and Joseph, 2005), and the development of innovative low- or non-verbal ways to measure false belief reasoning (Onishi and Baillargeon, 2005; Southgate et al., 2007). We hope that this process of evolution has led to a more precise account of the relationship between language and thought in general and language and theory of mind development in particular. But beauty remains in the eye of the beholder (or the parent).

references

Aksu-Koc, A., Avci, G., Aydin, C., Sefer, N. and Yasa, Y. (2005). The relation between mental verbs and ToM performance: evidence from Turkish children. Paper presented at the IASCL Convention, Berlin, July (2005).

Bickerton, D. (1984). The language bioprogram hypothesis. *Behavioral and Brain Sciences*, 7, 173–88.

Carlson, S. and Moses, L. (2001). Individual differences in inhibitory control and children's theory of mind. *Child Development*, 72, 1032–53.

Carruthers, P. (2007). An architecture for dual reasoning. In J. Evans and K. Frankish (eds), *In Two Minds: Dual Processes and Beyond*. Oxford: Oxford University Press.

Cheung, H. (2006). False belief and language comprehension in Cantonese-speaking children. *Journal of Experimental Child Psychology*, 9, 79–98.

Cheung, H., Hsuan-Chih, C., Creed, N., Ng, L., Ping Wang, S. and Mo, L. (2004). Relative roles of general and complementation language in theory-of-mind development: evidence from Cantonese and English'. *Child Development*, 75, 1155–70.

Chomsky, N. (1986). *Barriers*. Cambridge: MIT Press.

Chomsky, N. (2005). On phases. Unpublished paper, MIT. PDF available online at http://dmtr.ru/blog/omniling/.

Clements, W. and Perner, J. (1994). Implicit understanding of belief. *Cognitive Development*, 9, 377–95.

Collins, J. (2000). Theory of mind, logical form and eliminativism, *Philosophical Psychology,* 13, 465–90.

de Villiers, J. G. (1995). Steps in the mastery of sentence complements, Symposium paper, SRCD Convention, Indianapolis, March (1995).

de Villiers, J. G. (2001). Extension, intension and other minds. In M. Almgren, A. Barrens, M-J. Ezeizabarrena, I. Idiazabal and B. MacWhinney (eds) *Research in Child Language Acquisition: Proceedings of the 8th Conference of the IASCL*. Somerville, MA: Cascadilla Press.

de Villiers, J. G. (2005). Can language acquisition give children a point of view? In J. W. Astington and J. A. Baird (eds), *Why Language Matters for Theory of Mind*. Oxford: Oxford University Press.

de Villiers, J. G. (2007) The interface of language and theory of mind. *Lingua*, 117, 1858–78.

de Villiers, J. G. and de Villiers, P. A. (2000). Linguistic determinism and the understanding of false beliefs. In P. Mitchell and K. Riggs (eds) *Children's Reasoning and the Mind*. Hove: Psychology Press.

de Villiers, J. G., de Villiers, P. A. and Roeper, T. (in press). Wh-questions: Moving beyond the first phase. *Lingua*.

de Villiers, J. G. and Pyers, J. (1997). Complementing cognition: the relationship between language and theory of mind. In E. Hughes, M. Hughes and A. Greenhill (eds), *Proceedings of the 21st Annual Boston University Conference on Language Development*. Somerville, MA: Cascadilla Press.

de Villiers, J. G. and Pyers, J. (2002). Complements to cognition: a longitudinal study of the relationship between complex syntax and false-belief understanding. *Cognitive Development*, 17, 1037–60.

de Villiers, J. G., Roeper, T. and Vainikka, A. (1990). The acquisition of long distance rules. In L. Frazier and J. G. de Villiers (eds), *Language Processing and Acquisition*. Dordrecht: Kluwer.

de Villiers, J. G., Speas, P., Garfield, J. and Roeper, T. (2007). Preliminary studies of acquisition of Tibetan evidentials. Symposium paper, SRCD Convention, Boston, April (2007).

de Villiers, P. A. (2005). The role of language in theory-of-mind development: what deaf children tell us. In J. W. Astington and J. A. Baird (eds), *Why Language Matters for Theory of Mind*. Oxford: Oxford University Press.

de Villiers, P. A., Burns, F. and Pearson, B. Z. (2003). The role of language in the theory of mind development of language-impaired children: complementing theories. In B. Beachley, A. Brown and F. Conlin (eds), *Proceedings of the 27th Annual Boston University Conference on Language Development*. Somerville, MA: Cascadilla Press.

de Villiers, P. A. and Pyers, J. (2001). Complementation and false-belief representation. In M. Almgren, A. Barrens, M-J. Ezeizabarrena, I. Idiazabal and B. MacWhinney (eds), *Research in Child Language Acquisition: Proceedings of the 8th Conference of the IASCL*, Somerville, MA: Cascadilla Press.

de Villiers, P. A., Magaziner, K., Roman, W. and Sunderland, K. (2007). Dissociation of false belief reasoning, deception, executive functions and language in oral deaf children. Poster presentation, SRCD Convention, Boston, April (2007).

Dienes, Z. and Perner, J. (1999). A theory of implicit and explicit knowledge. *Behavioral and Brain Sciences*, 22, 735–808.

Evans, N. (2003). *Bininj Gun-wok: a Pan-Dialectal Grammar of Mayali, Kunwinjku and Kune*. Canberra: Pacific Linguistics.

Everett, D. (2005). Cultural constraints on grammar and cognition in Pirahã. *Current Anthropology*, 46, 621–46.

Felser, C. (1999). *Verbal Complement Clauses: A Minimalist Study of Direct Perception Constructions*. Amsterdam: John Benjamins.

Fisher, C., Gleitman, H. and Gleitman, L. R. (1991). On the semantic content of sub-categorization frames. *Cognitive Psychology*, 23, 331–92.

Fodor, J. (1975). *The Language of Thought*. New York: Harvester Press.

Fodor, J. (1992). A theory of the child's theory of mind. *Cognition*, 44, 283–96.

Gale, E., de Villiers, P. A., de Villiers, J. G. and Pyers, J. (1996). Language and theory of mind in oral deaf children. In A. Stringfellow, D. Cahana-Amitay, E. Hughes and A. Zukowski (eds), *Proceedings of the 20th Annual Boston University Conference on Language Development*. Somerville, MA: Cascadilla Press.

Gleitman, L. (1990). The structural sources of word meaning. *Language Acquisition*, 1, 3–55.

Hale, C. M. and Tager-Flusberg, H. (2003). The influence of language on theory of mind: a training study. *Developmental Science*, 6, 346–59.

Harris, P. (2005). Conversation, pretense, and theory of mind. In J. W. Astington and J. A. Baird (eds), *Why Language Matters for Theory of Mind*. Oxford: Oxford University Press.

Hollebrandse, B. and Roeper, T. (2007). Recursion and propositional exclusivity. Paper presented at conference, *Recursion in Human Languages*, Normal, Illinois, July, (2007).

Hollebrandse, B., Hobbs, K., de Villiers, J. G. and Roeper, T. (2007). Second order embedding and second order false belief. Paper presented at the GALA Conference, Barcelona, September, (2007).

Jensen de López, Kristine. (2005). The role of realis and irrealis complements in children's understanding of false-belief. Paper presented to the European Conference on Developmental Psychology, Tenerife, Spain.

Joshi, A. (2007). Does recursion in language work the same way as in formal systems? Paper presented at conference, *Recursion in Human Languages*. Normal, Illinois, July (2007).

Keen, R. (2003). Representation of objects and events: Why do infants look so smart and toddlers look so dumb? *Current Directions in Psychological Science*, 12, 79–83.

Kyuchukov, H. (2006). Evidentiality markers and ToM in bilingual Turkish-Bulgarian and Romani-Bulgarian speaking children. Colloquium presentation at Smith College, November (2006).

Leslie, A. M. (1994). Pretending and believing: issues in the theory of ToMM. *Cognition*, 50, 211–38.

Lohmann, H. and Tomasello, M. (2003). The role of language in the development of false belief understanding: a training Ssudy. *Child Development*, 74, 1130–44.

Moses, L. J. (2001). Executive accounts of theory of mind development. *Child Development*, 72, 688–90.

Nelson, K. (2005). Language pathways into the community of minds. In J. W. Astington and J. A. Baird (eds), *Why Language Matters for Theory of Mind*. Oxford: Oxford University Press.

Nevins, A., Pesetsky, D. and Rodrigues, C. (2007). Pirahã exceptionality: a reassessment, *LingBuzz/000411*.

Newton, A. and de Villiers, J. G. (2007). Thinking while talking: adults fail non-verbal false belief reasoning. *Psychological Science*, 18, 574–9.

Onishi, K. H. and Baillargeon, R. (2005). Do 15-month-old infants understand false beliefs? *Science*, 308, 255–8.

Perner, J. and Ruffman, T. (2005). Infants' insight into the mind: how deep? *Science*, 308, 214–16.

Perner, J., Sprung, M., Zauner, P. and Haider, H. (2003). *Want that* is understood well before *say that, think that,* and false belief: a test of de Villiers' linguistic determinism on German-speaking children. *Child Development*, 74, 179–88.

Peterson, C. C. and Siegal, M. (1999). Representing inner worlds: theory of mind in autistic, deaf and normal-hearing children. *Psychological Science*, 10, 126–9.

Povinelli, D. and Vonk, J. (2004). We don't need a microscope to explore the chimpanzee's mind. *Mind and Language*, 19, 1–28.

Pyers, J. (2004). The relationship between language and false-belief understanding: evidence from learners of an emerging sign language in Nicaragua. Doctoral dissertation, University of California, Berkeley.

Roeper, T. (2007). *The Prism of Grammar*. Cambridge, MA: MIT Press.

Ruffman, T., Slade, L., Rowlandson, K., Rumsey, C. and Garnham, A. (2003). How language relates to belief, desire, and emotion understanding. *Cognitive Development*, 18, 139–58.

Schick, B., de Villiers, P. A., de Villiers, J. G. and Hoffmeister, R. (2007). Language and theory of mind: a study of deaf children. *Child Development*, 78, 376–96.

Segal, G. (1998). Representing representations. In P. Carruthers and J. Boucher (eds), *Language and Thought*. Cambridge: Cambridge University Press.

Southgate, V. Senju, A. and Csibra, G. (2007). Action anticipation though attribution of false belief by 2-year-olds. *Psychological Science*, 18, 587–92.

Tager-Flusberg, H. and Joseph, R. (2005). How language facilitates the acquisition of false belief in children with autism. In J. W. Astington and J. A. Baird (eds), *Why Language Matters for Theory of Mind*. Oxford: Oxford University Press.

Tardif, T., So, C. and Kaciroti, N. (2007). Language and false belief: evidence for general, not specific, effects in Cantonese-speaking preschoolers. *Developmental Psychology*, 43, 318–40.

Varley, R. and Siegal, M. (2000). Evidence for cognition without grammar from causal reasoning and 'Theory of Mind' in an agrammatical aphasic patient. *Current Biology*, 10, 723–6.

Varley, R., Siegal, M. and Want, S. C. (2000). Severe impairment in grammar does not preclude theory of mind. *Neurocase*, 7, 489–93.

Wierzbicka, A. (1992). *Semantics, Culture and Cognition: Universal Human Concepts in Culture-Specific Configurations*. Oxford: Oxford University Press.

Wierzbicka, A. (2005a). Commentary on Everett, *Current Anthropology*, 46, 641.

Woolfe, T., Want, S. and Siegal, M. (2002). Signposts to development: theory of mind in deaf children. *Child Development*, 73, 768–78.

8
going beyond semantics:
the development of pragmatic enrichment

nausicaa pouscoulous and ira a. noveck

introduction

While the literal meanings of *or*, *and* and *some* are comparable to those found in classical logic (e.g. P *or* Q is inclusive and thus compatible with P *and* Q), each of these expressions is readily understood as having a richer meaning in context (e.g. the offer of 'coffee or tea' implies *not both*). The challenge for linguists, philosophers and psycholinguists has been to reconcile the two apparent meanings. While the difference between classical and everyday interpretations of logical terms could be viewed as a case of semantic ambiguity (e.g. by saying that *or* is ambiguous between the exclusive (A or B, but not both) and inclusive meanings (A or B including the possibility of A and B), philosopher Paul Grice insisted that, whenever possible, words and expressions should rather be assigned a single meaning (or at least as few senses as possible) (Grice, 1978/1989, p. 47). He thus proposed that part of the information conveyed through our utterances is not linguistically encoded, but pragmatically derived. For instance, the semantic meaning of connectives (such as *or*) and quantifiers (such as *some*) is separated from the pragmatic component which Grice termed *conversational implicatures*. His approach thus allows many expressions whose meaning varies from context to context to have a single core meaning, which may be enriched at the pragmatic level by context-dependent assumptions (i.e. conversational implicatures).

Although Grice's distinction between core linguistic and pragmatically derived meaning has been the topic of discussion among philosophers and linguists for several decades, it is only recently that his claims have been tested experimentally with children and adults. Here, we aim to show precisely how developmental studies support the pragmatic analyses of logical terms that Grice suggested. We begin by summarizing the developmental findings that have been critical in establishing the semantic-cum-pragmatic meanings of logical terms and in demonstrating just how general this Grice-inspired effect is. We then turn to data that show how pragmatic enrichments of logical terms (so-called *scalar implicatures*) can be encouraged among young children and suggest that children are more likely than adults to interpret terms literally rather than pragmatically. In order to show that this particular developmental trend is not limited to scalar implicatures, we then focus on another type of pragmatic enrichment: one linked to the conjunction *and*. Finally, we contrast the developmental trajectory linked to the pragmatic enrichments of logical terms with data on a genuine case of ambiguity (*All are not* sentences). We show that the latter produces a very different developmental profile, further demonstrating the uniqueness of the developmental trend associated with cases that rely on pragmatic enrichments of logical terms.

weak logical terms

Experimental studies of conversational implicatures have focused mostly on a paradigmatic case, known as scalar implicatures. An example illustrating this phenomenon is presented in (1) wherein a speaker uttering (1a) will typically be taken by the hearer to imply (1c).

(1)   (a) Some of the guests have arrived.
        (b) All of the guests have arrived.
        (c) Not all of the guests have arrived.

Under a Gricean analysis, the implication in (1c) would be seen as a conversational implicature. The reasoning is as follows: proposition (1b) is more informative than (1a) which it entails. Presumably, the more informative proposition would make a greater contribution to the common purpose of the conversation. Thus, when the speaker uses a weak term (e.g. *some*), the hearer thereby understands that she has reasons not to use a stronger one (i.e. *all*). Therefore, if someone says, 'Some of the guests have arrived', the hearer is entitled to infer that not all guests have arrived. The idea is that the hearer assumes that the speaker abides by Grice's (1975/1989) first sub-maxim of quantity ('Make your contribution as informative as is required'), at least so long as she can honour the second sub-maxim of quality as well ('Do not say that for which you lack adequate evidence'). Therefore, presumably, she either does not know whether (1b) is true or she knows that it is not.

Neo-Gricean researchers (e.g. Horn, 1972, 1989) have put forward slightly different analyses of effects such as that shown in (1) based on the notion of semantic scales. Semantic scales are a set of alternate terms or expressions of the same grammatical category ranked by order of informativeness from weaker to stronger; e.g. <or, and>, <possible, certain> and <some, all>. The use of a weaker term from one of these scales will tend to result in an implicature to the effect that the speaker is not in a position to use the stronger expression, either because she does not know whether her utterance would then still be true, or because she knows that it would be false. Similar accounts can be given for the everyday interpretation of utterances such as those in (2):

(2)   (a) Molly is going to be picked up by Mommy or Daddy (not *both* of
          them)
      (b) Steven might be home (it is not true that he *must* be there)
      (c) Yogi started to paint his house (he did *not finish*)

More recently, Noveck and Sperber (2007), working within the Relevance Theory paradigm (which is also inspired by Grice's work), put forward an alternative analysis of the phenomenon. Specifically, they have suggested that what are called 'scalar implicatures' do not, in fact, form a natural category. Rather, they maintain that the so-called scalar inferences are not specific to the highlighted terms and need not involve lexical or pragmatic scales. In addition, they have argued that 'scalar implicatures' should be divided into two distinct groups: scalar explicatures and true scalar implicatures.

Scalar explicatures are inferences that result from pragmatic adjustments to what is explicitly communicated by an utterance. This is where the hearer's expectations of relevance in a given context cause the *denotation* of the scalar term to be narrowed. Under this analysis, the inferences in (1c), and (2a–c) are:

> just ordinary illustrations of the fact that linguistic expressions serve to indicate rather than encode the speaker's meaning and that the speaker's meanings are quite often a narrowing down or broadening of the linguistic meaning. Taking 'some' to indicate not *at least two and possibly all* but *at least two and fewer than all* is a common narrowing down of the literal meaning of 'some' at the level of the *explicature* of the utterance. (Noveck and Sperber, 2007, p. 193)

Genuine scalar implicatures on the other hand are much less frequent than is generally assumed (and much less frequent than the kind of narrowing mentioned above) and will only be computed if there is a mutually manifest reason for the interlocutors to wonder about the more informative expression. Imagine for instance that Mary is about to offer several balloons to a neighbour's child after a party and Bill asks, 'Are those all of the balloons?' If Mary answers, 'These are some of them', Bill would be entitled to draw from this utterance the implicature that *these are not all the balloons* since Mary is answering a tacit question concerning all of the balloons and she does not provide an exhaustive response. In these cases, and in this sort of case only, the use of a scalar term will be taken to implicate the negation of a stronger one in the fashion of genuine scalar implicatures.

At the heart of a Relevance Theoretic approach is that both explicatures and implicatures (scalar or otherwise) are the result of highly context-dependent inferential processes guided by expectations of optimal relevance on the hearer's part. They take place 'when the consequences that render the utterance relevant as expected are characteristically carried by this narrowed down meaning' (Noveck and Sperber, 2007, p. 193). Therefore, the two types of scalar cases are very similar in psychological terms: crucially, they both proceed from highly context-dependent inferential processes. Like all other pragmatic inferences, those linked to scalar expressions are made by the hearer in order to meet contextually defined expectations of relevance.

Gricean and post-Gricean approaches (e.g. Sperber and Wilson, 1986/1995; but also Horn, 1989 and Levinson, 2000) all recognize the distinction between the literal meaning of terms and the various enrichments that they can offer. Although these authors do not make predictions as to how children fare with scalar implicatures, it seems plausible to hypothesize that within Relevance Theory as well as Grice's and Horn's frameworks (but not Levinson's) children should encounter more difficulty than adults when pragmatic enrichments are potentially called for. (For a discussion of the various theoretical analyses of scalar phenomena and their psychological implications, see Pouscoulous, 2006.)

experimental findings on scalar terms

Experimental work to date has focused on children's interpretation of so-called scalar expressions like *some* and *or*. This work has brought to light a developmental trend that at first seemed surprising, because it showed that children are more likely than adults to treat the weak term (e.g. *some*) as compatible with one that is stronger on the scale (*all*). The second author was in fact the first to conduct systematic experiments on children's treatment of scalar expressions; he showed that 8–10-year-olds do not make scalar inferences associated with *some* and *might* to the same degree as adults (Noveck, 2001). These results were supported at the time by classic studies that inadvertently included scalar expressions (Paris, 1973; Smith, 1980; Braine and Rumain, 1981) as well as by more recent studies that specifically aimed to replicate Noveck's effect (e.g. Chierchia et al., 2004; Guasti et al., 2005; Papafragou and Musolino, 2003). (For a review of experimental work on the acquisition of scalar terms see also Noveck, 2004; Pouscoulous and Noveck, 2004; and Siegal and Surian, 2004.)

a surprising developmental effect

Noveck's (2001) study of children's understanding of scalar expressions began by examining the inference generally associated with *might* – which excludes *must*. The experiment involved presenting children with three boxes; the first one contained a toy bear and a toy parrot, the second one had only a toy parrot while the content of the third one, which remained covered, was hidden from view. The child was told that the content of the third box was identical either to that of the first box or to that of the second box. The participant's task was to decide whether a puppet was right or wrong when it uttered the (critical) item: 'There *might* be a parrot in the box'. Clearly, in this context, the sentence 'There *must* be a parrot in the box' is more appropriate than 'There *might* be a parrot in the box'. Children answering 'correct' to '*might* be a parrot' were assumed to be interpreting the modal *might* as compatible with *must* – i.e. with its classical logical sense – and not to be making the pragmatic inference that prompts *might* to exclude *must*. Children who think the puppet is wrong in saying, 'There *might* be a parrot in the box', were seen as adopting a pragmatic interpretation of *might* (i.e. not *must*). The results with children aged 7 to 9 years old, shown in Figure 8.1, suggested that they gave the narrower 'logical' answers 80 per cent of the time. Adults, on the other hand, gave this answer only 35 per cent of the time, suggesting that children do not make the scalar inference associated with *might* to the same degree as adults. (Importantly, the children and adults responded correctly at high rates to the seven control items which demanded both true (e.g. 'There must be a parrot in the box') and false (e.g. 'There must be a bear in the box') responses.)

Another experiment, based on Smith (1980), explored the inference provoked by *some* (i.e. *but not all*). The critical items were of the form: 'Some elephants have trunks' or 'Some giraffes have long necks': this

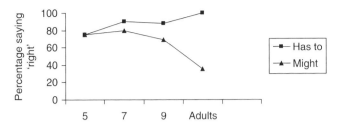

Figure 8.1 How participants respond to the utterance 'There has to be a parrot in the box' vs. 'There might be a parrot in the box' when the context determines that indeed there must be a parrot in the box

sentence is logically true, but it is pragmatically underinformative because we know that *'all* elephants have trunks' and *'all* giraffes have long necks'. Children (8- and 10-year-olds) had to say if these sentences were true or false. Most children who answered almost perfectly to the control questions (true quantified sentences, false quantified sentences, and absurd ones such as 'All crows have radios') accepted the pragmatically underinformative utterances (at rates of 89 per cent and 85 per cent, respectively), while adults tended to reject them as false (41 per cent accepted these as true). (See Noveck, 2001 for details.)

Unlike adults, children accept (rather than reject) utterances expressed with relatively weak terms (e.g. *might, some*) when a stronger one (*must, all*) is called for, and thus appear to be more (classically) logical than adults. But we must now ask how generalizable these results are to other scalar expressions and whether perhaps children are simply unable to draw pragmatic inferences in general.

developmental impediments in understanding scalar inferences?

Other developmental studies have extended our understanding of the developments described above. Noveck's (2001) findings have been generalized, with 5-year-old subjects, to other scalar expressions, such as *start* (not *finish*) and numerals (Papafragou and Musolino, 2003), as well as *or* (not *and*) (Chierchia et al., 2004). In all these experiments, the great majority of children accepted the weaker term as compatible with a stronger one, whereas adults would either consider them to be incompatible or at the very least equivocal.

Importantly, these researchers have found that, as it was hypothesized by Noveck (2001), when the circumstances are right, children are able to make appropriate pragmatic inferences. So their poor performance with scalar inferences is not due to semantic or pragmatic inability. In one set of studies, Papafragou and colleagues (Papafragou and

Musolino, 2003; see also Papafragou and Tantalou, 2004) showed that children as young as 5 are able to produce scalar inferences given the right conditions. In a first experiment, Papafragou and Musolino (2003), found, as indicated above, that 5-year-olds are less likely than adults to produce implicatures with *some*, *start* and number words. In a second experiment, they then went on to modify their experimental setup in two ways. First, children received training enhancing their awareness of pragmatic anomalies before they were tested. They were told that the puppet would say 'silly things' and that the point of the game was to help the puppet 'say it better' (e.g. they would be asked whether a puppet described a dog appropriately by saying 'This is a little animal with four legs'). In the event that the child did not correct the puppet, the experimenter did. Secondly, the modified paradigm put the focal point on a protagonist's performance. Unlike the original experiment, where children had been asked to evaluate a quantified sentence such as *Some horses jumped over the fence* (when in fact all the horses did), the modified paradigm raised children's expectations about the stronger case (*all*). Participants heard test sentences such as, 'Mickey put some of the hoops around the pole' (after having been shown to succeed with all of the hoops), but they were also previously told how Mickey claimed to be especially good at this task which is why another character challenged him to get all three around the pole. With these changes (training and a focus on a stronger contrast), 5-year-olds appeared more likely to produce scalar inferences than in the first experiment, though they still produced them less often than adults.

Guasti et al. (2005) took the investigation a step further. In a series of experiments on the understanding of *some* by 7-year-olds they first replicated Noveck's (2001) results with respect to the underinformative sentences such as *Some elephants have trunks*, and then used this as a baseline to tease apart the role of the two factors manipulated by Papafragou and Musolino (2003). First, they examined the role of training and found that training young participants to give the most specific description of a given situation did indeed have a major effect on their performances. While in the baseline experiment 7-year-olds rejected statements such as 'Some giraffes have long necks' only 12 per cent of the time (against 50 per cent for adults), when trained their rejection rate went up to 52 per cent, i.e. it matched the adult responses. Interestingly, however, this effect was short-lived and was not found when the same participants were tested a week later.

In their last experiment, Guasti et al. (2005) also tested whether the salience of the scalar inference influenced the interpretation of *some*.

They rendered the *all*-alternative more salient in context, for instance, by showing the participants a story featuring several characters deciding whether the best way to collect a treasure was to drive a motorbike or ride a horse. After some discussion, the scenario revealed that all of them chose to ride a horse. In this way it was made clearer that the sentence to be evaluated, 'Some of the characters chose to ride a horse', is underinformative. The results indicated that when the outcome of scalar inferences is highly relevant in context, children will compute them in an adult-like manner, at least by the age of 7.

To summarize, the evidence suggests that children's natural tendency is to interpret scalar expressions in context semantically, while adults are either equivocal between a semantic understanding and a pragmatic one, or prefer the pragmatic reading. However, when the contrast between the weak scalar term and a more informative one is made salient in context, children become more adult-like (Papafragou and Musolino, 2003; Guasti et al., 2005), suggesting that despite their semantic preferences, they do have the appropriate pragmatic capacity.

the effect of complexity on children's performance

There is evidence that even for adults scalar inferences involve additional processing costs (Noveck and Posada, 2003; Bott and Noveck, 2004; Breheny et al., 2006). Noveck (2001) and Guasti et al. (2005) therefore suggested that a plausible explanation for children's reluctance to interpret scalar inferences as adults do is that their cognitive resources have not yet reached the adult level. Pouscoulous et al. (2007) investigated this possibility by manipulating three complexity factors: the presence/absence of distractor items, the nature of the task (truth evaluation versus a novel manipulation task) and the choice of scalar expression (the existential French quantifiers *quelques* versus *certains*).

First, 9-year-olds were tested on the French equivalent of *some/all* (*certains/tous*) using four cardboard boxes placed in front of the children with different plastic animals displayed in and around the boxes. The main test item was 'Some turtles are in the boxes' when the scenario revealed that there was a turtle in each of the boxes. The 9-year-olds responded affirmatively 91 per cent of the time and adults 53 per cent to the test items. We thus reproduced the effect from earlier experiments using the standard truth-evaluation task with a weak quantifier *certains,* arbitrary materials, and plenty of distractor items (e.g. a statement such as 'There is a hippopotamus and a dolphin in the same box').

In the next experiment three changes were made to the above design. First, distractors were removed, i.e. only key and control items were kept. Second, the task was modified so that children's responses were determined by an action in response to a puppet's wish. For the critical underinformative item, participants were shown a set of five boxes each containing a token before hearing 'I would like some boxes to contain a token'. In this scenario, *inaction* (which is hard to do) would indicate accepting the statement as true with a minimal semantics whereas an action (removing a token or two) would indicate that the participant pragmatically enriched the statement. Finally, the French indefinite *certains* (meaning *some*) which was used in the first experiment was replaced by a simpler expression, *quelques*. The quantifier *quelques* is a more frequent word than *certains*, is more frequently used by younger children and it also seems to be semantically simpler than *certains* (i.e. *quelques* is a simple existential while *certains* is a partitive – for a detailed explanation see Pouscoulous et al., 2007). In order to establish whether the development of the inferencing in this case increases progressively with age, children of three age groups (4-, 5- and 7-year-olds) as well as adults were tested with this modified setup. The results are shown in Table 8.1.

The results reveal a dramatic increase in pragmatic responses among all participants, with children as young as 4 years of age successfully deriving implicatures, suggesting that when the paradigm is designed to reduce cognitive effort, it succeeds in affecting participants' responses. As the table shows, 4-, 5- and 7-year olds and adults make an action in response to the wish in 68 per cent, 73 per cent, 83 per cent and 86 per cent of the cases, respectively. Importantly, the data show that younger children (4- and 5-year-olds) can draw scalar implicatures spontaneously, i.e. without previous training (such as that used in Papafragou and Musolino, 2003). It is still the case, however, that even in a task which strongly encourages implicatures to be drawn, younger children are less likely to draw them, suggesting a developmental impact of cognitive processing.

experimental findings and pragmatic theories

The picture of children's understanding of scalar inferences sketched above suggests three conclusions. First, the literal, semantic meaning of scalar terms generally suffices for children, even in utterances where adults would generally draw the inference (at least to some extent), indicating that this reading is primary. Second, there is no threshold in the development of children's capacity to make scalar inferences: their

Table 8.1 Percentage of participants in Experiment 2 who provide logical responses with respect to each of the three different scenarios

	Age	N	Subset scenario ■□□■□	All scenario ■■■■■	None scenario □□□□□
All utterance: I would like all the boxes to contain a token	4	66	(LR: Change)	(LR: Keep as is)	(LR: Change)
	5	30	95	97	100
	7	54	100	97	100
	A	21	100	100	100
			100	100	100
Some utterance: I would like some boxes to contain a token	4		(LR: Keep as is)	(LR: Keep as is)	(LR: Change)
	5		64 (100)§	**32**	100
	7		67 (100)	**27**	100
	A		89 (100)	**17**	100
			80 (100)	**14**	100
None utterance: I would like no box to contain a token	4		(LR: Change)	(LR: Change)	(LR: Keep as is)
	5		78	69	64
	7		80	90	97
	A		94	98	98
			100	100	100
Some are not Utterance: I would like some boxes to not contain a token	4		(LR: Keep as is)	(LR: Change)	(LR: Keep as is)
	5		65 (100)*	64	41
	7		70 (100)	90	30
	A		91 (100)	98	41
			95 (100)	95	14

Notes: A black box indicates that there is a token. LR means Logical Response. § The values for the 'keep as is' response in the Subset condition are interpreted strictly; even harmless changes (e.g. adding a token to a box) are considered violations. However, the values in parentheses show the 'keep as is' responses when taken to mean 'keep the truth value the same'.

performances are not linked to specific ages, rather they depend on the relevance of the semantic expression in context, the effort required by the task, and probably the accessibility for them of the scalar expression in a given language; in fact, Pouscoulous et al. (2007, Experiment 3) reveal how pragmatic inferencing is more likely with *quelques* rather than *certains*). Third, young children before the age of 7 do not carry out scalar inferences with ease, i.e. younger (4- to 5-year-old) children have greater difficulty carrying out pragmatic enrichments than adults and have never been shown to do it at the same rate as their older cohorts.

These findings demonstrate the psychological reality of scalar inferences, as well as supporting specific pragmatic accounts of scalar terms over alternatives. Although, strictly speaking, the developmental findings reported here may be compatible with most pragmatic frameworks (Levinson's, 2000, and Chierchia's, 2004, being possible exceptions), Relevance Theory (Carston, 1998; Carston, 2002; Sperber and Wilson, 1986/1995; Wilson and Sperber, 2004) has certain explanatory advantages. In Relevance Theory, scalar implicatures are ordinary pragmatic inferences drawn by hearers in order to arrive at an interpretation of an utterance that meets their expectations of relevance. A non-enriched interpretation of a scalar term (the one that more closely coincides with the word's lexical meaning) will often suffice as a relevant-enough interpretation of the utterance in which it occurs, and in these cases no extra inferences are necessary. A scalar inference may be drawn by a hearer in an effort to make an utterance more informative and thus more relevant. How far the hearer goes in construing the utterance's interpretation is governed by considerations of effect and effort; hearers expect the intended interpretation to provide satisfactory effects for minimal effort. While a scalar implicature makes the utterance more informative, it will typically involve extra effort (for more discussion, see Bott and Noveck, 2004; Noveck, 2004).

The advantage of the Relevance Theory approach is that it predicts that implicature production should appear more readily when: a) its effects in contexts are greater, and b) when the effort required to derive them is not too strenuous (and this should be particularly true for children whose cognitive resources are not at adult levels). This, of course, is exactly what the data suggest. On one hand, studies such as Papafragou and Musolino (2003, Experiment 2) and Guasti et al. (2005, Experiment 4) demonstrate that children are more likely to draw scalar inferences when the given semantic scale is made highly relevant in context – i.e. when the expected effects of pragmatic enrichment are greater. On the other hand, the work reported in Pouscoulous et al. (2007) indicates that complexity is an important factor in the understanding of scalar terms – that is to say that effort plays a crucial role.

the case of conjunctions

Consider (3) below:

   (3)   (a) Mary got married and got pregnant.
          (b) Mary got pregnant and got married.

Whereas (3a) expresses a relatively standard series of events, (3b) can raise eyebrows in places where the order in (3a) is traditionally observed.

The implicit enrichment of both utterances, which is linked to the way the conjunction *and* is interpreted in each utterance (e.g. from *and* to *and then* or to *and thus*) make the two sentences seem rather different. This comparison highlights the contribution of pragmatics to sentence meaning. Without such enrichments the two utterances would be equivalent. In fact, logically speaking, they are.

An investigation into the pragmatic enrichment of *and* is an ideal complement to the studies on scalar expressions for two reasons. First, if one can find evidence showing that this sort of enrichment develops with age, it would show that the robust findings linked to scalar terms are just one example of linguistic-pragmatic development and that, in this respect at least, scalar inferences have no specific status among pragmatic phenomena. Second, early work on the conjunctions *before* and *after* (Clark, 1971) leave the impression that young children do not fully integrate conjunctions into their sentence processing and are rather sensitive to order-of-mention. For example, Clark found that 45 per cent of 5-year-olds act out kicking before patting despite having heard the sentence 'The boy kicked the rock after he patted the dog'. This would imply that children would readily reject a sentence as false when it presents two events in an order that is opposite to what was just read or heard.

We can now ask whether one will find children behaving differently with respect to the enrichment of *and* and in a way we saw with scalar terms. Initial experiments with *and* suggest that enrichments of sentences do indeed produce a developmental effect akin to scalars. An exploratory study (Noveck and Chevaux, 2002) presented 7-year-olds, 10-year-olds and adults with a small set of four very short stories (among fillers), each followed by a conjunctive comprehension question. For two of the comprehension questions, the order of its two conjuncts respected the sequence of events in the story and for the other two the conjuncts were inverted. For example, one story described a girl, Julie, who had answered a phone call in the second sentence and accepted an invitation to a birthday party in the fifth. Participants were then required to respond *Yes* or *No* to one of two kinds of follow-up questions:

(4) (a) Julie answered the phone and accepted an invitation?
      (b) Julie accepted an invitation and answered the phone?

Agreeing with (4b) indicates that the participant accepted the minimal meaning of the conjunctive sentence (that both conjuncts are simply true). Rejecting (4b) would indicate that the sentence was enriched, making the order of the two conjuncts relevant. Whereas the rates of agreement to (4a) were high and accurate for all participants, the authors found that 85 per cent of 7-year olds, 63 per cent of 10-year-olds and 29 per cent of the adults respond affirmatively to (4b). The adults' rates of affirmation were lower than those produced by the children while also defying chance predictions. The children were evidently less fussy than adults about the conjuncts' sequence. That 10-year-olds respond affirmatively to questions like the one in (4b) after having read (and while still having available) the story is impressive, indicating that they do not readily enrich such sentences.

In follow-up work, Noveck et al. (in press) are using reading times to further explore the cognitive impact of enrichment on interpretation. Results suggest that adults, as predicted, are more likely to reject inverted sentences like those in 4b (82 per cent of adults reject while only 56 per cent of 10-year-olds do). More interestingly, inverted sentences judged as true among the 10-year-olds are read significantly faster than inverted sentences judged as false. This is an indication that the enrichment is part of a time consuming process (see also Bott and Noveck, 2004).

Again Relevance Theory seems to provide a natural interpretation of the data: the minimal, linguistically encoded meanings of utterances containing *and* form the basis from which they are pragmatically enriched. Moreover, in this framework, sequential ordering of actions is only one possibility for enrichment of *and*. Carston (1993, 2002, pp. 223–4) provides the following as other examples:

(5)   (a)   Contrast: It's autumn in the US and it's spring in Chile.
            (b)   *Sequential*: She took the scalpel and made the incision.
            (c)   *Containment*: We spent the day in town and went to Macy's.
            (d)   *Causal*: She shot him in the head and he died instantly.

Thus Relevance Theory does not privilege sequential interpretations as enrichment. It also leaves open the possibility that a sentence could be perfectly meaningful without any enrichment. Finally, Relevance Theory makes no principled distinction between scalar inferences and pragmatic enrichments of *and*: both are examples of a listener's best efforts to make a speaker's utterance more informative (see Noveck and Sperber, 2007). The developmental story for both types of expression is that children are generally more likely than adults to accept the minimal, linguistically encoded meaning of *and*, while adults more consistently apply pragmatic enrichments. This suggests that developmental-pragmatic effect, associated with scalar terms, is generalizable to other pragmatic enrichments and that it is even more robust than previously imagined.

Indeed, some studies on metaphor suggest that the developmental patterns linked to it are akin to the patterns for the pragmatic enrichment of logical terms (see for instance Noveck et al., 2001; Winer et al., 2001). The comprehension of a word in its metaphoric sense requires an enrichment of the encyclopaedic entry of a critical term (i.e. from its literal meaning to its metaphorical meaning) (Wilson and Carston, 2007). In these cases, as for scalar inferences and the enrichment of *and*, sophisticated listeners, unlike unsophisticated ones, have the resources available to derive figurative meanings, thus suggesting that pragmatic enrichments of all sorts are not available for free.

a genuine case of ambiguity: *every ... not* sentences

Throughout this chapter, we have argued that instead of interpreting scalar terms and conjunctions as ambiguous, pragmatic theories (Grice's, neo-Gricean and Relevance Theory) provide motivation for the maintenance of a single core semantic meaning that is pragmatically enriched in context. This does not mean, however, that there is no such thing as ambiguous quantifier expressions. We turn to the case of *Every ... not* as exemplified in (7a) below:

(7)   (a) Every horse did not jump over the fence.
      (b) Not every horse jumped over the fence.
      (c) All horses are such that they did not jump over the fence.

Utterances such as (7a) can have two interpretations. When the negation takes scope over the quantifier (*Not > every*), one arrives at the interpretation in (7b) and when the quantifier takes scope over the negation (*Every ... not* or *None*) one arrives at the interpretation in (7c).

Musolino et al. (2000) reported that adults are more likely than children to accept the *Not every* interpretation, as in (7b), after being shown two of three horses jumping over a fence. Children, on the other hand, demonstrate ambiguity between the two readings (Musolino and Lidz, 2006) or a preference for a *None* reading, as in (7c) (Musolino et al., 2000). After several follow-up investigations, Musolino and Lidz (2003, 2006; Lidz and Musolino 2002) currently hypothesize that *Every ... not* sentences are syntactically ambiguous but that either performance factors play a role among children (Musolino and Lidz, 2006) or that scope relations favour a *None* reading among children (Musolino et al., 2000). That is, children either base their judgements on one of the two possible readings (chosen at random) or there are reasons (based on contextual factors or parsing mechanisms) that encourage a *None* reading. As Musolino and Lidz (2006) point out, the findings and suggestions from the papers on *Every ... not* sentences resonate with the work showing that young children are less likely than adults to produce scalar implicatures. Given that adults often prefer *Not every* interpretations in the same tasks where children tend to resist these makes them relevant to the current discussion.

To further explore these effects, Noveck et al. (2007) also investigated sentences like (7a). Their work aimed to replicate Musolino et al.'s results with 4-year-olds and adults while including verbally competent teenagers on the autistic spectrum. Syntactic skills among verbally competent participants on the autistic spectrum are assumed to be unimpaired while their pragmatic difficulties have been well documented. The experiment examines the way three different groups – 4-year-olds, teenagers on the autistic spectrum as well as adults – interpret a critical experimental item, as exemplified by (8):

(8)   All the children are not in the pool.

Participants were presented with stories in which ultimately 2-of-3 protagonists were shown doing something or in which 2-of-3 objects shared a feature (e.g. see Table 8.2). For example, in a story concerning the sentence above, the critical test sentence was presented in a context in which two of three children are in the pool (while a control item would present a scenario that ends with all three in the pool). If participants adopt the *None* reading, they ought to respond negatively, while if they adopt the *Not every* reading, they ought to respond positively. Given that the sentence is ambiguous, one would expect children and autistic participants to prefer either (a) the initial parse (the *None* reading), or else (b) to show evidence of being equivocal about the two interpretations. In any case, based on prior findings, one should expect typical adults to prefer the *Not every* reading, which leads to a true response in this context.

The results show an adult preference for the *Not every* reading in 2-of-3 contexts and equivocality among children and participants on the autistic spectrum. This is in line with the expectation that syntax makes the two readings equally available and that adults, unlike young children and autistic participants, are efficient at exploiting the context (i.e.

Table 8.2   Percentage of correct responses (correct response in parentheses) as a function of the quantified statements (QN and QP) and context (2-of-3 and 3-of-3)

Statement	Presentation condition	
	2-of-3	3-of-3
Children		
QN: All the children are not in the pool.	40%* (true)	81% (false)
QP: All the children are in the pool.	95% (false)	89% (true)
Teenagers on autistic spectrum		
QN: All the children are not in the pool.	47%* (true)	82% (false)
QP: All the children are in the pool.	93% (false)	87% (true)
Adults		
QN: All the children are not in the pool.	88%* (true)	93% (false)
QP: All the children are in the pool.	100% (false)	90% (true)

Notes: *For the sake of simplicity, this ambiguous item is considered 'correct' if participants treat it as 'not every'. It would be true with a *Not* > *every* reading (*Not all the children are in the pool*) and false with an *Every* > *not* reading (*None of the children are in the pool*).

pragmatic features) in order to come up with a single consistent reading. Although further studies are necessary to determine which pragmatic explanation best accounts for these sorts of data, it is clear that ambiguous structures do not produce the same sort of developmental profile as scalar terms or conjunction.

Although ambiguity and enrichment are both context-dependent phenomena, they also differ from each other, which is why linguistic theories distinguish between them and, arguably, why they yield different developmental profiles. In the case of ambiguous sentences, linguistic *decoding* – whether it be semantic or syntactic (as in the *every*-sentences discussed above) – gives rise to two interpretations. The context plays a crucial role in choosing the one that corresponds with the speaker's meaning. This is a mandatory process since, if one is not in the position to choose, the utterance cannot be properly understood. Additionally, there is no reason to assume *a priori*, that one interpretation is cognitively more costly than the other; one way or another the hearer must decide between the two possibilities and this is going to involve some amount of pragmatic inferencing.

In the case of pragmatic enrichment (whether linked to a scalar term, *and* or of another type), the form delivered by linguistic decoding is unambiguous (it is a single form) and sufficient for arriving at an interpretation. This form may, but need not, be enriched depending on the context. Furthermore, context also determines the *nature* of the enrichment; for instance, the conjunction 'and' can be interpreted as *and then* or *and thus*. In the case of ambiguity, processing is devoted to determining a valid interpretation. In the absence of a preference, the children (and the participants on the autistic spectrum) are left nonplussed. The difference between pragmatic enrichment and efforts at disambiguation is reflected in the developmental data we have presented. These theoretical distinctions are corroborated by the sharp contrast between response patterns elicited in on-line experiments by scalar expressions (e.g. Bott and Noveck, 2004; Breheny et al., 2006) and semantically ambiguous terms. (On the processing of ambiguous words, see Swinney, 1979; for more recent studies see for instance Kambe et al., 2001 and Swaab et al., 2003.) It is therefore not surprising that the developmental profile for ambiguous structures is distinct from developmental patterns that engage pragmatic enrichments of logical terms.

conclusions

It is now well established that, to begin with, children have problems making scalar inferences, which are often linked to the interpretation of logical terms such as *some*, *or* and *might*. There is no critical threshold such that children would start making scalar inferences at a certain age, although, as a group, children do not show adult-like behaviour in this respect before the age of seven. Rather, development appears to be gradual, and children's performance is linked to the effort required by the experimental task and to the relevance of narrowed-down meanings in context. Young children are not incapable of drawing what are currently called scalar inferences; they merely find it more difficult. Results reminiscent of the developmental trend linked to scalar expressions have also been found with another type of pragmatic inference: the enrichment of *and*. These data suggest that the semantic meanings of logical terms are the first to be accessible and that the pragmatic ability of drawing the relevant inferences develops later. Nonetheless, these findings contrast sharply with the developmental pattern observed for genuine cases of ambiguity, pointing to the specificity of the pragmatic processing and its development.

references

Bott, L. and Noveck, I. A. (2004). Some utterances are underinformative: the onset and time course of scalar inferences. *Journal of Memory and Language,* 51: 3, 437–57.

Braine, M. and Rumain B. (1981). Children's comprehension of 'or': evidence for a sequence of competencies. *Journal of Experimental Child Psychology*, 31, 46–70.

Breheny, R., Katsos, N. and Williams, J. (2006). Are generalized scalar implicatures generated by default? An on-line investigation into the role of context in generating pragmatic inferences. *Cognition* 100: 3, 434–63.

Carston, R. (1993). Conjunction, explanation and relevance. *Lingua,* 90, 27–48.

Carston, R. (1998). Informativeness, relevance and scalar implicature. In R. Carston and S. Uschida (eds), *Relevance Theory: Applications and Implications* (pp. 179–236). Amsterdam: John Benjamins.

Carston, R. (2002). *Thoughts and Utterances*. Oxford: Blackwell.

Chierchia, G. (2004). Scalar implicatures, polarity phenomena and the syntax/pragmatics interface. In A. Belletti (ed.), *Structures and Beyond*. Oxford: Oxford University Press.

Chierchia, G., Guasti, M.T., Gualmini, A., Meroni, L., Crain, S. and Foppolo, F. (2004). Adults and children's semantic and pragmatic competence in interaction. In I. A. Noveck and D. Sperber (eds) *Experimental Pragmatics*. Basingstoke: Palgrave Macmillan.

Clark, E. (1971). On the acquisition of the meaning of *Before* and *After. Journal of Verbal Learning and Verbal Behavior,* 10, 266–75.

Grice, H. P. (1975). Logic and conversation. In P. Cole and J. Morgan (eds), *Syntax and Semantics*. Vol. 3: *Speech Acts*. New York: Academic Press. Reprinted in Grice (1989) *Studies in the Way of Words* (pp. 22–40).

Grice, H. P. (1978). Further notes on logic and conversation. In P. Cole and J. Morgan (eds), *Syntax and Semantics*. Vol. 9: *Pragmatics*. New York: Academic Press. Reprinted in Grice (1989) *Studies in the Way of Words* (pp. 41–57).

Guasti, M. T., Chierchia, G., Crain, S., Foppolo, F., Gualmini, A. and Mernoni. L. (2005). Why children and adults sometimes (but not always) compute implicatures. *Language and Cognitive Processes*, 20: 5, 667–96.

Horn, L. (1972). On the semantic properties of logical operators in English. Unpublished dissertation, UCLA.

Horn, L. (1989). *A Natural History of Negation*. Chicago, IL: Chicago University Press.

Kambe, G., Rayner, K. and Duffy, S. (2001). Global context effects on processing lexically ambiguous words: evidence from eye fixations. *Memory and Cognition,* 29: 2, 367–72.

Levinson, S. (2000). *Presumptive Meanings*. Cambridge, MA: MIT Press.

Lidz, J. and Musolino, J. (2002). Children's command of quantification. *Cognition,* 84: 2, 113–54.

Musolino, J., Crain, S. and Thornton, R. (2000). Navigating negative quantifica-tional space. *Linguistics*, 38: 1, 1–32.

Musolino, J. and Lidz, J. (2003). The scope of isomorphism: turning adults into children. *Language Acquisition,* 11: 4, 277–91.

Musolino, J. and Lidz, J. (2006). Why children aren't universally successful with quantification. *Linguistics*, 44: 4 817–52.

Noveck, I. A. (2001). When children are more logical than adults: experimental investigations of scalar implicature. *Cognition,* 78: 2, 165–88.

Noveck, I. A. (2004). Pragmatic inferences related to logical terms. In I. A. Noveck and D. Sperber (eds), *Experimental Pragmatics* (pp. 301–22). Basingstoke: Palgrave.

Noveck, I. A., Bianco, M. and Castry, A. (2001). The costs and benefits of meta-phor. *Metaphor and Symbol*, 16: 1, 2, 109–21.

Noveck, I.A., Chevallier, C., Chevaux, F., Musolino, J. & Bott, L. (in press). Children's enrichments of conjunctive sentences in context. In M. Khissine (ed.) *Semantics and Pragmatics*. Emerald Group (Elsevier).

Noveck, I. and Chevaux, F. (2002). The pragmatic development of *and*. *Proceedings of the 26th annual Boston University Conference on Language Development*. Somerville, MA: Cascadilla Press.

Noveck, I. A., Guelminger, R., Georgieff, N. and Labruyere, N. (2007). What aut-ism can tell us about *Every…not* sentences. *Journal of Semantics,* 24: 1, 73–90.

Noveck, I. A. and Posada, A. (2003). Characterizing the time course of an impli-cature: an evoked potentials study. *Brain and Language,* 85, 203–10.

Noveck, I. A. and Sperber, D. (2007). The why and how of experimental prag-matics: the case of 'scalar inferences'. In N. Burton-Roberts (ed.), *Pragmatics* (pp. 184–212). Basingstoke: Palgrave.

Papafragou, A. and Musolino, J. (2003). Scalar implicatures: experiments at the semantics-pragmatics interface. *Cognition,* 86: 3, 253–82.

Papafragou, A. and Tantalou, N. (2004). Children's computation of implicatures. *Language Acquisition,* 12: 1, 71–82.

Paris, S. G. (1973). Comprehension of language connectives and propositional logical relationships. *Journal of Experimental Child Psychology,* 16: 2, 278–91.

Pouscoulous, N. (2006). *Processing Scalar Inferences*. Doctoral dissertation, EHESS, Paris.

Pouscoulous, N. and Noveck, I. (2004). Implicature et développement. *Psychologie Française*, 49, 193–207.

Pouscoulous, N., Noveck, I., Politzer, G. and Bastide, A. (2007). Processing costs and implicature development. *Language Acquisition,* 14:4, 347–75.

Siegal, M. and Surian, L. (2004). Conceptual development and conversational understanding. *Trends in Cognitive Sciences*, 8, 534–8.

Smith, C. L. (1980). Quantifiers and question answering in young children. *Journal of Experimental Child Psychology,* 30: 2, 191–205.

Sperber, D. and Wilson, D. (1986/1995). *Relevance: Communication and Cognition*. Oxford: Basil Blackwell.

Swaab, T., Brown, C. and Hagoort, P. (2003). Understanding words in sentence con-texts: the time course of ambiguity resolution. *Brain and Language*, 86, 326–43.

Swinney, D. A. (1979). Lexical access during sentence comprehension: (re) con-sideration of context effects. *Journal of Verbal Learning and Verbal Behavior,* 18, 645–59.

Wilson, D. and Carston, R. (2007). Lexical pragmatics. In N. Burton-Roberts (ed.), *Pragmatics* (pp. 230–59). Basingstoke: Palgrave.

Wilson, D. and Sperber, D. (2004). Relevance Theory. In L. Horn and G. Ward (eds), *The Handbook of Pragmatics*. Oxford: Blackwell.

Winer, G. A., Cottrell, J. E., Mott, T., Cohen, M. and Fournier, J. (2001). Are children more accurate than adults? Spontaneous use of metaphor by children and adults. *Journal of Psycholinguistic Research*, 30: 5, 485–96.

9
the acquisition of phrasal vocabulary
koenraad kuiper, georgie columbus and norbert schmitt

introduction

Corpus research has demonstrated that formulaic sequences are ubiquitous in both the written and spoken discourse of native speakers (Cowie, 1998; Biber et al., 1999; Erman and Warren, 2000; McCarthy and Carter, 2002; Kuiper, 2004; Biber et al., 2004). Although idioms have attracted perhaps the greatest research attention, there are many types of formulaic language, varying in degree of fixedness, institutionalism/conventionality and opacity/non-compositionality. This heterogeneity is reflected in the wide range of terminology in the area. Wray (2002, p. 9) found over fifty terms to describe the phenomenon of formulaic language, including *chunks*, *formulaic speech*, *multi-word units*, *collocations*, *formulas*, *prefabricated routines*, *conventionalised forms*, *holophrases* and *ready-made utterances*. The choice of term depends on the focus of the analysis, and many of them will be used in this chapter.

Although much of the research has been done on English, formulaic sequences have been found in a range of languages, including Russian, French, Spanish, Italian, German, Swedish, Polish, Arabic, Hebrew, Turkish, Greek and Chinese (Conklin and Schmitt, 2008). One reason for their pervasiveness may be that formulaic sequences serve a wide range of different functions in discourse. They can be used to express a concept (*get out of Dodge* = get out of town quickly, usually in uncomfortable circumstances), state a commonly believed truth or advice (*Too many cooks spoil the soup/broth* = it is difficult to get a number of people to work well together), provide phatic expressions which facilitate social interaction (*Nice weather today* is a non-intrusive way to open a conversation), signpost discourse organization (*on the other hand* signals an alternative viewpoint), and provide technical phraseology which can transact information in a precise and efficient manner (*2-mile final* is a specific location in an aircraft landing pattern) (Schmitt and Carter, 2004). Formulaic sequences also realize a variety of conversational routines, gambits and discourse objectives (Coulmas, 1981) and occur at places of topic-transition and as summaries of gist (Drew and Holt, 1998). Likewise, Nattinger and DeCarrico (1992) argue that formulaic language fulfils the functions of maintaining conversations (*How are you?*, *see you later*), describing the purposes for which the conversations take place (*I'm sorry to hear about X*, *would you like to X?*), and realizing the topics necessary in daily conversations (*When is X?* (time), *How far is X?* (location)). In fact, practically every conventional activity or function in a culture has its associated phrasal vocabulary. (Cell phones now come ready equipped with a lexicon of phrases for users.) Because members of a speech community know these expressions, they serve as a quick and reliable way to achieve the desired communicative effect.

Formulaic sequences also often have a type of register marking function known as *semantic/collocational prosody* (Sinclair, 2004; Stubbs, 2002). For example, *bordered on X* (*bordered on the pathological*, *bordered on apathy*) often has a negative evaluation, while the collocations that form around the word *provide* (*provide information*, *provide services*) tend to be positive. Semantic prosody is one means of showing a speaker/writer's attitude, evaluation or stance; for example, the knowledge status of the proposition following the formulaic item (*I don't know if X* indicates uncertainty about X), their attitude towards an action or event (*I want you to X* shows a positive attitude towards this action), or their desire to avoid personal attribution (*it is possible to* avoids a directly attributable suggestion) (Biber et al., 2004). Likewise, the choice of formulaic sequences can reflect an author's style and voice, as well as encoding cultural ideas.

In addition to socio-functional motivations for formulaic language, there is also a commonly held psycholinguistic explanation for their existence, which has perhaps been articulated most clearly by Pawley and Syder (1983) and Kuiper and Haggo (1984), and tested by Kuiper (1996): formulaic sequences offer processing efficiency because single memorized units, even if made up of a sequence of words, are processed more quickly and easily than the same sequences of words generated creatively. In effect, the mind uses an abundant resource (long term memory) to store prefabricated chunks of language that can be used 'ready made' in language production. This compensates for a limited resource (working memory), which can potentially be overloaded when generating language online from individual lexical items and syntactic/

discourse rules. In essence, the mind uses formulaic sequences to ease its processing load. This load can be considerable, especially in speech production, as de Bot (1992) illustrates:

> When we consider that the average rate of speech is 150 words per minute, with peak rates of about 300 words per minute, this means that we have about 200 to 400 milliseconds to choose a word when we are speaking. In other words: 2 to 5 times a second we have to make the right choice from... [all the words in the productive lexicon]. And usually we are successful; it is estimated that the probability of making the wrong choice is one in a thousand. (p. 11)

The use of formulaic language seems particularly widespread and essential in spoken discourse that occurs under heavy time constraints, such as auctioneering and sports announcing, suggesting that hearer processing can be facilitated by the predictability of formulaic language (Kuiper, 1996, 2004).

The ubiquity of phrasal vocabulary has led some to suggest there may even be a larger number of phrasal items than single word vocabulary. Sinclair (1991) has gone so far as to argue that the dominant structuring feature of language is the *idiom principle*, rather than the rule-based *open-choice principle*. Pawley and Syder (1983, p. 213) suggest that the number of 'sentence-length expressions familiar to the ordinary, mature English speaker probably amounts, at least, to several hundreds of thousands'. Benson et al.'s (1986) collocational dictionary contains over 90,000 entries, and Moon (1997, p. 48) has suggested that 'the largest specialist dictionaries of English multi-word items... contain some 15,000 phrasal verbs, idioms and fixed phrases, but the total number of multi-word items in current English is clearly much higher'.

formulaic language in first language acquisition

Study of the acquisition of phrasal vocabulary in children was initiated by Peters (1983) (see Wray, 2002; Weinert, 1995), who argued that, for some children, knowledge of grammar and individual words comes to a large degree from the segmentation of phrasal (gestalt) chunks into smaller components. [See Peters, this volume: SFC.] Thus when a child realizes that the phrase *I wanna cookie* (previously used as a holistic unit) is actually *I wanna + noun*, he or she gains information about the way syntax works in the language, as well as the independent new word *cookie*. Children with these 'gestalt' tendencies make more use of formulaic sequences to communicate than children with more referential tendencies (Nelson, 1973). In the course of acquisition, however, some sequences will cease to be used and are lost, while others are refined into adult-like forms.

Wray (2002) argues that there is an interaction between the fate of early formulae and the rule system: developing formulaic sequences will only be retained if they appear to the learner to conform to the developing rule system. However, knowing whether to keep a formulaic sequence poses an interesting acquisition question. Children are exposed to many formulaic sequences in their input, but how do they decide what to analyse and what to keep at the holistic level? Wray (2002) suggests a 'needs-only analysis' mechanism. Rather than segmenting every sequence into the grammar system, children will operate with the largest possible unit, and only segment sequences when useful for social communication. Thus the segmentation process is driven by pragmatic concerns, rather than an instinctive urge to segment in order to push grammatical and lexical acquisition. The default would be to not analyse, and to retain holistic forms. Thus children maintain many formulaic sequences into adulthood, even though the components of those sequences are likely to be stored individually as well (perhaps being acquired from the segmentation analyses of other formulaic sequences). This suggests that dual storage, as both individual lexical items and as formulaic sequences, is the norm.

Relying on holistic versus analytical approaches to language acquisition and use has long been understood not to be an either/or proposition, and children use both approaches to varying degrees. However, Wray and Perkins (2000) and Wray (2002) suggest that the relative ratios between the approaches may change with age. Schmitt and Carter (2004) summarize Wray and Perkins' views:

During Phase 1 (birth to around 20 months), the child will mainly use memorized vocabulary for communication, largely learned through imitation. Some of this vocabulary will be single words, and some will consist of sequences. At the start of Phase 2 (until about age 8), the child's grammatical awareness begins, and the proportion of analytic language compared to holistic language increases, although with overall language developing quickly in this phase, the amount of holistically-processed language is still increasing in real terms. During Phase 3 (until about age 18), the analytic grammar is fully in place, but formulaic language again becomes more prominent. 'During this phase, language production increasingly becomes a top-down process of formula blending as opposed to a bottom-up process of combining single lexical items in accordance with the specification of the grammar' (Wray and Perkins, 2000: 21). By Phase 4 (age 18 and above), the balance of holistic to analytic language has developed into adult patterns. (pp. 12–13)

According to Locke and Bogin (2006, p. 265), native adolescent language learning is characterized by the following features: the acquisition of more nuanced grammatical operations, and an increase in the acquisition of idiomatic phrases. Social talking becomes more sophisticated including gossiping in young women and teasing in young men, 'joking, deceiving, mollifying, negotiating and persuading, with increases in the use of sarcasm'. These 'facilitate achievement of two things that matter a great deal to adolescents and adults: status and relationships'. It is clear that all these can involve and help to facilitate increased acquisition of phrasal lexical items (Kuiper, 2006).

formulaic language in a second language

Given the importance of formulaic sequences in native speaker language it is not surprising that they are increasingly seen as an important aspect of language and language use in second language (L2) studies. Some research suggests second language learners handle this part of the language quite well. Schmitt, Dornyei, Adolphs and Durow (2004) found that L2 postgraduate students at the beginning of their study at a British university knew 16.84 out of 20 formulaic sequences (84 per cent) measured receptively with a multiple-choice test. The target items were formulaic sequences found frequently in academic writing, including the type of lexical bundles which Biber et al. (1999) describe (*in the long run, it is clear that, there is no evidence that*). The participants were also able to produce, on average, 12.83 (64 per cent) of the formulaic items in a modified C-test.

In a study using a multiple-choice test of formulaic sequences, Spöttl and McCarthy (2004) found that 14 Austrian multilingual learners were also relatively successful at selecting the correct formulaic sequence for the context. Although only eleven sequences were measured, over 70 per cent of the participants selected correct answers on seven items, and over 90 per cent on two items. This is further evidence that L2 learners have some knowledge of formulaic language. However, other studies have been less impressive. Nesselhauf (2003) extracted 1,072 English verb-noun combinations from 32 essays in the International Corpus of Learner English (ICLE) written by German university students and found that almost one-quarter of these collocations were judged to be incorrect.

The learners in Spöttl and McCarthy (2004) had relatively good perceptions of their knowledge of the target formulaic sequences, although in some cases they tended to overestimate it. Other studies suggest such self-knowledge is not always as accurate. Phongphio and Schmitt (2006) found that 21 Thai university undergraduates were quite confident of their ability to recognize multi-word verbs when listening or reading, but scored only 55 per cent on a multiple-choice test. Indeed, there was little relationship between the self-rating scores and multiple-choice test percentages. Despite this, when given a context to guess the meaning of the verbs, the learners were able to produce a Thai definition 75 per cent of the time, suggesting they were able to use the context relatively successfully to infer the meanings of many of the unknown multi-word verbs. This is encouraging, as guessing from context is one of the strategies commonly promoted for learning individual words (Nation, 1990, 2001). When specifically asked what strategies they found helpful in discovering the meaning of unknown multi-word verbs (on a 5-point scale), the Thai students reported guessing from textual context (3.62) as one of their top three strategies, along with the use of bilingual dictionaries (3.67) and asking the teacher to translate or to give synonyms (3.52). However, this result must be tempered by the fact that the ratings given hovered around the non-committal middle of the scale.

Despite these modestly good results in written contexts, non-native speakers have been found not to do well when required to produce phrasal items orally. Even when asked to reproduce from dictation (Schmitt, Grandage and Adolphs 2004), only two out of 25 formulaic sequences were reproduced fully correctly by a majority of non-native participants. (Further details of this study are given below.) Similarly, Siyanova and Schmitt (2007) used a questionnaire of 26 multi-word/ one-word verb pairs and found that non-native speakers were less likely to use multi-word verbs in informal spoken contexts. High frequency verbs like *make*, *look* and *do* are used in numerous formulaic sequences and are an important feature of informal spoken discourse. However, Altenberg and Granger (2001) found that EFL learners had great difficulty with formulaic sequences based on the verb *make*, especially the de-lexicalized uses, such as *make a distinction* and *make a decision*. (Biber et al., 1999).

Overall, the evidence is that spoken production of formulaic language is difficult for second language learners and tends to lag behind other aspects of language development (Irujo, 1993). Some researchers find that learners often simply avoid using these forms (Laufer, 2000). One can assume that formulaic sequences are frustrating for learners given that some, such as multi-word verbs (*work out* at the gym), usually have single word alternatives (*train* at the gym), and therefore appear to be easy candidates for avoidance. However, the multi-word verbs tend to be colloquial in tone and are a particular feature of informal spoken discourse.

Others have found that learners overuse a small number of formulaic sequences (Granger et al., 2006); possibly because they stick with familiar and 'safe' sequences they feel confident using (Granger, 1998). Oppenheim (2000) found that the speech of her six non-native participants contained between 48 per cent and 80 per cent recurrent sequences with an overall mean of 66 per cent. This is further evidence that non-native speakers rely heavily on formulaic language in their efforts to produce fluent speech. Similarly, Bolander (1989) found that her learners of Swedish commonly relied on formulaic sequences in their speech. De Cock (2000), on the other hand, found some formulaic sequences were overused, some underused, and others simply misused by non-native speakers when compared to native norms.

Proficiency also seems to play a role in the use of formulaic sequences. Levy (2003) found that the more proficient of two groups studied in a university context were more likely to use bundles from the academic register, while the less proficient group used more bundles from the conversational register. The more proficient group also used more bundles to structure discourse and for pragmatic purposes; the less proficient group used bundles that were syntactically simpler and literal in meaning. The conclusion must be that while L2 learners are capable of producing mainly acceptable collocations, the underlying intuitions and fluency with collocations of even advanced learners do not seem to match those of native speakers.

The processing advantages of formulaic speech can be exploited by learners to increase fluency. For example, Dechert (1983) studied the spoken output of a German learner of English as she narrated a story from six cartoons. He found that some of her output was marked with hesitations, fillers and corrections, while other output was smooth and fluent. The fluent output was characterized by what Dechert labelled 'islands of reliability', which essentially describe formulaic language. Dechert suggests that islands of reliability may anchor the processes necessary for planning and executing speech in real time. Conklin and Schmitt (2008) found a similar advantage in reading by non-native speakers who read formulaic sequences more quickly than non-formulaic phrases, even while the non-native speakers read more slowly overall.

The processing advantage of formulaic sequences for native speakers is argued to be that they are stored as ready-made wholes. However, some evidence suggests this may not be the case for non-native speakers. Schmitt, Grandage and Adolphs (2004) embedded recurrent sequences derived from a corpus analysis into a passage that was then used in a dictation task wherein the individual dictation bursts were deliberately long enough to overload working memory. This meant that the dictated language had to be reconstructed rather than being repeated rote from memory. Since the task was to repeat the dictated bursts exactly, it was assumed that the non-native participants would draw upon any of the target formulaic sequences they had stored in memory. Since they would be stored as wholes in memory, it was also assumed that they would be repeated fully intact, without hesitation, and with a normal stress profile. The results showed that many of the recurrent sequences were not repeated in such a manner, or even produced at all by the speakers. This suggests that these recurrent sequences may not in fact be stored as formulaic sequences in the minds of these participants.

the acquisition of phrasal vocabulary in L2

Non-native speakers, particularly adults who are classroom based, are more often expected to learn words rather than phrases, which is unlikely to give them the chance to learn and produce phrasal vocabulary. Even in naturalistic L2 learning contexts, 'there is little evidence … of a progression of the kind identified for first language acquisition, from using formulaic sequences as an aid to initial communication, through a process of segmentation, to nativelike abilities' (Wray, 2002, p. 176). With respect to collocational pairs, Wray suggests non-native speakers acquire separate words which they must then pair for correct collocation. Thus, while formulaic sequences seem to be useful for natives throughout the learning process, non-native speakers begin by focusing more on words than sequences because they are more manageable and give a feeling of control over the language. 'The consequence [of focusing on word-sized units in L2 learning] is a failure to value the one property of native-like input which is most characteristic of the idiomaticity to which the learner ultimately aspires: words do not *go* together, having first been apart, but, rather, *belong* together, and do not necessarily need separating' (Wray, 2002, p. 212).

While it is a common recommendation for students to memorize for-mulaic sequences as a basis for more fluent and idiomatic language, Wray (2004) found that this may not always be possible. Her case study subject was required to learn a number of Welsh formulaic sequences in a week in order to present a cooking show on Welsh television. In this case, the most efficient method would be just to learn the phrases and repeat them verbatim without any analysis. However, in interviews five and nine months after the learning, Wray found the subject had introduced many errors typical of an early stage learner of Welsh into the sequences as a result of faulty linguistic analysis. (See also Schmitt et al., 2004, described above.) This suggests that people may not have the capability to bypass linguistic analysis, even when it is in their interest to do so. It seems to be difficult to simply memorize formu-laic sequences without them becoming involved in the larger language acquisition process.

When we ask what factors can facilitate the acquisition of formulaic sequences, we find, surprisingly, that the size of the mental lexicon in terms of individual word forms does not seem to be a strong predictor. Schmitt et al. (2004) correlated formulaic sequence gain scores over 2 to 3 months of intensive English for Academic Purposes pre-sessional study with the students' vocabulary size (in word families), and found no significant relationship. Similarly, correlations between the stu-dents' word family size and their phrasal item size showed only modest correlations, ranging mainly between .26 and .37, although the cor-relations between the 3,000 level vocabulary (Schmitt et al., 2001) and productive formulaic sequences ranged between .42 and .54. It seems that having acquired a larger vocabulary consisting of words does not necessarily translate into having acquired a large phrasal lexicon.

The Schmitt et al (2004) study also found that gains in formulaic lan-guage did not correlate with language aptitude, language motivation, or language attitudes, even though these factors have been shown to be generally important in language acquisition (Dörnyei, 2002; Dörnyei and Csizér, 2002). However, an in-depth case study has suggested that integration into the L2 environment and culture can make a diffe-rence. Dörnyei et al. (2004) interviewed and tested four 'good' formu-laic sequence learners and three 'poor' learners over the course of six months. They found that the ability to integrate into the 'host national networks' was a key factor in learning formulaic sequences:

Success in the acquisition of formulaic sequences appears to be the function of the interplay of three main factors: language aptitude, motivation and sociocultural adaptation. Our study shows that if the latter is absent, only a combination of particularly high levels of the two former learner traits can compensate for this, whereas successful sociocultural adaptation can override below-average initial learner characteristics. Thus, sociocultural adaptation, or acculturation, turned out to be a central modifying factor in the learning of the international students under investigation ... (p. 105)

This finding is reminiscent of Wong-Fillmore's study (1976) of the naturalistic acquisition of a second language by elementary school children. She found that the child who had the most integrative orientation to the target culture used the most formulaic language and was creative with its use.

The impact of language aptitude, motivation and socio-cultural adaptation was further explored by Adolphs and Durow (2004), who looked at the interview transcripts of one high-integration (≈ 9,500 words) and one low-integration student (≈ 11,500 words) from the Dörnyei et al. study. They compared the ten most frequent three-word sequences in the initial interview with the final interview given seven months later to see if the students progressed in using common sequences over time. It transpired that the high-integration student increased the percentage of these three-word formulas from 2.38 per cent to 3.53 per cent, while the low-integration student showed virtually no increase (1.34 per cent to 1.48 per cent). Furthermore, when three-word sequences of all frequencies were analysed (not just the top 10), the high-integration student produced a higher percentage (18.93 per cent to 20.98 per cent of the total text) compared to the low-integration student (9.55 per cent to 12.66 per cent). When the three-word sequences from the interviews were compared to a native spoken corpus (CANCODE), the high-integration student progressed towards using the more native-like forms, while the low-integration student did not. Overall, the analysis suggested that the student with better social integration improved more compared to the student who had difficulty integrating. Some potentially contradictory evidence (Siyanova and Schmitt, 2007) suggesting that the amount of exposure to native-speaking environments did not have an effect on the likelihood of using multi-word verbs could be resolved by acknowledging that it is not exposure per se that is important, but the kind of high-quality exposure that occurs in a socially integrated environment.

The availability of Cross Linguistic Influence (CLI) may also play a role in successful or less successful acquisition of formulaic sequences.

Spöttl and McCarthy (2004) found that their multilingual participants were largely able to transfer the meaning of formulaic items across L1, L2, L3 and L4 (see also Siyanova and Schmitt, 2008). Zalasiewicz (1991) carried out an analysis of 205 English idioms translated into Polish. Seven percent of the English idioms translated directly into Polish with full semantic and lexical equivalence, while 17 per cent could not be translated effectively at all. The majority of the idioms (75 per cent) could be effectively translated, because there was usually a semantic correlate available in Polish, but often the lexical form (words/syntax) was quite different. She interpreted the generally high level of similarity between Polish and English idioms in two ways:

> Some instances, particularly involving close similarity, could be accounted for by a common origin, the result of shared historical or cultural roots. In most cases, though, the parallels may be the result of a general tendency to construct idioms about the same general topics, with reference to a common set of metaphors. The overall differences were largely the result of reference to specifically English national, cultural or historical phenomena. (p. 1)

One of the few studies to explore whether formulaic sequences can be successfully taught was carried out on university pre-sessional students. Jones and Haywood (2004) highlighted formulaic sequences during a ten week course, and found that they were largely successful in raising their students' awareness of formulaic sequences, but that this awareness did not translate into any substantial increase in the usage of the sequences in the student output. The researchers did note however, that while there was no definite improvement in group performance, 'there were instances where individual students used phrases accurately and appropriately in their own unsupported writing' (p. 289). This suggests that it may not be easy to increase the number of formulaic sequences produced by students. On the other hand, instruction may have more effect on the accuracy and appropriacy of use of formulaic sequences. This is one area which clearly requires more research.

Along these lines, Phongphio and Schmitt (2006) looked at Thai university undergraduates and their impressions of learning strategies and formulaic language. Their 21 participants considered seven strategies which are potentially useful for discovering the meaning of new multi-word verbs. Overall, the students appeared rather lukewarm towards strategies for discovering the meaning of these verbs, with an average rating very near to the non-committal middle of a 5-point rating scale.

Even the top three strategies failed to gain particularly strong ratings: the use of bilingual dictionaries (3.67), guessing from textual context (3.62) and asking the teacher to translate or to give synonyms (3.52). Similarly, the participants were asked to consider strategies potentially useful for consolidating or enhancing knowledge of multi-word verbs which are already partially acquired. Again, the average score was not overwhelmingly positive (3.48), with the exception of 1) connecting multi-word verbs to personal experience (4.19), and 2) using the target multi-word verbs which have just been learnt in real conversation (3.90). Given these relatively modest scores, it seems important to increase learners' awareness of the value of such strategies.

a study of native speaker and l2 acquisition of formulaic vocabulary

It is clear from the foregoing discussion that many questions relating to the acquisition of formulaic vocabulary remain. These include the difficulty of estimating the size of a typical native speaker's phrasal vocabulary and of recognizing what the statistical threshold is after which corpus evidence would establish that an expression is formulaic as opposed to analytic (Altenberg, 1998; Moon, 1998). Currently, taxonomic theories of the linguistic properties of phrasal lexical items predominate (Burger, 2003; Kuiper, 2007) and few established theories exist as to how multi-word lexical items are stored and retrieved from the mental lexicon (Cutting and Bock, 1997; Sprenger et al., 2006; Kuiper et al., 2007). Since theories of language acquisition rely on an understanding of what is acquired and how it is stored and retrieved, these are serious shortcomings.

Cloze testing, however, holds out promise as a method for investigating whether or not a speaker has acquired a formulaic lexical item. Asking a reader to complete an expression (cloze testing) assumes that context and some of the constituents can activate the expression in the mental lexicon, allowing the speaker to supply the missing words (Jackendoff, 1995). Thus, if a respondent can produce the missing word(s) which conventionally fill(s) the gap, then they can be taken to know the expression, i.e. to have acquired it and stored it in their mental lexicon.

An appropriate model of lexical access for phrasal lexical items is superlemma theory (Sprenger et al., 2006; Kuiper et al., 2007). Part of a larger model of lexical access (Levelt, 1989; Levelt and Meyer, 2000), superlemma theory presupposes that a phrasal lexical item has a single lexical concept. If this is activated, then its superlemma node, in which are found all the idiosyncratic syntactic properties of the item, is activated, including, for example, whether it is flexible under movement, and whether it can take internal modification and so forth. The activation of the superlemma node in turn activates the lemma nodes of all its constituent words. These nodes contain the syntactic properties of individual words on which, for example, the phrase structure of the expression, in part, depends. In turn, the lemma nodes are related to and thus activate their phonological, phonetic and graphological form(s). Under superlemma theory formulaic expressions are unitary, i.e. stored holistically, with a single associated concept in the mental lexicon and in their superlemma representation, rather than being stored as their constituent words.

In responding to a cloze test, a respondent accumulates evidence as to what (s)he is reading incrementally in the normal way through eye fixations at various points along the lines of print. The graphic forms activate their associated lemmas and then the associated concept of each lemma. Parsing proceeds on the basis of the syntactic information contained in the lemma, and the accumulated syntactic properties the parser creates. In the case of a phrasal lexical item, the reader has two options, the lemmas can either add up to a freely produced expression or a lexicalised expression. The activation of a superlemma node, where one is available for the sequence of words being perceived, aggregates the syntactic information gained from the parser until such a point that the activation level is higher than that of the homophonous, non-lexicalized counterpart. Once the superlemma is sufficiently activated, all its constituent lemmas are also activated, thus allowing the respondent to retrieve the missing word. Note this latter process moves from perception to production since the entering of a filler in the gap is a production process.

The situation can be more complex, as indicated earlier, where there is more than one conventional option in the gap. The formulaic expression *enter the fray* has *join* also available as the initial verb. It is an open question as to which of the two is more likely to be selected since both may be activated when the superlemma for *enter/join the fray* is activated. These processes are of course not failsafe, and slips of the pen, misreadings and misunderstandings can occur. And if the respondent does not know the formulaic expression, i.e. if it is not represented in his/her mental lexicon, they must attempt to guess what an appropriate gap filler would be from the context. This will be a best guess on the basis of the compositional evidence available either side of the gap.

Thus if one did not know the expression *worship the ground someone walks on* and the gap was the word *ground*, then any plausible walking surface such as *earth, floor* or *carpet* might be selected.

The study to be reported below used cloze testing to explore when formulaic expressions are learned by native speakers and how native and non-native speakers differ in their acquisition. The gapped expressions were all familiar to mature native speakers and were designed to provide subjects with the best linguistic conditions for 'success'. Significant clues were present as to the meaning of the whole expression while at the same time providing contexts for more than one plausible filler. We selected only VPs as test cases and in all cases it was the verb that was gapped in line with Mel'čuk's (1998) proposal that, in the case of lexicalized predicate argument structures, it is often the predicate which is idiomatic while the argument retains its literal meaning. Gapping the same item in each case also created syntactic parallelism and thus clear syntactic priming (Smith and Wheeldon, 2001).

subjects

Respondents for the age grading experiment were selected into four sets of ten: 16 ± 1 years of age, between 20 and 30, between 40 and 50, and over 65. All were New Zealanders. The high-school students were selected from an academic stream while the adult participants were generally university educated. No attempt was made to control for gender or socio-economic status on the (falsifiable) assumption that this would not be relevant.

For the non-native subjects, two groups of EFL speakers were selected. The first group were a set of ten German secondary students aged around 16 who had been studying English at secondary school. These were selected for comparison with the high-school cohort of native speakers. The second group were native speakers of a variety of languages other than English; all were adult EFL speakers over the age of 20 selected for comparison with the adult native speakers between 20 and 50 from the age grading experiment.

procedure

Respondents were asked to read a story about a social event written in a vernacular style such as one might find in a popular magazine. The aim was to maintain stylistic homogeneity throughout the task and provide sufficient narrative interest to encourage respondents to continue to the end of the story. The context for each expression being investigated was thus extensive. The instructions to participants were as follows: 'Thank you for taking the time to help us with our research. Please read the story and when you find a gap (____), write in the verb you think should go there. For example: Wow! It's really <u>raining</u> cats and dogs out there! Don't worry if you can't think of a word straight away, just put in your best guess.' Appendix A provides the first part of this story.

The expressions being targeted were given in bold type. Nothing was said as to why they were in bold but the aim was to provide a visual clue that the gap was related to the bolded sequence of words which was usually the complement of the verb. The test items are shown in Table 9.1, ordered by the frequency of their head verb.

The cloze items were selected on the basis of their membership in four categories: light (or de-lexicalized) verbs (Grimshaw, 1990), non-light high frequency verbs, mid-frequency verbs and low frequency verbs. The frequencies were derived as follows. A random selection of phrasal lexical items were selected from the *Syntactically Annotated Dictionary of Idioms* (Kuiper et al., 2003), and the verbs were divided into three frequency bands and four categories based on a combined evaluation of verb frequency rankings in the Brown Corpus (accessed via edict. com.hk), Kilgarriff's BNC rankings (Kilgarriff, 1995), the Most Frequent

Table 9.1 Test items by descending order of frequency of the head verb

1. do things by halves
2. make tracks (for)
3. take a fancy to NP
4. give NP the creeps
5. keep a straight face
6. let NP into a secret
7. join/enter the fray
8. drive NP to drink
9. act the goat
10. avoid NP like the plague
11. wipe NP off the map
12. tighten NP's belt
13. seal NP's fate
14. spare no expense
15. scrape the bottom of the barrel
16. worship the ground NP walks on
17. wring NP's neck
18. pluck/summon up courage
19. goad/spur NP into action
20. toe the company line

Note: NPs are noun phrases which were filled in the story. The verbs were gapped.

Word lists (Nation, 2000) and the discussion in (Nation and Waring, 1997). The phrasal lexical items themselves could not be ordered by frequency, because, as indicated earlier, reliable measures of frequency are currently unavailable. The four categories were classified as shown in Table 9.2.

Table 9.2   Categorization of verbs

Category	Frequency criterion
High frequency light verbs (HL)	appearing in the top 1–3,000 words in the MFW lists (as words). Note that light verbs are also higher in frequency than the other high frequency verbs.
High frequency lexical verbs (H)	appearing in the top 1–3,000 words in the MFW lists (as words)
Medium frequency lexical verbs (M)	appearing in the 3,000–5,000 word list in the MFW lists (as words)
Low frequency lexical verbs (L)	not appearing in any lists

Table 9.3   Frequency data and band allocation of head verbs

Verb	Rank number	Total occurrences	Frequency band
do	18	559,596	HL
make	46	217,268	HL
take	54	179,220	HL
give	76	131,417	HL
keep	189	50,092	HL
let	330	29,768	H
join	594	17,331	H
drive	618	16,477	H
act	654	15,620	H
avoid	866	11,750	H
wipe	3,122	2,367	M
tighten	4,178	1,548	M
seal	4,249	1,512	M
spare	5,457	1,023	M
scrape	6,011	865	M
worship	no rank	0 (as verb)	L
wring	no rank	0	L
pluck	no rank	0	L
goad	no rank	0	L
toe	no rank	0 (as verb)	L

Table 9.4   BNC frequencies of alternate verbs

Verb	BNC freq. per million words
join	173.91
enter	142.69
summon	14.02
pluck	6.29
spur	3.97
goad	1.55

Twenty items were then selected using these criteria to create the short story, five from each category. These 20 verbs were subsequently checked against Kilgarriff's lemmatized BNC frequency list, and the results showed that the original allocations were largely accurate. Items ranked highly were largely in the 'High' category, and with a high total number of occurrences. The frequency bands were also checked against frequency data from the CELEX database (Baayen et al., 1993) and the BNC corpus data (www.natcorp.ox.ac.uk/). With minor ranking exceptions the allocation of verbs to frequency bands was confirmed. (For example, in the BNC data *worship* ranked one higher than *scrape* while *seal* ranked one higher than *tighten*.)

The initially employed frequency data and band allocation of each head verb are contained in Table 9.3.

As can be seen in Table 9.1, some cloze items allowed for more than one conventional option. There were three selected for investigation here: *enter/join the fray, goad/spur NP into action* and *pluck/summon up courage*. The alternates appeared in the same frequency bands, i.e. they were relatively close in their frequency as is shown in their BNC frequency (Table 9.4).

results

Differences among the four native speaker groups as a function of age were not large as shown in Figure 9.1.

Perhaps this result is not surprising considering that the items chosen were vernacular, non-specialized items, likely to be known to individuals from teenage onwards. However, given that enculturation is lifelong, the acquisition of often low frequency phrasal vocabulary items could be expected to continue, though presumably at a decreasing rate, throughout the life course. One would also expect that lexical retrieval becomes slightly less efficient after 65.

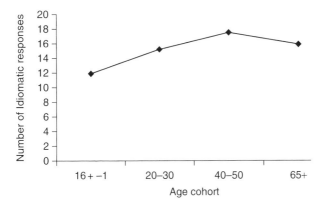

Figure 9.1   Native speaker recall of verb heads of verb phrasal lexical items by age group

The cloze tests of the native and EFL adolescents and adults yielded the comparisons in Table 9.5. These data suggest that EFL speakers' acquisition of vernacular phrasal vocabulary items is an order of magnitude lower than that of native speakers. Note, however, that given the very large phrasal vocabulary of native speakers, non-native speakers even in adolescence have still acquired a sizable phrasal vocabulary. Note too that the cloze procedure is likely to underestimate non-native speaker recognition of phrasal vocabulary; a multi-choice methodology would be anticipated to yield a significantly larger number of recognized phrases.

The impact of the frequency of the gapped head verb was consistent across all the age-graded native speaker respondents with more successful retrieval of light and higher frequency verbs as compared to lower frequency verbs (Figure 9.2).

It was to be expected that retrieval of mid- and low-frequency heads would show the attrition in the older age cohort it appears to. Non-native speakers show similar preference for clozing on high frequency verb heads as is shown in Figure 9.3.

The cloze testing process has, therefore, corroborated previous hypotheses that acquisition of phrasal lexical items is age graded and that non-native speakers have a lower rate of acquisition. It has also corroborated the hypothesis that the frequency of a head word which is gapped affects its recall, the more frequent items being easier to recall than low frequency items. There were, however, some exceptions. Some lexicalized VPs seem to have high saliency, notwithstanding the low frequency of their head verb. A clear case is *worship the ground NP walks*

234 languagelanguage acquisition

TableTable 9.5* Native and EFL adolescent and adult cloze test results.

Native adolescents	EFL adolescents
11.9	0.8
Native adults	**EFL adults**
16.4	1.8

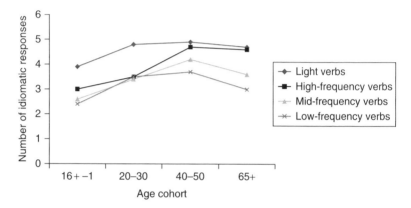

Figure 9.2 Native speaker recall of heads of phrasal lexical items (Frequency plotted against age)

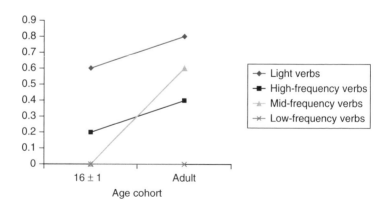

Figure 9.3 Non-native speaker recall of heads of phrasal lexical items (Frequency plotted against age)

on which was correctly clozed by 10/10 of the over-65-year-old native speakers, 9/10 of the 40–50-year-olds, 9/10 of the 20–30-year-olds and 8/10 of the 16-year-olds.

The verbs which were scored as being correctly recalled were those which are the conventional heads of the phrasal lexical item. In three cases there was more than one of these. Cloze testing of native speakers revealed the selectional patterns favouring particular heads of phrase, as Table 9.6 shows.

These selectional preferences are not exclusively related to the relative frequency of the respective verbs in text, however, as shown in Table 9.7.

We can therefore infer that phrasal lexical items with alternative selectional preferences may have those alternatives independent of the frequency of their head, as shown by *enter* vs. *join* and *pluck* vs. *summon*. Such preferences may be dialectally determined. However, cloze testing, by forcing a single response, cannot show acquisition of the alternatives. On the other hand from this small data set it would seem that speakers differ in their preference for particular words from a selection

Table 9.6 Selection of alternative idiomatic heads

	Word 1	Word 2	
	enter the fray	*join* the fray	Total
Times selected	3 *goad* NP into action	27 *spur* NP into action	30/40
Times selected	5 *pluck* up the courage to	10 *summon* up the courage to	15/40
Times selected	9	4	15/40

Table 9.7 BNC frequencies of alternative idiomatic heads

	Word 1	Word 2
	enter	*join*
BNC fr	142.69	173.91
	goad	*spur*
BNC fr	1.55	3.97
	pluck	*summon*
BNC fr	6.29	14.02

set, and that populations of speakers can, through cloze testing, reveal normative preferences. It is an interesting question whether such preferences are also found in the frequencies with which the alternatives are manifest in large corpora.

conclusion

In addition to revealing learners' knowledge of phrasal vocabulary at a particular point in time, as here, cloze testing could be used iteratively to explore acquisition over a period. One might use it, for example, to see if early phrasal vocabulary learning undergoes a learning burst at some stage in language development and if acquisition order is related to the acquisition of the head which would imply that verb phrases with low frequency heads would be acquired in the order of the frequency of their heads. These and other questions will have to await further research.

appendix a

Shannon walked into the vast, badly decorated function room and looked around for faces she knew. Tom's hand waved frantically at her from a table near the coat check. *Thank goodness!* she thought to herself, *I'm not the only one from Data Entry here!* Shannon normally _____ **these kind of events like the plague**, but her pushy new flatmate had convinced her a night out might be in order, especially considering she'd only been at the firm for a few weeks. She walked towards Tom and was further relieved to see familiar faces from Accounts, which had its offices on the same floor as her department. On closer inspection, she realised she knew a few others at the table – Jenny, who had a tendency to _____ **the goat** at inter-departmental health and safety meetings, pulling faces and telling stupid jokes; Annabel, who always looks like a startled deer when you ask her anything that isn't work-related, her face going blotchy at the prospect of real conversation; and Jonno, who _____ **every woman on the floor the creeps** with his fake smile and lame innuendo.

references

Adolphs, S. and Durow, V. (2004). Social-cultural integration and the development of formulaic sequences. In Schmitt, N. (ed.), *Formulaic Sequences* (pp. 107–26). Amsterdam: John Benjamins.

Altenberg, B. (1998). On the phraseology of spoken English: the evidence of recurrent word-combinations. In A. P. Cowie (ed.), *Phraseology: Theory, Analysis and Applications* (pp. 101–22). Oxford: Oxford University Press.

Altenberg, B. and Granger, S. (2001). The grammatical and lexical patterning of *make* in native and non-native student writing. *Applied Linguistics 22*, 2, 173–94.

Baayen, R. H., Piepenbrock, R. and van Rijn, H. (1993). The CELEX Lexical Database.

Benson, M., Benson, E. and Ilson, R. (1986). *The BBI Combinatory Dictionary of English*. Amsterdam: John Benjamins.

Biber, D., Conrad, S. and Cortes, V. (2004). Lexical bundles in university teaching and textbooks. *Applied Linguistics 25*, 377–405.

Biber, D., Johansson, S., Leech, G., Conrad, S. and Finegan, E. (1999). *Longman Grammar of Spoken and Written English*. Harlow: Longman.

Bolander, M. (1989). Prefabs, patterns and rules in interaction? Formulaic speech in adult learners' L2 Swedish. In K. Hyltenstam and L. Obler (eds), *Bilingualism across the Lifespan* (pp. 73–86). Cambridge: Cambridge University Press.

Burger, H. (2003). *Phraseologie: Eine Einführung am Beispiel des Deutschen* (2nd edition). Berlin: Erich Schmidt Verlag.

Conklin, K. and Schmitt, N. (2008).Formulaic sequences: are they processed more quickly than nonformulaic language by native and nonnative speakers? *Applied Linguistics*, March, 29: 72–89.

Coulmas, F. (1981). *Conversational Routine*. The Hague: Mouton.

Cowie, A. (ed.) (1998). *Phraseology: Theory, Analysis and Applications* (pp. 125–43). Oxford: Oxford University Press.

Cutting, J. and Bock, K. (1997). That's the way the cookie bounces: syntactic and semantic components of experimentally controlled idiom blends. *Memory and Cognition 25*: 1, 57–71.

de Bot, K. (1992). A bilingual production model: Levelt's 'speaking' model adapted. *Applied Linguistics*, 13, l–25.

De Cock, S. (2000). Repetitive phrasal chunkiness and advanced EFL speech and writing. In C. Mair and M. Hundt, M. (eds), *Corpus Linguistics and Linguistic Theory* (pp. 51–68). Amsterdam: Rodopi.

Dechert, H. (1983). How a story is done in a second language. In C. Faerch and G. Kasper (eds), *Strategies in Interlanguage Communication* (pp. 175–95). London: Longman.

Dörnyei, Z. (2002). The motivational basis of language learning tasks. In P. Robinson (ed.) *Individual Differences and Instructed Language Learning* (pp. 137–58). Amsterdam: John Benjamins.

Dörnyei, Z. and Csizér, K. (2002). Some dynamics of language attitudes and motivation: results of a longitudinal nationwide survey. *Applied Linguistics*, 23, 421–62.

Dörnyei, Z., Durow, V. and Zahran, K. (2004). Individual differences and their effects on formulaic sequence acquisition. In N. Schmitt (ed.), *Formulaic Sequences* (pp. 87–106). Amsterdam: John Benjamins.

Drew, P. and Holt, E. (1998). Figures of speech: figurative expressions and the management of topic transition in conversation. *Language in Society*, 27, 495–522.

238 language acquisition

Erman, B. and Warren, B. (2000). The idiom principle and the open-choice principle. *Text*, 20, 29–62.

Granger, S. (1998). Prefabricated patterns in advanced EFL writing: collocations and formulae. In A. P. Cowie (ed.), *Phraseology: Theory, Analysis and Applications* (pp. 145–60). Oxford: Oxford University Press.

Granger, S., Paquot M. and Rayson P. (2006) Extraction of multi-word units from EFL and native English corpora. The phraseology of the verb 'make'. In A. Häcki Buhofer and H. Burger (eds), *Phraseology in Motion I: Methoden und Kritik. Akten der Internationalen Tagung zur Phraseologie (Basel, 2004)* (pp. 57–68). Baltmannsweiler: Schneider Verlag Hohengehren.

Grimshaw, J. (1990). *Argument Structure*. Cambridge, MA: MIT Press.

Irujo, S. (1993). Steering clear: avoidance in the production of idioms. *International Review of Applied Linguistics in Language Teaching*, 31, 205–19.

Jackendoff, R. (1995). The boundaries of the lexicon. In M. Everaert, E. van der Linden, A. Schenk and R. Schreuder (eds), *Idioms: Structural and Psychological Perspectives* (pp. 133–66). Hillsdale, NJ: Erlbaum.

Jones, M. and Haywood, S. (2004). Facilitating the acquisition of formulaic sequences. In N. Schmitt (ed.), *Formulaic Sequences* (pp. 269–300). Amsterdam: John Benjamins.

Kilgarriff, A. *BNC Database and Word Frequency Lists* 1995 [cited 24 August 2006. Available from www.kilgarriff.co.uk/BNC_lists/lemma.al].

Kuiper, K. (1996). *Smooth Talkers*. Mahwah, NJ: Erlbaum.

Kuiper, K. (2004). Formulaic performance in conventionalised varieties of speech. In N. Schmitt (ed.), *Formulaic Sequences* (pp. 37–54). Amsterdam: John Benjamins.

Kuiper, K. (2006). Knowledge of language and phrasal vocabulary acquisition. *Behavioral and Brain Sciences*, 29, 291–2.

Kuiper, K. (2007). Cathy Wilcox meets the phrasal lexicon. In J. Munat (ed.), *Lexical Creativity, Texts and Contexts* (pp. 93–112). Amsterdam: Benjamins.

Kuiper, K. and Haggo, D. C. (1984). Livestock auctions, oral poetry and ordinary language. *Language in Society*, 13, 205–34.

Kuiper, K., McCann, H., Aitchison, T. and van der Veer, K. (2003). *SAID: A Syntactically Annotated Idiom Database*. Linguistics Data Consortium, University of Pennsylvania.

Kuiper, K., van Egmond, M-E., Kempen, G. M. and Sprenger, S. (2007). Slipping on superlemmas: multiword lexical items in speech production. *The Mental Lexicon*, 2: 3, 313–57.

Laufer, B. (2000). Avoidance of idioms in a second language: the effect of L1-L2 degree of similarity. *Studia Linguistica*, 54, 186–96.

Levelt, W. J. M. (1989). *Speaking: from Intention to Articulation*. Cambridge, MA: MIT Press.

Levelt, W. J. M. and Meyer, A. S. (2000). Word for word: multiple lexical access in speech production. *European Journal of Cognitive Psychology*, 12: 4, 433–52.

Levy, S. (2003). *Lexical Bundles in Professional and Student Writing*. Unpublished Ph.D. dissertation, University of the Pacific, Stockton, CA.

Locke, J. L. and Bogin, B. (2006). Language and life history: a new perspective on the development and evolution of human language. *Behavioral and Brain Sciences*, 29, 259–325.

McCarthy, M. and Carter, R. (2002). This that and the other: multi-word clusters in spoken English as visible patterns of interaction. *Teanga* (Yearbook of the Irish Association for Applied Linguistics), 21, 30–52.

Mel'čuk, I. (1998). Collocations and lexical functions. In A. P. Cowie (ed.), *Phraseology: Theory, analysis, and applications.* Oxford: Clarendon Press.

Moon, R. (1997). Vocabulary connections: multi-word items in English. In N. Schmitt and M. McCarthy (eds), *Vocabulary: Description, Acquisition and Pedagogy* (pp. 40–63). Cambridge: Cambridge University Press.

Moon, R. (1998). *Fixed Expressions and Idioms in English: A corpus based approach.* Oxford: Clarendon Press.

Nation, I. S. P. (1990). *Teaching and Learning Vocabulary.* Cambridge: Cambridge University Press.

Nation, I. S. P. (2001). *Learning Vocabulary in Another Language.* Cambridge: Cambridge University Press.

Nation, I. S. P. (2000) *Most Frequent Words* [cited 8 August 2006. Available on www.edict.com.hk/lexiconindex/frequencylists/words2000.htm].

Nation, P. and Waring, R. (1997). Vocabulary size, text coverage, and word lists. In N. Schmitt and M. McCarthy (eds), *Vocabulary: Description, acquisition, pedagogy.* New York: Cambridge University Press.

Nattinger, J. R. and DeCarrico, J. S. (1992). *Lexical Phrases and Language Teaching.* Oxford: Oxford University Press.

Nelson, K. (1973). *Structure and Strategy in Learning to Talk.* Monographs of the Society for Research in Child Development, Serial no. 149, nos 1–2.

Nesselhauf, N. (2003). The use of collocations by advanced learners of English and some implications for teaching. *Applied Linguistics*, 24, 2, 223–42.

Oppenheim, N. (2000). The importance of recurrent sequences for nonnative speaker fluency and cognition. In H. Riggenbach (ed.), *Perspectives on Fluency* (pp. 220–40). Ann Arbor: University of Michigan Press.

Pawley, A. and Syder, F. (1983). Two puzzles for linguistic theory: nativelike selection and nativelike fluency. In J. Richards and R. Schmidt (eds), *Language and Communication* (pp. 191–225). London: Longman.

Peters, A. (1983). *The Units of Language Acquisition.* Cambridge: Cambridge University Press.

Phongphio, T. and Schmitt, N. (2006). Learning English multi-word verbs in Thailand. *Thai TESOL Bulletin*, 19, 2, 122–36.

Schmitt, N. and Carter, R. (2004). Formulaic sequences in action: an introduction. In N. Schmitt (ed.), *Formulaic Sequences* (pp. 1–22). Amsterdam: John Benjamins.

Schmitt, N. Dornyei, Z., Adolphs, S. and Durow, V. (2004). Knowledge and acquisition of formulaic sequences. In N. Schmitt (ed.), *Formulaic Sequences.* Amsterdam: John Benjamins.

Schmitt, N., Grandage, S. and Adolphs, S. (2004). Are corpus-derived recurrent clusters psycholinguistically valid? In N. Schmitt (ed.), *Formulaic Sequences* (pp. 127–51). Amsterdam: John Benjamins.

Schmitt, N., Schmitt, D. and Clapham, C. (2001). Developing and exploring the behaviour of two new versions of the Vocabulary Levels Test, *Language Testing* 18,1, 55–88.

Sinclair, J. (1991). *Corpus, Concordance, Collocation.* Oxford: Oxford University Press.

Sinclair, J. (2004). *Trust The Text: Lexis, Corpus, Discourse*. London: Routledge.

Siyanova, A. and Schmitt, N. (2007). Native and nonnative use of multi-word vs one-word verbs. *International Review of Applied Linguistics*, 45, 109–39.

Siyanova, A. and Schmitt, N. (2008). L2 learner production and processing of collocation: a multi-study perspective. *Canadian Modern Language Review*, 64, 3, 429–58.

Smith, M. and Wheeldon, L. (2001). Syntactic priming in spoken sentence production – an online study. *Cognition*, 78, 123–64.

Spöttl, C. and McCarthy, M. (2004). Comparing knowledge of formulaic sequences across L1, L2, L3, and L4. In N. Schmitt (ed.), *Formulaic Sequences*. Amsterdam: John Benjamins. pp. 190–225.

Sprenger, S., Levelt, W. J. M. and Kempen, G. (2006). Lexical access during the production of idiomatic phrases. *Journal of Memory and Language*, 54, 161–84.

Stubbs, M. (2002). *Words and Phrases: Corpus Studies of Lexical Semantics*. Oxford: Blackwell.

Weinert, R. (1995). The role of formulaic language in second language acquisition: a review. *Applied Linguistics*, 16, 180–205.

Wong-Fillmore, L. (1976). *The Second Time Around*. Doctoral dissertation, Stanford University.

Wray, A. (2002). *Formulaic Language and the Lexicon*. Cambridge: Cambridge University Press.

Wray, A. (2004). 'Here's one I prepared earlier': Formulaic language learning on television. In N. Schmitt (ed.), *Formulaic Sequences* (pp. 249–68). Amsterdam: John Benjamins.

Wray, A. and Perkins, M. R. (2000). The functions of formulaic language: an integrated model. *Language and Communication*, 20, 1–28.

Zalasiewicz, K. (1991). English and Polish Idioms: A Comparative Study. Unpublished MA dissertation: University of Nottingham.

part 3.
language acquisition, culture and linguistic diversity

10
language development in simultaneous bilingual children

natascha müller

introduction

While the European Union officially favours multilingualism, the reality is that teachers and other pedagogically engaged people harbour deep-seated prejudices against multilingualism. They fail to recognize code-switching as normal behaviour for a bilingual; assume that every bilingual must have a dominant language; and worry that many children may be semilingual, unable to function in either of their languages. This chapter reviews these issues in light of data from a study of bilingual first language acquisition (in which children are exposed to two languages from birth) with a focus on Romance languages in combination with German.[1]

Identifying bilingual first language acquisition means distinguishing *simultaneous* acquisition of two languages from *successive* acquisition, whether this is the native German speaker learning English in school or the child of immigrant parents meeting German for the first time on entry into compulsory education. In either case, successive acquisition involves learning the second language in a *tutored* environment. Simultaneous acquisition of two languages, on the other hand, always happens in a *natural* setting. The dichotomies simultaneous vs. successive and natural vs. tutored are further complicated by another contrast, namely between *early* and *late* onset of acquisition. Researchers usually assume that second languages are learned much more easily the earlier the learner is exposed to them. However, as we will see below, there are children acquiring a second language in early childhood who nonetheless develop it rather slowly and with significant influence from their other language.

Many researchers claim that the age of onset of acquisition defines the difference between simultaneous and (child) successive bilingualism. These researchers have appealed to neuroscientific findings about the language faculty, and to the notion of a critical period for first language acquisition. McLaughlin (1978), for example, proposed that after the age of 3, languages are no longer learnt in the same manner as first languages, and others have since argued that after three a variety of linguistic developments are limited by neurological changes in the brain. Long (1990), Hyltenstam and Abrahamsson (2003), Obler et al. (1982) and Hahne and Friederici (2001), for example, have all argued that learners exposed to a second language after the age of 3 represent this language differently in the brain from their mother tongue.

If this link between the language faculty and neurophysiology is correct, in the sense that a window is closed after a certain age for particular linguistic abilities and that afterwards the developmental process happens in a qualitatively and quantitatively different way, we would be forced to conclude that acquisition which starts after the age of 3, whether it is a first or a second language, can never access the same devices as language acquisition which starts before that age. However, there are a number of similarities between successive and simultaneous bilingualism which suggest that age of onset of acquisition does not in fact distinguish between the different types of acquisition. In what follows, we will review the literature on the relationships between the two languages of a simultaneous bilingual. Cross-linguistic influence will be observed in simultaneous bilinguals, relating simultaneous and successive bilingualism.

overview of the literature: fusion or separation?

Based on a longitudinal study of the simultaneous acquisition of German and Italian by two girls raised in Italy, Volterra and Taeschner (1978) proposed the three-stage-model of bilingual language acquisition shown in Figure 10.1.

Stage 1 is characterized by the existence of one lexicon and one syntactic system (or grammar) as a fused system, with properties from both languages. The existence of a single lexicon predicts that the child will not be able to refer, for example, to a book with the equivalent words in the two languages – buch (German)/libro (Italian) – but will use the word of language A (German) in order to refer to a book both when producing language A and when speaking language B (Italian). This results

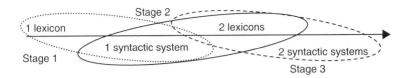

Figure 10.1   The three-stage-model

in either monolingual (buch$_G$ kaputt$_G$ = book broken) or 'mixed' utterances (buch$_G$ voglio$_I$ = book (I) want).

Stage 2 is characterized by the development of two language-specific lexicons while the syntactic system remains shared by both languages. This results in, for example, both children placing attributive adjectives post-nominally, which gives target-like results for Italian (scarpe marrone scuro = shoes brown-dark / il riso buono = the rice good) and target-deviant placements in German (schuhe dunkelbraun = shoes dark-brown / reis gut = rice good). During the third and final stage, both lexicons and syntactic systems are separate, resulting in, for example, pre-nominal placement of adjectives in German (ein kleines haus = a small house) and post-nominal placement in Italian (un sole rosso = a sun red).

Even at stage 3, however, Volterra and Taeschner did not characterize the children as truly bilingual because language choice was strongly determined by addressee, i.e. they used German with the (German) mother and Italian with the (Italian) father. Volterra and Taeschner argue that this person-dependent language use was a strategy to avoid interference between the two syntactic systems; and only when the children were able to speak both languages 'with the same linguistic competence as a monolingual child, with any person' (p. 326) were Volterra and Taeschner prepared to say that the children were truly bilingual.

Volterra and Taeschner's research subjects were raised according to the ONE PERSON–ONE LANGUAGE[2] strategy. However, there are other strategies that result in successful bilingualism (for an overview, cf. Romaine, 1995, p. 183ff. and Müller et al., 2006, Chapter 3). Another common approach is ONE LANGUAGE–ONE ENVIRONMENT[3] where the language depends on the setting. Other possibilities are ONE LANGUAGE WITHOUT COMMUNITY SUPPORT–ONE ENVIRONMENT,[4] where parents with different native languages speak one of these at home and the ambient language, which is neither of their native languages, outside the home or TWO LANGUAGES WITHOUT

COMMUNITY SUPPORT–ONE ENVIRONMENT[5] where the child will be exposed to three languages, two at home (one natively from each parent/caregiver) and a third outside. Two further possibilities have been described. One type, labelled BILINGUAL,[6] is characteristic of parents who are bilingual themselves and who speak both languages to the child at home, i.e. they mix languages. The other is when one parent decides to address the child in a second language which s/he has mastered well, despite being in a monolingual community, which we can call NON-NATIVE PARENTS.[7]

The existence of these other successful strategies calls into question Volterra and Taeschner's claim that separating language use by person is an attempt to minimize interference between the two languages, since we have no evidence that there is more (syntactic) interference between the languages in children whose parents link language use to the environment. This then means that Volterra and Taeschner's claims for the causes of so-called language 'mixing' must be re-examined. Perhaps the 'mixing' is not a result of early fused systems.

In opposition to Volterra and Taeschner's claims, two seminal works argued that bilingual first language children are able to separate their two languages from early on. The first study (Genesee, 1989) suggested that there are other reasons for language mixing at the lexical level than the absence of an equivalent word in the lexicon of the other language. In support of this, Cantone (2007) observed that while some bilingual children mix a lot in both languages, others mix only in one language and still others do not mix at all or very rarely. Figures 10.2 and 10.3 show data collected on a fortnightly basis in both languages from a German–Italian bilingual child, Marta, up to the age of 2;4,0 (years;months,days). As the figures show, Marta mixes a lot more in her exchanges with the German interviewer, than in her Italian. Marta's preferred language during this early stage of development is clearly Italian. However, a lack of mixing does not necessarily indicate the preferred language. Italian is also the stronger language in another bilingual German–Italian child, Aurelio (from whom data will be presented below), even though he mixes his languages as much as 50 per cent of the time during the earliest stages.

In another key study, Meisel (1989) also criticized Volterra and Taeschner's view on an early fused syntactic system. He studied syntactically contrasting grammatical domains in bilingual German–French children, including word order and expression of subject-verb-agreement. He showed that from the very beginning these domains were acquired differently in the two languages. Word order was also

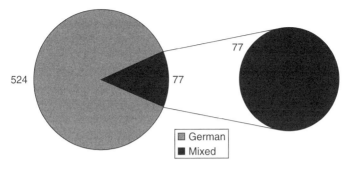

Figure 10.2   Marta, German context (taken from Müller, Kupisch, Schmitz and Cantone, 2006, 195)

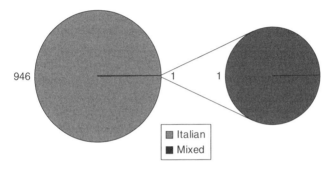

Figure 10.3   Marta, Italian context (taken from Müller, Kupisch, Schmitz and Cantone, 2006, 196)

examined by Müller et al. (2002) in their study of the acquisition of the verb-second property of German.[8] They found that bilingual children use verb-second constructions from very early on in German, as illustrated in Figure 10.4 below for the German–Italian bilingual child Carlotta. Verb-second constructions, in which the first constituent is not the subject, are indicated as VS in Figure 10.4. These data support Meisel's contention that young bilinguals use language-specific word orders from early on.

Italian and German also differ in the behaviour of grammatical subjects. In German, the subject is generally lexically realized (cf. Müller et al., 2006, p. 150ff.).[9] In Italian, a null-subject language, it is generally omitted (between 60 and 70 per cent in the adult language). Figure 10.5 shows evidence from the development of subject realizations in the two languages of one of our subjects, a German–Italian bilingual child, Jan. The development of subject realisations in the two languages is clearly different.

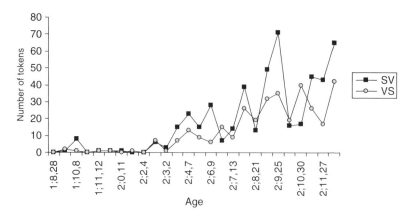

Figure 10.4   SV and VS in Carlotta's German (taken from Müller, Kupisch, Schmitz and Cantone, 2006, 121)

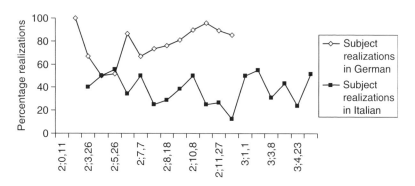

Figure 10.5   Realization of subject position in Jan (taken from Müller, Kupisch, Schmitz and Cantone, 2006, 157)

In sum, the two studies, by Genesee and by Meisel, suggest that bilingual children do not necessarily pass through a stage of fusion in either their lexicon or syntactic systems. However, Genesee and Meisel's claim of separate paths for each language was also taken to be a denial of the existence of cross-linguistic influence because (like Volterra and Taeschner) they assumed that separation and cross-linguistic influence are mutually exclusive: either the languages are combined and cross-linguistic influence occurs, or they are separate, and it does not. The problem arises because all four researchers were conceiving of separation and influence from the perspective of a language as a single system, not from the perspective of *subsystems* such as finite verb placement in Italian vs. German, or the realization of subjects in Italian vs. German.

Below we adopt a subsystems approach to bilingual development and examine a number of vulnerable grammatical phenomena,[10] showing that cross-linguistic influence and language separation can co-occur.

cross-linguistic influence and separation

Research suggests that all combinations of influence and separation are possible when a grammatical sub-systems perspective is taken. Gawlitzek-Maiwald and Tracy (1996) observed that while some grammatical domains developed separately in an English–German bilingual child, other domains involved the child using language A to bootstrap aspects of the syntactic system of language B. Similarly, Hulk and Müller (2000) and Müller and Hulk (2001) described grammatical domains which are vulnerable to cross-linguistic influence, while other syntactic properties are acquired without reference to the other language.

In response to these possibilities, Hulk and Müller (2000) examined the conditions under which cross-linguistic influence affects bilingual first language acquisition and concluded that it is the linguistic properties or characteristics of the grammatical phenomenon in question which allow us to predict cross-linguistic influence. Language dominance or language preference is not the driving force for influence. Rather, Hulk and Müller's two conditions for cross-linguistic influence to occur are

(1) The vulnerable grammatical phenomenon is an *interface* property, i.e., a grammatical property located at, e.g. the interface between syntax and pragmatics (Pillunat et al., 2006); and
(2) The surface strings of the two languages are similar for the expression of the vulnerable grammatical phenomenon.

When both conditions are satisfied, the bilingual child will have recourse to the least computationally complex analysis of the grammatical property in question. So if language A offers a less complex analysis than language B for a given grammatical phenomenon Z (which meets the above two conditions), the child will use the less complex analysis for both languages. That complexity has an effect on acquisition can be seen in data from monolingual children acquiring the language with the 'more complex' phenomenon who show delays in the acquisition of that phenomenon compared with the monolingual acquisition of the same phenomenon in the other language (Müller and Hulk, 2001).

To see what is meant by an 'interface property' in the conditions given above, we can look at object pronouns in Romance languages. In these languages, clitic pronouns ('weak' pronouns which cannot be stressed, coordinated, modified etc., *le/l'* in the following examples) can be construed with noun phrases containing an indefinite article and assume a type-reading, as in (1).

(1) Un homme, on le reconnait par sa façon de parler.
    'A man, one recognizes him by his way of speaking.'

Here, the antecedent, the noun phrase that the pronoun (le) refers to (i.e. un homme), must be an entity that can be presupposed. This explains why (2) is impossible.

(2) Je voudrais boire du vin. – D'accord. *Un verre, je l'ai dans l'étagère.
    'I'd like to drink some wine. – All right. A glass, I it have on the shelf.'

Here, the noun phrase 'un verre' cannot be presupposed and so the pronoun (l') cannot refer to it.

López (2003) noticed that Romance clitics occur in constructions which are typically analysed as presuppositional. The examples presented below come from López (2003, p. 199) but have been translated into Italian and French. The two constructions discussed are CLLD (CLitic Left Dislocation, in which a noun phrase has been moved to the left of the clause, as in 3) and CLRD (CLitic Right Dislocation, in which a noun phrase has been moved to the right of the clause, as in 4). In both cases, the clitics appear in order to mark the dislocated noun phrase as presupposed either in the discourse or by the hearer.

(3) *Speaker A* French: Qu'est-ce que tu as fait avec les meubles?

    Speaker A Italian: Cosa hai fatto con i mobili?
                           'What did you do with the furniture?'

    Speaker B French: Les tables, je les ai réparées le matin, mais les chaises je les ai réparées le soir.

    Speaker B Italian: Le tavole, le ho riparate la mattina, ma le sedie le ho riparate la sera.

    Lit.: The tables I them repaired in the morning, but the chairs I them repaired at night.

(4)   *Speaker A*   French: Qu'est-ce que tu as fait avec le stylo?
      Speaker A   Italian: Che cosa hai fatto con la penna?
                               'What did you do with the pen?'

(a)   *Speaker B*   French: Je l'ai oublié sur la table, ton crétin de
                               stylo.
      Speaker B   Italian: L'ho dimenticata sulla tavola, la tua stupida
                               penna.
      Lit.: I it forgot on the table, your stupid pen.

(b)   *Speaker B*   French: *J'ai oublié sur la table, ton crétin de
                               stylo.
      Speaker B   Italian: *Ho dimenticata sulla tavola, la tua
                               stupida penna.
      Lit.: I forgot on the table, your stupid pen.

(5)   *Speaker A*   French: Qu'est-ce qu'il y a?
      Speaker A   Italian: Che cos'è?
                               'What happened?'

(a)   *Speaker B*   French: J'ai oublié ton crétin de stylo sur la table.
      Speaker B   Italian: Ho dimenticata la tua stupida penna sulla
                               tavola.
      Lit.: I forgot your stupid pen on the table.

(b)   *Speaker B*   French: *Je l'ai oublié sur la table, ton crétin de
                               stylo.
      Speaker B   Italian: *L'ho dimenticata sulla tavola, la tua
                               stupida penna.

These examples illustrate that an antecedent can be presupposed either
in the discourse or by the hearer. Both CLLD and CLRD constructions
share the *pragmatic* property that they are presuppositional. In other
words, French and Italian clitics are not only syntactic elements which
are used under pragmatic conditions which favour pronominalization,
but they mark that the antecedent (overt or covert) is presupposed by
the speaker. The ungrammaticality of (4b) and (5b) show that object
clitics mark certain constituents as presuppositional, and their use or
absence may result in ungrammatical sentences, not just pragmatically
odd constructions. The choice of object clitics, however, is determined
not by pure syntactic factors but by pragmatic ones. In other words,
pragmatics and syntax interact in a way that pragmatic factors restrict

the possibilities offered by the syntactic system. It is this that makes the behaviour of clitics an interface phenomenon.

Given their interface status, the prediction is that clitic systems will be ripe for cross-linguistic influence when there is a mismatch of complexity between one language and the other. The bilingual child is predicted to use the grammatical analysis of the less complex language for both languages. Such a case arises when the two languages are German and a Romance language.

German is a language with a less complex system than the Romance languages. As (6) shows, it possesses normal (non-clitic) pronouns which, although they are used under certain pragmatic conditions, are not obligatory in syntax. Instead of a normal pronoun, a noun phrase can be used and the sentence remains grammatical, as in (6), although it becomes pragmatically odd, marked as '?'.

(6) *Speaker A* German: Hast du das Buch auf dem Tisch schon gelesen?
                          'Have you already read the book on the table?'

     Speaker B German: Das habe ich schon gelesen, ja.
                          'It have I already read, yes'

     Speaker B German: ?Das Buch auf dem Tisch habe ich schon gelesen, ja.
                          'The book on the table have I already read'

The prediction is thus that until they have mastered the more complex clitic analysis, the bilingual German–Romance child will use the German analysis for both languages and treat clitic pronouns as regular pronouns in the sense that they are not obligatory in syntax.

Let's look at the other condition on cross-linguistic influence. The second condition concerns similarity of surface strings. Although German is a verb-second language, and Italian is generally treated as an SVO language, with verbs in final position in subordinate clauses, both languages share the word order SVO. (Maria liest das Buch = 'Maria reads the book' can be translated directly into Maria legge il libro.) In other words, two otherwise syntactically different languages may share surface word orders. A child acquiring these two languages may thus opt for one syntactic analysis of SVO constructions in both languages, the less complex analysis, because the German analysis would require both SVO *and* SOV, whereas Italian requires only SVO.

The impact of the two conditions (interface and simplicity/complexity) on acquisition can be expected to be either quantitative or qualitative, or both. Quantitative impact would result in acceleration or delay in the bilingual's developmental process in comparison with monolingual peers. Qualitative impact would result in transfer. Thus, we can suggest that acceleration, delay and transfer may all be epiphenomenal products of conditions on cross-linguistic influence.

Evidence for acceleration shows in the placement of finite verbs in German. From monolingual language acquisition we know that children pass through a stage during which they place the finite (and non-finite) verb clause-finally, including in main clauses (Clahsen, 1982) despite it being ungrammatical in the adult language. For example, Figure 10.6 shows data from Chantal, a monolingual German learner (Schmitz, 2006).

Until the age of 2;7, the verb-final pattern prevailed in Chantal's speech, and she produced utterances such as 'ich auch mache' = 'I also make' and 'die puppe schlafen will' = 'the doll to-sleep wants'. Figure 10.7, on the other hand, shows data from Lukas, typical of German–Italian bilingual children, who does *not* show a stage in the development of his German characterized by the predominance of verb-final patterns. Rather, he uses verb-second placement (VS) earlier than the monolingual child. Between them, Figures 10.6 and 10.7 show that bilingual Lukas has reached a developmental stage at 2;3 which monolingual Chantal reaches more than six months later at the age of 2;10. Thus in this case we have an acceleration effect of bilingualism.

Delay effects also occur. Examining gender marking, for example, Kupisch et al. (2002) concluded that while monolingual French and Italian learners master their gender systems very early (before 2;3), this is not the case for bilingual children. Figure 10.8 compares the development of gender by the German–Italian child Marta and the German–French child Amélie, and shows both of them are quite late in mastering the gender systems.

We can also view the bilingual data quantitatively and qualitatively. My review of the literature on the acquisition of German finite verb placement in subordinate clauses by bilingual children with a Romance language or English (Müller, 1998) concluded that half of the bilingual population is late in acquiring the correct word order in finite subordinate clauses in German, but have no problems in either the Romance language or English. Examples of bilingual children showing this effect are provided for Carlotta in Figure 10.9 (Italian–German) and for Alexander in Figure 10.10 (German–French). Both children pass through a stage

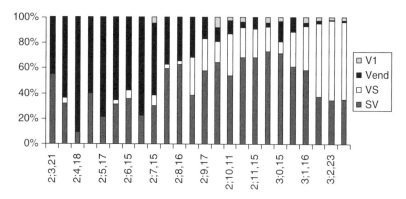

Figure 10.6   Verb placement in Chantal's German (taken from Müller, Kupisch, Schmitz and Cantone, 2006, 120)

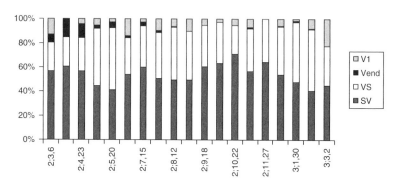

Figure 10.7   Verb placement in Lukas' German (taken from Müller, Kupisch, Schmitz and Cantone, 2006, 122)

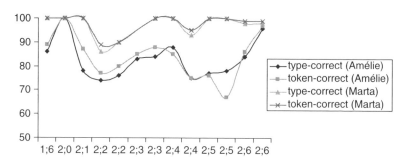

Figure 10.8   Gender marking accuracy in Amélie (French–German) and Marta (Italian-German) in the Romance language, taken from Kupisch (2006)

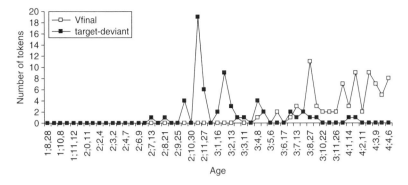

Figure 10.9   Finite verb placement in Carlotta's German subordinate clauses (taken from Müller, Kupisch, Schmitz and Cantone, 2006, 167)

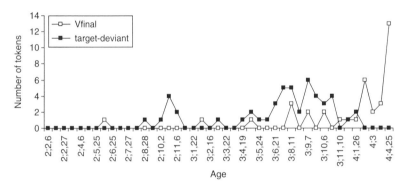

Figure 10.10   Finite verb placement in Alexander's German subordinate clauses (taken from Müller, Kupisch, Schmitz and Cantone, 2006, 170)

in which they almost exclusively use target-deviant placements of the finite verb. Only after the age of 4 in the data from these children do target-deviant word orders disappear.

Independent of the second language, the bilingual children placed the finite verb in the position following the subject in German subordinate clauses, e.g. 'Wenn ich war baby...' = 'When I was a baby ...' In other cases, however, there are constructions whose emergence depends on the second language. If a German-speaking child acquires Italian as the second first language, the verb is often placed in second position in the subordinate clause, i.e. in the position immediately following the clause-introducing conjunction: 'Wenn hab ich geburtstag...' = 'When have I birthday'. This does not happen when the second first language is French or English. These children place the finite verb in third pos-ition in subordinate clauses, even if the second structural position is not the subject of the clause: 'Wenn geburtstag hab ich gehabt...'/ 'wenn ich hab geburtstag gehabt...' = 'when birthday have I had'/'when I have birthday had'. For a discussion of how the linguistic differences between the languages might cause this difference see Müller (2006, 2007). The observation that the second language determines the kind of construc-tion used in German subordinate clauses clearly indicates a qualitative effect of cross-linguistic influence.

To summarize, cross-linguistic influence and language separation are not mutually exclusive and cross-linguistic influence affects only some grammatical domains, while others develop separately from the very beginning. The nature of the cross-linguistic influence depends on the vulnerability of the domain and the complexity of the alternative ana-lyses with which the child is presented. The bilingual child initially uses the less complex syntactic analysis for both languages, an effect that disappears as the children's language develops. Moreover, as the preceding discussion has shown, it is not always one language or the other that is the subject of cross-linguistic influence. This suggests that the effect is unrelated to language dominance, the latter being defined for whole languages during a particular period in development. We explore the issue of language dominance further below.

language dominance

In a review of the definition and use of the term 'language domin-ance' in the literature, Müller et al. (2006) found it in use by researchers investigating their own bilingual children from early in the last century (Ronjat, 1913; Leopold, 1949a, 1949b; Taeschner, 1983; and Fantini, 1985). These studies were diary reports and the observations on lan-guage dominance were not intended to be theoretical. Unfortunately, language dominance remains poorly understood. While attempts to define it in the 1980s and 1990s used both quantitative and qualita-tive measures, the criteria for distinguishing one from the other were unclear. On one hand, despite the variation in cross-linguistic influence we have examined above, the investigation of grammatical phenomena in each language (considered to be areas of competence), were taken to be qualitative, and language dominance was considered to be a type of 'grammatical predominance' (see e.g. Lindholm and Padilla, 1978; Petersen, 1988; Schlyter, 1993). Quantitative criteria, on the other hand, were associated with language performance and linguistic production, with MLU (= mean length of utterance) being a popular criterion (see e.g. Genesee et al., 1995; Döpke, 1992). Müller and Kupisch (2003) suggest, however, that MLU is a qualitative criterion, while the number of utterances used by each child per recording session is associated with language performance and is thus a quantitative criterion.

Another problem with the definition of language dominance arises from the fact that attempts to define it were largely motivated by the search for correlations between language dominance and language separation (de Houwer, 1990), code-switching patterns (Petersen, 1988; Genesee et al., 1995) and cross-linguistic influence (Döpke, 1992). Nearly all researchers who observed cross-linguistic influence claimed (usually without systematic measurement) that the influenced language was less frequently spoken by the child, did not develop as quickly (as measure by MLU), and/or was not the language of the community and thus did not provide sufficient input (see Kupisch, 2006). Common across all studies is the assumption that 'language dominance' could explain other phenomena such as language separation, cross-linguistic influence and code-switching patterns.

MLU (mean length of utterances) (Brown, 1973) is the best known, most adopted and at the same time most criticized criterion (Genesee et al., 1995) for measuring language dominance. Figures 10.11 and 10.12 show a 'balanced' German–Italian child (Lukas), and a German 'dominant' German–French child (Céline) respectively.

A related measure to MLU is the 'upper bound', i.e. the longest utterance in a recording or transcript. It is argued (Brown, 1973) to reflect the child's capacity to produce syntactically complex utterances even more clearly than the MLU, because it does not represent a mean. Figures 10.13a and b show the upper bound data for Lukas and Céline. The number of multi-morphemic utterances is a third dominance criterion used by Genesee et al. (1995). It can be particularly informative during the largely one-word stage when a word-based MLU is not yet appropriate (Loconte, 2001).

The number of mixed utterances and the direction of mixing have also been integrated into studies on language balance/dominance on the grounds that some authors found a correlation between language mixing and language dominance (e.g. Berman, 1979; Genesee et al., 1995). Furthermore some authors claimed that mixing is unidirectional (e.g. Petersen, 1988). Cantone (2007), however, argued against this view, pointing out that mixing also occurs from the weaker into the stronger language, as discussed above.

Some authors have attempted to make sense of the notion of language dominance by measuring the size and nature of the bilingual

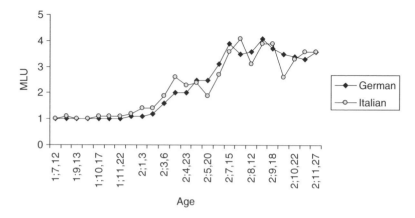

Figure 10.11   MLU development in Lukas (taken from Müller, Kupisch, Schmitz and Cantone, 2006, 71)

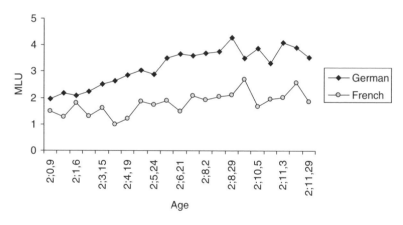

Figure 10.12   MLU development in Céline (taken from Müller, Kupisch, Schmitz and Cantone, 2006, 71)

lexicon. Genesee et al. (1995) measured the full range of word types in a fairly small dataset. Other authors have limited their investigations to a particular word-class, such as verbs or nouns. Cordes (2001) and Loconte (2001) examined verb types and tokens to establish language balance. For our part, we have looked at the cumulative growth of the verb lexicon (Müller and Kupisch, 2003). Figures 10.14 and 10.16 show the lexicon growth for 'balanced bilingual' Lukas, Figures 10.15 and 10.17 for 'unbalanced bilingual' Céline.

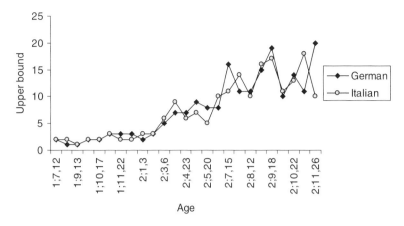

Figure 10.13a   Upper bound development in Lukas (taken from Müller, Kupisch, Schmitz and Cantone, 2006, 72)

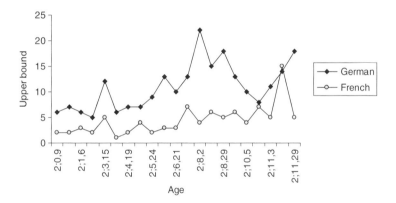

Figure 10.13b   Upper bound development in Céline (taken from Müller, Kupisch, Schmitz and Cantone, 2006, 72)

The number of utterances per recording session is another criterion often used to measure dominance (e.g. Paradis et al., 2000). Loconte (2001, p. 26), however, remarks that this criterion measures the children's readiness to speak rather than language dominance (Cantone and Müller, 2005). Figure 10.18 for Marta shows that she likes to speak both languages. Figure 10.19 for Aurelio indicates that his readiness to speak German is very low until the age of 3;6.

A better term for these data than language dominance is 'language preference' which can be used when bilinguals feel more at ease using

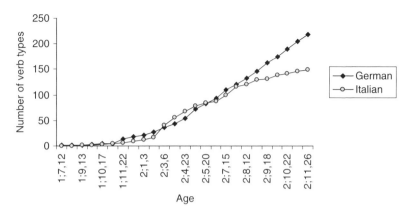

Figure 10.14   Development of verb lexicon in Lukas (taken from Müller, Kupisch, Schmitz and Cantone, 2006, 74)

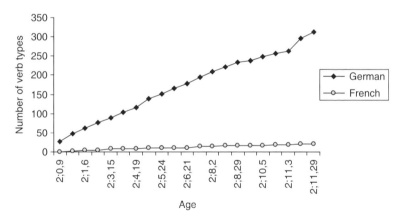

Figure 10.15   Development of verb lexicon in Céline (taken from Müller, Kupisch, Schmitz and Cantone, 2006, 74)

one of their languages for a particular activity rather than the other (Baetens-Beardsmore, 1982; Dodson, 1985).

Thus, although each of these measures (MLU, upper bound, multi-morphemic utterances, number and direction of mixed utterances, size and nature of the lexicon, and number of utterances per session) provide some statistical data, it is not clear that they constitute evidence of language dominance.

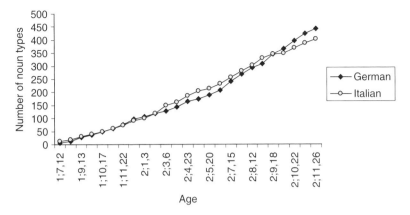

Figure 10.16   Development of noun lexicon in Lukas (taken from Müller, Kupisch, Schmitz and Cantone, 2006, 75)

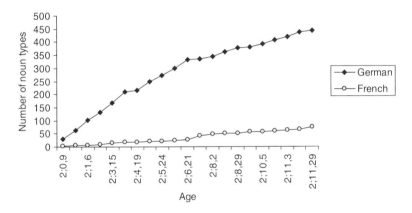

Figure 10.17   Development of noun lexicon in Céline (taken from Müller, Kupisch, Schmitz and Cantone, 2006, 75)

language dominance and correspondence to a norm

So far we have examined the notion of language dominance/preference between the languages of a bilingual. However, we might want to know how each language's speed of acquisition compares with some kind of norm. The most commonly used norms have to this point been those based on monolingual development. However, in a recent proposal (Kupisch et al., 2005), we have suggested a *bilingual norm* established by using mean values of the different dominance/preference measures in several bilingual children. Taking the mean values of a language

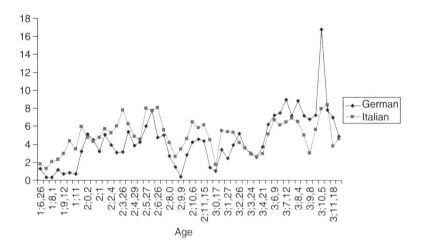

Figure 10.18   Number of utterances in Marta (taken from Arecibia Gurra, 2008)

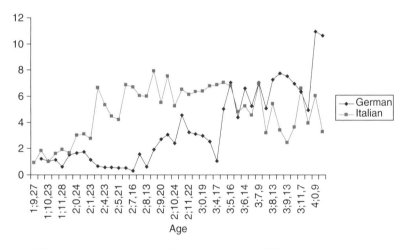

Figure 10.19   Number of utterances in Aurelio (taken from Arecibia Gurra, 2008)

in a larger population of bilinguals as the norm for that language in a bilingual individual, one can compare and measure each of the two languages in one individual with the mean values for the respective language. By this method, we have suggested (Müller and Pillunat, 2006) that there are bilingual children with two languages which range below an established norm for each of the languages. We have also shown that some children start out with one language dominant and become balanced in later stages, and balanced bilinguals who become dominant in one language. Or it may be the case that one of the languages ranges below the norm for that language but that they catch up to the norm over the course of development. Clearly, language dominance is not an explanatory prime, but a feature of bilingualism deserving of study in its own right.

If we can establish language dominance as an independent measure based on bilingual norms, as suggested above, we can then ask whether language dominance is related to the kind of cross-linguistic influence we examined earlier. Although there is not space here to enter into a detailed discussion of this issue, there are a number of reasons to suppose that they are not, in fact, related. These include that perfectly balanced bilingual children show signs of cross-linguistic influence; that cross-linguistic influence occurs in different languages during the same developmental stage for different grammatical phenomena; that cross-linguistic influence may go in both directions at the same time; that some forms of cross-linguistic influence only ever go in one direction irrespective of dominance patterns; that children with clear dominance patterns have areas of grammar that are never subject to cross-linguistic influence; and that the weaker language in bilingual children may influence the stronger language for vulnerable grammatical phenomena.

Although all of the above situations bear careful scrutiny, there is another important question left unanswered: if language dominance does not account for the occurrence of cross-linguistic influence, then why is it that not all vulnerable interface grammatical phenomena are subject to cross-linguistic influence? In other words, it seems to be true that in order for cross-linguistic influence to occur, some criteria have to be met. However, the inverse is not true, namely that if the criteria are met, cross-linguistic influence necessarily follows. Why is this the case? We turn to this now.

different paths to bilingualism?

As we have suggested, non-vulnerable domains develop in bilingual children the same way that they do in monolinguals. Vulnerable domains, on the other hand, may or may not show cross-linguistic influence in bilingual children. Above we saw that finite verb placement in German subordinate clauses is vulnerable for some children (e.g. Carlotta and Alexander). For other children such as Jan, Lukas and Céline, this grammatical domain is acquired in an error-free way, as it is for monolingual children. Figure 10.20 shows the error-free development for Jan, the German–Italian bilingual child.

Certainly Jan's data when compared with that of other bilingual children suggests there is individual variation in the way each child approaches acquisition. However, is this really the case or could there be another explanation for the variation we see? We suggest that there are in fact two strategies: a *monolingual strategy* and a *bilingual strategy* and children apply one or the other to each subsystem of language. The monolingual strategy could be defined as an initial assumption that the two languages are similar (even if they are not, and this guess will be visible as cross-linguistic influence). The bilingual strategy could be defined as an initial assumption that the languages are different (even if they are not, although this guess will never be visible for the psycholinguist). These two strategies would then be domain-specific so that one child may apply a monolingual strategy to syntax but show cross-linguistic influence in the development of the two lexicons; while another child would show the reverse application. Still other children might apply one strategy to both domains, the lexicon and the syntax.

Ultimately, the choice between the two strategies and the choice as to where the strategies apply (lexicon, syntax) is probably regulated by the processing costs placed on the child by the production and comprehension demands of the two languages. Data from Jan, Carlotta and Alexander show the different possible paths of development and also

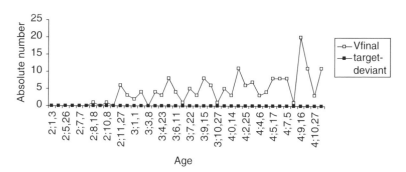

Figure 10.20   Finite verb placement in Jan's German subordinate clauses (taken from Müller, Kupisch, Schmitz and Cantone, 2006, 168)

give an idea of how the impact of processing demands may be revealed in the children's data.

Jan has been characterized above as a child who does not show effects of cross-linguistic influence in the development of word order in German, i.e. in syntax. Interestingly, his lexical development does not show signs of cross-linguistic influence either. Blal (2004) has suggested that in monolingual development, the German lexicon is characterized by a noun–verb symmetry (no preference of nouns or verbs) between the ages 2 and 3, whereas in the Romance language (French), a noun–verb asymmetry in the form of a noun preference can be observed. In line with this, Jan's German lexicon shows Blal's symmetry for German and asymmetry for French, as shown graphically in Figure 10.21. However, we know that Jan is a bilingual child with a strong imbalance; his German is the dominant language as measured using the bilingual norm protocol. Thus we might want to say that language dominance is a third strategy in addition to the monolingual and bilingual strategies that, unlike the latter two is not domain-specific but is language-specific. We might then say that children like Jan 'benefit' from language dominance in the sense that their processing costs are reduced as a function of one language not being developed as quickly as the other language.

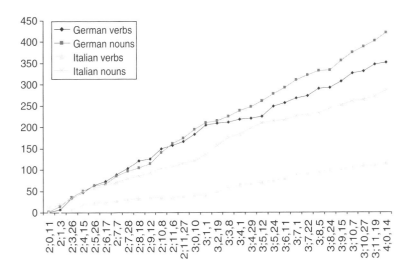

Figure 10.21   Development of the lexicon in Jan (noun and verb types)

Carlotta is a bilingual child exhibiting signs of cross-linguistic influence in syntax whenever predicted by the criteria. Her lexicon does not develop in the way predicted for monolingual children either, as shown in Figure 10.22. Note however that Carlotta is a well-balanced bilingual child at all times in her development. In other words, she makes use of

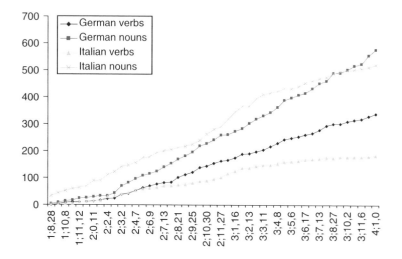

Figure 10.22   Development of the lexicon in Carlotta (noun and verb types)

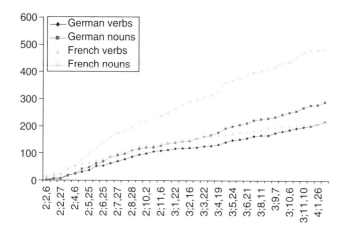

Figure 10.23   Development of the lexicon in Alexander (noun and verb types)

the monolingual strategy whenever possible. As a consequence, there is no need to develop one language less quickly than the other language.

Finally, Alexander is a child whose corpora exhibit signs of a bilingual strategy in the development of his syntax, while his lexicons develop monolingually, as shown in Figure 10.23. Alexander is a slightly imbalanced bilingual; his French is a little stronger at all times in his development.

Summarizing, Jan seems to make use of the bilingual strategy (assuming the languages are independent) in both the acquisition of syntax and of the lexicon. As such he appears to be learning each language monolingually, even though he has a preferential imbalance between the languages. Carlotta on the other hand uses a monolingual strategy in both domains (assuming there is only a single system), and Alexander uses the bilingual strategy (separate systems) in syntax and the monolingual strategy (same system) in the lexicon.

Further research will be needed to reveal whether language dominance might be reinterpreted as a bilingual strategy to cope with the simultaneous acquisition of two languages and to reduce the processing costs created by the production and comprehension of two languages simultaneously. That language dominance might be seen this way is supported by the observation made by Kupisch et al. (2005) that language imbalance is a characteristic of some bilingual children during early stages of language development (before age 4). During later stages, most of the strongly imbalanced children minimize the mismatch between their languages and become fairly balanced bilinguals (as in the case of Céline).

what other factors play a role?

The preceding sections have shown that separation and cross-linguistic influence in bilingual children do not affect whole languages but have to be analysed with fine-grained linguistic tools, the outcome being that there are some robust grammatical domains not affected by language influence and other domains which are vulnerable to cross-linguistic influence. Appeal to language dominance cannot explain these different patterns of influence. Rather the explanations lie in the grammatical phenomena involved, which, once analysed linguistically, will allow predictions about how the developmental path proceeds. In addition, as we have seen, bilingual children may develop certain strategies in order to acquire the two languages in the most efficient way. Other factors may play a role, however, including socio-economic background, the attitude towards bilingualism and education, and the relative prestige of the languages involved in the societies in question. This last can be seen in the German context where French is a highly prestigious language, while Italian (like Spanish, Portuguese) is often associated with Gastarbeiter ('working-class migrant') families. While the difference does not seem to be apparent in the data of bilingual French–German and Italian–German children we have looked at above, it is a general assumption in Germany that children with a Romance background are able to become very successful bilinguals, whereas children with a Turkish background often fail to do so. It remains to be seen if this difference is reflected in bilingual data.

notes

1. The empirical results reported here stem from a research project which has been (and still is) financed by the Deutsche Forschungsgemeinschaft starting in 1999. The project has been (and still is) directed by Natascha Müller (research assistants until 2005: Katja Cantone, Tanja Kupisch, Katrin Schmitz) and is currently conducted at Bergische Universität Wuppertal (current research assistants: Lastenia Arencibia Guerra, Nicole Hause-Grüdl, Estelle Leray, Franziska Witzmann).
2. Ronjat (1913) French–German, Kielhöfer and Jonekeit (1985) French–German, Meisel (1990, 1994) French–German, Genesee et al. (1995) French–English (with bilingual community), Leopold (1949a, b) English–German, Tracy (1995) English–German, Döpke (1992) English–German, Taeschner (1983) Italian–German, deHouwer (1990) English–Dutch.
3. Fantini (1985) English–Spanish, Tracy (1995) English–German.
4. Haugen (1953) Norwegian–English, Oksaar (1977) Estonian (parents) – Swedish/German (community), Ruke-Dravina (1967) Serbian–French, Pavlovitch (1920) Serbian–French.
5. Elwert (1959) English–German–Italian, Hoffman (1985) German–Spanish– English.
6. Tabouret-Keller (1962) French–German, Ellul (1978) Maltese–English.
7. Döpke (1992) English–German, Saunders (1982) English–German.
8. German is a verb-second language, i.e. the finite verb (which inflects for person, number and tense) occurs in second position in main clauses, following the first constituent. The first constituent in German main clauses can be the subject – S_{ubj} V_{fin} X (Y) 'Maria liest das Buch im Garten' = 'Mary reads the book in-the garden' – as well as the object, an adjunct, etc. – X V_{fin} S_{ubj} (Y) 'Das Buch liest Maria im Garten' = 'The book reads Mary in-the garden', where X is the object and Y an optional constituent. If the first constituent is not the subject, the subject immediately follows the finite verb. Italian is not a verb-second language, but an SVO language. The finite verb precedes the subject in declarative main clauses. If a non-subject constituent is fronted, the order between subject and finite verb remains: X S_{ubj} V_{fin} (Y). Bilingual German–Italian children do not use German verb-second order when they speak Italian, e.g. an utterance like 'il libro legge Maria nel giardino' = 'the book reads Mary in-the garden does not occur'.

9. The subject can be omitted in the first structural position of German main clauses if it is the topic and recoverable from the linguistic context or if it is an expletive element, i.e. an element without semantic content. In the following examples, the omitted subject has been marked as xxx: (1) Omitted subject recoverable from the linguistic context, Speaker A: 'Ich kann zwei Bücher an einem Tag lesen' = 'I can read two books in one day' – Speaker B: 'ich muss das mal ausprobieren' = 'have it PARTICLE to-out-try', (2) Omitted expletive subject, 'Es regnet ganz schön lange in dieser Stadt' = 'rains quite a long-time in this town'. Italian is often characterized as a null-subject-language; the pronominal subject is omitted in about 67 per cent of cases in spontaneous speech (cf. Müller et al., 2006, 150ff.). Pronominal subjects are realized only if they carry contrastive stress: The sentence 'Io vado alla festa (non lei)' = 'I go to-the party (not her)' means in Italian that it is me who goes to the party, not any other person.

10. For the robust, i.e. non-vulnerable phenomena, we refer the interested reader to Müller et al. (2002), Müller and Pillunat (2008), Schmitz and Müller (2008).

references

Arencibia Guerra, L. (2008). Sprachdominanz bei bilingualen Kindern mit Deutsch und Französisch, Italienisch oder Spanisch als Erstsprachen. Unpublished doctoral thesis, Bergische Universität Wuppertal.

Baetens-Beardsmore, H. (1982). *Bilingualism: Basic Principles*. Clavedon: Tieto Ltd.

Berman, R. (1979). The re-emergence of a bilingual: a case study of a Hebrew-English speaking child. *Working Papers on Bilingualism* 19, 158–80.

Blal, A. (2004). Das Lexikon im Erwerb des Französischen. Unpublished Master's thesis, Universität Hamburg.

Brown, R. (1973). *A First Language: The Early Stages*. Cambridge, MA: Harvard University Press.

Cantone, K. F. (2007). *Code-switching in Bilingual Children*. Dordrecht: Springer.

Cantone, K. F. and Müller, N. (2005). Code-switching at the interface of language specific lexicons and the computational system. *International Journal of Bilingualism* 9 (2), 205–25.

Clahsen, H. (1982). Spracherwerb in der Kindheit. Eine Untersuchung zur Entwicklung der Syntax bei Kleinkindern. Tübingen: Narr.

Cordes, J. (2001). Zum unausgewogenen doppelten Erstspracherwerb eines deutsch-französisch aufwachsenden Kindes: Eine empirische Untersuchung. Unpublished Master's thesis, Universität Hamburg.

de Houwer, A. (1990). *The Acquisition of Two Languages from Birth: A Case Study*. Cambridge: Cambridge University Press.

Dodson, C. J. (1985). Second language acquisition and bilingual development: A theoretical framework. *Journal of Multilingual and Multicultural Development* 5 (6), 325–46.

Döpke, S. (1992). *One Parent One Language. An Interactional Approach*. Amsterdam/ Philadelphia: Benjamins.

Ellul, S. (1978). *A Case Study in Bilingualism. Code-switching between Parents and their Pre-school Children in Malta*. St Albans: The Campfield Press.

Elwert, W. T. (1959). *Das zweisprachige Individuum: Ein Selbstzeugnis.* Wiesbaden: Franz Steiner Verlag.

Fantini, A. (1985). *Language Acquisition of a Bilingual Child: A Sociolinguistic Perspective.* San Diego: College Hill Press.

Gawlitzek-Maiwald, I. and Tracy, R. (1996). Bilingual bootstrapping. *Linguistics* 34, 901–26.

Genesee, F. (1989). Early bilingual development: One language or two? *Journal of Child Language* 16, 161–79.

Genesee, F., Nicoladis, E. and Paradis, J. (1995). Language differentiation in early bilingual development. *Journal of Child Language* 22, 611–31.

Hahne, A. and Friederici, A. (2001). Processing a second language: late learner's comprehension mechanisms as revealed by event-related brain potentials. *Bilingualism: Language and Cognition* 4 (2), 123–41.

Haugen, E. (1953). *The Norwegian Language in America: A Study in Bilingual Behavior.* Philadelphia: University of Pennsylvania Press.

Hoffman, C. (1985). Language acquisition in two trilingual children. *Journal of Multilingual and Multicultural Development* 6, 479–95.

Hulk, A. and Müller, N. (2000). Crosslinguistic influence at the interface between syntax and pragmatics. *Bilingualism: Language and Cognition* 3 (3), 227–44.

Hyltenstam, K and Abrahamsson, N. (2003). Maturational constraints in second language acquisition. In C. Doughty and M. Long (eds) *Handbook of Second Language Acquisition* (pp. 539–88). Oxford: Blackwell.

Kielhöfer, B. and Jonekeit, S. (1985). *Zweisprachige Kindererziehung.* Tübingen: Stauffenburg.

Kupisch, T. (2006). *The Acquisition of Determiners in Bilingual German-Italian and German-French Children.* München: Lincom.

Kupisch, T., Cantone, K., Schmitz, K. and Müller, N. (2005). Rethinking language dominance in bilingual children. Manuscript Universität Hamburg / Bergische Universität Wuppertal. Submitted.

Kupisch, T., Müller, N. and Cantone, K. (2002). Gender in monolingual and bilingual first language acquisition: comparing Italian and French. *Lingue e Linguaggio* 1, 107–49.

Leopold, W. (1949a). *Speech Development of a Bilingual Child. A Linguist's Record III: Grammar and General Problems in the First Two Years.* New York: AMS Press.

Leopold, W. (1949b). *Speech Development of a Bilingual Child. A Linguist's Record IV: Diary from Age 2.* New York: AMS Press.

Lindholm, K. J. and Padilla, A. M. (1978). Language mixing in bilingual children. *Journal of Child Language* 5, 327–35.

Loconte, A. (2001). Zur Sprachdominanz bei bilingual deutsch-italienischen Kindern. Unpublished Master's thesis, Universität Hamburg.

Long, M. (1990). Maturational constraints on language development. *Studies in Second Language Acquisition* 12, 251–68.

López, L. (2003). Steps for a well-adjusted dislocation. *Studia Linguistica* 57 (3), 193–231.

McLaughlin, B. (1978). *Second Language Acquisition in Childhood.* Hillsdale, NJ: Erlbaum.

Meisel, J. M. (1989). Early differentiation of languages in bilingual children. In K. Hyltenstam and L. Obler (eds), *Bilingualism Across the Lifespan: Aspects of*

Acquisition, Maturity, and Loss (pp. 13–40). Cambridge: Cambridge University Press.

Meisel, J. M. (ed.) (1990). *Two First Languages. Early Grammatical Development in Bilingual Children*. Dordrecht: Foris.

Meisel, J. M. (ed.) (1994). *Bilingual First Language Acquisition. French and German Grammatical Development*. Amsterdam/Philadelphia: Benjamins.

Müller N. (1998). Transfer in bilingual first language acquisition. *Bilingualism: Language and Cognition* 1 (3), 151–71.

Müller N. (2006). Emerging complementizers. German in contact with French/ Italian. In C. Lefevre, L. White and C. Jourdan (eds) *L2 Acquisition and Creole Genesis* (pp. 145–65). Amsterdam/Philadelphia: Benjamins.

Müller N. (2007). Some notes on the syntax-pragmatics interface in bilingual children: German in contact with French/Italian. In J. Rehbein, C. Hohenstein and L. Pietsch (eds) *Connectivity in Grammar and Discourse* (pp. 101–35). Amsterdam/Philadelphia: Benjamins.

Müller N., Cantone, K., Kupisch, T. and Schmitz, K. (2002). Zum Spracheneinfluss im bilingualen Erstspracherwerb: Italienisch – Deutsch. *Linguistische Berichte* 190, 157–206.

Müller, N. and Hulk, A. (2001). Crosslinguistic influence in bilingual language acquisition: Italian and French as recipient languages. *Bilingualism: Language and Cognition* 4 (1), 1–21.

Müller, N. and Kupisch, T. (2003). Zum simultanen Erwerb des Deutschen und des Französischen bei (un)ausgeglichen bilingualen Kindern. *Vox Romanica* 62, 145–69.

Müller, N., Kupisch, T. Schmitz, K. and Cantone, K. (2006). *Einführung in die Mehrsprachigkeitsforschung*. Tübingen: Narr.

Müller, N. and Pillunat, A. (2008). Balanced bilingual children with two weak languages: a French-German case study. In P. Guijarro-Fuentes, P. Larrañaga and J. Clibbens (eds) *First Language Acquisition of Morphology and Syntax: Perspectives across Languages and Learners* (pp. 269–94). Amsterdam/Philadelphia: Benjamins.

Obler, L. K., Zatorre, R. J., Galloway, L. and Vaid, J. (1982). Cerebral lateralization in bilinguals: methodological issues. *Brain and Language* 15, 40–54.

Oksaar, E. (1977). On becoming trilingual. In C. Molony (ed.) *Deutsch im Kontakt mit anderen Sprachen* (pp. 296–306). Kronberg: Scriptor Verlag.

Paradis, J., Crago, M., Genesee, F. and Rice, M. (2000). Dual language impairment: Evidence from French-English bilingual children with SLI. Talk given at the 25th Boston University Conference on Language Development, Boston, Mass.

Pavlovitch, M. (1920). *Le langage enfantin: acquisition du serbe et du français par un enfant serbe*. Paris: Champion.

Petersen, J. (1988). Word-internal code-switching constraints in a bilingual child's grammar. *Linguistics* 26, 479–93.

Pillunat, A., Schmitz, K. and Müller, N. (2006). Die Schnittstelle Syntax-Pragmatik: Subjektauslassungen bei bilingual deutsch-französisch aufwachsenden Kindern. *Zeitschrift für Literaturwissenschaft und Linguistik LiLi* 143, 7–24.

Romaine, S. (1995). *Bilingualism*. Oxford: Blackwell.

Ronjat, J. (1913). *Le développement du langage observé chez un enfant bilingue*. Paris: Champion.

Ruke-Dravina, V. (1967). *Mehrsprachigkeit im Vorschulalter.* Lund: Gleerup.

Saunders, G. (1982). *Bilingual Children: Guidance for the Family.* Clevedon: Multilingual Matters.

Schlyter S. (1993). The weaker language in bilingual Swedish-French children. In K. Hyltenstam and Å. Viberg (eds) *Progression and Regression in Language* (pp. 289–308). Cambridge: Cambridge University Press.

Schmitz, K. (2006). *Zweisprachigkeit im Fokus. Der Erwerb der Verben mit zwei Objekten durch bilingual deutsch-französisch und deutsch-italienisch aufwachsende Kinder.* Tübingen: Narr.

Schmitz, K. and Müller, N. (2008). Strong and clitic pronouns in the monolingual and bilingual acquisition of French and Italian. *Bilingualism: Language and Cognition* 11, 1, 19–41.

Tabouret-Keller, A. (1962). L'acquisition du langage parlé chez un petit enfant en milieu bilingue. *Problèmes de Psycholinguistique* 8, 205–19.

Taeschner, T. (1983). *The Sun is Feminine. A Study on Language in Bilingual Children.* Berlin: Springer.

Tracy, R. (1995). *Child Languages in Contact: Bilingual Language Acquisition in Early Childhood.* Habilitationsschrift, Tübingen.

Volterra, V. and Taeschner, T. (1978). The acquisition and development of language by bilingual children. *Journal of Child Language* 5, 311–26.

11
universals and cross-linguistic variability in children's discourse

maya hickmann

introduction

First language acquisition requires learning rules of well-formedness at two levels of linguistic organization, the sentence and discourse. Full linguistic competence comprises grammatical knowledge, as well as a vast repertoire of skills inherent to native language use in varied situations – conducting a job interview, conversing with a neighbour, explaining route directions or a recipe. Irrespective of the language to be acquired, these rules are as much part of children's developing linguistic competence as their knowledge of how to produce, recognize and comprehend grammatical sentences.

The present chapter focuses specifically on *discourse cohesion* in child language. This aspect of children's linguistic competence pertains to their ability to regulate the flow of information as it unfolds across utterances in discourse. It is inherent to all types of discourse, but particularly crucial in narrative discourse where references to entities, states, and events contribute to the construction of some kind of 'story'. The survey below examines several referential domains of narrative discourse (reference to entities, time, space) across child languages, highlighting three main conclusions. First, discourse development is partially driven by general and presumably universal cognitive determinants. Second, structural and functional factors jointly determine how children become fully competent native speakers at different levels of linguistic organization. Third, each language confronts children with particular problems to solve, thereby influencing how they proceed to acquire their native language. Suggestions are made for future research directions necessary to examine the implications of these results for our understanding of linguistic and cognitive development.

discourse cohesion: general principles

The grammaticality of sentences clearly does not guarantee their well-formedness when they are embedded among other sentences in cohesive discourse. Discourse cohesion implies a variety of rules that regulate the flow of information across utterances, following at least two general principles. The first principle consists of marking the relatively *new* or *given* status of information in order to integrate what is said at a given point with what is already mutually known (e.g. Halliday and Hasan, 1976). Second, information may be more or less central at a given point, requiring discourse to be organized into a *foreground* and a *background* (e.g. Hopper, 1982). Mastering these discourse principles invites children to acquire a variety of linguistic devices, illustrated below in several referential domains.

denoting entities in discourse

When denoting entities, we simultaneously mark several distinctions. For example, *subjecthood* is marked in English sentences by position (pre-verbal and/or sentence-initial) and by morphological means (e.g. subject–verb agreement, case distinctions in pronouns). At the discourse level the continuum in (1) illustrates (in underlined italics) indefinite forms introducing referents that are not mutually known (new) and other forms denoting entities that are mutually known to various degrees (given to most presupposed or topical). In addition, many languages (especially if SVO) provide a variety of structures, such as existentials (3) or subject-verb inversions (4), that place new information towards the end of the sentence, rather than before the verb (as in (2)).

(1)   indefinite nominal < definite nominal < overt pronoun < zero pronoun
     NEW   GIVEN   GIVEN +   GIVEN ++
     <u>a boy</u> and <u>a girl</u> came... <u>the boy</u> was sad...   <u>he</u> cried...   and <u>0</u> left...
(2)   A boy was standing behind the window.
(3)   There was a boy standing behind the window.
(4)   Behind the window stood a boy.

time in discourse

Temporality in language is constructed by means of several categories briefly illustrated in (5) to (8). *Tense* presents an event (John's eating) as occurring either during speech time (5) or before ((6) and (7)), while *aspect* presents this event either as an interval (e.g. overlapping with immediate speech in (5) and situating Mary's arrival in (6)) or as a point (e.g. ordered in relation to her arrival in (7)). In (8) *modality* also marks the speaker's evaluation of truth (prediction) or a particular speech act on the part of the denoted speaker (promise), and in both cases the sentence denotes events expected to occur after speech time.[1] Finally, these markings serve to ground information in discourse by differentiating main events in the foreground from surrounding information in the background. Thus, (6) foregrounds Mary's arrival and backgrounds John's eating, while (7) describes two successive foregrounded events.

(5) John is eating an apple (as I am talking right now).

(6) John was eating an apple when Mary walked in (at noon yesterday).

(7) John ate an apple (at noon yesterday), then Mary walked in (five minutes later).

(8) John will eat an apple tomorrow (I predict, he promised ...).

space in discourse

All languages mark a number of distinctions in the spatial domain, for example between situations that are static (9) vs. dynamic ((10) and (11)) or between dynamic situations that imply a change of location (from outside to inside in (11)) vs. a general location (10). In addition, organizing spatial information in discourse requires the management of presuppositions in relation to denoted spatial entities. For example, in some cases the speaker must provide *spatial anchors* that enable the interlocutor to interpret locations or location changes across utterances in discourse. As illustrated in (12), once locations have been introduced in the universe of discourse (*roof*), they can serve as spatial anchors for further discourse (*jump all the way down*).

(9) John is sitting in the office.

(10) John is running in the office.

(11) John is running into the office.

(12) Look at the cat on top of the roof! It's going to jump all the way down!

discourse and linguistic diversity

In all three referential domains, then, devices mark syntactic, semantic and pragmatic distinctions, thereby simultaneously organizing information at the sentence and discourse levels. However, as illustrated below, their properties are quite variable across languages, presenting children with different problems to solve.

denoting entities across languages

In order to mark discourse status, languages rely to different extents on devices that may be obligatory or optional and relatively 'local' (referring expressions) or 'global' (utterance structure). As illustrated for English above, nominal determiners may be obligatory and clause structure variations optional for discourse purposes in some languages. In Romance languages determiners are also obligatory, but discourse status is further grammaticalized by clause structure, which requires (clitic) pronouns to be pre-verbal (13).[2] Yet other structural factors constrain word order in a language such as German (*V2-language*), where subject–verb inversions may be obligatory merely to ensure that the verb be in second position (14).[3]

(13) Pierre a acheté un lit. Il l'a transporté chez lui.
      ('Pierre bought a bed. He it carried home.')
(14) Ein/das Kind kam herein. Dann kam ein/der Lehrer herein
      ('A/the child came in. Then came a/the teacher in.')

Consider now a language such as Chinese, which lacks morphology and therefore heavily relies on word order. Determiners may serve to mark information status in discourse (numeral 'yi' 'a/one', demonstrative 'zhei' 'this/the'), but they are entirely optional. In contrast, clause structure is an obligatory marking of discourse status, according to the following rule: new information must be placed in post-verbal position, for example in subject–verb inversions such as (15a) or in existential constructions such as (15b), and it is ungrammatical in pre-verbal position (16a), which is reserved for given information (16b).[4]

(15) a. POST-VERBAL – Inversion   b. POST-VERBAL – Existential
         lai le yi-ge ren.   You yi-ge ren.
         (come-PERF one-CL person)   (have one-CL person)
         ('A person came'.)   ('There is/was a person'.)
(16) a. PRE-VERBAL – Indefinite   b. PRE-VERBAL – Definite
         *yi-ge ren lai-le.   [zhei-ge] ren lai2 le.
         (one-CL person come PERF)   ([this-CL] person come PERF)
         (*'A person came.')   ('The person(s) has/have
                                        come.')

Choosing among discourse devices also depends on a number of syntactic, semantic and pragmatic factors that partially differ across languages (see Hickmann, 2003). For example, grammatical *pro-drop* properties govern some uses of null subjects and discourse context determines when reference must be disambiguated. In addition, nominal determiners present children with a highly multifunctional system, that may, depending on the language, carry morphology (gender and number in French), serve to count (French indefinite 'un/une' = 'a/one'), mark non-specific reference ('I want a dog'), or label referents ('This is a dog').

time across languages

Temporal-aspectual systems vary along several dimensions, such as complexity, transparency and grammaticalization (e.g. Comrie, 1976, 1985; Dahl, 1985; Smith, 1983). For example, among the languages that provide morphological markings, variations occur with respect to how aspect is grammaticalized. English provides a productive progressive (-ing in (17)), whereas French and German aspect is marked in the past (18) and neutralized in the present, notwithstanding the existence of (optional and rather marked) periphrastic progressive constructions (19).[5] Finally, in the quasi-absence of any morphology, Chinese provides some aspectual devices (particles, adverbials) but no grammaticalized tense forms, so that events are temporally located by means of optional adverbials or through inferences based on aspect and on context (20).

(17)   He is, was, has been, will be, would be, will have been…running.

(18)   Il a couru. / Il courait.
       Er ist gelaufen. / Er lief.
       ('He has run[ran]. / He ran[was running].')

(19)   Il court. / Il est en train de courir. /
       Er läuft. / Er ist dabei zu laufen.
       ('He runs[is running]. / He is [in the midst of] running.')

(20)   Pao-le. / Pao-zhe.
       (run-PERF / run-IMP)
       ('[He] ran [away]. / [He] is/was running.')

space across languages

Languages display considerable variations in the spatial domain (e.g. Grinevald, 2006; Gumperz and Levinson, 1996; Levinson, 2003; Lucy, 1992). Among these variations, Talmy's typology (2000) differentiates

Satellite-framed and *Verb-framed* languages (hereafter S and V), illustrated below for motion events by English (21) and its French literal translation (22). S-languages (e.g. Germanic) typically lexicalize the manner of motion in the verb root (*to run*) and encode its path in particles and prepositions (*up, across, away* ...). In contrast, V-languages (e.g. Romance) lexicalize path in the verb (*monter* 'to ascend', *traverser* 'to cross', *partir* 'to leave' ...) and express manner peripherally, if at all (*en courant* 'by running'). Such patterns run through each language well beyond the expression of motion, for example also affecting the expression of causality and of resulting states in (23) and (24). As discussed further below, recent proposals (e.g. Bowerman, 2007; Slobin, 2006) have even suggested that they constitute strong prototypical paradigms that have cognitive implications for how speakers organize their internal representations.

(21)   He ran into the house, up the stairs, across the living room, down again, out into the garden, and away.

(22)   Il est entré dans la maison [en courant], il a monté les escaliers [en courant], il a traversé le

salon [en courant], il est redescendu [en courant], il est ressorti dans le jardin [en courant] et il est parti [en courant].

(23)   He kicked the door open.

(24)   Il a ouvert la porte à coups de pied.
('He opened the door by kicking it.')

discourse in first language acquisition

Such universal and variable properties of languages have implications for children's discourse development during first language acquisition. For each referential domain, we illustrate below some recurrent vs. language-specific developmental sequences in the acquisition of particular devices necessary for discourse organization across child languages.

denoting entities across child languages

As discussed in detail elsewhere (Hickmann, 2003), early findings suggesting that local and/or obligatory markings are acquired more easily than global and/or optional ones must be examined with care in the light of methodological problems and of all (sentence/discourse-internal) functions of these devices. Our findings (Hickmann and

Hendriks, 1999; Hickmann et al., 1996) based on picture-elicited narratives in several languages (English, German, French, Chinese) and age groups (adults, children from four to ten years) showed the following main results. First, in all languages structural and functional factors both determined children's uses of local and global markings, given that these devices simultaneously marked syntactic–semantic distinctions (subject, agent) and discourse relations (given/new, role maintenance/switch across clauses). Second, with increasing age, appropriate discourse uses of these markings followed similar developmental progressions across languages, showing the impact of general cognitive factors. Third, the narratives in all languages displayed a strong attraction between local/global discourse markings (indefinite/post-verbal, definite/pre-verbal), but global markings varied more than local markings as a function of language-specific properties. Finally, contrary to what could be expected from previous research, obligatory markings were not necessarily the first ones to be acquired in all languages. Some examples from children's narratives illustrate these findings below.

Notwithstanding significant functional changes with age, French children massively relied on global markings from early on, suggesting that they were sensitive to the partial grammaticalization of information status in their language. As illustrated below (first and subsequent mentions FM and SM in underlined italics), they used varied structures to mark 'topic switches' at all ages. However, they first did so inappropriately at younger ages (dislocated FM in (25)) and later on with great delicacy, as shown in (26) where information is new (existential FM), then given (dislocated SM), then topical (pronominalized SM).[6]

(25)   Et après _le chien il_ [FM] arrive. (5 years)
       ('And then the dog it comes.')

(26)   _Il y a un chat_ [FM] _qui arrive_, _le chat il_ [SM] regarde le nid, _il_ [SM] voit les oiseaux. (10 years)
       ('There's a cat coming, the cat he looks at the nest, he sees the birds.')

In contrast, children did not use utterance structure for discourse purposes until 10 years of age in other languages for two distinct reasons (relevant expressions in underlined italics below). First, German children (27) used frequent spatio-temporal connectives that resulted in post-verbal expressions, irrespective of discourse status (obligatory subject–verb inversions in V2-languages). Second, in languages displaying a morphology that is weak (English) or non-existent (Chinese), children reserved global markings for grammatical relations within the sentence, producing pre-verbal first mentions of animate referents in subject/agent roles, irrespective of discourse status ((28) to (31)). In this respect, Chinese children first marked newness by means of nominal determiners (local and optional), rather than by means of structural variations (global and obligatory), which are more complex from a functional point of view.[7] In addition, they were increasingly sensitive to constraints on subject–verb inversions (only allowed with particular predicates, e.g. *lai* 'come'), using inappropriate pre-verbal first mentions with all types of predicates at young ages (30), but exclusively with predicates that did not allow inversions at age ten (31).

(27) (...) Und da war *eine Katze* [FM]. Da waren *die Vögelchen* [FM] alleine. Und dann geht *die Katze* [SM] hoch zu den Vögelchen [SM]. Und da kam *der Hund* [FM] (...) (4 years)
('And there was a cat. There were the little birds alone. And then goes the cat up to the little birds. And there came the dog ...')

(28) *The cat* [FM] comes to the tree. (5 years)

(29) *A cat* [FM] comes and sees the birds. (10 years)

(30) *Yi-zhi gou* [FM] lai-le (6 years)
(NUM-CL dog come-PERF)
('A dog came.')

(31) *Yi-zhi mao* [FM] lai-dao shu xia (10 years)
(NUM-CL cat come-arrive tree under)
('A cat arrived under the tree.')

time across child languages

A number of hypotheses have been proposed concerning children's acquisition of verbal morphology. Among them the *defective tense hypothesis* suggests that children's use of verbal morphology is determined by universal situation types, leading them to mark at first aspect and not tense. According to this hypothesis, children's cognitive immaturity leads them to focus on the immediately perceptible results of events and therefore to associate the past perfective with resultative verbs. However, other findings strongly suggest the need to modify this hypothesis. For example, unpredicted variations occur across languages (Berman and Slobin, 1994; Weist et al., 1984) and discourse functional factors partially determine acquisition (e.g. Bamberg, 1987; Bazzanella and Calleri, 1991).

In our cross-linguistic corpora of picture-elicited narratives (Hickmann, 2003), the predicted association (past, perfective, resultative) was clearly observed among Chinese speakers (at all ages) and among the youngest English speakers (four years), but not in other age and language groups. For example, French and German speakers heavily anchored their narratives in the non-past, presumably because the present tense is aspectually unmarked in their language, thereby leaving few 'degrees of freedom' for variations in tense-aspect forms. Furthermore, with increasing age, children of all language groups used a greater variety of tense-aspect forms that were largely determined by discourse factors. From about age seven on, temporal-aspectual markings differentiated the discourse foreground and background in a variety of contexts (referent introductions, event overlaps, narrators' comments, internal states). In addition, connectives also became more varied in these contexts, showing a decrease in 'sequential' devices marking temporal succession (e.g. English 'then', German 'dann', French 'puis', Chinese 'ranhou' 'then') and an increase in 'regional' devices marking overlaps (English 'while', German 'in der Zwischenzeit' 'in the meantime', French 'pendant que' 'while'), which were used more frequently and earlier in Chinese than in other languages (e.g. 'de shihou' 'while'). Examples (32) and (33) show verbal morphology and connectives (relevant sentences in underlined italics) situating events in the same temporal region, while (34) shows verbal morphology that marks a referent introduction (initial stage setting) and an event overlap (subsequent discourse).

(32)   The cat comes to the tree, sits down and starts to climb. And the dog's just walking along and the dog bites the cat's tail _when the cat just about got up there_ and the bird's coming. (7 years)

(33)   Elle va chercher à manger pour ses petits mais en dessous y'a un chat et pendant qu'elle est partie le chat i regarde le nid (...). _Au moment où il atteint la branche_ pour attraper les trois petits oiseaux, y'a un chien qui arrive par derrière, qui lui mord la queue et même à ce _moment-là y'avait la mère qui arrivait_ et après le chat i retombe. (10 years)
       ('She goes to get food for her little ones but underneath there's a cat and while she is gone the cat it looks at the nest (...). _At the moment when he has reached the branch_ to catch the three little birds, there's a dog that comes from behind, that bites its tail and _just at this moment there was the mother that was arriving_ and then the cat it falls back down.')

(34) Ein Vogel <u>hat</u> Kinder <u>bekommen</u> und der Vogel fliegt weg und
      die Katze will ein Vogel essen und da läuft die Katze hoch, und
      dort schaut der Hund und dann <u>war</u> die Katze fast aufm Baum
      und der Hund zieht se mit Schwanz runter, und dann kommt
      en Vogel mit einer Raupe. (7 years)
      ('A bird <u>has gotten</u> children and the bird flies away and the
      cat wants to eat a bird and there the cat runs up and there
      the dog looks and then the cat <u>was</u> almost on the tree and the
      dog pulls it down with the tail and then a bird comes with a
      caterpillar.')

space across child languages

During the last decade the spatial domain has been quite controversial in the light of considerable variations across child languages that
have revived fundamental questions concerning language acquisition
and cognitive development. Given the recent explosion of developmental studies focusing on space, we present this domain in some detail
below.

the development of spatial representations: a paradox

The ability to represent space is central to a variety of behaviours that
are fundamental for the survival of all species, such as finding food,
returning home, escaping from predators or avoiding obstacles. Some
developmental theories, for example in the Piagetian tradition, have
stressed the crucial contribution of spatial representations as founding
stepping stones for human cognition. More recent research now suggests that spatial knowledge is a fundamental component of children's
earliest cognitive capacities from a few months of life onwards. This surprisingly precocious knowledge has been either attributed to children's
active perceptual processes (Mandler, 1998) or assumed to be available
at birth as part of their innate 'core knowledge' (Carey and Spelke, 1994;
Spelke, 1998). Furthermore, it has been claimed (Jackendoff, 1996;
Landau and Jackendoff, 1993) that all languages comprise two basic
systems (*What* and *Where*) devoted either to identifying entities or to
locating them, which might reflect two related systems in the neuronal substrate of the brain. In general, approaches focusing on universal determinants of language acquisition argue that language-specific
factors only have a superficial impact on restricted aspects of verbal
behaviour and/or on relatively late phases of development (Clark, 2003;
Munnich and Landau, 2003).

In contrast, a growing number of studies show striking cross-linguistic differences in children's spatial language that raise some questions about universals in this domain. Such differences can be observed in relation to how speakers express both static spatial relations and motion events over a wide age range that includes the pre-linguistic period, the emergence of language, later phases of child language, and adulthood (Allen et al., 2007; Berman and Slobin, 1994; Bowerman, 2007; Bowerman and Choi, 2001, 2003; Choi and Bowerman, 1991; Slobin, 1996, 2003, 2006). Such findings have revived the old Whorfian hypothesis of *linguistic determinism*, now available in new versions (cf. Gumperz and Levinson, 1996), according to which languages filter information and invite learners to pay attention to some aspects of reality, that thereby become more salient and accessible.

The findings summarized below illustrate both recurrent and variable aspects of children's spatial reference in their narratives, suggesting that cognitive and language-specific factors both determine how children organize spatial information. In all languages, references to locations show general developmental progressions with respect to spatial anchoring in discourse, while references to motion events show highly quite language-specific patterns.

spatial anchoring: universal determinants of children's discourse

Spatial anchoring in discourse seems to be a late development in all languages. In our sample, only adults and some 10-year-old children introduced spatial anchors in the initial stage setting of their narratives ('a field', 'a fence' in (35)), thereby providing a frame that anticipated locations and changes of location in subsequent discourse. At around age 7 potential spatial anchors occurred only as they became relevant deep into discourse ('the fence' in (36)) and before this age narratives provided no anchoring, making it difficult to interpret some events (e.g. 'jumped over' and 'fell in' (37)). This progression reflects the development of children's capacity to plan reference in discourse, which is presumably driven by general cognitive development.

> (35) First there's a horse running around in <u>a field</u> and he comes to <u>a fence</u> and he looks at it. And there's a cow on the other side. And he decides to jump over the fence and he falls and the cow looks at him and then the cow helps him bandage his leg. That's all. (10 years)

> (36) Once there was a horse running and he saw a cow and then he stopped and then he jumped over <u>the fence</u> and he broke the

fence and got hurt. And then a bird came along and with a doctor's kit and bandaged the horse up. (7 years)

(37)   The horse is running and sees the cow and the bird. And the horse runs, jumped over, then he fell. Then the birdie got bandage. Then he puts it on. (4 years)

structural constraints on children's spatial language

In contrast to this general progression, children's spatial reference in discourse shows wide cross-linguistic variations along at least three dimensions that follow language-specific properties of S- or V-languages: speakers' *focus* on different types of spatial information, the relative *density* of their utterances when expressing this information, and the *compactness* of the structures they use to encode this information. With respect to focus, research shows cross-linguistic differences in what speakers (adults, children of 3 to 10 years) choose to express in varied situations. In narratives (Berman and Slobin, 1994; Slobin, 1996, 2003, 2006) S-speakers generally elaborate information concerning motion but presuppose information concerning locations, while V-speakers provide fewer details about motion and more elaborate descriptions of locations in stage settings. An experiment (Hickmann and Hendriks, 2006) comparing how English vs. French speakers described caused motion (actions causing the displacements of objects, e.g. putting a lid onto a pan, one piece of Lego into another) also showed two main results: a general developmental progression, whereby children expressed increasingly specific types of information in both languages; as well as significant cross-linguistic differences in information focus at all ages, for example a focus on manner of attachment in French ('accrocher 'lit' = 'to hook', 'emboîter' = 'to in-fit') and on manner of causing motion in English ('to push into', 'to pull off').

With respect to density, analyses of picture-elicited narratives (Hickmann, 2003) showed denser utterances about motion events in English, German or Chinese (S-languages) than in French (V-language). At all ages S-speakers frequently used varied predicates expressing multiple types of information (manner, path, cause, e.g. 'to fly off', 'to jump across', 'to run down', 'to pull down', 'to chase away'). In contrast, French speakers typically encoded one piece of information at a time (e.g. 'voler' = 'to fly', 'courir' = 'to run', 'partir' = 'to leave', 'monter' = 'to ascend'), notwithstanding semantically denser predicates from age 10 onwards (e.g. 'grimper' = 'to climb up', 'faire tomber' = 'to make fall'). Longitudinal analyses of early spontaneous productions (Hickmann et al., 2008) further showed that this difference in utterance density could be observed from the emergence of language onwards (before age 2). Young English learners encoded more information within each clause, e.g. manner + path ('run away'), cause + manner ('fly a kite'), or cause + path ('put down') than French learners (e.g. manner 'voler' = 'to fly', path 'monter' = 'to ascend', cause 'mettre' = 'to put').

Finally, focus and density are related to the linguistic means that are used across languages to present spatial information in discourse. It is because speakers rely on the most accessible structures in their (S or V) language that they represent motion differently in their narratives. In our corpus of picture-elicited narratives, English speakers of all ages systematically used dense and compact structures, while French speakers strung less dense structures across utterances in discourse. Given this observation, an experiment about voluntary motion (Hickmann, 2006) systematically compared how speakers of English vs. French (adults and children from 3 to 7 years) narrated animated clips showing agents' displacements along different paths and manners. Irrespective of age and of event types, English speakers (38) encoded both manner and path (in verb roots and satellites, respectively) systematically and more frequently than French speakers. French responses depended on age and event type, encoding path and manner among adults (in main verbs vs. adverbials, prepositions, subordinate clauses, see (39)), path only at all ages (40) or manner only among children (41). In contrast to English children, French children also produced disjoint references to path and manner across utterances in discourse (42).

(38) The boy walks to the river, swims across, and walks away. (5 years)

(39) Il traverse en courant. (adult)
('He crosses by running.')

(40) *Il a passé sur l'herbe et il a passé sur la route et il a passé sur l'herbe.* (3 years)
('He passed on the grass and he passed on the road and he passed on the grass.')

(41) *C'est un petit garçon qui a couru sur la neige, après il a glissé et après il a couru sur la neige.* (5 years)
('It's a little boy that ran on the snow, then he slid and then he ran on the snow.')

(42) *Ça parle d'un grand monsieur qui a couru, couru, couru, il est allé sur la route et puis il est allé de l'autre côté.* (3 years)
('It talks about a big man that ran, ran, ran, he went on the road and then he went to the other side.')

Similarly, an experiment (Hendriks et al., 2008) examined how French vs. English speakers (adults and children between ages 3 and 10) narrated animated clips showing caused motion events that involved too much information to be expressed within a single clause (an agent's action causing the displacement of an object, the manner and path of his own motion, the manner and path of the objects' displacement).[8] As predicted, narratives differed with age and language. Utterance density increased with age in both languages, but it was clearly higher at all ages in English and showed a striking increase with age in French (and not in English). Furthermore, English speakers typically expressed Cause and Manner in the main verb, Path in satellites, and (eventually) other information peripherally (e.g. (43) and (44)). In French they distributed information within and across sentences in much more varied ways (e.g. (45) to (47)) and children produced some idiosyncratic uses suggesting that the task presented a challenge to them.[9]

(43) *He pushes the tyre into the cave.*

(44) *He rolls the ball down the hill by pushing it with both hands.*

(45) *Il descend en poussant la valise.*
      ('He descends while pushing the suitcase.')

(46) *Il monte un paquet cadeau sur le toit.*
      ('He ascends[transitive] a gift on the roof.')

(47) *Il tire un gros sac sur la dune en marchant du bas de la dune jusqu'en haut.*
      ('He pulls a big bag on the sand dune while walking from the bottom of the dune to the top.)

discussion: discourse development and linguistic diversity

This overview shows that multiple factors determine the course of discourse development during first language acquisition. As first summarized below for different referential domains (entities, time, space), these determinants include structural and functional factors, as well as general and language-specific factors, none of which alone can account for the patterns observed across child languages. Second, recognizing the existence of multiple determinants raises further questions about the ways in which these different factors come to interact and the timing of this complex process during first language acquisition. Third, these conclusions open new lines of research that are necessary to examine deeper implications for the relation between language and other aspects of cognition during human development.

When referring to entities, children simultaneously learn to express grammatical and semantic relations within sentences (subjecthood, agency) and to mark the changing status of information (new, given, topical) across utterances in discourse. The way in which they integrate these two levels of organization depends on the properties of the relevant markings in their language (local/global, optional/obligatory, sentence/discourse-internal functions), which present different levels of cognitive complexity. For example, Chinese children first mark newness by means of optional local markings, rather than by means of obligatory global means that are functionally more complex since they crucially contribute to sentence-internal organization in the absence of morphology. As a result, children begin to use local markings for referent introductions at about the same age in all languages, including in languages that are rather distant. In contrast, their uses of global markings vary across languages, given a number of language-specific factors constraining clause structure, such as a weak or absent morphology (reliance on word order in English and Chinese), obligatory structural constraints (V2-constraint in German) or the partial grammaticalization of discourse status (French clitic pronouns).

With respect to temporality, children gradually learn to use a variety of grammatical and lexical means to represent and to temporally locate different types of situations, while simultaneously establishing temporal relations among them and grounding information in discourse. At around age 7 they begin to use particular morphological markings (tense-aspect) and connectives (regional) in order to construct the foreground and background of discourse. This development is observed in all languages, despite wide differences across temporal-aspectual systems, suggesting that general cognitive factors also drive discourse development in this referential domain. However, unlike previous studies focusing only on universal cognitive determinants, the predicted morphological/lexical association (between past, perfective, resultative) was not observed to the same extent across languages (Chinese, English > German, French) and across ages in some languages (young children > older children or adults in English), a result that partially follows from the different types of temporal anchoring adopted by speakers as a function of their language. Therefore, although cognitive immaturity may invite children to focus on immediate results in some languages and at some ages, it does not account for the cross-linguistic differences that were otherwise observed.

Finally, children's narratives show a progression in their ability to provide spatial anchors in discourse. This ability follows a very gradual development in all languages that barely emerges at around age 7 and continues to develop after age 10. Such a development suggests again the impact of general cognitive factors in this third domain, contributing to how children learn to plan discourse in such a way as to construct an initial frame when representing space in discourse. However, space also shows considerable variation across child languages. Children's speech about location or motion varies along several dimensions (focus, density, compactness) that directly follow from typological constraints. In particular, such constraints determine what information (path, manner, cause) is lexicalized or grammaticalized in different types of structures, some of which are more 'prototypical' and therefore more accessible than others within a given system. Such structural constraints affect how children organize semantic information both within the sentence and in discourse.

determinants of language acquisition in a cross-linguistic perspective

This interplay of multiple determinants must be further explored in a cross-linguistic perspective that highlights both recurrent and variable phenomena in child language. Irrespective of the language to be acquired, development implies learning a system of form–function relationships that organize sentences and discourse, a task that requires growing cognitive capacities in all domains. However, depending on the particular language and domain to be learned, this multi-functionality also presents children with different problems to solve, which constrain the process whereby they become competent native speakers.

Cross-linguistic comparisons show that discourse functions develop very gradually and follow partially similar developmental progressions in very different languages and in all referential domains, supporting hypotheses concerning the cognitive bases of language acquisition. At the same time, cognitive complexity is related to functional complexity for young learners faced with a highly multifunctional system to acquire. Therefore, discourse functions are an integral part of how, when and where children learn grammar. Thus, until age 10 Chinese children still produce some ungrammatical utterances (pre-verbal new information) because they have not yet integrated the sentence and discourse levels of linguistic organization. Furthermore, the cross-linguistic differences that were observed in all domains indicate that general cognitive factors do not constitute the only determinants driving language acquisition. In particular, children are sensitive to the properties of their native language from very early on and these properties affect how they go about the process of acquiring language. Despite similar developmental progressions in discourse functions across languages, structural constraints affect how children organize information, resulting in very different types of sentence and discourse organization across child languages.

These conclusions lead to two more general implications. They first exclude any conception of development that cannot account for two fundamental aspects of language: multi-functionality and structural diversity. Functional approaches capture well how children acquire form–function relationships in their language, but must also take into account structural constraints on how these relationships are systemically organized. Inversely, in their accounts of how children uncover abstract rules of grammar, structural approaches cannot ignore discourse functional determinants of how they go about this discovery procedure. Furthermore, developmental theories – particularly in the Vygotskian tradition – have stressed the fact that human language provides all children in our species with a special semiotic medium that has implications for cognitive and communicative development. As argued in more recent discussions, this semiotic system invites particular types of cognitive processes (e.g. Gentner, 2003), while also displaying variable properties that influence language acquisition and perhaps also cognitive representations more generally (e.g. Bowerman, 2007; Slobin, 2006).

Second, a major issue among models of language acquisition is whether the capacities underlying children's growing linguistic competence are innate and domain-specific or whether they are gradually acquired through more general perceptual and cognitive processes that apply to all domains of development. In this respect, results concerning discourse development partially support models that postulate developmental changes that go from general to specific knowledge (e.g. Karmiloff-Smith, 1992), but they also indicate the early impact of language-specific factors on development (e.g. Bowerman, 2007) that cannot be accounted for in such models. Such language-specific factors imply knowledge that is both specific to language (rather than to other domains of knowledge), variable across language domains (entities, time, space), and variable across linguistic systems (e.g. as a function of typological constraints). Thus, although universal communicative rules (e.g. joint attention) and cognitive categories (of entities or events) may first guide development, they may be rapidly transformed by the acquisition of a new system of representation that displays general properties (shared by all languages) but also provides different ways of organizing incoming information (variable across languages).

future directions

The implications of these conclusions must be further tested along several research directions. First, research is necessary over a wider range of languages within and across linguistic families in order to test the hypothesis that language-specific factors partially determine the process of language acquisition. Only large-scale comparisons of child languages in specific domains can allow a precise account of how cognitive and linguistic factors interact during children's language development. Second, it is necessary to compare a variety of learners in order to evaluate the role of distinct factors that are normally confounded during development. For example, to determine the relative weight of increasing cognitive maturity, of developing linguistic competence, and of language-specific factors, it is necessary to compare monolingual children acquiring their first language with children acquiring two languages simultaneously, children and adults acquiring a second language, as well as speakers suffering from various pathologies that show dissociations among some of these factors (e.g. agrammatic aphasic patients).

Finally, it is urgent to examine simultaneously linguistic and non-linguistic cognition during different developmental phases in order to address deeper questions concerning the relation between language and thought. With respect to early phases of development, the 'prelinguistic' period is of particular interest for the study of whether and when language(s) (in general and in particular) begin(s) to influence human cognitive development. Similarly, with respect to later developmental phases in child language and adulthood, complementary measures of linguistic behaviours (production, comprehension) and of other processes (co-verbal gestures, non-verbal categorization) are necessary to access speakers' internal representations in relation to their speech representations. It is only by means of such varied methods that we might hope to seriously test the hypothesis that language influences human cognition beyond language use.

notes

1. Some uses of tense are atemporal (*The earth is round*). Terminologies vary with respect to lexical dimensions of aspect (e.g. *resultativity, boundedness, Aktionsart*). Modality includes the future, which is strictly speaking not a 'tense'.

2. Clitics are unstressed non-contrastive pronouns that typically denote given information, notwithstanding non-specific uses.
3. In V2-languages it is the tensed part of the verb that must be in second position.
4. Pre-verbal position also allows non-specific reference. Classifiers (abbreviated as –CL in all examples) are obligatory with determiners and include the 'general' classifier –ge (possible with all nominals), as well as 'specific' classifiers that vary with lexical class. Other particles are abbreviated as PERF (perfective) and IMP (imperfective). Tones were not transliterated.
5. French and German provide different aspectual distinctions in the past that cannot be directly translated in such examples (roughly a strict perfective/imperfective distinction in French and a distinction between perfective and unmarked in German).
6. Left-dislocations only allow definite forms (*'Un chien il arrive' = 'A dog it comes').
7. Chinese children in fact used two types of local markings. When marking new information with numeral determiners, they also used specific classifiers (e.g. –zhi in examples (31) and (32)), rather than the general classifier –ge (used for subsequent mentions).
8. This study also included adult English speakers learning French and showed the impact of source and target languages in how speakers selected and organized spatial information.
9. French idiosyncratic uses typically involved the expression of causativity with path or manner, which frequently requires complex causative constructions (*faire* 'to make/do' + infinitive), for example *'Il traverse le cheval' (Lit. 'He crosses the horse' [rather than 'Il fait traverser le cheval' 'He makes the horse cross']) or *'Il enroule le ballon' (Lit. 'He wraps up the balloon' [rather than '*Il* fait rouler le ballon' 'He makes the balloon roll']).

references

Allen, S., Özyürek, A., Kita, S., Brown, A., Furman, R., Ishizuka, T. and Fujii, M. (2007). How language-specific is early syntactic packaging of Manner and Path? A comparison of English, Turkish, and Japanese. *Cognition*, 102: 1, 16–48.
Bamberg, M. G. W. (1987). *The Acquisition of Narratives: Learning to Use Language*. Berlin: Mouton de Gruyter.
Bazzanella, C. and Calleri, D. (1991). Tense coherence and grounding in children's narratives. *Text*, 11: 2, 175–87.
Berman, R. A. and Slobin, D. I. (eds) (1994). *Different Ways of Relating Events in Narrative: A Crosslinguistic Developmental Study*. Hillsdale, NJ: Erlbaum.
Bowerman, M. (2007). Containment, support, and beyond: constructing topological spatial categories in first language acquisition. In M. Aurnague, M. Hickmann and L. Vieu (eds), *Spatial Entities in Language and Cognition*. Amsterdam/Philadelphia: John Benjamins.
Bowerman, M. and Choi, S. (2001). Shaping meanings for language: universal and language-specific in the acquisition of spatial semantic categories. In M. Bowerman and S. C. Levinson (eds), *Language Acquisition and Conceptual Development* (pp. 475–511). Cambridge: Cambridge University Press.

Bowerman, M. and Choi, S. (2003). Space under construction: language-specific categorization in first language acquisition. In D. Gentner and S. Goldin-Meadow (eds), *Language in Mind: Advances in the Study of Language and Thought* (pp. 387–427). Cambridge, MA: MIT Press.

Carey, S. and Spelke, E. (1994). Domain-specific knowledge and conceptual change. In L. A. Hirschfeld and S. A. Gelman (eds), *Mapping the Mind: Domain Specificity in Cognition and Culture* (pp. 169–200). New York: Cambridge University Press.

Choi, S. and Bowerman, M. (1991). Learning to express motion events in English and Korean: the influence of language-specific lexicalization patterns. *Cognition* 41, 83–121.

Clark, E. V. (2003). Language and representations. In D. Gentner and S. Goldin-Meadow (eds), *Language in Mind: Advances in the Study of Language and Thought*. Cambridge, MA: MIT Press.

Comrie, B. (1976). *Aspect: An Introduction to the Study of Verbal Aspect and Related Problems*. Cambridge: Cambridge University Press.

Comrie, B. (1985). *Tense*. Cambridge: Cambridge University Press.

Dahl, O. (1985). *Tense and Aspect Systems*. Oxford: Basil Blackwell Ltd.

Gentner, D. (2003). Why we're so smart. In D. Gentner and S. Goldin-Meadow (eds), *Language in Mind: Advances in the Study of Language and Thought* (pp. 195–235). Cambridge, MA: MIT Press.

Grinevald, C. (2006). The expression of static location in a typological perspective. In M. Hickmann and S. Robert (eds), *Space in Languages: Linguistic Systems and Cognitive Categories*. Amsterdam/Philadelphia: John Benjamins.

Gumperz, J. J. and Levinson, S. C. (eds) (1996). *Rethinking Linguistic Relativity*. Cambridge: Cambridge University Press.

Halliday, M. A. K. and Hasan, R. (1976). *Cohesion in English*. London: Longman.

Hendriks, H., Hickmann, M. and Demagny, A-C. (2008). How children and adult learners express caused motion in French and in English. *AILE*, 27, 15–41.

Hickmann, M. (2003). *Children's Discourse: Person, Space and Time across Languages*. Cambridge: Cambridge University Press.

Hickmann, M. (2006). The relativity of motion in first language acquisition. In M. Hickmann and S. Robert (eds), *Space in Languages: Linguistic Systems and Cognitive Categories*. Amsterdam: Benjamins.

Hickmann, M. and Hendriks, H. (1999). Cohesion and anaphora in children's narratives: a comparison of English, French, German, and Chinese. *Journal of Child Language* 26, 419–52.

Hickmann, M. and Hendriks, H. (2006). Static and dynamic location in French and in English. *First Language*, 26: 1, 103–35.

Hickmann, M., Hendriks, H. and Champaud, C. (2008). Typological constraints on motion in French and English child language. In J. Guo et al. (eds), *Crosslinguistic Approaches to the Psychology of Language* (pp. 209–24). Hillsdale, NJ: Lawrence Erlbaum.

Hickmann, M., Hendriks, H., Roland, F. and Liang, J. (1996). The marking of new information in children's narratives: A comparison of English, French, German, and Mandarin Chinese. *Journal of Child Language* 23, 591–619.

Hopper, P. J. (ed.) (1982). *Tense and Aspect: Between Syntax and Semantics*. Amsterdam: Benjamins.

Jackendoff, R. (1996). The architecture of the linguistic-spatial interface. In P. Bloom, M. Peterson, L. Nadel and M. Garrett (eds), *Language and Space* (pp. 1–30). London, Cambridge, MA: MIT Press.

Karmiloff-Smith, A. (1992). *Beyond Modularity: A Developmental Perspective on Cognitive Science*. Cambridge, MA: MIT Press.

Landau, B. and Jackendoff, R. (1993). *What* and *Where* in spatial language and spatial cognition. *Behavioral and Brain Sciences*, 16:2, 217–38.

Levinson, S. C. (2003). Language and mind: Let's get the issues straight! In D. Gentner and S. Goldin-Meadow (eds), *Language in Mind: Advances in the Study of Language and Thought*. Cambridge, MA: MIT Press.

Lucy, J. (1992). *Language Diversity and Thought: A Reformulation of the Linguistic Relativity Hypothesis*. Cambridge: Cambridge University Press.

Mandler, J. M. (1998). Representation. In W. Damon, D. Kuhn and R. S. Siegler (eds), *Handbook of Child Psychology*, Vol. 2 (pp. 255–308). New York: Wiley.

Munnich, E. and Landau, B. (2003). The effects of spatial language on spatial representation: setting some boundaries. In D. Gentner and S. Goldin-Meadow (eds), *Language in Mind: Advances in the Study of Language and Thought*. Cambridge, MA: MIT Press.

Slobin, D. I. (1996). From 'thought and language' to 'thinking for speaking'. In J. J. Gumperz and S. C. Levinson (eds), *Rethinking Linguistic Relativity* (pp. 70–96). Cambridge: Cambridge University Press.

Slobin, D. I. (2003). The many ways to search for a frog. In S. Strömqvist and L. Verhoeven (eds), *Relating Events in Narrative: Typological and Contextual Perspectives* (pp. 219–57). Hillsdale, NJ: Lawrence Erlbaum.

Slobin, D. I. (2006). What makes manner of motion salient? Explorations in linguistic typology, discourse, and cognition. In M. Hickmann and S. Robert (eds), *Space across Languages: Linguistic Systems and Cognitive Categories*. Amsterdam/Philadelphia: John Benjamins.

Smith, C. (1983). A theory of aspectual choice. *Language* 59, 479–501.

Spelke, E. S. (1998). Nativism, empiricism, and the origins of knowledge. *Infant Behavior and Development*, 21, 181–200.

Talmy, L. (2000). *Towards a Cognitive Semantics*. Cambridge, MA: MIT Press.

Weist, R. M., Wysocka, H., Witkowska-Stadnik, K., Buczowska, E. and Konieczna, E. (1984). The defective tense hypothesis: On the emergence of tense and aspect in child Polish. *Journal of Child Language,* 11, 347–74.

12
trends in research on
narrative development*

ruth a. berman

introduction

In the post(-post) modern twenty-first century, the notion 'narrative' is so all-encompassing as to be almost vacuous. Here the term is confined to a special genre of *verbal discourse* that is agent-oriented, focused on people, their actions and motivations, and expresses the unfolding of events in a temporal framework (Labov, 1972; Longacre, 1996). As such, narratives contrast with, say, expository discourse, which focuses on concepts and issues or with descriptive discourse, which characterizes the properties of objects, people and places. Bruner (1986) characterizes narrative as a distinct 'mode of thought', while Turner proposes that '*Story* is a basic principle of mind' (Turner, 1996, p. v). Also relevant to characterizing the narrative genre is the distinction between narrative as a type of mental representation and storytelling as an activity (Berman, 1995; Clark, 2004).

This chapter considers both narrative as a type of discourse and narration as the act of storytelling, from early pre-school age across adolescence and into adulthood. It takes account of different sub-genres of narrative – fictive (e.g. mystery, romance, fables) and veridical (news reports, personal adventures, hassle stories) – that are produced under different circumstances – picture-based and personal-experience accounts, conversation-embedded and monologic. These different types of stories share underlying properties and principles, even though differences in setting have been shown to affect the task of narration, particularly among younger children (Berman, 2004; Hickmann, 1998). The chapter starts with a brief review of socio-cultural, cognitive and psycholinguistic approaches to the study of narrative development followed by a survey of form-function relations in different domains of developing narrative production, and concluding with a summary of the developmental path from interactive, conversation-embedded narration to autonomous text construction.

approaches to narrative and narrative development

Children's stories have been of concern to researchers from different perspectives over the past 50 years or so. Before that, narratives were studied primarily as a genre of *literature*, and analysed aesthetically as works of art produced by specially talented or creative individuals. While such studies in themselves are of marginal interest for language acquisition research, a literary perspective had an impact on children's narratives until the 1970s, resulting in a focus on the *content* of the stories that they told (e.g. Ames, 1966; Pitcher and Prelinger, 1963). Such analyses were concerned mainly with make-believe stories and children's fantasies as reflecting their (unconscious) fears and wishes, what kinds of characters appeared in their stories, and how they represented the key figures in their lives. These were complemented by projective psychological analyses of the content of stories written *for* children, such as nursery stories and fairy tales, to ascertain the effect of children's literature on children's psyche (e.g. Bettelheim, 1970). These motifs and the concern for how children project their inner life onto fantasy in the stories they tell, hear and, later, read are echoed in a resurgence of interest in narratives as relating to children's symbolic and pretend play (e.g. Galda and Pellegrini, 1990).

socio-cultural studies of children's narratives

One socio-cultural perspective on children's narratives views narrative knowledge as part of a general *cultural heritage*, deriving from the largely oral traditions of folk tales, fairy stories and bedtime storytelling and merging with the later development of literacy in society and in individuals (e.g. Bruner, 1986). There is also a growing body of *anthropologically motivated* research comparing narrative development cross-culturally (Invernezzi and Abouzeid, 1995; Pesco and Crago, 1996; Stein, 2004) that questions universalistic claims that a single 'narrative schema' governs how stories are construed, and constructed. The Strömqvist and Verhoeven (2004) collection of 'frog story' studies presents other directions for cross-cultural comparison of children's storytelling. For example, Aksu-Koç and Tekdemir (2004) found differences in reference to inner states among Turkish compared with English-speaking children, while Küntay and Nakamura (2004) demonstrate the impact of cultural conventions on the use of evaluative language by Japanese

compared with Turkish children. Other, typologically motivated analyses in the same volume (by Bavin (2004) on Walpiri, and Brown (2004)
on Tzeltal) reveal a focusing on 'where' and the centrality of positioning
in the languages spoken in two different non-Western (rather, non-in-
dustrialized) cultures. Such findings reflect Slobin's (1996, 2003a) idea
of 'thinking for speaking': that the way speakers give verbal expression
to situations in discourse is directly affected by the linguistic structures
available and preferred in their native language. Other research that is
cross-linguistic rather than cross-cultural in conception (e.g. Berman
and Slobin, 1994; Hickmann, 1996; Hickmann and Hendriks, 1999;
Kupersmitt, 2006) reveals that deeply embedded typological properties
of a particular language are mirrored from early on in the narratives
produced by children from linguistically distinct backgrounds.

Other, sociologically motivated, cross-cultural research suggests that
family practices in storytelling (Blum-Kulka, 1997; Heath, 1982; Minami
and McCabe, 1995) and 'home support for narrative talk' (Chang, 2003)
have an impact on how, when and how much children are encouraged
to engage in narration. A related class of studies, also under the heading
of 'socio-cultural', compares groups of speakers from different *social-class
or educational backgrounds* within a given society, reflecting an interest
in the interrelations between children's stories and their social as well
as educational development. These include comparisons of narratives
told to and by children from different backgrounds and more or less
literate segments of the population (e.g. Gee, 1989; Heath, 1983, 1986;
Snow and Dickinson, 1990; Snow and Ninio, 1986). Such investigations
have largely pedagogical motivations in their concern for the way children read and how this affects their success at school, with narrative
development seen as impinging directly on the domain of emergent and
developing literacy (Aksu-Koç, 2004; Minami, 2002; Tolchinsky, 2003).
Cross-cultural studies of children's narratives thus range from ethnographic and typological to sociological and educational concerns.

Proponents of a socio-cultural approach to language and narrative
acquisition relate to conversation-embedded narratives as an integral
part of children's *pragmatic development* (e.g. Blum-Kulka, 2004a, b;
Ninio and Snow, 1996). In this view, the ability to tell a story is an
important facet in the development of 'communicative competence',
and constitutes part of a more general process of socialization that is
achieved first and foremost through interaction – initially mainly with
adult caretakers, subsequently with peers (e.g. Nicolopolou, 1996, 1997).
Such research reflects a reaction against what Nicolopolou terms 'for-
malist approaches to narrative analysis' by psycholinguists who take

their lead from 'functional linguistics' in contrast to the socio-cultural approach that she advocates. A similar motivation underlies current concern with the narratives of older children, particularly adolescents, as reflecting issues of self-perception and identity. These in a sense go back full cycle to the earlier, projective concern with narratives as vehicles for the expression of emotional and social issues, including such themes as 'counter-narrative' (e.g. Bamberg and Andrews, 2004), social incongruence (Smorti, 2004), and narrative as 'autobiography' (Sanderson and McKeough, 2005).

cognitive and psycholinguistic approaches to narrative structure

A very different perspective on narrative development has its under-pinnings in the emergence of cognitive psychology as a domain of inquiry in the 1970s. This yielded rich research on narrative and narrative development concerned with the knowledge base that ena-bles people to understand and construct stories rather than with the thematic content of what children talk about or the impact of socio-cultural background factors. The shift to a cognitively oriented approach is reflected, for example, in the structuralist analyses of children's folktales by Botvin and Sutton-Smith (1977), Sutton-Smith (1981), and in Applebee's (1978) Piagetian cum Vygotsky-based ana-lysis of the Pitcher and Prelinger (1963) corpus. The central claim here is that a narrative is not merely a string of utterances, but a piece of discourse with specific structural properties, and that knowledge of narrative involves mental representations of a narrative schema which people internalize as a result of experience with storytelling (Bartlett, 1932).

Researchers in cognitive psychology and discourse analysis in the 1970s viewed narrative text as a construct with an obligatory internal structure, consisting of a beginning, middle and end, realized in different surface forms in any given story. Three broad approaches emerged out of these insights, each with a distinct impact on the study of narrative development: concern with categories of narra-tive content, structural features of a well-formed story, and relations between linguistic forms and narrative functions (see below).

types of narrative content: scripts, high points and evaluation

The focus on 'content' as developed in the cognitive psychology of the 1970s had two rather different points of departure: the idea of 'scripts' (Shank and Abelson, 1977), and of 'narrative evaluation' (Labov, 1972). With respect to the first, Katherine Nelson and associates (Nelson,

1986) analysed children's narrative abilities as reflecting general cognitive underpinnings, arguing that a script-like representation of generic, prototypical sequences of events (for example, a trip to the beach, a birthday party, baking cookies) anchored in general mental schemata is a necessary precursor to the ability to tell a story (see also Berman and Katzenberger, 1998). Nelson's research demonstrates that older children entertain a more complex range of routes to any specific realization (e.g. a birthday party might begin or end with opening of presents, it can be held at home, in school, at a restaurant). Moreover, with age, children make reference to more and more elaborated categories of general script-based knowledge (participant roles, activities, props and locations) in verbalizing a specific narrative account.

The groundbreaking work of Labov (1972; Labov and Waletzky, 1967) underlies the second type of content-based narrative analysis. On the basis of over 600 narratives elicited from inner-city adolescents asked to tell about a life-threatening experience, Labov and Waletzky (1967) defined narratives as 'one method of recapitulating past experience by matching a verbal sequence of clauses to the sequence of events which actually occurred' (1967, p. 20). Their focus on the *temporal sequencing* of linguistic strings as critical to narrative accounts of events inspired much subsequent work on narrative acquisition. Researchers from different backgrounds analysed narrative development as having its antecedents in the ability of very young children to string together events that took place in the past (e.g. Bauer and Mandler, 1989; Miller and Sperry, 1988; Veneziano and Sinclair, 1995).

Importantly, Labov made a distinction between referential versus *evaluative* elements of narrative content. Referential elements convey information about the characters and events in the story and move the plotline forward from background orientation, via a complicating action to a high point, the cardinal or focal event of the narrative, its climax, reached just before the resolution; and narrators typically mark this point – or the fact that they are approaching it – by some 'evaluative' comment, affective or interpretive. The best-known application of 'high-point analysis' to children's narratives is Peterson and McCabe's (1983) study of the personal-experience accounts of 4- to 10-year-olds who were asked to tell about incidents such as when they got hurt and had to go to the doctor, or an adventure they had with a pet. The authors identified six patterns of storytelling, with only the older children being consistently able to construct the canonical pattern, while younger children often ended at the high point, or used a simple 'chronological' pattern. They also found that with age, children make reference to more, and more different types of, evaluative elements to flesh out the narrative backbone of the story. (See below.)

In sum, content-based narrative analyses have focused on narrative production rather than comprehension, taking into account the event representation underlying the script-like prototypical situation in which a narrative is anchored or considering narrative texts as pieces of discourse that lead up to a high point and that embed a sequential chain of events in a network of evaluative commentary. Such analyses have informed the study of narrative development along several lines. First, children need to recognize a familiar script for them to succeed in interpreting or producing a narrative text (Berman and Katzenberger, 1998; Nelson, 1986). They must also, minimally, be able to verbalize past events in sequences of at least two predications, an ability shown to develop early on (Eisenberg, 1985; Sachs, 1983). Subsequently, children need to recognize that a canonic narrative consists of events that lead up to a 'high point' before culminating in a final outcome or resolution (Peterson and McCabe, 1983). And fully mature narratives include an explicit background setting and concluding coda and are interspersed with the narrator's evaluative commentary.

structure-based analyses: story grammars and causal networks

Structuralist approaches to narrative derive from two main traditions: analysis of the structural regularities of oral folktales and fables (Propp, 1958), and concern with mental representations and mechanisms of information processing in cognitive psychology. The latter take two main forms: story grammars and causal networks. Both argue for story schemata as abstract knowledge made up of shared expectations about how narratives are organized, what kind of story is at issue (e.g. a fairy tale, romance or adventure story), and whether the story is a good one. Story grammars aimed to specify what constitutes a 'possible' or well-formed story, as a rule system with constituent categories – analogous to the generative phrase-structure grammar of the 1960s and, subsequently, to syntactic X-bar theory (de Beaugrande, 1982; Mandler, 1982; Shen, 1988). In this framework, the units or constituents composing the narrative (e.g. setting, episodes, outcome) are defined as purely abstract categories with each episode subdivided (e.g. into initiating event, goal, plot, resolution) to yield a narrative structure that is both hierarchical and recursive.

The story-grammar approach had a strong impact on narrative development research in the 1970s and 1980s, moving it away from thematic to structural issues and from the act of narration to psycholinguistic processing (e.g. Mandler, 1987; McConaughy et al., 1983). In a series of studies on narrative comprehension and recall, Nancy Stein and her associates found that children are sensitive to story structure from an early age (Stein, 1982) and that they rely on this internal representation when asked to retell a story. In one well-known study, Stein and Glenn (1979) had first- and fifth-grade children retell short simple stories they had heard, after a few minutes and a week later. The older children remembered better than the younger; they all remembered better immediately rather than after a week; and first-graders tended to recall mainly actions, while older children also related to internal responses of protagonists. Relatedly, Poulsen et al. (1979) found that when children were presented with pictures arranged in canonic story-structure order, even 4-year-olds, but especially older children, produced much better stories. The fact that children did less well when the pictures violated structural well-formedness led the researchers to conclude that their responses reflect existence or lack of an internalized narrative schema.

The consensus of story-grammar research on children's developing narrative abilities is that by around age 6 years, children demonstrate knowledge of a narrative schema, since they can recount stories they have encountered in the canonic order of a story grammar, although they may fail to use the exact wording of the original. The fact that in recall studies, children change the words and syntactic structures of the original more than the order of its constituents does not necessarily indicate inadequate command of an internalized story schema. Rather, what is retained in memory is the actual sequence of events rather than how they were verbalized in the original. The tendency to adapt the wording of the original version in story retelling or rewriting shows that these tasks reflect a knowledge-based transformational operation of reconstruction rather than mere rote repetition of input (Bereiter and Scardamalia, 1987; Sandbank, 2004).

The 'causal-networks' approach to narrative structure and development of Trabasso and his associates (e.g. Trabasso et al., 1981; Trabasso et al., 1989) highlights the story-grammar view of narrative as a system of problem-solving episodes centring on the protagonist's efforts to achieve a central goal. In contrast to the earlier work of Labov, which treats temporal sequencing as critical in defining relations between story constituents, advocates of the causal-networks approach focus on 'causal inferences that link the states and actions of a story' (Trabasso and Rodkin, 1994, p. 87). For them, then, a narrative is essentially causal in structure and content.

Developmental research deriving from such structure-based orientations to narrative analysis and concern with the mental representation of events and the interrelations between events has generally focused on children's comprehension and recall of stories rather than on narrative production. In this, 'structure-based analyses' of the kind reviewed here differ from research concerned with children's developing abilities in the construction of narrative discourse and their ability to recruit the appropriate linguistic means for this purpose.

form-function approaches to narrative development

Form-function approaches to the development of narrative abilities (Berman, 2009; Berman and Slobin, 1994; Hickmann, 2003) are concerned with the relationship between linguistic forms (free and bound grammatical morphemes; content words and multilexemic expressions; grammatical constructions like noun phrases, passives, relative clauses; and syntactic processes like word order changes or nominalizations) and the functions that these forms perform in narrative discourse (e.g. reference, temporality, connectivity). [See Hickmann, this volume: SFC.] Current research on narrative development in the framework of 'functional psycholinguistics' (Nicolopolou, 1997) derives from several domains of inquiry, including Discourse Analysis (van Dijk, 1980; Shen, 1988), Usage-based Cognitive Linguistics (Tomasello, 1998, 2003), Linguistic Typology (Berman and Verhoeven, 2002; Hickmann and Hendriks, 1999; Slobin, 2004a, b; Strömqvist and Verhoeven, 2004), Contrastive Rhetoric (Berman and Nir-Sagiv, 2008; Berman and Slobin, 1994; Slobin, 2003a, b, 2004a, b) and, most crucially in the present context, Developmental Psycholinguistics (Slobin, 1973; Karmiloff-Smith, 1979)) and are briefly reviewed below for five domains of narrative discourse: Reference, Temporality, Evaluation, Connectivity, and Global Text Structure.

reference

In narratives, reference serves the function of introducing participants, and then of maintaining reference to them or shifting reference to other participants. Developing command of narrative reference is of interest for several reasons from a form-function perspective. First, the linguistic forms needed for this domain – referring expressions such as proper nouns, indefinite and definite noun phrases, pronouns, and null elements (by ellipsis) – are available even to pre-school children. Yet research shows that the ability to make appropriate reference is a late-developing ability, continuing into middle childhood and beyond (Hickmann, 1981, 1995, this volume; Karmiloff-Smith, 1981). One reason is the cognitive difficulty involved in keeping in mind across an entire piece of discourse what/who has been mentioned, when and how. Also cognitively demanding is the need to take into account shared speaker–hearer knowledge, to provide hearers with enough information so that they can identify exactly who is being referred to at each point, while at the same time not providing them with too much information (Hickmann et al., 1995; Warden, 1976). A third difficulty is that different strategies may, and sometimes must, be used in order to refer to participants both unambiguously and appropriately (Berman and Katzenberger, 1998; Kail and Sanchez y Lopez, 1997; Wigglesworth, 1990). This domain has thus been the topic of considerable research on narrative development in different languages, pioneered by Karmiloff-Smith's (1979, 1980, 1981) demonstration that from around the age of 6 years, children rely on 'a thematic subject strategy' in order to link utterances by using the same pronoun across the text to refer to a single major protagonist. Research in this domain from a functional psycholinguistic perspective has also been conducted by Hickmann (1981) and extended in cross-linguistic studies by Hickmann and her associates on two picture series (summarized in Hickmann, 2003, pp. 235–9). Other research in this domain by Bamberg (1986), Berman (1990) and Wigglesworth (1990) uses the 'frog story' picture book as a means of elicitation in German, Hebrew and English respectively (and see earlier references to Kail and her associates for French and Spanish). These studies show that it takes until middle childhood and even beyond to achieve full command of this complex domain which requires a unique integration of local and global processes (Hickmann, 2003, pp. 86–106), tapping into the concurrent emergence and consolidation of linguistic knowledge with key cognitive abilities (Berman and Slobin, 1994, p. 609).

temporality

The notion of temporality is expressed linguistically by a combination of grammatized encodings of the categories of Tense, Mood and Aspect (TMA) together with lexical means, including temporal adverbials like 'at first, later on, eventually' or phasal verbs like 'begin, go on'. Although the domain has been studied intensively in developmental psycholinguistics since the 1960s, until fairly recently it was dealt with only marginally in narrative development, largely to demonstrate the ability of very young children to string together events that took place in the past (e.g. Miller and Sperry, 1988; Sachs, 1983; Veneziano and Sinclair, 1995).

Berman and Slobin's (1994) comparison of temporal markings in the narratives of pre-schoolers, schoolchildren and adults in five languages represents an important departure in this domain, since it covers a wider age range and reflects the view that language development of temporality as of other domains needs to be considered in discourse-embedded contexts. Taking as a point of departure Labov's (1972) insight that narrative discourse is based on the principle of temporal *sequentiality* combined with discourse-based analyses of notions of foreground and background, we analysed narrative texts as encoding three possible temporal relations: the default case of Sequentiality – where one event follows another in temporal sequence, realized as consecutive, typically past tense and/or perfective finite clauses; Simultaneity – where two events co-occur or overlap in time; and Retrospection – where past events are encoded subsequent to their antecedent events.

The study highlighted the notion of narrative sequentiality as indeed critical to both encode and reflect an internalized narrative schema in the form of an 'anchor tense' – typically past and/or perfective forms (or, in picture book storytelling, ongoing present tense) – used consistently across the text. Five-year-old children generally manifested a 'narrative mode' of text production by such means, whereas 3-year-olds typically adopted a picture-by-picture descriptive mode. (Note that in other tasks, such as recounting personal experiences, even three-year-olds can generally adhere to a single timeline across a sequence of events (Berman, 1995, 2004)). Aksu-Koç and von Stutterheim (1994, p. 451) explain the shift in the frog story narratives from 3-year-olds' use of spatial deictics like *here*, *there* to markers of sequentiality like *and then* by older children as reflecting a development from 'a spatio-perceptually based to an abstract-representational conceptualization of time', noting that with age, children 'learn to distinguish the different functions of Simultaneity in relation to foregrounding and backgrounding' (ibid.).

Across the languages in the Berman and Slobin study, marking of Retrospection emerged even later than that of Simultaneity, and reflected a shift from local to more global functions (first in adjacent clauses, e.g. *the boy saw that his frog had escaped*) and subsequently tying in the end of the narrative with its beginning (e.g. *in the end, the boy found the frog he had lost*). Cross-linguistically, this was marked by an age-related increased in use of past perfect forms in Spanish and English, whereas languages like German and Hebrew relied on sequence of tense marking in complement clauses or on relative clause constructions for encoding the temporal function of 'flashbacking' in narrative.

Other research confirms that with age, narrative texts reflect a more variegated temporal texture and a shift from local to global marking of temporal relations. Thus, tense marking is increasingly used to encode both more local cohesive and more global coherence relations (e.g. Bazzanella and Calleri, 1991; Hickmann, 2003). On the other hand, the distinction between perfective past tense and imperfective aspect is early on mastered for encoding background/foreground relations in languages that mark this distinction grammatically (e.g. Kern, 1997, for French; Sandbank, 2004, for Spanish). And the ability to deploy TMA marking as a means of distinguishing between narrative and other types of discourse is well established by early school-age. Thus, children from late pre-school through middle childhood adhere rigidly to use of past tense and, where relevant, perfective aspect in their narratives, while they rely extensively on timeless present tense and irrealis, future-oriented expressions of modality in producing non-narrative texts (Berman and Nir-Sagiv, 2004; Reilly et al., 2002). This contrasts with adolescents and adults, who show a shift from 'dichotomy to divergence', by inserting present-tense or future-oriented generalizations in their narratives (Berman and Nir-Sagiv, 2007). That is, with age, narrators show greater reliance on 'storytelling' versus 'story time' (Berman and Katzenberger, 2004; Kupersmitt, 2006). Moreover, among 9- and 12-year-olds, such departures occur mainly in codas and subsequently in story openings, and they relate directly to the events themselves, whereas the narratives of older speaker-writers are fleshed out by distanced generalizations and inferential commentary (Ravid and Berman, 2006).

Current research thus throws new light on developmental facets of 'tense-aspect switching', as first noted in the Berman and Slobin (1994) study. Such studies show that the ability to intersperse 'non-narrative' or 'story-external' expository-like generalizations for purposes of effective storytelling and for 'creating texture within text' (Fleischmann, 1990) develops well beyond the time when the relevant linguistic forms are mastered. And they suggest that narrative temporality interacts in non-obvious ways with the function of narrative evaluation.

evaluation

Young children tend to focus on events and changes of states, paying relatively little attention to the *when*, *where* and especially the *why* things happened, where the 'when' and 'where' would be taken as descriptive, and the 'why' is typically interpretive (Berman, 1997; Peterson, 1990). This reflects the fact that young children are as yet not fully cognizant of what is informative and how much background information the listener needs. Research based on Labov's definition of evaluative elements shows that these forms increase from pre-school to middle childhood in amount, and change in distribution, both in personal-experience accounts (Petersen and McCabe, 1983) and in 'frog story' narratives (Bamberg and Damrad-Frye, 1991). Other studies reveal a progression from affective comment on the protagonist – e.g. *the little boy was mad at his frog* – rather less so from the narrator's point of view – e.g. *The giant really scared me* (Bamberg and Reilly, 1996; Reilly, 1992), with some local attribution of mental states to characters by around the age of 4 to 5 years (Bokus, 2004; Eaton et al., 1999; Richner and Nicolopoulou, 2001). Only from middle childhood, around 8 to 9 years of age, will children refer to the beliefs and motivations of other characters (Aksu-Koç and Tekdemir, 2004; Küntay and Nakamura, 2004; Veneziano et al., 2008). And, as noted earlier, it takes until adolescence for narrators to move outside of the narrative mode to express 'story-external' generalizations that go beyond the events recounted. That is, while narrative structure is achieved quite early on, the evaluative function continues to develop across adolescence.

For example, Segal's (2001) analysis of evaluative elements in the narratives of older Hebrew-speaking (pre-)adolescents and adults asked to recount a personal experience revealed that the 12-year-olds related mainly to concrete facets of everyday routines, adolescents talked more about emotional stress, while adults comment cognitively on their interpretation of the events and their possible consequences. Other studies show that the narratives of older children, particularly from adolescence on, include longer, more detached, and more elaborate background information in the opening and closing parts of the text (Berman, 2001; Berman and Katzenberger, 2004; Tolchinsky et al., 2002). Further light is thrown on these developments by subdividing narrative evaluation into factual descriptive information on the circumstances that serve as background to sequential narrative events compared to interpretive or attitudinal elements that comment on narrator perception of these events (Berman, 1997). Research shows that the narratives of adolescents and adults include more, and more reflectively distanced interpretative material than those of younger children in middle childhood (Ravid and Berman, 2006), while as many as two-thirds of the narratives produced by proficient adolescent and adult storytellers consist of descriptive and interpretive as against eventive material.

In sum, development in narrative evaluation reveals a shift from reporting events to emotional responses of how the narrator or the protagonists felt via reference to internal cognitive states of their own and others, on to motivations for actions, leading eventually to the ability to adopt a meta-cognitive stand on the events reported. This ability to express the storyteller's attitude to and perspective on events in the form of story-external generalizations noted in the preceding section reflects a capacity to move outside of events and to explicitly construe and present stories as 'having a point'. The studies surveyed here, across different elicitation contexts, languages, and age groups, thus point to a long developmental route to full narrative proficiency. And they highlight the role of evaluation as a narrative function in going beyond 'structural well-formedness' to 'effective storytelling' (Berman and Nir-Sagiv, 2007). While the former appears to derive from general cognitive development and hence to be shared across children and languages, the ability to adopt an evaluative discourse stance reflects individual skills and personal propensities that flourish in adolescence as the hallmark of effective storytelling performance.

connectivity

Investigations of connectivity in children's narratives go beyond earlier, sentence-based studies of how children use temporal and causal conjunctions to concern with how connectives are used in extended discourse. Such studies highlight the multi-functionality of a term like 'and' in different languages (Berman, 1996; Jisa, 1985; Peterson and McCabe, 1988), and the fact that with age, this all-purpose coordinator is increasingly supplemented by other, semantically more specific markers of narrative discourse functions such as temporality and causality (Berman and Slobin, 1994; Jisa, 1987; Peterson and McCabe, 1987, 1991; Silva, 1995). [See also Pouscoulous and Noveck, this volume: SFC.] Initially, young children use words like 'and' or 'then' as pragmatic discourse markers to indicate that they have more to say, or that their account is still proceeding. Subsequently, such forms combine with common subordinating conjunctions like those meaning 'when' or 'because' to mark semantically motivated and syntactically conventional inter-clausal temporal and causal relations. In a kind of U-shaped developmental curve, children around the age of 5 or 7 years often over-use markers like 'and then', 'after that' as indicators of narrative sequentiality, whereas older, more proficient narrators relate to these as 'default' markers and use them far more sparingly. With age, these early connectives are supplemented and even replaced by semantically more specific, lower-frequency markers of global discourse segments, such as sequential 'at first', 'later on', 'eventually' or subordinators like 'since', 'while', 'although' and the everyday sentence-modifying conjunctions 'so', 'but' are replaced by higher register, semantically more specific counterparts like 'thus', 'however'.

A rather different approach to the development of narrative connectivity was initiated by Berman and Slobin's (1994) notion of clause combining 'syntactic packaging'. This perspective derives from functional linguistic approaches to how complex syntax functions in discourse, and relies critically on the 'clause' (defined in semantico-syntactic terms by Berman and Slobin, 1994, p. 660, as a 'unified predication') rather than the notion of an 'utterance' in the study of early child language or of a 'proposition' as the rather vaguely specified unit of analysis in much research on narrative discourse. Such analyses go beyond prior research on children's use of connectives in producing narratives as well as more traditional school-based studies of discourse connectivity based on 'T(erminable)-Units' (Hunt, 1965) or 'C(ommunication)-Units' (Loban, 1976). Concern is with the general 'syntactic architecture' of developing narratives, rather than with the distribution or use of specific connective terms. Research along these lines reveals, for example, that with age, children package more clauses together within a single unit of discourse and that, in different languages, they show increasing reliance on more cohesive strategies of syntactic connectivity in the form of relative clauses and non-finite subordination (Berman, 1998; Dasinger and Toupin, 1994).

Current analyses of 'clause packaging' shed light on complex syntax as interacting with other facets of more advanced narrative abilities. In cross-linguistic terms, children from a young age reflect similar trends in linking together clauses as those favoured by adolescent and adult narrators in different native languages: For example, they rely relatively more on paratactic stringing of clauses together in Hebrew, as against broader use of complement and non-finite subordinate clauses in English, and complex stacking and centre-embedding of clauses in Spanish (Berman and Nir-Sagiv, 2008). As was earlier shown for the oral 'frog story' sample in Berman and Slobin (1994), older school-age children's personal-experience narratives reveal clear age-related differences in the number of clauses packaged together into a single unit of narrative connectivity. Moreover, from middle childhood across adolescence, there are marked differences in the types of 'syntactic architecture' used for linking clauses together in a single narrative package. Perhaps most importantly, development of narrative connectivity emerges as more than simply moving from more linear (juxtaposed or coordinated) structures to more hierarchical means of subordination (relative and adverbial clauses). Rather, complex clause-linkage in narrative is realized by stacking together of different *types* of clauses, such as by coordination on complement clauses or complementation on adverbial clauses, and so on. Developmentally, while even young pre-school children have command of these different kinds of clause structures and can use them in individual utterances to produce complex sentences, it takes until late school-age or adolescence to skilfully interweave these different options within a single discursive unit in order to meet the function of text-embedded narrative connectivity.

narrative structure

This domain has been examined in developing narrative abilities from different points of view, including in terms of coherence relations (Hickmann, 2003), the distinction between macro- and micro-level structures (van Dijk, 1980) and Karmiloff-Smith's (1986, 1992) insights into the need to achieve a level of 're-representation' in order to integrate early, item-based 'bottom-up' events with later-developing 'top-down' overall discourse structure. The study of narrative development from these various perspectives sheds light on general cognitive abilities in moving from a local to a more global level of organization and structuring of information.

   Different avenues of research reveal a consistent picture of this progression from local to global narrative construction. For example, analysis of picture-series based texts shows a progression from 'pre-narrative' via 'local narration' to 'global action-structure' (Berman and Katzenberger, 1998; Katzenberger, 1994). Texts at the most basic level show no obvious connection between the contents of the pictures and the child's verbal output or else describe the pictures in static, non-action terms, related only to objects (mainly 4-year-olds); at an intermediate level they express a linear, temporal relation, by two consecutive clauses for the events depicted in two adjacent pictures; while at the third and highest level, texts express a global action-structure organized hierarchically around a general goal specified at the outset (a level achieved by only some 6-year-olds on some but not all the picture-series, and commanded by all the 10-year-olds investigated).

Analysis of the 'frog story' oral picture book narratives produced in different languages revealed a similar age-related progression from 3 to 9 years: from isolated events in picture-description mode to local, linearly connected events (first temporally, then causally related) by age 5 to 6 years, and on to hierarchically organized, global action structure shown by most 9-year-old and all adult narrators (Berman, 1988, 1995; Berman and Slobin, 1994). Specifically, 3-year-olds are able to translate static visual pictures into dynamic verbal expression, but they are typically not able to interpret spatial arrays as temporally related sequences of events. At the next phase, of connecting events locally, children give expression to temporal sequentiality, the default case for narrative, at which stage, as noted earlier, they may overmark this explicitly by repeatedly chaining clauses by connectives like 'and then'. The third level reveals a causal relating of events, increasingly motivated by an overall action structure, but still largely local, e.g. *they went into the forest to look for the frog, the boy climbed the tree because the frog might be up there*. Finally, some 9-year-olds, and all the adults, express a hierarchical organization at the global level of action structure, for example, *the boy had lots of adventures in his search for the frog, in the end, he found the frog that had run away*. That is, although basic plot structure is established by age 5 to 9 years, children's texts are still typically organized online by local chaining. Their construals of events are limited in not being able to adopt different 'perspectives on a scene' (Berman, 1993; Berman and Slobin, 1994, pp. 515–38), and they refer to relatively few components within a given episode. Relatedly, younger children do little in the way of retrospective looking back or prospective looking forward to earlier or later points in the unfolding narrative. All these facets of developing narrative abilities from pre-school across early school-age and beyond reflect more general, cognitively motivated development of hierarchical principles of discourse organization, and are shared by speakers of different language backgrounds.

Current analysis of global discourse structure in both narrative and non-narrative texts produced by native speakers of different languages from school-age across adolescence reveals that the youngest children in the sample (9-year-old fourth-graders) were nearly all able to produce what we termed 'well-formed narratives', where this is defined as integrating bottom-up events within an overall, top-down narrative structure, including an initial background setting, one or more episodes, and a concluding resolution (Berman and Nir-Sagiv, 2007). This level of global narrative organization was achieved by all 12-year-old seventh-grade children across the sample, well before the same children were able to construct a well-structured piece of expository discourse. However, it took to adolescence and beyond for narrators to go 'beyond structural well-formedness' – departing from canonic narrative elements by means of expository-like 'story-external' generalizations and by skilled deployment of rhetorical devices to elaborate and reflect meta-cognitively on the events recounted.

conclusions: the developmental path

The preceding form-function analysis of different domains of narrative development underscores the 'usage-based' view that acquisition and development of linguistic knowledge needs to be considered in text-embedded contexts rather than in isolated utterances. Narratives provide a particularly appropriate frame for such analyses since they are a universal and early emerging form of discourse, they occur in conversational interchanges across the life span, they may take the shape of monologic texts in both speech and writing and, in the case of specially skilled individuals, they constitute an expressive means of artistic creativity. In addition, the study of narrative acquisition reveals a general developmental progression from interactive, highly scaffolded, conversation-embedded narration to autonomous text construction.

Among younger children, storytelling is communicative and interactive, representing the desire to participate in the social activity of telling an interested party about something that happened, largely triggered by caretaker input. That is, the ability to 'tell a story' develops very early, and children can give verbal expression to their personal (autobiographical) experiences as young as age 20 months, certainly by the age of 2 years, when they first start talking about events in the recent past, demonstrating the cognitive recognition of actions as completed. However, 2- and 3-year-olds cannot sustain their accounts of past events autonomously, but require scaffolding to continue the unfolding of events in linear sequence. And even when scaffolded by external stimuli such as pictures or a storybook, 3-year-olds persist in engaging their interlocutor as a participant in an interactive co-production.

By late pre-school age, around 5 years, narrative structure – where stories have some minimal introductory setting, at least one episode, and some kind of closure – appear to be well established, but this is largely context- and task-dependent: Children may do quite well at recounting personal experiences, but they will have a hard time telling a coherent make-believe story, and will not be able to provide adequate background information or evaluative content to produce a well-motivated, picture-based narrative. Middle childhood, around 9 years of age, represents a watershed in narrative development. At this stage, children are able to integrate top-down narrative structure with bottom-up individual events irrespective of the particular communicative context or elicitation task, and they can elaborate on this by commenting on internal states of their own and others.

Current research shows that such global, hierarchical organization of extended discourse emerges relatively early in the narrative genre compared with other genres. A combination of factors explains this. First, in experiential terms, narrative is a universal type of discourse, existing in all types of cultures – oral and literate, less and more educated – with very young children having stories told and read to them from early pre-school age. Second, stories deal with concrete people, objects and events rather than with abstract ideas or concepts, and even in fictive contexts, they include protagonists with whom narrators can identify emotionally. Third, in cognitive terms, narratives are organized by a straightforward underlying principle of chronological sequentiality. However, as this chapter has shown, despite the naturalness of narratives, it takes until adolescence and beyond to establish a proficient narrative style, even though most of the necessary linguistic forms are available from early childhood.

note

*I am grateful to Irit Katzenberger and Bracha Nir-Sagiv for their helpful comments on an earlier draft.

references

Aksu-Koç, A. (2004). Role of the home context in relations between narrative abilities and literacy practices. In D. Ravid and H. Bat-Zeev Shyldkrot (eds), *Perspectives on Language and Language Development* (pp. 257–74). Dordrecht: Kluwer.

Aksu-Koç A. and von Stutterheim, C. (1994). Temporal relations in narrative: simultaneity. In R. A. Berman and D. I. Slobin, *Relating Events in Narrative: A Crosslinguistic Developmental Study* (pp. 393–456). Hillsdale, NJ: Lawrence Erlbaum.

Aksu-Koç A. and Tekdemir, G. (2004). Interplay between narrativity and mindreading: A comparison between Turkish and English. In S. Strömqvist and L. Verhoeven (eds), *Relating Events in Narrative: Typological and Contextual Perspectives* (pp. 307–28). Mahwah, NJ: Lawrence Erlbaum.

Ames, L. B. (1966). Children's stories. *Genetic Psychology Monographs*, 73, 337–96.

Applebee, N. (1978). *The Child's Concept of Story*. Chicago: University of Chicago Press.

Bamberg, M. (1986). A functional approach to the acquisition of anaphoric relationships. *Linguistics*, 23, 227–84.

Bamberg, M. and Andrews, M. (eds) (2004). *Considering Counter Narratives: Narrating, Resisting, Making Sense*. Amsterdam: John Benjamins.

Bamberg, M. and Damrad-Frye, R. (1991). On the ability to provide evaluative comments: Further explorations of children's narrative competencies. *Journal of Child Language*, 18, 689–710.

Bamberg, M. and Reilly, J. S. (1996). Emotion, narrative, and affect: How children discover the relationship between what to say and how to say it. In D. Slobin, J. Gerhardt, A. Kyratzis and J. Guo (eds), *Social Interaction, Social Context, and Language* (pp. 329–42). Mahwah, NJ: Lawrence Erlbaum Associates.

Bartlett, F. C. (1932). *Remembering: A Study in Experimental and Social Psychology*. Cambridge: Cambridge University Press.

Bauer, P. J. and Mandler, J. M. (1989). One thing follows another: Effects of temporal structure on one- to two-year-olds' recall of events. *Developmental Psychology*, 25, 197–206.

Bavin, E. (2004). Focusing on 'where': An analysis of Walpiri frog stories. In S. Strömqvist and L. Verhoeven (eds), *Relating Events in Narrative: Typological and Contextual Perspectives* (pp. 17–36). Mahwah, NJ: Lawrence Erlbaum.

Bazzanella, C. and Calleri, D. (1991). Tense coherence and grounding in children's narrative. *Text*, 11, 175–87.

de Beaugrande, R. (1982). The story of grammars and the grammar of stories. *Journal of Pragmatics*, 6, 383–422.

Bereiter, C. and Scardamalia, M. (1987). *The Psychology of Written Composition*. Hillsdale, NJ: Lawrence Erlbaum.

Berman, R. A. (1988). On the ability to relate events in narratives. *Discourse Processes*, 1: 1, 469–97.

Berman, R.A. (1990). Acquiring an (S)VO language: Subjectless sentences in children's Hebrew. *Linguistics*, 28, 1135–66.

Berman, R. A. (1993). The development of language use: Expressing perspectives on a scene. In E. Dromi (ed.), *Language and Cognition: A Developmental Perspective* (pp. 172–201). Norwood, NJ: Ablex.

Berman, R. A. (1995). Narrative competence and storytelling performance: How children tell stories in different contexts. *Journal of Narrative and Life History* 5: 4, 285–313.

Berman, R. A. (1996). Form and function in developing narrative abilities: The case of 'and'. In D. Slobin, J. Gerhardt, A. Kyratzis and J. Guo (eds), *Social Interaction, Context, and Language: Essays in Honor of Susan Ervin-Tripp* (pp. 243–68). Mahwah, NJ: Lawrence Erlbaum.

Berman, R. A. (1997). Narrative theory and narrative development: The Labovian impact. *Journal of Narrative and Life History*, 7, 235–44.

Berman, R. A. (1998). Typological perspectives on connectivity. In N. Dittmar and Z. Penner (eds), *Issues in the Theory of Language Acquisition* (pp. 203–24). Bern: Peter Lang.

Berman, R. A. (2001). Setting the narrative scene: How children begin to tell a story. In A. Aksu-Koç, C. Johnson and K. Nelson (eds), *Children's Language*, Vol. 10 (pp. 1–31). Mahwah, NJ: Erlbaum.

Berman, R. A. (2004). The role of context in developing narrative abilities. In S. Strömqvist and L. Verhoeven (eds), *Relating Events in Narrative: Typological and Contextual Perspectives* (pp. 261–80). Mahwah, NJ: Lawrence Erlbaum.

Berman, R. (2009). Language development in narrative contexts. In Edith Bavin (ed.) *The Cambridge Handbook of Child Language*, (pp. 355–75). Cambridge: Cambridge University Press.

Berman, R. A. and Katzenberger, I. (1998). Cognitive and linguistic factors in development of picture-series narration, *Studia Italiani i Linguistica Teorica e Applicata*, 27, 21–47.

Berman, R. A. and Katzenberger, I. (2004). Form and function in introducing narrative and expository texts: A developmental perspective. *Discourse Processes*, 38, 57–94.

Berman, R. A. and Nir-Sagiv, B. (2004). Linguistic indicators of inter-genre differentiation in later language development. *Journal of Child Language*, 31, 339–80.

Berman, R. A. and Nir-Sagiv, B (2007). Comparing narrative and expository text construction across adolescence: A developmental paradox. *Discourse Processes*, 43: 2, 79–120.

Berman, R.A. and Nir-Sagiv, B. (2008). Clause-packaging in narratives: a crosslinguistic developmental study. In J. Guo, E. Lieven, S. Ervin-Tripp, N. Budwig, S. Özçalişkan and K. Nakamura (eds), *Crosslinguistic Approaches to the Psychology of Language: Research in the Tradition of Dan I. Slobin*, (pp. 149–62). Mahwah, NJ: Lawrence Erlbaum.Berman, R. A. and Slobin, D. I. (1994). *Relating Events in Narrative: A Crosslinguistic Developmental Study*. Hillsdale, NJ: Lawrence Erlbaum

Berman, R. S. and Verhoeven, L. (2002). Developing text production abilities in speech and writing: Aims and methodology. *Written Languages and Literacy*, 5, 1–44.

Bettelheim, B. (1970). *The Use of Enchantment: The Meaning and Importance of Fairy Tales*. New York: Knopf.

Blum-Kulka, S. (1997). *Dinner-Talk: Cultural Patterns of Sociability and Socialization in Family Dinners*. Mahwah, NJ: Lawrence Erlbaum.

Blum-Kulka, S. (2004a). I will tell you the whole story now: Sequencing the past, present, and future in children's conversational narratives. In D. Ravid and H. Bat-Zeev Shyldkrot (eds), *Perspectives on Language and Language Development* (pp. 275–88). Dordrecht: Kluwer.

Blum-Kulka, S. (2004b). The role of peer interaction in later pragmatic development: The case of speech representation. In R. A. Berman (ed.), *Language Development across Childhood and Adolescence* (pp. 191–210). Amsterdam: John Benjamins.

Bokus, B. (2004). Inter-mind phenomena in child narrative discourse. *Pragmatics*, 14, 391–408.

Botvin, G. J. and Sutton-Smith, B. (1977). Development of structural complexity in children's fantasy narratives. *Developmental Psychology*, 13, 377–88.

Brown, P. (2004). Position and motion in Tzeltal frog stories: The acquisition of narrative style. In S. Strömqvist and L. Verhoeven (eds), *Relating Events in Narrative: Typological and Contextual Perspectives* (pp. 37–58). Mahwah, NJ: Lawrence Erlbaum.

Bruner, J. (1986). *Actual Minds, Possible Worlds*. Cambridge, MA: Harvard University Press.

Chang, C-J. (2003). Talking about the past: How do Chinese mothers elicit narratives from their young children across time? *Journal of Narrative Inquiry*, 13, 99–126.

Clark, H. H. (2004). Variations on a ranarian theme. In S. Strömqvist and L. Verhoeven (eds), *Relating Events in Narrative: Typological and Contextual Perspectives* (pp. 457–76). Mahwah, NJ: Lawrence Erlbaum.

Dasinger, L. and Toupin, C. (1994). The development of relative clause functions in narrative. In R. A. Berman and D. I. Slobin, *Relating Events in Narrative: A Crosslinguistic Developmental Study* (pp. 457–514). Hillsdale, NJ: Erlbaum.

van Dijk, T. (1980). *Macrostructures: An Interdisciplinary Study of Global Structures in Discourse, Interaction, and Cognition*. Hillsdale, NJ: Lawrence Erlbaum.

Eaton, J. H., Collis, G. N. and Lewis, V. A. (1999). Evaluative explanations in children's narratives of a video sequence without dialogue. *Journal of Child Language*, 26, 699–720.

Eisenberg, A. R. (1985). Learning to describe past experiences in conversation. *Discourse Processes*, 8, 177–204.

Fleischman, S. (1990). *Tense and Narrativity: From Medieval Performance to Modern Fiction*. Austin: University of Texas Press.

Galda, L. and Pellegrini, A. D. (eds) (1990). *Play, Language, and Stories: The Development of Children's Literate Behavior*. Norwood, NJ: Ablex.

Gee, J. (1989). Two styles of narrative construction and their linguistic and educational implications. *Discourse Processes*, 12, 287–308.

Heath, S. B. (1982). What no bedtime story means: Narrative skills at home and at school. *Language in Society*, 11, 49–76.

Heath, S. B. (1983). *Ways with Words: Life and Work in Communities and Classroom*. Cambridge: Cambridge University Press.

Heath, S. B. (1986). Taking a cross-cultural look at narratives. *Topics in Language Disorders*, 7: 1, 84–94.

Hickmann, M. (1981). Creating referents in discourse: A developmental analysis of linguistic cohesion. In J. Kreiman and E. Ojeda (eds), *Papers from the Parasession on Pronouns and Anaphora* (pp. 192–203). Chicago: Chicago Linguistic Society.

Hickmann, M. (1995). Discourse organization and the development of reference to person, space, and time. In P. Fletcher and B. MacWhinney (eds), *Handbook of Child Language* (pp. 194–218). Oxford: Basil Blackwell.

Hickmann, M. (1996). Information status and grounding in children's discourse: A crosslinguistic perspective. In J. Costermann and M. Fayol (eds), *Processing Interclausal Relationships in the Production and Comprehension of Texts* (pp. 221–43). Mahwah, NJ: Lawrence Erlbaum.

Hickmann, M. (1998). Form, function, and context in narrative development. *Journal of Pragmatics*, 29, 33–56.

Hickmann, M. (2003). *Children's Discourse: Person, Time, and Space across Languages*. Cambridge: Cambridge University Press.

Hickmann, M. and Hendriks, H. (1999). Cohesion and anaphora in children's narratives: A comparison of English, French, German, and Chinese. *Journal of Child Language*, 26, 419–52.

Hickmann, M., Kail, M. and Roland, F. (1995). Cohesive anaphoric relatios in French children's narratives as a function of mutual knowledge. *First Language*, 15, 177–300.

Hunt, K. W. (1965). Grammatical structures written at three grade levels. *National Counters of Teachers of English Research Report #3*. Champaign, IL: National Council of Teachers of English.

Invernezzi, M. A. and Abouzeid, M. P. (1995). One story map does not fit all: A cross-cultural analysis of children's written story retellings. *Journal of Narrative and Life History*, 5, 1–19.

Jisa, H. (1985). French preschoolers' use of *et pis* ('and then'). *First Language*, 5, 169–84.

Jisa, H. (1987). Sentence connectors in French children's monologue performance. *Journal of Pragmatics*, 11, 607–21.

Kail, M. and Sanchez y Lopez, I. (1997). Referent introductions in Spanish children's narratives as a function of contextual constrains. *First Language*, 17, 103–30.

Karmiloff-Smith, A. (1979). *A Functional Approach to Child Language: A study of Determiners and Reference*. Cambridge: Cambridge University Press.

Karmiloff-Smith, A. (1980). Psychological processes underlying pronominalization and non-pronominalization in children's connected discourse. In J. Kreiman and A. Ojeda (eds), *Papers from the Parasession on Pronouns and Anaphora* (pp. 231–49). Chicago: Chicago Linguistic Society.

Karmiloff-Smith, A. (1981). The grammatical marking of thematic structure. In W. Deutsch (ed.), *The Child's Conception of Language* (pp. 121–47). London: Academic Press.

Karmiloff-Smith, A. (1986). Language and cognitive processes from a developmental perspective. *Language and Cognitive Processes*, 1, 61–85.

Karmiloff-Smith, A. (1992). *Beyond Modularity: A developmental perspective on cognitive science*. Cambridge, MA: MIT Press.

Katzenberger, I. (1994). Cognitive, linguistic, and developmental factors in the development of picture-series narration. Unpublished doctoral dissertation [in Hebrew], Tel Aviv University.

Kern, S. (1997). *Comment les enfants jonglent avec les contraintes communicationelles, discursives, et linguistiques dans la production d'une narration*. Unpublished doctoral dissertation. Université Lumière, Lyon 2.

Küntay, A. C. and Nakamura, K. (2004). Linguistic strategies serving evaluative functions: A comparison between Japanese and Turkish Narratives. In S. Strömqvist and L. Verhoeven (eds), *Relating Events in Narrative: Typological and Contextual Perspectives* (pp. 329–58). Mahwah, NJ: Lawrence Erlbaum.

Kupersmitt, J. (2006). Temporality in texts: A crosslinguistic developmental study of form-function relations in narrative and expository discourse. Unpublished doctoral dissertation, Bar-Ilan University.

Labov, W. (1972). The transformation of experience in narrative syntax. In W. Labov. *Language in the Inner City* (pp. 355–96). Philadelphia: University of Pennsylvania Press.

Labov, W. and Waletzky, J. (1967). Narrative analysis. In J. Helm (ed.), *Essays on the Verbal and Visual Arts* (pp. 12–44). Seattle, WA: American Ethnological Society.

Loban, W. (1976). Language development: Kindergarten through grade twelve. *Research Report 12*. Urbana, IL: National Council of Teachers of English.

Longacre, R. E. (1996). *The Grammar of Discourse*. (2nd edition). Topics in Language and Linguistics. New York: Plenum.

Mandler, J. (1982). Some uses and abuses of a story grammar. *Discourse Processes*, 5, 305–18.

Mandler, J. (1987). On the psychological reality of story structure. *Discourse Processes*, 10, 1–30.

McConaughy, S., Fitzhenry-Coor, I. and Howell, D. (1983). Developmental differences in schemata for story comprehension. In K. E. Nelson (ed.), *Children's Language*, Vol. 4 (pp. 385–421) Hillsdale, NJ: Lawrence Erlbaum.

Miller, P. J. and Sperry, L. L. (1988). Early talk about the past: Origins of conversational stories of personal experience. *Journal of Child Language*, 15, 293–315.

Minami, M. (2002). *Culture-specific Narrative Styles: The development of Oral Narrative and Literacy*. Tonawanda, NY: Multilingual Matters.

Minami, M. and McCabe, A. (1995). Rice balls versus bear hunts: Japanese and Caucasian family narrative patterns. *Journal of Child Language*, 22, 423–46.

Nelson, K. (ed.) (1986). *Event Knowledge: Structure and Function in Development*. Hillsdale, NJ: Lawrence Erlbaum.

Nicolopolou, A. (1996). Narrative development in social context. In D. I. Slobin, J. Gerhardt, A. Kyratzis and J. Guo (eds), *Social Interaction, Context, and Language* (pp. 369–90). Mahwah, NJ: Lawrence Erlbaum.

Nicolopolou, A. (1997). Children and narratives: Toward an interpretive and sociocultural approach. In M. Bamberg (ed.), *Narrative Development: Six approaches* (pp. 179–216). Mahwah, NJ: Lawrence Erlbaum.

Ninio, A. and Snow, C. E. (1996). *Pragmatic Development*. Oxford: Westview Press.

Pesco, D. and Crago, M. (1996). We went home, told the whole story to our friends: Narratives by children in an Algonquin community. *Journal of Narrative and Life History*, 6, 293–321.

Peterson, C. (1990). The 'who', 'when', and 'where' of early narratives. *Journal of Child Language*, 17, 433–55.

Peterson, C. and McCabe, A. (1983). *Developmental Psycholinguistics: Three Ways of Looking at a Child's Narrative*. New York: Plenum.

Peterson, C. and McCabe, A. (1987). The connective 'and': Do older children use it less as they learn other connectives? *Journal of Child Language*, 14, 375–81.

Peterson, C. and McCabe, A. (1988). The connective 'and' as discourse glue. *First Language*, 8, 19–28.

Peterson, C. and McCabe, A. (1991). Linking connective use to connective macrostructure. In A. McCabe and C. Peterson (eds), *Developing Narrative Structure* (pp. 29–54). Hillsdale, NJ: Erlbaum.

Pitcher, G. and Prelinger, E. (1963). *Children Tell Stories: An Analysis of Fantasy*. New York: International Universities Press.

Poulsen, D., Kintsch, E., Kintsch, W. and Premack, D. (1979). Children's comprehension and memory for stories. *Journal of Experimental Child Psychology*, 28, 379–403.

Propp, V. (1958). *Morphology of the Folktale*. Bloomington: Indiana University Press.

Ravid, D. and Berman, R. A. (2006). Information density in the development of spoken and written narratives in English and Hebrew. *Discourse Processes,* 41, 117–49.

Reilly, J. S. (1992). How to tell a good story: The intersection of language and affect in children's narratives. *Journal of Narrative and Life History 2,* 355–77.

Reilly, J. S., Jisa, H., Baruch, E. and Berman, R. A. (2002). Propositional attitudes in written and spoken language. *Written Language and Literacy,* 5, 183–218.

Richner, S. and Nicolopoulou, A. (2001). The narrative construction of differing conceptions of the person in the development of young children's social understanding. *Early Education and Development,* 12, 393–432.

Sachs, J. (1983). Talking about the there and then: The emergence of displaced reference in parent-child discourse. In K. Nelson (ed.), *Children's Language,* Vol. 4 (pp. 1–48) New York: Gardner Press.

Sandbank, S. (2004). Writing narrative text: A developmental and crosslinguistic study of fable reconstruction. Unpublished doctoral dissertation, Tel Aviv University.

Sanderson, A. and McKeough, A. (2005). Narrative analysis of behaviorally troubled adolescents' life stories. *Journal of Narrative Inquiry,* 15, 127–60.

Segal, M. (2001). Form-function relations in the expression of narrative evaluation across adolescence. Unpublished doctoral dissertation [in Hebrew], Tel Aviv University.

Shank, R. C. and Abelson, R. P. (1977). *Scripts, Plans, Goals, and Understanding.* Hillsdale, NJ: Lawrence Erlbaum.

Shen, Y. (1988). The X-Bar grammar for stories: Story grammar revisited. *Text,* 9, 415–67.

Silva, M. N. (1995). Simultaneity in children's narratives: The case of *when, while* and *as. Journal of Child Language,* 18, 641–62.

Slobin, D. I. (1973). Cognitive prerequisites for the development of grammar. In C. A. Ferguson and D. I. Slobin (eds), *Studies of Child Language Development* (pp. 175–208). New York: Holt, Rinehart and Winston.

Slobin, D. I. (1996). From 'thought and language' to 'thinking for speaking'. In J. J. Gumperz and S. C. Levinson (eds), *Rethinking Linguistic Relativity* (pp. 70–96). Cambridge: Cambridge University Press.

Slobin, D. I. (2003a). Language and thought online: Cognitive consequences of linguistic relativity. In D. Gentner and S. Goldin-Meadow (eds), *Language in Mind: Advances in the Investigation of Language and Thought* (pp. 157–91). Cambridge, MA: MIT Press.

Slobin, D. I. (2003b). How people move. In C. L Moder and A. Martinovic-Zic (eds), *Discourse across Languages and Cultures* (pp. 195–210). Amsterdam: John Benjamins.

Slobin, D. I. (2004a). The many ways to search for a frog: Linguistic typology and the expression of motion events. In S. Strömqvist and L. Verhoeven (eds), *Relating Events in Narrative: Typological and Contextual Perspectives* (pp. 219–57). Mahwah, NJ: Lawrence Erlbaum.

Slobin, D. I. (2004b). Relating events in translation. In D. Ravid and H. B. Shyldkrot (eds), *Perspectives on Language and Language Development* (pp. 115–30). Dordrecht: Kluwer.

Smorti, A. (2004).Narrative strategies for interpreting stories with incongruent endings. *Journal of Narrative Inquiry,* 14, 141–68.

Snow, C. E. and Dickinson, D. K. (1990). Social sources of narrative skills at home and at school. *First Language*, 10, 87–103.

Snow, C. E. and Ninio, A. (1986). The contracts of literacy: What children learn from learning to read books. In W. Teale and E. Sulzby (eds), *Emergent Literacy: Writing and Reading* (pp. 116–37). Norwood, NJ: Ablex.

Stein, N. L. (2004). Analysis of narratives of Bhutanese and rural American 7-year-old children: Issues of story grammar and culture. *Narrative Inquiry*, 14, 369–94.

Stein, N. L. (1982). What's in a story: Interpreting interpretations of story grammars. *Discourse Processes*, 5, 319–35.

Stein, N. L. and Glenn, C. G. (1979). An analysis of story comprehension in elementary school children. In R. O. Freedle (ed.), *New Directions in Discourse Processing* (pp. 55–120). Norwood, NJ: Ablex.

Strömqvist, S. and Verhoeven, L. (eds) (2004) *Relating Events in Narrative: Typological and Contextual Perspectives*. Mahwah, NJ: Lawrence Erlbaum.

Sutton-Smith, B. (1981). *The Folkstories of Children*. Philadelphia: University of Pennsylvania Press.

Tolchinsky, L. (2003). *The Cradle of Culture: What Children Know about Writing and Numbers before Being Taught*. Mahwah, NJ: Lawrence Erlbaum.

Tolchinsky, L., Johansson, V. and Zamora, A. (2002). Text openings and closings in writing and speech: Autonomy and differentiation. *Written Language and Literacy*, 5, 219–54.

Tomasello, M. (ed.) (1998, 2003). *The New Psychology of Language: Cognitive and Functional Approaches to Language Structure*, Vols 1 and 2. Mahwah, NJ: Lawrence Erlbaum.

Trabasso, T. and Rodkin, P. (1994). Knowledge of goals/plans: A conceptual basis for narrating 'Frog, where are you?'. In R. A. Berman and D. I. Slobin, *Relating Events in Narrative: A Crosslinguistic Developmental Study* (pp. 85–107). Hillsdale, NJ: Lawrence Erlbaum.

Trabasso, T., Stein, N. L. and Johnson, L. R. (1981). Children's knowledge of events: A causal analysis of story structure. In G. Bower (ed.), *Learning and Motivation*, Vol. 15. New York: Academic Press.

Trabasso, T., van den Broek, P. and Suh, S. (1989). Logical necessity and transitivity of causal relations in stories. *Discourse Processes*, 12, 1–25.

Turner, M. (1996). *The Literary Mind: The Origins of Thought and Language*. Oxford: Oxford University Press.

Veneziano, E., Albert, L. and Martin, S. (2008). Learning to tell a story of false belief: A study of French-speaking children. In J. Guo, E. Lieven, S. Ervin-Tripp, N. Budwig, S. Özçalişkan and K. Nakamura (eds), *Crosslinguistic Approaches to the Psychology of Language: Research in the Tradition of Dan I. Slobin* (pp. 277–90). Mahwah, NJ: Lawrence Erlbaum.

Veneziano, E. and Sinclair, H. (1995). Functional changes in early child language: Appearance of references to the past and of explanations. *Journal of Child Language*, 22, 557–82.

Warden, D. (1976). The influence of context on children's use of identifying expressions and reference. *British Journal of Psychology*, 67, 101–12.

Wigglesworth, G. (1990). Children's narrative acquisition: a study of some aspects of reference and anaphora. *First Language*, 10, 105–25.

13
family literacy activities: what is, what ought to be and the role of parents' ideas

stuart mcnaughton, meaola amituanai-toloa, and 'ema wolfgramm-foliaki

introduction

This chapter examines how family literacy practices change, and specifically the role of parents' ideas in that change. The rationale for this examination is that changing family practices is as much about shifting cultural identity as it is about demonstrating developmental relationships (McNaughton, 2005). Our concern comes from an applied developmental perspective (Lerner et al., 2000); that is, from a need to understand how best to optimize the conditions for socialisation. In our case this is optimizing circumstances to increase schooling success for children in families whose practices do not take the canonical forms which are developmentally associated with success in school literacy. But if we are right about how family interventions are cultural interventions then the relationship with what 'is' the case and what 'ought' to be the case needs very careful consideration; particularly in terms of the conditions under which change is both effective and justified. In the following discussion we examine this issue from the point of view of the ideas of the parents in the change process.

First we make a case for the role of parents' ideas in family literacy practices and the sources of those ideas. Then we use two studies of family literacy practices and parents' ideas to illustrate our argument by describing the interface between parents' ideas and multiple sources of information and guidance. This enables us to conceptualise the variety of forms that interface takes and from which we can draw some developmental implications, linking the case studies with research about programmes that have attempted to change family practices.

parents' ideas in family literacy practices

We know a lot about the relationships between family literacy practices and literacy achievement at school. We would not expect to find a simple unitary developmental progression for school forms of reading and writing generally. But there is a degree of consensus over the general picture, of how the components of reading and writing as conventional school-based print skills develop through family practices in the early years and over the transition to school, given instructional activities at school that define conventional school literacy practices, such as the activities within which instruction for decoding and comprehension occur. Some family practices are more directly developmentally linked with school practices than others and use of specific activities by families may enhance the development of aspects of conventional literacy both before school and when a child goes to school (Heath, 1983). For example, developmental relationships between particular sets of knowledge and skills before school and subsequent progress at school can be linked to specific family activities such as how books are read with children (Whitehurst and Lonigan, 2001). This relationship comes about because of relationships between expertise on entry to school and achievement in reading over the first grades of schools.

We also know that family literacy practices vary in two ways. One is variation between cultural groups where there are differences between groups shown by qualitative case studies or in terms of direct sample comparisons. The latter also indicate the presence of a second form of variation about which there is less known: that within groups (McNaughton, 2005). Cultural groups, defined generally as groups having common practices and meanings associated with those practices (Greenfield and Cocking, 1994), may differ from each other in terms of the characteristics of their language and literacy practices, both in the types of activities which form their practices as well as the frequency of occurrence of those activities (Greenfield, 1994). But cultural groups are internally heterogeneous with respect to those activities and their occurrence too. That is, family literacy activities are variable in terms of type and occurrence of particular activities, so that within any given cultural group families differ one from another also (McNaughton,

1996; Neuman et al., 1995). Applied to child-rearing practices, Reese and Gallimore (2000) refer to this within-group variation as composed of both idiosyncratic and widely shared features of the group's cultural model of children's literacy development. This is similar to a view of a group's cultural practices which involve core and more peripheral practices, the latter of which may be changing (McNaughton, 1996).

Additionally, individual families within a cultural group may vary in their own practices. The variations can be short-term fluctuations as the purpose of reading and the text genre change (Pellegrini et al., 1990). Or the variations may be more long-term as families have access to new ideas as well as types of texts and incorporate these into their practices.

Heath et al. (1986) describe how a researcher and a teacher collaborated with a young African American mother in a low socio-economic community. She incorporated the reading of narrative texts with her 2-year-old child into their language practices, adding new interactional forms such as expansions of text words and commentaries on text topics and oral narratives to previous types of interactions which were, in the main, directives or questions to label or imitate. Other more deliberate interventions with particular families such as 'dialogic reading' (Whitehurst and Lonigan, 2001) also involved a shift in roles and patterns of interaction for individual families as, for example, parents add the discussing of narrative events and life-to-text relationships when reading narrative texts with their children. Even more generally, changes in social circumstance such as increased experience and familiarity with formal education can be associated with changing practices across generations (Greenfield and Cocking, 1994; Reese and Gallimore, 2000). What differs between these variations is the degree to which they involve short- or long-term changes in family members' beliefs and ideas and related practices, a topic explored further below.

The reason for the variability in literacy activities is that while socialization practices are structured, they are also dynamic. The structure comes from how parents' ideas and actions guide children, creating 'channels' of development for children, which increase the likelihood of some activity settings for children occurring and decrease the probability of others (Valsiner, 1988). However, caregivers are not passively reproducing cultural practices, and their ideas and actions change. New ideas and practices are constructed using messages and models available from multiple sources within family, community and institutional settings, particularly school settings (Reese and Gallimore, 2000).

Within the channels children develop expertise situated in recurring activity settings, which involves coming to know the goals, the actions and the conditions relevant to those activities (Gee, 2001; Rogoff, 1990). But children too are not passive in this process and the resulting co-construction between children and parents also impacts on the nature of activities. For example, Heath et al. (1986) also describe how dialogue patterns changed between the mother and her child as the child developed ways of telling stories co-opted from the activity of hearing stories being read. In a similar way, early childhood settings and schools have been identified as sources of new ideas about written and oral language that subsequently alter family activities, especially those school tasks that require parental responding to children (Royal-Tangaere and McNaughton, 1994; Reese and Gallimore, 2000). Thus, both the commonalities and the diversity of practices within cultural groups can be attributed to the dynamic nature of the ideas and actions of both socialization agents and children (McNaughton, 1996).

An analysis of activities as sites of socialization needs to consider the ideas participants hold about those activities. Goodnow and Collins (1990) outlined the notion of parent's ideas. They argued that parents hold ideas about children, parents and family relationships. They maintained 'that we cannot understand parents' ideas unless we consider parents in the context of particular responsibilities, particular social conditions, particular relationships, and a cultural history of ideas about childhood, parenting, and the course of development' (1990, p. 7). Family members construct ideas about the nature of children's development and appropriate forms of teaching and learning. These include beliefs about developmental goals and stages. The ideas can be seen as part of activities (Wertsch, 1991) but, as noted earlier, they are not static. They change over the course of child-rearing and across generations, a process that contributes to cultural shifts. Like their children, parents' ideas develop through processes of personal construction from ambient events, personal problem solving and through co-construction in joint activities with others.

A number of ideas about early literacy are possible. In the following two studies we examined parents' ideas about specific literacy activities. In the case of Pacific Island families living in New Zealand, family members may have thought about these activities and the functions activities perform in meeting the needs of the family system and may even be able to describe and explain them clearly (Tagoilelagi-Leota et al., 2003; Tanielu, 2004). However, the actual guidance of these activities might be driven and expressed not only by the need to retain certain cultural and social identities but also by the need to address issues that might be hindering educational achievement for their children.

These activities reflect cultural and social identities as well as how guidance might be implemented and channelled in such a way as to create opportunities for adapting and adopting certain cultural ways of knowing and particular ways of acting. The culturally based variability in activities is an inherent property of parenting and cultural identity because the ways of knowing and the ways of acting which constitute a culture are constructed both at a collective and at a personal level. For example, parents and caregivers might employ and display activities which pertinently carry the school's 'right' way of providing guidance for reading, but they might also employ and display those activities which have nothing to do with school initiatives but everything to do with (cultural) codification by language, gestures and gaze which are channelled by voice, body and sight (Duranti, 1992).

case studies of two cultural groups

We know very little about the literacy activities various immigrant Pacific Island families engage in with their children and how children learn from the specific activities in these contexts. Yet children from these Pasifika communities living in New Zealand are over represented in the 'tail' of the achievement distribution in literacy at school and a national literacy strategy has been in place which has promoted specific educational interventions for these families and their children (McNaughton, 1996). In the following two case studies we examine parents' ideas about specific literacy activities. The first study describes Tongan parents reading books with their pre-school children. The second examines Samoan mothers and their primary school-age children in the activity of hearing their children read at home.

reading to pre-schoolers in tongan families

Six Tongan pre-school children, together with their families, took part in the study led by Wolfgramm-Foliaki (2006). The families all attended the same church and all of the children attended the same Tongan pre-school run by professional educators where the nationwide New Zealand early childhood curriculum (known as Te Whāriki) was delivered in Tongan. The pre-school served two purposes. One was to prepare children for compulsory schooling (available to children from age 5; mandated from age 6 in New Zealand). Parents expressed in interviews a desire for their children to learn school-related skills. Secondly, the pre-school was seen as an additional site where the children could learn more about cultural values and the Tongan language. Both goals were believed to be crucial elements in their children's literacy development.

Observations of reading, writing and oral narrative activities at home were complemented by interviews with the parents (or the primary caregiver or primary participant in literacy activities), and also with teachers. The aim was to identify and analyse these activities across three sites: home, pre-school and church. The wider study describes how the activities created a developmental cohesion in terms of shared goals, ideas and the characteristics of the activities (Wolfgramm-Foliaki, 2006). Here we describe how one specific activity, reading books with children, was underpinned by parents' ideas about learning and literacy development.

Each of the families read books with their children, in a combination of Tongan and English for all but one family. When they read narrative texts they used combinations of styles (McNaughton, 1995). A performance style occurred through modelling and imitation routines where the parent provided a model for a word or longer text sequence and the child copied. A display style occurred usually in classic Initiation Response Evaluation (IRE) routines (Cazden, 2001) with the parent initiating a question requiring item knowledge about such things as shapes and colours in the illustrations, the child responding and the parent evaluating through affirming or correcting the label. A narrative style involved routines which were more conversational in format and involved discussion of such features as character and plot, and in which life-to-text connections are made.

The parents held specific ideas about the use of these routines. For example, they claimed that books were for learning, *'a way of gaining knowledge'*,[1] and in this respect they were also a preparation for school. This belief was directly linked with the display style.

> *'first of all we look at the pictures and then I ask [child] questions relating to the pictures such as, 'what is this object?' and 'do you know what this is? [then I say] 'very good' [or] 'no! it is a rabbit'. (Mother H)*

The parents attributed different routines and their features to different sources of information. One source was their memories of teaching and learning from their own childhood. Parent 'K' said her reading activities stemmed directly from how she learned to read as a child in

Tonga, saying her use of performance routines and display routines had been used extensively by her teachers. She further recalled that reading was not a very interactive process at school and Sunday school, as children were always expected to sit quietly and listen to the reader. However, after migrating to New Zealand, she learned from observing children's television programmes and through the teachers at the pre-school that a more interactive style was appropriate. She now believed that the reader should allow the child to ask questions and for the reader to also answer the child's questions. During reading it was acceptable also now for her and her daughter to discuss and negotiate the various meanings of texts.

The influence of the professionally based knowledge derived from the teachers at the pre-school could be seen in very specific attributes of the routines. For example, praise occurred frequently often as part of the third term of the IRE sequence. For Mother O praise was deliberately given to affirm correct responses and to encourage saying: '*you are very clever!*' This mother traced her practices to the pre-school where she had observed that '*the teachers encouraged the children all the time*'. In Parent H's case, the belief in reading as a pathway towards success at school now included '*Talking about it (story)*', and '*allowing the child to question what they may not understand and giving feedback which further reinforces the child's understanding of the story*'. This adoption of a more interactive style also occurred with a grandmother, who was the reader in one family. She used a combination of performance and narrative routines and encouraged her grandson to talk about the stories read and to ask questions about them. She believed that discussion about what they had read promoted literacy and language skills.

Readers in all the families had adopted the use of questions at the end of book reading. They saw the questions as having several functions. They were a way of ensuring that the children listened carefully. All the parents highly valued good memory skills, and during the reading activities the children were constantly reminded of the need to pay attention as they would be questioned at the end. Parent K, who used both the display style and the narrative style, believed that '*Questions aid memory skills and children remember events and characters from stories if they are asked questions at the end.*' But the parents also used the questions as a means of checking whether children had understood the story.

It was clear that the parents had put different combinations of ideas and actions together and that they discriminated between their actions using these ideas. For example, they all distinguished the styles of reading narrative books from the way church texts were read. When reading the Bible Mother O pointed out that her children knew what was expected of them, *'when we read the Bible they sit very quietly and listen'*. In Parent K's family there were no English reading books at home and regular reading primarily involved the Tongan Bible and hymns. There were parts of these texts that the child needed to memorize for Sunday school which were learned through recitation using the performance style. However, this parent too had adopted a question and answer format, and her child liked to be questioned at the end of their reading activity often requesting to be questioned if the parent did not do so, which the parent traced to the pre-school. This parent explained further that children love to hear stories read to them, and according to a radio programme she had heard, parents should encourage reading at home. Furthermore, through her experiences at the pre-school with her son, she had seen that, through reading, children *'learned a variety of skills such as memory skills and knowledge about words and letters'*.

Aspects of the styles used by the parents can be traced to the framework provided by Tongan cultural values. For example, the use of recitation in the performance style can be linked with beliefs about authority and the hierarchical structure of Tongan society (McNaughton, 1995; Wolfgramm-Foliaki, 2006). The point we draw here from these case studies is that the ideas that the parents held were dynamic and were derived from several different sources. They had reconceptualized ideas about literacy and styles of guidance using memories of 'traditional' patterns from their childhood as well as contemporary sources of information. A very powerful source was the pre-school and the models for guidance available from the teachers (who were very familiar members of the same church and community). Ideas from this source were coordinated with their existing ideas. The significance of the pre-school source for new ideas was also found by Utumapu (1998) in her study of Samoan mothers and their involvement in early childhood education through Samoan pre-schools.

The parents in this study actively sought new ideas, partly motivated by their belief in the importance of early childhood education and of their children's participation in it. Like other studies of new immigrant families there was a strong belief in the value of education as having a crucial role in their children's future status in the new society (Matuti-Bianchi, 1986; Ogbu, 1991), This desire, according to Edwards (1995), shows a willingness to create a new identity socially, and studies of immigrant families in the United States have found this to be the case (Greenfield and Cocking, 1994). However, for these Tongan parents the development of ideas was also associated with deliberate decisions to preserve cultural and language values and access a pre-school education site where these were being upheld. The second study, to which we now turn, examined the sources in greater detail and how they are mapped on to existing culturally based beliefs.

samoan mothers hearing school children read at home

This study, led by Amituanai-Toloa (2002), focused on six Samoan mothers of 6- to 7-year-old children, examining their patterns of guidance and ideas about that guidance in the activity of hearing their children reading school books in English. In New Zealand a standard practice is for teachers to send books home for children to read to a more mature reader for further practice and consolidation and to establish home–school links (McNaughton, 1996). Previous research in New Zealand has shown that the practice is initiated by the schools and is widespread. Parents' guidance which matches core school forms, such as pausing at the point of a miscue to enable self-corrections to occur, praising accurate reading and prompting children to solve miscues, is more likely to occur if specific guidance has been given or if the parents have some relationship with teaching, either through their own occupations or through family connections (McNaughton, 1996). In the current study no direct guidance for this activity had occurred so it enabled us to examine ideas and practices that the mothers had constructed for themselves. The results discussed here are based on audio recordings of sessions between the children and their mothers. The primary language of the home was Samoan but the children were bilingual and were being taught in bilingual classrooms at the local primary school.

In general, the mothers in this study did not act in ways consistent with generally effective tutorial techniques established by schools who give guidance to parents on such matters (e.g. 'pause, prompt and praise'). Rather, they corrected 97 per cent of the 116 miscues that occurred, and did so immediately in 93 per cent of the cases. When they intervened, the mothers tended to tell their child what the word was rather than prompt using graphophonemic, syntactic or semantic cues. Praise was relatively infrequent, and two of the mothers did not praise their child at all. There was a strong emphasis on pronouncing each word correctly through telling (modelling). In addition, all six mothers had added a further activity that had not come from the school, or at least is not part of standard school forms of guidance to parents. This involved requiring the child to retell the story in Samoan after having read it in English, with the specific goal of testing comprehension/understanding. Three mothers used illustrations in the book and on the cover to prompt the child to retell the story. Two mothers asked questions only.

All mothers were aware of what they were attempting to teach and from where their ideas had come. Four non-exclusionary sources were clearly identified in their explanation of their guidance. In the current study, the first source mothers identified was culturally preferred ways of acting their Samoan based folk pedagogical beliefs (Olson and Bruner, 1996). For example, respect in the Samoan culture requires that children listen to their parents and their elders in order to learn. According to the mothers, instruction that is direct and explicit is advantageous for the child because it is part of the child's sensitisation into cultural practices from an early age (Meleisea and Schoffel, 1996). One mother explained it this way (in English):

> *I really believe that it is difficult for children to say the word unless we tell them. Until we do that, the child will not be able to write that word. I also believe that the majority of children want to know but they are not told…what's the point of hiding it? What about our children? Children don't know if they're not told. If children don't know how to pronounce, their pronunciation will be different to ours and we, as mother and father and as first teachers, must tell them. Yes we can tell them. There is no sense in hiding it. (Mother 2)*

When asked why they did not seem to praise when their child attempted a word correctly, they said praising was not appropriate.

> *In Samoa there is no praise…When you look at the palagi (Europeans), obviously they praise their children…But in our case, when we praise some parents say we're praising our <u>own</u> children and so on…that's why I'm reluctant to show her that I'm happy…because the child might get puffed up…then… (Mother 1)*

A second major source for the parents' styles of guidance came from their experiences of being taught either at school or at home. Four out of six mothers taught their child in the way they claimed that they themselves were taught at school. The mothers utilized methods of teaching they believed were present in their school days (e.g. look and say; repetition, recitation and rote learning). All mothers listened for correct pronunciation of words and had strategies put in place should the pronunciation be incorrect:

> If [he] doesn't know the word, then spell and say it. For example, the word 'lucky' l-u-c-k-y lucky five times … like that. If they don't know the word, and I get tired of them not catching up quickly then they say and spell it ten times … (Mother 1)

A third source was the mothers' views about their current context as members of cultural groups who have minority language status. A telling aspect of these mothers' guidance was the retelling strategy that they used to assess their child's understanding of texts. The common rationale was to confirm comprehension/understanding:

> Usually after reading [I] go back to the beginning of the book and say, 'retell the story in Samoan' so that the child understands the story. Go back and translate the story in Samoan … that's all. Then by retelling in Samoan I know she understands. (Mother 1)

Three mothers used pictures in the book and on the cover to prompt the child to retell story. Two mothers deliberately tested the child's memory.

> I go back to the cover of the book and ask him questions as with the beginning to see if he understands … Usually I tell him to look at the cover of the book, point to the pictures and tell me: who, what, where etc, of the story. I ask him again about the author, illustrator … like at the beginning before he reads. Then I turn the pages and tell him to retell the story as on each page in Samoan. When he's too slow I say, 'tell me' … but I have to ask question after question to prompt him. (Mother 3)

The pattern of telling then asking with little or no praise at all during the reading contextualizes reading as 'fagogo' or ancient tales where the teller tells and the hearer hears. Subsequently, the teller is assured that hearers have heard and that hearers would eventually retell the same story to another audience or another generation. Consolidating the hearing, the teller asks questions to ensure that hearers understand.

The fourth and final source was school-related experiences which were a distinct source of variations between the mothers. Two mothers, both of whom were teachers, tended to pause more often, prompt rather then tell their children when difficulties arose, and praise; 21 of the 34 instances of praise in the data were provided by these mothers. Ideas sourced from their professional training are in their accounts of the tutorial style:

> *Correct pronunciation. Correct voice and sounding out. Recognising full stops…the voice accordingly…like surprise or animal cry e.g. dog. He usu-ally initiates the cries or shouts – but it is you who should do it first to set him an example for him to know? If a little difficult, or whatever from what he sees in the book, I don't tell him etc…I try to leave it to him…I cover the part (of the word) look for the syllable, what's the first letter, the second letter and so on then try to say the word. Most of the time I don't interrupt. (Mother 3)*

> *Pronunciation of words. Syllables help him for words he can't say…Help such as, not to say the whole word but just syllable by syllable then he tells the whole word. Especially pictures like…when that idea fails…then I ask, what can you see in the picture? Then he tells me the word. So the pictures help…I start to sound out and pronounce a word…I won't say what the whole word is, but syllable by syllable then he works it out and try to say it. So when he says it and it's correct then it's correct but if not I tell him. One thing is full stop. He knows it's a full stop but keeps reading, or a comma, but… (Mother 5)*

These changes in parents' ideas are like those described in the child-rearing literature where immigrant parents tend to adopt more school-like patterns in their guidance with increasing educational experience (Greenfield and Cocking, 1994). This educational effect has been found with mothers in minority communities living in the United States (Greenfield and Cocking, 1994; Laosa, 1989) and indigenous Māori mothers in New Zealand (Podmore and St George, 1986). Similarly, there is some evidence for this effect among Samoan mothers living in New Zealand reading to pre-schoolers (Tagoilelagi-Leota et al., 2003). Interestingly this pattern of using multiple sources and preparedness to consider new information including that related to school, does not match Delpit's (1996) description of parent styles in the United States adopted by members of groups without economic power who, she argues, reject learner-centred methods as not being effective.

changing family practices

Despite the dynamic reconstruction of ideas and use a variety of sources, the case studies presented above can be seen as illustrating why educational programmes for families need to be designed to change practices. In the case of the families described, this might mean that practices which are more directly supportive of school success could be systematically enhanced and made more consistent.

Research evidence suggests that family literacy practices can be changed, including modifying how parents read to their children before school and how parents hear their children read at school in ways that enhance the skills and knowledge their children need for more effective engagement in the literacy instruction and discourse of schools. Examples include increasing the frequency or the style of reading (typically narrative) texts with children before school (e.g. Pellegrini and Galda, 1998; Whitehurst and Lonigan, 2001). In some instances this has been in the home language of a minority language group (Gallimore and Goldenberg, 1993; Wolfgramm et al., 1997; Yaden et al., 2000). Other interventions have adopted a broader focus, by extending literacy activities to include writing and oral storytelling; or by creating inter-generational family literacy programmes (Morrow, 1995). Other research has evaluated programmes for parents with school-age children hearing their children read school texts and providing guidance (Hannon, 2003).

The research has shown that family members can be taught to increase the use of specific activities and that these can impact positively on beginning reading instruction at school (Whitehurst and Lonigan, 2001). However, difficulties have been reported including the incomplete adoption and sustaining of patterns within families (McNaughton, 1996). Gallimore and Goldenberg (1993), for example, reported an intervention to increase the educational success of children in Hispanic families. Immigrant families in Los Angeles were given specially written beginning reading texts which they could read with their kindergarten level children. The families had not typically read story books with children, so with these specially designed texts they were asked to read for enjoyment together and to concentrate on the story. However, sending linguistically and culturally appropriate narrative texts home did not result in the predicted increase in targeted exchanges (i.e. those involving elaborating , extending and negotiating meanings). Rather, the families' interactions were like those described earlier as a performance style and a style for learning items. Just like the Tongan and Samoan parents in the two studies presented here, the Hispanic parents interpreted the task in terms of their ideas about appropriate school pedagogy and how they themselves had learned to read. The researchers, reflecting on this outcome, argued that the ideas and beliefs held by participants in educational programmes were important determinants of how activity settings develop, and other researchers have noted the significance of developing shared understanding in interactions between family members and researchers in research contexts (Edwards, 1995; Renshaw, 1992).

Studies in New Zealand have shown that through specific training programmes, mothers in Pasifika communities can engage in, or increase the frequency of, exchanges which have a focus on text meaning by using language which elaborates and extends. In one study Tongan mothers read narrative texts in Tongan to their 2- to 4-year-old children (Wolfgramm et al., 1997). Patterns of exchanges (narrative, performance and display) with children and instances of 'non-immediate' talk (Dickinson and Tabors, 2001) were analysed from tape recordings over several days. This 'baseline' provided evidence for the use of multiple exchanges by mothers, although there were generally low frequencies of narrative exchanges and non-immediate talk.

In several collaborative sessions using illustrative exchanges drawn from recordings, Tongan researchers and educators have provided a rationale and models for the differential use of exchanges across texts to suit different purposes they might have for their children's reading, thus developing their 'textual dexterity'. The mothers reported relatively easily changing their patterns, based on shared understanding of goals and recognizing examples from their own experience or that of other members of the community group. This was borne out by analyses of their interactions with children before the educational programme and subsequent recordings of reading after the educational programme. For example, the mean frequency of use of narrative exchanges increased by between two and seven exchanges per book reading representing an increase in proportionate usage to between 10 and 50 per cent of the combined exchanges used by mothers.

This research base together with the earlier case studies provide evidence for how family literacy practices change and the role of ideas in those changes. Using these case studies and the existing research evidence we can conceptualize the conditions under which these changes take place along two dimensions. One is the relationship between external agents or information sources and parents, which can vary from being incidental to being direct. At one end of this dimension parents access and use information about activities which are available in the immediate contexts within which they live. While the form and content of the information may be fixed, say in a national television advertising campaign to promote parents' reading to their children (Research

Solutions, 1999) or the creation of new libraries and services to increase families' access to texts (Neuman and Celano, 2004) the selection, utilization and development of ideas and practices is primarily under the control of the parent and incidental to the external sources. The other end of the dimension is direct provision of knowledge initiated by an external agent who directs and systematises it for the parent. This might be in the form of a specific intervention programme that approaches families and provides specific training, such as Dialogic Reading (Whitehurst and Lonigan, 2001).

A second dimension concerns the process of exchange or negotiation of ideas from the perspective of the parents. We would see parents as actively constructing their ideas and developing the specific forms that literacy activities take with their children from the variety of sources described by the first dimension. But the relationship with the source of new ideas can vary. At one end of the continuum, these sources enable an active reflection on the relationship between existing ideas and practices and those externally available. At the other end, no opportunity exists to negotiate and reflect, to reconceptualize ideas in a meaningful dialogue. This latter end involves the attempted replacement or modification of existing ideas and practices by the external agent. Parents continue to actively construct ideas under these conditions too, but there are few degrees of freedom and the implied or deliberate message from external agents is that existing practices are deficient or inadequate and need to be replaced.

We assume there are developmental sequelae from different combinations of these dimensions. In general we predict that the more parents' ideas are directly engaged and the relationships between sources of new ideas and parents is one of negotiation and dialogue the more that new ideas are able to be effectively adopted. More importantly, such a process is more likely to enable parents to add to their culturally based repertoires of practice (Gutiérrez and Rogoff, 2003) and produce what we have called 'dexterity' in the use of different activities for different purposes, to provide a basis for sustainability of new literacy practices and be less intrusive or undermining of cultural identity.

This analysis is not unlike that proposed by Cummins (1981) for analysing bilingual educational programmes. There are those that are additive to L1 and those that replace an L1 (either intentionally or unintentionally) with developmentally and educationally problematic consequences. In our case, we are arguing that because literacy activities are essentially part of cultural practices that any attempt to change those practices is an act of cultural change. Further we are arguing that there are conditions under which such cultural interference is warranted and these conditions are the combination of high reflection and directness so that caregivers understand both the import of a message but also how it relates to their own current practices, and there is opportunity to negotiate how the new ideas can be located in their practices.

note

1. All direct quotes are translations from Tongan

references

Amituanai-Toloa, M. (2002). Samoan pedagogy: Teaching and learning and the practice of hearing children read at home. Unpublished Master's thesis. University of Auckland.

Cazden, C. (2001). *Classroom Discourse*. (2nd ed). Portsmouth, NH: Heinemann.

Cummins, J. (1981). *Bilingualism and Minority Language Students*. Ontario: Ontario Institute of Studies in Education.

Delpit, L. (1996). *Other People's Children: Cultural Conflict in the Classroom*. New York: New York Press.

Dickinson, D. and Tabors, P. O. (2001). *Beginning Literacy and Language: Young Children Learning at Home and at School*. Baltimore: Paul Brooks Publishing.

Duranti, A. (1992). Language and bodies in social space: Samoan ceremonial greetings. *American Anthropologist*, 94, 3, 657.

Edwards, P. A. (1995). Combining parents' and teachers' thoughts about story-book reading at home and at school. In L. M. Morrow (ed.), *Family Literacy: Connections in Schools and Communities* (pp. 54–69). Newark, DE: International Reading Association.

Gallimore, R. and Goldenberg, C. (1993). Activity settings of early literacy: Home and school factors in children's emergent literacy. In E. A. Forman, N. Minick, and C. A. Stone (eds), *Contexts for Learning: Sociocultural Dynamics in Children's Development* (pp. 315–35). New York: Oxford University Press.

Gee, J. P. (2001). A sociocultural perspective on early literacy development. In S. B. Neuman and D. K. Dickinson (eds), *Handbook of Early Literacy Research* (pp. 30–42). New York: The Guilford Press.

Goodnow, J. J. and Collins, W. A. (1990). *Development According to Parents: The Nature, Sources, and Consequences of Parents' Ideas*. Hillsdale, NJ: Lawrence Erlbaum.

Greenfield, P. (1994). Independence and interdependence as developmental scripts: implications for theory, research and practice. In P. Greenfield and R. Cocking (eds), *Cross-Cultural Roots of Minority Child Development*. New York: Earlbaum.

Greenfield, P. and Cocking, R. (eds) (1994). *Cross-Cultural Roots of Minority Child Development*. New York: Earlbaum.

Gutiérrez, K. D. and Rogoff, B. (2003). Cultural ways of learning: individual traits or repertoires of practice. *Educational Researcher*, 32: 5, 19–25.

Hannon, P. (2003). Family literacy programmes. In N. Hall, J. Larson and J. Marsh (eds), *Handbook of Early Childhood Literacy* (pp. 99–111). London: Sage.

Heath, S. B. (1983). *Ways with Words: Language, Life, and Work in Communities and Classrooms*. Cambridge: Cambridge University Press.

Heath, S. B., Branscombe, A. and Thomas, C. (1986). The book as a narrative prop in language acquisition. In B. Schieffelin and P. Gilmore (eds), *The Acquisition of Literacy: Ethnographic Perspectives* (pp. 16–34). Norwood, NJ: Ablex.

Laosa, L. M. (1989). Social competence in childhood: toward a developmental, socioculturally relativistic paradigm. *Journal of Applied Developmental Psychology*, 10, 447–61.

Lerner, R. M., Fisher, C. B. and Weinberg, R. A. (2000). Toward a science for and of the people: Promoting civil society through the application of developmental science. *Child Development*, 71: 1, 11–20.

Matuti-Bianchi, M. (1986). Ethnic identities and patterns of school success and failure among Mexican descent and Japanese-American students in a California high school: An ethnographic analysis. *American Journal of Education*, 95, 233–55.

McNaughton, S. (1995). *Patterns of Emergent Literacy: Processes of Development and Transition*. Auckland: Oxford University Press.

McNaughton, S. (1996). Ways of Parenting and Cultural Identity. *Culture and Psychology*, 2: 2, 173–201.

McNaughton, S. (2005). Considering culture in research-based interventions to support early literacy. In D. Dickinson and S. Neuman (eds), *Handbook of Early Literacy Research*, Vol. 2 (pp. 229–40). New York: Guilford.

Meleisea, M. and Schoffel, P. (1996). Pacific Island Polynesian attitudes to child training and discipline in New Zealand: some policy implications for social welfare and education. Paper presented at the National Symposium on Pacific Islands Learning, 15–16 February, Auckland.

Morrow, L. (ed.) (1995). *Family Literacy: Connections in Schools and Communities*. Newark, DE: International Reading Association.

Neuman, S. B. and Celano, D. (2004). Save the libraries. *Educational Leadership*, 61: 6, 82–5.

Neuman, S. B., Hagedorn, T., Celano, D. and Daly, P. (1995). Toward a collaborative approach to parent involvement in early education: A study of teenage mothers in an African-American community. *American Educational Research Journal*, 32: 4), 801–27.

Ogbu, J. U. (1991). Cultural mode, identity and literacy. In J. W. Stigler, R. A. Shweder and G. Herdt (eds), *Cultural Psychology: Essays on Comparative Human Development* (pp. 520–41). Cambridge: Cambridge University Press.

Olson, D. R. and Bruner, J. S. (1996). Folk psychology and folk pedagogy. In D. R. Olson and J. S. Bruner (eds), *The Handbook of Education and Human Development* (pp. 9–27). Oxford: Blackwell.

Pellegrini, A. and Galda, L. (1998). *The Development of School-based Literacy: A Social Ecological Perspective*. London: Routledge.

Pellegrini, A. D., Perlmutter, J. C., Galda, L. and Brody, G. H. (1990). Joint book reading between black head start children and their mothers. *Child Development*, 61, 443–53.

Podmore, V. N. and St George, R. (1986). New Zealand Maori and European mothers and their three-year-old children: Interactive behaviour in pre-school settings. *Journal of Applied Development Psychology*, 7, 273–82.

Reese, L. and Gallimore, R. (2000). 'Immigrant Latinos' cultural model of literacy development: an evolving perspective on home-school discontinuities. *American Journal of Education*, 108: 2, 103–34.

Research Solutions (1999). *Benchmark Research into the Attitudes of Various Ethnic Groups to Helping Their Children Learn*. Wellington: NZ Ministry of Education.

Renshaw, P. D. (1992). Reflecting on the experimental context: Parent's Interpretations of the Education Motive during Teaching Episodes. In L. T. Winegar and J. Valsiner (eds), *Children's Development within Social Context*, Vol. 2 (pp. 53–74). Hillsdale, NJ: Lawrence Erlbaum.

Rogoff, B. (1990). *Apprenticeship in Thinking: Cognitive Development in Social Contexts*. Oxford: Oxford University Press.

Royal-Tangaere, A. and McNaughton, S. (1994). From preschool to home: Processes of generalisation in language acquisition from an indigenous language recovery programme. *International Journal of Early Years Education*, 2: 1, 23–40.

Tagoilelagi-Leota, F., McNaughton, S., MacDonald, S. and Farry, S. (2003). The precious threads: bilingual and biliteracy development over the transition to school. *Language Acquisition Research*. NZ Ministry of Education Research Division, Wellington.

Tanielu, L. S. (2004). O le A'oa'oina o le Gagana, Faitautusi ma le Tusitusi i le A'oga a le Faifeau: Ekalesia Fa'apotopotoga Kerisiano Samoa (EFKS). Literacy Education, language, reading and writing in the Pastor's school: Congregational Christian Church of Samoa. Unpublished doctoral dissertation, University of Auckland, New Zealand.

Utumapu, T. L. P. (1998). O le Poutu: women's roles and Samoan language nests. Unpublished Ph.D. thesis, University of Auckland.

Valsiner, J. (1988). Ontogeny of co-construction of culture within socially organised environmental settings. In J. Valsiner (ed.), *Child Development within Culturally Structured Environments*, Vol. 2. Norwood, NJ: Ablex.

Wertsch, J. V. (1991). *Voices of the Mind: A Sociocultural Approach to Mediated Action*. Cambridge, MA: Harvard University Press.

Whitehurst, G. J. and Lonigan, C. J. (2001). Emergent literacy: Development from pre-readers to readers. In S. B. Neuman and D. K. Dickinson (eds), *Handbook of Early Literacy Research* (pp. 11–29). New York: The Guilford Press.

Wolfgramm, 'E., Afeaki, V. and McNaughton, S. (1997). Story-reading in a Tongan language group. *SET Special: Language and literacy*, 7, 1–4.

Wolfgramm-Foliaki, 'E. A. (2006). Ko e Hala Kuo Papa. Pathways and Sites for Literacy Development in Tongan Families. Unpublished doctoral thesis, The University of Auckland, New Zealand.

Yaden, D. B., Tam, A., Madrigal, P., Brassell, D., Massa, J., Altamirano, S. and Armendariz, J. (2000). *The Reading Teacher*, 54, 186–90.

index